D0629424

FLOODTIDE IN EUROPE

Floodtide in Europe

DON COOK

G. P. Putnam's Sons

NEW YORK

Member of the Authors League of America

The author acknowledges with thanks the kind permission of Dean Acheson and Harper and Row to quote from *Sketches from Life,* © 1961 by Dean Acheson; Mr. Acheson and Harvard University Press to quote from *Power and and Diplomacy,* © 1958 by Dean Acheson; Robert D. Murphy and Doubleday to quote from *Diplomat Among Warriors,* © 1964 by Robert D. Murphy; and The Times Publishing Co., Ltd., copyright owners of the Eden papers, to quote from *Full Circle,* Volume II of the memoirs of the Rt. Hon. the Earl of Avon. Copyright of the documents quoted from the Eden Memoirs is vested in Her Majesty's Stationery Office, London.

 Published simultaneously in the Dominion of Canada by Longmans Canada Limited, Toronto.

Library of Congress Catalog Card Number: 64-18004

Printed in the United States of America

For CHERRY
Who has shared it all
and much more

There is a tide in the affairs of men,
Which, taken at the flood, leads on to fortune.
—*Julius Caesar*

Contents

PART I

FROM MONNET TO DE GAULLE

1. ". . . A Tide in the Affairs of Men"

In the hilly wooded countryside of the Grand Duchy of Luxembourg, a few miles from the French border, lies the city of Esch-sur-Alzette —100,000 people in a valley of small stone houses with gray slate roofs clustered around the smokestacks and blast furnaces and sprawling sheds and clanking machinery of Luxembourg's biggest industrial complex, the Arbed-Belval Steel Company.

If you put a pin on the map of Europe at Esch and draw a circle with a radius of 150 miles through France, Germany, Holland and Belgium, you encompass the heartland of European production and industry and the scene of most of its decisive military history as well. At the center of the circle, extending south from Esch across the Luxembourg border into France, lies the great Lorraine iron ore basin, and next to it the rich coal fields of that vale of European contention, the Saar. Surrounding this coal and iron are the mountain ranges which for centuries have formed the shifting borders and battlegrounds of Western Europe: on the west the Argonne Woods and to the south the Vosges Mountains of France; in the north the Ardennes Forest of Belgium; on the east the Eifel and Hunsruck ranges of Germany which guard the approaches to the Rhine, and across the Rhine the Taunus Mountains and the Westerwald stretching toward central Europe.

Tourists usually bypass this heart of Western Europe except to visit its battlefields and its monuments. Its towns and cities are mainly small dingy industrial centers like Esch, with little to offer in culture or comfort. Its mountains and hills are short and covered with scrub forest of thick underbrush and small trees. There are few vistas, and none of the sweeping dramatic grandeur of the Alps or the Dolomites, or the old-world charm of the spa-towns of the Black Forest or the Jura or the Haute-Savoie.

More battles have been fought, more blood spilled, more lives lost in this 300-mile circle of geography than anywhere else on the globe: Waterloo in 1815; Sedan in 1870; Verdun in 1916; the invasion of Belgium and the encirclement of the French armies in 1940; Bastogne in 1944; the bombing of the Ruhr, the destruction of Cologne and the crossing of the Rhine in 1945. With the tide of war, national frontiers have shifted endlessly back and forth across these battle-scarred mountains. Alsace-Lorraine was ruled by Germany from 1870 until 1918 and then restored to France. The Saar Valley was detached from Germany in 1919 until it voted to rejoin Hitler's Reich in 1935. It was detached again by France in 1946 and returned to Germany by peaceful agreement in 1956. Since 1700, Luxembourg has been ruled in turn by Spain, Austria, France, The Netherlands and the German Confederation, then linked to modern Germany by a customs union until 1919, neutral and linked to Belgium until 1940, incorporated by Hitler into the Third Reich until the liberation in 1944, and now is one of the three members of the Benelux Customs Union. History has not been kind to the people, their cities or their land.

Nor will a traveler driving across this country, from Paris east to Cologne, or south from Brussels to Strasbourg, gain much impact or impression of industrial output and productive wealth. The feel of the country is pastoral—not industrial. You speed through most of these factory towns in ten minutes or less, barely conscious of their existence except perhaps to wonder why people would want to live in such a place, before you are back on the wooded mountain roads. Much of the heavy commerce moves on rivers and canals which link the towns and cities to the open sea: the Rhine, the Moselle, the Meuse, the Sambre, the Saar, the Maas, the Ruhr, the Main. These are the industrial highways, along with the roads and the railroads, and barges loaded with iron ore, coal, limestone, oil, cement, raw materials and finished products push placidly through vine-covered river valleys and along canals with cows grazing on the banks.

Only when a traveler reaches the belching smokestacks and the pulsating truck traffic of the Ruhr Valley on the northeastern edge of this 300-mile circle in Germany does he find a visual concentration of industrial power which is comparable to Pittsburgh and the Allegheny Valley, or the endless string of factories along the Pennsylvania Railroad from New York to Delaware. The Ruhr echoes names like Krupp, I. G. Farben, Flick, Frick, Thyssen. The cities of

Düsseldorf, Essen, Bochum, Dortmund, Solingen, Wuppertal, Mülheim, Duisburg, merge from one to the next almost without a break in the industrial skyline—the most concentrated single productive area in Europe and the world.

But the collective wealth and manufacturing of the rest of this circle far exceeds that of the Ruhr. South of Esch lie the main French steel centers of Metz and Thionville, linked by canal to the coal and coke ovens of Saarbrücken. Farther south is the city of Nancy, and on the banks of the Rhine the fine old Alsatian capital of Strasbourg.

North of Strasbourg along the Rhine in Germany are the chemical and engineering centers of Mannheim, Ludwigshafen, Karlsruhe and Mainz. On the Main River are Frankfurt and Russelsheim, where nearly a fifth of Germany's automobiles are made. The circle next takes in the West German capital at Bonn, and the cathedral towers of Cologne, where yet another 20 percent of Germany's cars are produced. Then comes the Ruhr, and the circle swings north into Holland to include the city of Eindhoven with Europe's largest single electrical manufacturing industry. On into Belgium lie the big port of Antwerp, the light industry of Brussels, the coal mines and limestone pits, steel and engineering plants of Liège, Namur and Charleroi. Back in France on the northwestern perimeter of the circle is the textile center of Lille and the factory towns of Laon, St.-Quentin, Maubeuge and Douai.

At the Arbed-Belval Steel Company works in Esch-sur-Alzette on a late spring afternoon a little more than a decade ago a group of diplomats, politicians, civil servants, steel company executives, journalists and photographers gathered to watch one of those anticlimactic ceremonies by which great events of history are so often set in motion. The date was April 30, 1953. Jean Monnet, the "Father of Europe," had come to Esch to tap the first blast furnace of pig iron to be produced under the control and direction of the High Authority of the European Coal and Steel Community, of which he was the first president.

Europeans had dreamed of this moment for decades, and had been actively working toward it for three years—ever since May 9, 1950, when French foreign minister Robert Schuman, at Jean Monnet's inspiration and instigation and later with his guidance and negotiating skill, had launched the famous Schuman Plan at a press conference in Paris. Now on that April afternoon in 1953, the six-nation Coal and Steel Community was about to go into business.

The Arbed-Belval steel works was a happy if obvious choice for the ceremonies. At the heart of Western Europe it had for years been producing steel from French iron ore, Belgian limestone, coking coal from Holland and West Germany, with a sprinkling of Italian workmen employed by the company to ease the chronic labor shortage in little Luxembourg. In the molten pig iron bubbling inside that blast furnace, the six nations of Europe were already joined.

Amid the heat and noise, Jean Monnet cast an anxious glance over his shoulder at the smiling audience in the flag-decorated blast furnace shed. A man who prefers private offices and the back rooms of power, conversation and contemplation to ceremonials and the public eye, Monnet looked as he felt—uncomfortable and out of place in this Dante-like setting of dust and dirt, sulphur fumes, screaming air compressors, gas, soot and smoke. A brawny foreman in freshly laundered blue denim work clothes heaved a long steel spike into place opposite the thin wall of firebrick that sealed off the taphole at the base of the blast furnace. He shoved a pneumatic hammer into the reluctant hands of the president of the High Authority, and shouted instructions in his ear over the roar of the air compressors. Monnet inched gingerly forward, and as flashbulbs popped he managed to muster two croquet-like taps at the big spike. Then with a self-deprecating little smile he motioned the foreman to finish the job. Monnet's work toward this moment had long since been done, and like the scratch of a signature on a treaty or the bottle of champagne on the bow of a ship, this was only the recording act, the simplest of all.

The firebrick quickly gave way. The first trickle of orange-red ore spilled out like a licking tongue into a trough of sand across the sloping floor of the furnace shed almost at Monnet's feet. The foreman produced a huge ladle, and with an artistic flourish worthy of a *chef de cuisine* he dipped it into the flowing pig iron and poured the molten ore into a special mold for Monnet bearing the word EUROP—not the "Europe" of the French spelling or the "Europa" of the German, but a "Europ" of the supranational Six: France, Belgium, Holland, Luxembourg, Italy and West Germany. Then everybody trooped off in the spring sunshine to the company dining hall for a glass of champagne and some conversational chatter about the future of Europe.

"This is not just coal and steel." Monnet waved an admonishing finger at one of the steel company executives. "It's the beginning of a process—a dynamic process to build a great market for all the people of Europe. Then the day that a vote takes place in Paris and in Brussels and in Bonn for a European legislature—that day you will have linked the people to this process. Coalitions are no longer enough. Europe must unite. . . ."

The steel company man nodded knowingly but somewhat uncomprehendingly. After all, they had been tapping blast furnaces of "European pig iron" at Esch in exactly the same way made of exactly the same combination of raw materials for years before Jean Monnet came along. It was not easy to sense how different things were going to be in Europe. But the long ebb of war which had all but drained the life out of the old continent was over now. The years of Europe's dependence on the United States were ending. After six years of war and seven years of recovery, the tide had turned and Europe was resuming life on its own, taking up its own destiny, moving forward to forge its own future. Monnet's "dynamic process" was underway.

Today the tide has carried Europe to a plateau of peace and prosperity unmatched in any era in all its long history. There is political stability everywhere and the internal threat of Communism has all but disappeared. Never have the nations of Western Europe lived in an atmosphere so free of territorial disputes, the threat of aggression or even the thought of war. No propaganda campaign of hate shatters its airwaves or stifles the vast and animated flow of its peoples across rivers and borders where so much blood has been shed. No war of nerves, no maneuvering of armies, no secret manipulations of an ephemeral balance of alliances, no vows of national revenge, threaten the relations of its member states. Europe has reached this plateau of peace through a process of historic exhaustion—the physical, political, economic and spiritual exhaustion of a century and a half of despotic conflict and revengeful territorial strife, climaxed by the bloodletting of two world wars. But with exhaustion, Europe has entered a new age of reason and common sense, and war or the threat of war has ceased to be an instrument for settling its differences.

In this atmposhere of peace, the nations of Western Europe have shown the world how to adapt democratic government to a new twentieth-century standard of economic and social responsibility to meet the needs of the people. This, indeed, was a major political and economic test of the postwar period. Everywhere governments faced the enormous complications of recovery and rebuilding, and at the same time meeting the demands of the people for something better out of life than the dreary cycle of depression, hunger, war and death. The people wanted jobs, houses, security and a share of the national wealth. If democracy could not provide it, then everywhere in postwar Europe militant Communism was active and waiting, sabotaging democracy, hoping to prove its failure.

But democracy did not fail. Today, every important political party in Western Europe accepts that government must provide the solutions for an ever-growing range of economic, social and human problems. If these are not solved, then society as a whole begins to stagnate and democracy is doomed. Europe has by no means solved all its problems. But it has resolved the central political argument between Left and Right about the responsibility of government, and it has equipped itself with the means of democratic action. In so doing, Europe has not followed any particular ideology or embraced any doctrinaire attitude or approach. Systems vary from one capital to the next. Norway and Sweden, with long Socialist traditions, place the emphasis on social security systems and government direction. In France, President Charles de Gaulle inherited the economic planning machinery of the Commissariat du Plan from the Leftist governments of the old Fourth Republic—but none of the old Leftist regimes was more vigorous in the use of state planning than the economists under De Gaulle's Rightist government. In West Germany, the Christian Democrats have eschewed any kind of centralized state planning and relied instead on guiding free enterprise through taxation and monetary policies. But at the same time, 30 percent of Germany's national budget is spent on social services. The Conservatives in Britain followed much the same approach as the Germans, but now under a Labour Government, state economic planning is being introduced in Britain. In Italy, a coalition of left-wing Socialists and liberal Christian Democrats is working to keep the "Italian economic miracle" in forward motion. All over Europe, it is no longer a question of whether political parties are for or against strong management of national economies. The political battles are fought over who can manage better, and who is going to do the most with the resources available.

The common denominators of economic policy are broadly the same in Western Europe, whatever the country, the politics or the government: maintenance of full employment, a strong rate of economic growth, and an equitable distribution of national wealth through social security, nationalized industries, government spending, public works and other means. During the decade from 1953, after Monnet's dynamic process had begun, Europe averaged an economic growth of 5 percent each year, and some countries bounded ahead at the phenomenal rate of 8 or 10 or even 12 percent. The population of Western Europe has grown by 35,000,000 since 1953 to a total of 340,000,000 today, but unemployment averages only a little over 2 percent and in many countries there is literally no unemployment at all.* In the democracies of Europe, this growth rate, plus the absence of unemployment and the enforced distribution of national wealth, creates economic advance and improvement spread over society as a whole. There is no longer in Europe the sense of a widening social gap between "haves" and "have-nots"—of wealth and income growing on one side of the social scale while unemployment, stagnation and deterioration mount on the other. There is a leveling out of society, but there is also a leveling up.

Europe's productive wealth has grown enormously. When Jean Monnet tapped that first blast furnace of European pig iron at Esch in April, 1953, steel production for all of Europe stood at barely 60 million tons a year. Five years later, in 1958, Europe surpassed the steel output of the United States and today is averaging 95 million tons annually. Automobile output has risen from 1,560,000 cars in 1953 to nearly 6,000,000 in 1964.

Aluminum production has climbed from 450,000 tons a year to well over a million. Electricity consumption has more than doubled. Vast new fields of natural gas have been brought into production in southwest France, in Holland, Italy and Germany and, most important of all, under the North Sea. Natural gas, like coal and oil before it, is creating a whole new pattern of industry and productivity in Europe; consumption is six times the level of 1953 and going up every day. This industrial expansion has carried Europe's gross national product from $184 billion in 1953 to $390 billion in 1964. When the Coal and Steel Community was launched, Europe was exporting only $2.3 billion worth of goods each month; today the total is over $5 billion. As the biggest and most concentrated single consumer market in the world, Europe buys to the tune of $6 billion

* OECD statistics for Austria, Belgium, Luxembourg, Denmark, France, Germany, Greece, Ireland, Italy, Netherlands, Portugal, Spain, Sweden, Turkey and United Kingdom. The U.S. averaged a 3 percent growth rate from 1953 to 1963, and only in 1964 did the American economy begin to expand again at a pace matching the average in Europe.

in monthly imports today against $2.2 billion in 1953. From the hapless position of economic dependence on America, Europe's combined gold and dollar reserves have climbed from $7.6 billion to more than $20 billion today—some $6 billion more than all the gold in Fort Knox.

The prosperous democracies of Western Europe stand as a particular economic and social example for the rest of the world. They are providing their people with both security and freedom—the economic benefits that Communism claims to offer, and much that the free enterprise system does not attempt. As a result, the classic political struggle between Left and Right extremism which continuously wracked and often wrecked every government in Europe for the last half-century has quietly faded away in the prosperity and well-being of the 1960's. Just as Europe has arrived at a plateau of peace among its member states, so are the nations of Europe enjoying almost unparalleled political stability and internal harmony.

No longer are "match kings" and "merchants of death" manipulating the finances of government to their private profit and the delight of the Communist and anarchist propagandists. No longer need a starving little shipbuilding town like Jarrow, on the bleak northeast coast of England, organize a hunger march of its 75 percent unemployed, as it did in 1936, to walk 250 miles to London in an effort to stir a Stanley Baldwin to act about its plight. No longer can a Stavitsky financial scandal bring a Leftist mob pouring into the Place de la Concorde of Paris, leaving twenty-one dead from the gunfire of the gendarmes, as happened in 1934. No longer can a Hitler count on battalions of German unemployed to don brown shirts and bring democracy down with mass hysteria. Nowhere in Western Europe today can the Communists call an effective political strike. They can and do exploit labor troubles, but militant Communist labor leadership and strike action for political ends has become a thing of the past. Communist bellies are as full as those of the Socialists, the Christian Democrats, the Conservatives, the farmers and the independents. The moderation of a paycheck and the policies of responsible democratic government are triumphing over the attractions of a picket line or the fading fervor of agitprop lectures on the iniquities of capitalism and democracy.

For the last twenty years, while United States nuclear power has held Communism in military check, Western Europe has revived and prospered and in the process has won its victory over Communism too—a victory of political moderation and economic success. And in the years ahead this may well prove to have been a more decisive and substantive defeat for the Communist system than the stalemate in arms and military power.

In the world at large in the last decade, Europe has liquidated its imperial past and relinquished all but the last of its colonial possessions to self-government. Most of the process has been managed so skillfully that old flags have been lowered and new ones raised all but unnoticed by the rest of the world. Sometimes little wars have been involved: Kenya, Malaya, Cyprus. Sometimes big wars of international political repercussion: Indochina and Algeria. Sometimes the colonial powers have left in bitterness and chaos: the Congo and Indonesia. But whether the process has been rough or smooth, a phase of history is over and the great powers of Europe are no longer encumbered or fettered with a dying past. No fewer than fifty-five former European colonies have joined the ranks of free and independent self-governing nations, and the list grows almost monthly. Moreover, not one single colony where Europeans once ruled has yet adopted the Communist system of government. There have been flirtations with Communism, and there have been Communist movements and subversion and influence in Africa, Asia and elsewhere, but nowhere have the Communists yet been strong enough to take over one of the emerging nations and impose their system and regime. Today only Portugal is left in Europe with a colonial problem on its hands.

Twenty years after the end of World War II, Western Europe is emerging from a long period of historic decline. European power rose with the Industrial Revolution of the mid-1800's, which brought with it war, human exploitation, economic and political rivalry, colonialism and empire-building—problems which democratic government has only painfully found the means to resolve a century later. Today a new spirit of fundamental and abiding peace has come to Europe, and its masses are enjoying security, well-being and a sharing of national wealth as it has never been shared before.

Never have Europe's three great powers—Britain, France and Germany—been in such fundamental accord on the maintenance of peace. Never have they been as free of political or territorial rivalries on the European continent or in the world at large. Never before have they been members of the same military alliance.

There has not, indeed, been a comparable time of peace and well-being for Europe's peoples and its states since the early eighteenth century—the beginning of the expansive and civilized Age of Reason, the years of the peaceful ascendancy of the Court of Versailles in Europe and the easy movement of men and ideas from country to country; the days of Voltaire, Jean-Jacques Rousseau, Frederick the Great, Goethe, John Wesley, Sir Robert Walpole, Dr. Johnson, the elder Pitt, Catherine the Great; the decades of history before Napoleon, Bismarck, the Kaisers, the Hapsburgs, the Romanoffs and Hitler came to dominate the next century and a half with blood and iron. A floodtide of history is running in Europe, carrying an old civilization and old nations not merely to new heights of material prosperity but to a new epoch, a renewal and reassertion of Europe's independent strength, influence, economic power and political role around the globe.

In this emergent Europe of today, national politics, foreign policies and diplomacy revolve around three main competing political forces or causes: European unity, European nationalism and European independence of the United States. Paradoxically, the success of the postwar policies which restored Europe to health and security has also released the new European nationalism. Europe could not have survived without the protection and leadership of the United States, and $45 billion in postwar American aid. Nor could it have gone forward from recovery to prosperity without European unity. But the renewed strength of Europe, and of France in particular, has enabled President Charles de Gaulle to assert his vigorous policies of nationalism and "European independence," and to challenge American leadership in Europe and the concepts of Atlantic unity which have held sway since the Marshall Plan and the signing of the North Atlantic Treaty in 1949.

At the same time there has been a shift in the power alignments of the Atlantic Alliance. Great Britain, which held a predominant position of leadership in Europe in 1953, has declined in power and influence. France under De Gaulle has reasserted itself with a political force and determination not felt in Europe since the last century. Germany has emerged from two wars to take its place as a treaty ally of its old enemies. The nations of Europe are no longer dependent client states of the United States. Europe's gold reserves have climbed since 1953 to more than $20 billion today, while American reserves have fallen in that period from about $18 billion to below

$15 billion. The gold figures are the simple, dramatic evidence of the radical shift in the economic balance between Europe and America. Although the nuclear power of the United States is still the bulwark of NATO security, the economic and political relationship between America and its Allies has altered completely in the sixteen years since the NATO treaty was signed.

These changes in the power structure of the Atlantic Alliance have brought parallel changes in the political atmosphere. The old comfortable intimacy and cohesiveness which existed among the leading powers of NATO amid the political conditions of European recovery and the Cold War belong to the past. The assertion of national interests and national policies has replaced the harmony of the 1950's, when NATO interests usually could be relied upon to take priority over national interests.

During the decade from 1953 to 1963, the goal and the common interest of the NATO governments was unity—European unity and Atlantic unity. The Monnet concept shaped national policies of the Alliance: step-by-step economic integration of Europe, attracting other European nations to join, leading eventually to political federation in Europe and an Atlantic partnership with the United States. Differences and difficulties of course arose in various capitals along the way. The European Defense Community treaty to create a European Army was killed by the French in 1954. Britain waited and debated until 1961 before deciding at last that it was time to try to join Europe. But despite setbacks and arguments, the Monnet concept held sway as Alliance policy and was not seriously challenged or checked. Progress toward the Monnet goals was steadily maintained. Dozens of men worked together in the Europe of the 1950's for these common aims: Schuman, Pineau, Pinay, Bidault in France; De Gasperi, Sforza, Segni, Sarragat in Italy; Adenauer, Hallstein, Von Brentano in Germany; Spaak, Van Zeeland in Belgium; Stikker, Luns, Mansholt in Holland; Joseph Bech in Luxembourg.

It was Jean Monnet's particular role to have been a catalyst around whom the cause of European federalism has revolved since the end of World War II. A man of influence rather than power, Monnet has never even been a cabinet minister in France. He is an economist and expert in finance, and he has worked as an adviser to governments everywhere, from Peking to Warsaw, on every kind of national economic problem. Across the years, Monnet has built a tremendously wide range of friendships and associations in the world of diplomacy, government, politics, and finance in every capital of NATO and beyond. From this vast experience and range of contacts, Monnet has a particular sense of Bismarck's "art of the possible." At decisive points along the way, he has defined the goals and outlined the practical plans and objectives toward which governments should be working to give structural reality to the dream of European unity.

Monnet first broached the idea of a European coal and steel community in 1943 in Washington, where he was serving as head of the wartime Free French Supply Mission. He discussed it with Paul-Henri Spaak, who was visiting Washington as foreign minister of the Belgian government-in-exile. Finally, in 1950, Monnet found the historical moment and above all, the man who could turn his idea into political reality: Robert Schuman, a kindly, ascetic Alsatian lawyer who had spent his boyhood as a subject of the Kaiser, speaking German before he spoke French, and who managed to establish a remarkable four-year tenure as Foreign Minister of France under one Fourth Republic government after another from 1949 to 1953. Schuman's shrewdness and political skill carried the plan through the French cabinet and the National Assembly. Monnet headed the six-nation negotiating committee which drafted the treaty, and then spent two years as first president of the High Authority until the Coal and Steel Community was a going concern. Subsequently he turned to the Euratom Treaty, the six-nation atomic organization. At this same time, Spaak took the initiative in the crowning achievement of economic integration, the European Common Market.

In these treaties, the Europeans set out to build unity around common solutions to common economic problems which could not be solved inside national borders—the creation of bigger markets for everybody; the establishment of supranational authorities with power to hack away at the jungle of European trade restrictions; the creation of international funds to finance such projects as the closing down of unproductive coal mines and the transfer of miners to new jobs; the harmonizing of freight rates and tariffs. These are problems which do not touch upon national pride and honor or national security, do not involve the sanctity of borders or national territory, do not impinge on patriotism or rouse political emotions. At the same time, economic decisions do involve national political policies, particularly in any area which touches on agriculture and the farmers. It was Monnet's vision that in uniting to deal with economic problems, Europe inevitably would move toward greater and greater political unity. From coal and steel to atomic energy, and from atomic energy to the Common Market, and from the Common Market for industrial goods to a Common Market for agriculture in which the farmers in Europe from Normandy to Sicily would all receive the same price for their grain—in this process, it seemed, Europe would wake up one day to find that it had united by stealth.

Today the subsurface "infrastructure" of European unity is enormous. It is composed not merely of the Six, with the big supranational commissions in Brussels and Luxembourg. In addition to the Six there are dozens of intergovernmental technical committees and organizations which meet endlessly and never produce a paragraph of news, working on such problems as fishing rights, railroad schedules, road signs, telecommunications and standards for university degrees.

Europe today is somewhere in the middle of the Monnet concept of the federalist process. It is too early to say that the thesis is going to work, and that economic integration is going to lead to a federated Europe. But it is too late to say that it will not work. What can be said with certainty at this point in postwar history is that the new European nationalism, as epitomized by General de Gaulle, has checked the federalist momentum, and more especially it has checked the Atlanticist concept of forging closer links of partnership between the United States and a united Europe.

General de Gaulle's new European nationalism bears no relationship at all to the old nationalism of Hitler's Germany or Mussolini's Italy. It is not a nationalism which threatens Europe's peace, or involves *lebensraum* or territorial questions, or stifles trade, commerce or the movement of peoples. But it is a nationalism which seeks to re-emphasize and assert the identity and the power of the nation-state, at a time when economies are becoming more and more entwined and when national borders have all but ceased to have meaning. Jean Monnet looked to this process of economic integration as the healthy submerging of nationalism in a common European identity. De Gaulle seeks just the opposite—to maintain and reinforce national policies and national leadership, the political feelings of Frenchmen, Germans, Italians, Poles, Czechs, Roumanians, while still gaining the benefits of economic integration. De Gaulle has based his nationalistic appeal primarily on the theme of European independence from the United States. It is a theme which strikes a very strong subsurface response in Europe, and cannot lightly be dismissed as part of the General's posing and search for grandeur.

When Europeans talk about independence from the United States, it is no doubt difficult for Americans to understand what it is all about. After all, the United States did not spend $45 billion in postwar aid and send six divisions to Europe to build some kind of a European hegemony for itself. There were reasons of enlightened self-interest for this American policy of help for Europe, but the United States certainly had no aim except to preserve freedom and independence. Nevertheless, the very process of restoring Europe to economic health drew the United States into the day-by-day affairs of every government it was assisting. Sometimes the involvement was very deep. United States missions were in a position to force decisions which basically shaped the policies of governments and even the naming of cabinet ministers. The fact that the exercise of this power often was necessary and inevitable does not change the experience of a postwar generation of European civil servants and political leaders of being frequently dependent upon decisions in Washington. What was true in the economic field was equally true in the military sphere. America picked up a huge portion of the bill for rebuilding Europe's defenses, provided the equipment, schooled the officers and pilots, named the generals and set up the military staff machinery, and of course decided the strategy for the defense of Europe. The fact that this was all done in Europe's interest and that it was on the whole judiciously handled with due regard to the participation of others does not change the fact that NATO and Supreme Allied Headquarters in Europe have been essentially American-run operations. For Europe, this American dominance has meant a certain suffocation of independence of foreign policy.

American policies and political leadership were often challenged in the 1950's and early 1960's There were frequent divergencies over the Cold War attitudes, and whether or not to go to the conference table with the Russians. The United States and its Allies in Europe differed constantly over colonialism and neutralism in the world. There were major policy clashes over the ending of the Indochina war in 1954, over the European Defense Community treaty that same year, and most dramatically of all over Suez in 1956. In each of these affairs, Europe asserted a line of independence which the United States opposed. Nevertheless, there was no fundamental or lasting break in the overall strategic harmony of the Atlantic Alliance.

That break came with General de Gaulle's press conference of January 14, 1963, in which he vetoed British entry into the European

Common Market, and rejected President Kennedy's project for the creation of a multilateral nuclear force in NATO. But De Gaulle's actions went far beyond these specific points. His strategic aim was the establishment of a second independent foreign policy in the Atlantic world where there had been only one policy and one leadership before. He was out to force a complete change in the postwar structure of the Atlantic Alliance. Just as France had regained its economic independence and had achieved political stability, so De Gaulle was now determined to assert an independent Gaullist foreign policy, including, of course, nuclear independence for France. De Gaulle does not pretend that France is capable of defending herself without allies, but he does assert that it is essential that a decision on whether or not to launch a nuclear weapon can be made in Europe by Europeans and not controlled solely from Washington.

General de Gaulle is not against European unity. But he is against the Monnet concept of growing European federalism, and the idea that the North Atlantic Treaty Organization should be strengthened into an Atlantic partnership. He has no wish to see the European Common Market of the Six enlarged. He made this bluntly clear in the manner and timing and the reasons which he gave for vetoing British entry in 1963. But on the other hand, since his return to power in France in 1958, he has been able to take stronger and more determined decisions to strengthen French participation in the Common Market than could possibly have been taken by the weak governments of the Fourth Republic. He has also forced the other partners—West Germany in particular—to make concessions in the field of agricultural policy which have put the Market two and a half years ahead of its schedule for economic integration. There is no question of the Europe of the Six going back on what has been achieved, or dismantling its unity. The question centers on how it will go forward.

Here De Gaulle strives to re-create in the world the identity of Europe, the image and personality of the foreign policies of Europe which the world felt before the old continent was submerged by the destruction of the Second World War and then held in the background by the Cold War confrontation of the two superpowers. This does not mean the "third force" idea, which has no reality for the Europeans and no practical political meaning. Europe could become a third force only as a result of the breakup of the Atlantic Alliance, which would leave the continent a military hostage to the Soviet Union.

Nor does neutralism have any political appeal or reality in Europe. Whatever General de Gaulle might be, he is far from a neutralist.

General de Gaulle plays his theme of European independence in the cynical certainty that there will be no war in Europe, that there is no political reason of any kind for a European conflict, and that in any case the nuclear might of the United States makes war impossible. He therefore feels very safe in espousing the new nationalism, in withdrawing France's military forces from NATO and asserting that the Organization must be overhauled, in exercising the newfound French economic strength, and in setting out relentlessly to prove that France is not tied to supporting United States policies in the world. The rest of Europe is caught between the challenge of Gaullist nationalism and loyalties to NATO and the United States, wariness of the realities of the nuclear world in which strong American involvement is the only ultimate guarantee of security. Gaullism does not, therefore, attract much open support in Europe, but this has not prevented the General from working a very considerable change in the European outlook twenty years after the war. Just below the surface lies Europe's latent anti-American frustrations. While these should not be exaggerated, neither should they be underrated. Anti-Americanism used to burst out in the "Ami Go Home" and "Ban the Bomb" campaigns, but today it is more sophisticated, involving such issues as the flow of American investment into Europe. The Gaullist themes of nationalism and independence offer an outlet for a wide variety of European frustrations.

Even without Gaullism, Europe would be taking its own independent place in the world again. Its economic recovery since 1953 has been one of the most remarkable expansions in industrial history. Gaullism sharpens and accentuates the great change in the political and economic balance between the United States and Europe, but the change would have produced its challenges to the old postwar order in any case. In the new era which is underway, three basic problems remain to be solved:

The future organization of Europe and European unity, and in particular the role that Britain eventually will play;

The German question and German reunification;

The future organization of the Atlantic Alliance and America's relations with Europe as the NATO treaty approaches the end of its first twenty-year span in 1969.

None of these problems will be solved quickly or easily. The struggle between Monnet's federalist Europe and De Gaulle's nationalist Europe will be played out subtly over a long time. German reunification, which has been frozen in the confrontation of the Cold War, is becoming an active problem which will involve a long process of diplomacy, with slow evolution rather than dramatic change. As the NATO Alliance moves toward 1969, General de Gaulle will be increasing his political pressures for a dismantling of the present military organization and its replacement with a new structure which reflects the changed power relationship between the United States and Europe.

These problems have their roots in past decisions and past attitudes and events, and this book, therefore, is first of all about the men and the affairs that have shaped the present state of Europe since Jean Monnet tapped that first blast furnace at Esch-sur-Alzette in 1953.

It is about Eden, Dulles, Churchill, Pierre Mendès-France, Adenauer, Bidault, Mollet, Selwyn Lloyd, Macmillan, Eisenhower, Gaitskell, Erhard, De Gaulle and Kennedy;

About the ending of the Indochina war in 1954 with the negotiations at Geneva that divided Vietnam into North and South;

About the death of the European Defense Community and how the pieces were picked up afterwards;

The death of the Fourth Republic, the De Gaulle revolution, the Fifth Republic and the rebirth of France;

The Adenauer era and the return of Germany;

The unending testing of the West in Berlin;

The Suez affair, the end of British imperialism and then Britain's thwarted efforts to join Europe;

The climactic De Gaulle press conference in January, 1963, and the ten days that shook the western world.

From this crowded and dramatic evolution of Europe in the decade from 1953 to 1963 new problems, new forces, new faces have moved into world focus. Where does De Gaulle seek to lead Europe? Will the British, who have lost an Empire, find a new role? What will the new generation in Germany bring to this new era in Europe? This book looks cautiously at the future, and the problems of America's relations with Europe at floodtide—perhaps the most hopeful time of two centuries.

2. France: The Fourth Republic

In the antiseptic political atmosphere of present-day France, it is regarded as bad taste to remember with sympathy or nostalgia the days of that impossible wreck of democracy, the Fourth Republic. Whenever President de Gaulle—proud, imperious, secure and almost uninhibited in the exercise of power in the Fifth Republic—mentions the Fourth Republic, he usually contrives to introduce the word "*nostalgie,*" and then he pronounces it as if he were holding his nose, sardonic scorn dripping from every syllable.

All the same, with all of its calamitous faults, bitter failures and built-in weaknesses—with its twenty-three different governments headed by nineteen different men in the twelve years and eight months of its life from October 1945 to May 1958—the poor old despised Fourth Republic was much more of a mirror of France, of French individualism and political personality than the present extraordinary once-in-a-century one-man rule of Charles de Gaulle. Moreover, it accomplished a great deal more for France and for Europe than it is popularly given credit for. Looking back across those years, the wonder is not that the Fourth Republic was such a failure, but that it accomplished as much as it did.

In France, an acute sense of personal independence, liberty and freedom is constantly at war with the kind of political self-discipline essential to successful parliamentary government. The French make a clear distinction in attitude between the French *nation,* to which they owe patriotism and honor, and the French *government,* to which they owe taxes. A Frenchman will render the former obligations with all of the heartfelt passion and fervor of his race. He is ready to die for France. But he cheats on his obligations to the latter. He evades the tax collector, thinks nothing of violating or circumventing the law, resists authority, and undermines or even sabotages the workings of the state. For the Frenchman, his democracy was born in 1789 as a revolution against tax collectors, the gendarmes, the law, authority, the moneyed class and oppressive government. A Frenchman does not look upon government as "his government." He views government and the law not as regulators of society for the common good, but as restrictions on liberty and an incursion on freedom.

Yet France is not a lawless anarchy. In fact a great deal more "law" and red-tape regulation surround daily life in France than in England or Germany, let alone the United States. But the law in France is relative—to what one can get away with, rather than absolute in its regulation or application. That is why a municipal bus barreled through a red light one night at a deserted Paris street corner as I, the law-abiding Anglo-Saxon, sat in my car patiently waiting for the light to turn green. And that is why the Paris police finally had to make a bonfire of a staggering four-year backlog of 3,000,000 parking violations at the end of 1963. A Frenchman will pay a parking fine quite readily if it is ever assessed, but in the meantime he cheerfully breaks the law against the odds that he may never be asked to pay up.

This ambivalent attitude toward the law exists, moreover, on both sides in France. You can never be certain whether the police will be brutally ruthless or excessively tolerant. Once a friend of ours visiting Paris drove up to a policeman in the center of the Champs-Élysées and asked in appealing schoolgirl French if she could make a forbidden left turn.

"Madame," the gendarme replied with French logic and exquisite courtesy, "were I not here it might be possible, but as I am here I am afraid that it is not."

The problem of democracy in France—of which the Fourth Republic offered a continuous thirteen-year example—begins, then, with the individualism of French character and the French suspicion and resentment of government, the law and authority. As a nation of individuals, the French are simply not used to the idea of public service or public spirit. They seldom organize themselves into community groups, service clubs, betterment societies, improvement movements, voluntary public service organizations—the kind of community welfare activities which abound in England and the United States. They give sparingly of their money to charities or universities or social institutions. A Frenchman works to achieve economic self-sufficiency, and he resents being expected or asked to share the fruits of his labor with the community or the government. He may well be personally generous, but that is a matter of his individualism—not any call of public spirit. Charity or philanthropy is handled with discretion rather than public attention. There are no great French institutions such as the Ford Foundation or England's Nuffield Foundation. Wealth in France does not carry with it the same traditional social obligations that it does in Britain or the United States.

The French Revolution, with its assault on tax collectors and the power of monarchical wealth, also served to strengthen the determination of the wealthy to cling to property, possessions and privilege and guard their riches as jealously as any peasant guards his meager life. The provincial château continues to remind the French peasant that he still has a long way to go before there is full "liberty, equality and fraternity" for him, and he uses his vote accordingly. François Mauriac, France's Nobel Prize writer, has written: "Those who are familiar with the provinces know that contemporary France was born of the mortal sin of envy. The peasant shuts his eyes and casts his vote for the Left, certain that he can make no mistake if he votes against those who wash and go to Mass. He loathes any distinctions in dress, occupation or ideas."

Thus, the revolution, which well served the cause of human liberty, has left France with a strong Leftist orientation in politics. By voting for the Communists, the Socialists, or other Leftist parties, the Frenchman acts in the revolutionary tradition to enlarge his social gains and resist the power of the wealthy. That is why in a nation of great individualism, resistant to authority, the Communists, authoritarian and anti-democratic, continue methodically to collect their usual 21 to 25 percent of the national vote—even today when France, under President de Gaulle, is the most firmly Rightist oriented that it has been in this century.

Until the return of De Gaulle and the death of the Fourth Republic, the consistent Leftist orientation of French politics made virtually impossible any normal political swing between a strong Right and a strong Left—the kind of pendulum movement which occurs from Republican to Democrat in the United States, or Conservative to Labour in England, and is the real essence of parliamentary democracy. But why did this firm Leftist orientation of French politics fail to produce stable government in both the Third and the Fourth Republics?

The answer lies in yet another of the political paradoxes of France.

While the French voted Left to protect themselves against the wealth and power of the monarchical Right, they also contrived to protect themselves against too much authority from anybody in the Fourth Republic by electing an incredible multiplicity of left-wing parties, groupings and factions. Being individualists, the French tend to follow individual political leaders rather than parties. Political movements in France can spring up like mushrooms or dandelions and disappear just as fast. The Poujadist Movement of the Fourth Republic was a classic example—launched in 1953 by an anarchistic wild-eyed young middle-class shopkeeper named Pierre Poujade from a small town in southwest France on a platform of refusal to pay certain sales taxes, which he declared to be intolerable for small businesses. By 1956, he had 2,446,000 Frenchmen voting with him to elect 53 deputies to the National Assembly. He was swept away, however, with all the other headline names of the 1950's in the collapse of the Fourth Republic, and today few Frenchmen can tell you what ever happened to Poujade, where he is living or what he is doing. The individualism and political fragmentation of the Fourth Republic reached a kind of mad apogee in the case of Canon Felix Kir, a venerable and salty Burgundian priest now nearing the age of ninety, a wartime resistance leader who has been deputy mayor of the city of Dijon for more than half a century and has served in the National Assembly for decades. The complete individualist, Canon Kir was a member of an Assembly grouping known as the National Council of Independents until he quarreled with the leadership and boldly declared himself to be an "Independent Independent." With the appealing nuance of this political label, he achieved the French politician's dream. He headed a one-man political party which was elected in the national voting of 1951.

As Charles de Gaulle once burst out to one of his aides: "How can you govern a country that produces 242 different kinds of cheese!"

When the Fourth Republic breathed its last, there were twelve different political parties in the National Assembly, ranging in strength from the Communists with 144 seats to the Progressives who held 6 seats out of a total membership of 695. A vicious political rhythm characterized the way France was governed. Under one government after another, conditions would deteriorate, problems would accumulate and the country would stagger toward chaos. Then, near the disaster point, the political leaders would select a temporary strong man, and back him in power sufficiently long to solve the particular problem of the moment. After that the knife would be wielded, the government would fall, and the old game resumed. The only concerted period of Rightist-led government in the Fourth Republic occurred from March to December of 1952, when Antoine Pinay, leader of the Independent Peasants, took over as head of a coalition with the unpleasant but necessary task of imposing stringent anti-inflation measures on the country. No Leftist coalition could brace itself to tackle the job. But as soon as Pinay's measures began to bear success, the Assembly dumped him and things went back to normal. A Leftist coalition was patched together which could pick up enough votes in the Center and Right to govern.

There was, however, one highly important, fundamental rule of the political game in the Fourth Republic. The Communists were never invited to share in the government. Democracy was weak and futile in the Fourth Republic, but it was never so weak that a government had to depend on the Communists for support. They usually held the largest bloc of Assembly votes, and this made coalition-forming extremely difficult and complicated, but once they were turned out of the government in 1947, they never got back in again.

Across the erratic comings-and-goings of politicians and governments, the sustaining elements in French national life ever since Napoleon have been the civil service and the Army. A civil service career offers not merely a stable job, but the attraction of continuing power. And in a purely technical sense, France undoubtedly has one of the most brilliantly directed government machines in Europe. Its hothouse civil service training schools—the École Nationale de'Administration which was established on De Gaulle's orders after the war, the École Polytechnique, the École Normale Superieure—are unique in the world, established for the prime purpose of training the best brains in France to run the country. Though power corrupts in France as much if not more than anywhere else in the world, and though on its petty levels the French bureaucracy can be as venal, unpleasant and dishonest as any, in the creative echelons of higher government administration the French civil service is in a class by itself for intelligence, skill, diplomatic technique and strength in depth. (It is strength in depth and skill, for example, which enables the French to dispatch men of caliber to Brussels to dominate the workings of the European Common Market.) In the absence of cohesive political leadership in the Fourth Republic, the civil service gave French policy a kind of lurching consistency. Thus, the ultimate anomaly of French democracy is that a nation of individualists, with the most passionate feelings about liberty and independence, allows itself to be run most of the time by the very elements of government which should be its servants and not its masters. The civil service gave France such stability as it had in the Fourth Republic, and then it was the Army which administered the deathblow and supported the "De Gaulle revolution" in Algeria.

There could be no more poignant example of this paradox of strength and weakness—the orderly civil service maintaining its routines in the midst of disaster—than the scene which General de Gaulle found when he returned to Paris on the day of its liberation, August 25, 1944. He made his way to the Ministry of War first, to establish both the symbolic and practical reality that a French government had returned to the seat of power. He reached the quadrangle on the rue Saint-Dominique at 5 o'clock in the evening, while there was still gunfire in the Paris streets. In his war memoirs, he recorded:

> I was immediately struck by the impression that nothing had changed inside these venerable halls. Gigantic events had overturned the world. Our Army was annihilated. France had virtually collapsed. But at the Ministry of War, the look of things remained immutable. In the courtyard, a unit of the Garde Republicaine presented arms as in the past. The vestibule, the staircase, the arms hanging on the walls, all these were as they had been. Here in person were the same stewards and ushers. I entered the "Minister's Office" which M. Paul Reynaud and I had left together on the night of June 10, 1940. Not a piece of furniture, not a rug, not a curtain had been disturbed. On the desk the telephone was in the same place and exactly the same names on the call buttons. Soon I was to learn that this was the case in all the other buildings in which the Republic housed itself. Nothing was missing except the State. It was my duty to restore it; I installed my staff at once and got down to work.*

Amid such political conditions, it is little to be wondered that a man of the ability, insight and vision of Jean Monnet should have elected to remain outside the arena of French politics and political life, and concentrate instead on serving in the machinery of power. Monnet, who has never been elected to public office in France, never served in a French cabinet and for many years of his life has not even been directly associated with French governments, nevertheless gave to the Fourth Republic two great basic achievements which

* De Gaulle's Memoirs, Vol. II, *Unity*.

establish its place in history. The first was the French system of national economic planning, which Monnet began organizing as soon as the French Government returned to Paris in 1944, and which has become the envy of Europe and a model of modern democratic governmental operation for all the world. The second was the concept of the European Coal and Steel Community, by which France took the lead in postwar European foreign policy and brought the ideal of "united Europe" out of the realm of political slogan and into practical action.

Orderly, concerted economic planning would probably have been the last thing anyone would have expected to find amid the muddled, anarchic political life of the Fourth Republic. It was self-evident when the war ended that French recovery would be impossible without government planning. All the same, every kind of interest and orthodoxy and political pressure threatened to hamstring economic planning. Should a special planning ministry be established? Should there be political and government control over planning? Should it be purely civil service? The Communists and the extreme Left pressed for a Marxist approach of state take-over and state control, while the conservative wealth and private industry of France loomed just as powerfully to sabotage any planning that did not take private interests into account.

Monnet devised a flexible "middle way" based on cooperation rather than power. First of all, he insisted that planning should operate outside the regular channels of government. He established the small, independent Commissariat du Plan, staffed by about 150 people. Its operation was and is decentralized. It brings diverse political elements and economic groups together to sit down with interested government departments and work to achieve the maximum ground of common consent. In effect, Monnet created a kind of partnership of government, industry, agriculture, trade unions, finance and business in national planning under the direction of his Commissariat. By keeping the operation outside the machinery of government, he insured that planning would not suffer at every political change. By making it a cooperative effort, he avoided political resistance in the National Assembly and economic resistance in the country. (Four years later, when Monnet turned his attention to drafting the European Coal and Steel Community treaty in 1950, he adopted a completely different approach. He dropped the "cooperative" idea and deliberately excluded private industry or the trade unions from any direct role. He ordained that power and decision be invested in a single supranational High Authority—an example of what one of his long-time associates calls "part of a higher consistency—conformity to his own instinct.")

In twenty years since the end of World War II, thirty French governments have come and gone,* but there have been only three Commissioners of the Plan: Monnet from 1946 until 1952 when he became first president of the High Authority of the Coal and Steel Community at Luxembourg; Étienne Hirsch, who followed Monnet until 1959; and the present commissioner, Pierre Massé (who is working on the Fifth Plan to shape the French economy into the 1970's).

France's economic plan for 1966 to 1970 calls for an expansion of the national economy at an annual rate of 5 percent. Within this basic framework, it has also been laid down by the planners that investment in a *"civilisation des gadgets"* will be avoided or discouraged, and that emphasis will be on social investment—new schools, hospitals, playgrounds and sports facilities, the development of ports, harbors and roads, and regional investments to obtain a better distribution of industry. In the immediate postwar period, the planners gave priority to restoration of the French railway system, expansion of electric power and provision of machine tools for industry.

It falls to the state to carry out the main lines of the plan through directing expenditure on public works, through control of capital and credit to insure that money going into private industry is going where the planners want it to go. Finally, of course, the government controls the operations of the nationalized state industries—the railroads, gas, water and electricity, the tobacco industry, oil, the nationalized Renault automobile works, the airlines. In private fields, the plan will fix such targets as a 6 percent increase in steel capacity, or a boost in textiles. Nothing is "dictated" or ordered, but a blueprint has been drawn. Like any blueprint, it is subject to changes and alterations while the building is going up. But it brings government, industry, agriculture, the banks, the trade unions and local authorities together to agree on a program for investment and expansion in accordance with a coherent economic concept.

Thus, for example, total public expenditure in France was only 5 percent higher in 1950 than it was in 1938. But under the economic planning system, the government had directed its spending in such a

* France had four provisional governments after the war; twenty-three governments under the Fourth Republic constitution, and three under the Fifth Republic as of the end of 1964.

way that 38 percent of its money was going into direct productive purposes in 1950 as against only 5 percent in 1938.

France regained her prewar level of industrial production under the Fourth Republic within three years after the end of the war. It had taken twice as long for her to recover after the Armistice of 1918. When Marshall Plan aid began to flow to Europe in 1948, the French, with a coordinated economic plan, were well poised to state their priority needs and lay down a program which formed the base for renewal of their whole economy and the "great leap forward" which followed from 1953. It is perfectly true that the headlines out of Paris during the Marshall Plan days usually centered on inflation, the black-market rate of the French franc, the incredible cost of lunch at Maxim's as compared with the wages of the secretary back in the office, the laxity of tax collections and the slowness of housing construction. But behind such headlines, successive governments were in fact sticking to the recommendations of the economic planners at constant political risk, and France was pouring money into machine tools for industry, rebuilding its railway system into the most modern in Europe, damming the Rhone Valley for power and a new waterway, modernizing its steel industry and expanding its productivity per worker by 4 percent each year from 1949 to 1958 when the Fourth Republic fell.

Today, under De Gaulle, state economic planning goes right on. In fact, the Fifth Republic has even managed to balance France's national budget for the first time in thirty-five years. Planning is not without its critics, and in the Fifth Republic the economic problems are entirely different, so that the emphasis on what to plan and how to plan is changing. The main criticism lies in the fact that planning tends to carry with it the seeds of built-in inflation by demands for expansion which cannot always be met.

All the same, even with its weaknesses and even though French postwar recovery depended on many other factors besides economic planning, the French Government today has at its disposal the most effective and coherent economic planning machinery of any modern democratic state. In the words of Monnet's present-day successor, Pierre Massé: "I am still waiting for the moment when someone in this country openly demands the abolition of The Plan."

But unhappily for France, political stability and the life and eventually death of the Fourth Republic never turned on the economic management of the nation—else the Fourth Republic would certainly still be alive. It is true that governments often fell and were re-formed in those merry-go-round days on what narrowly amounted to "economic issues." The economic problem, however, was not in Paris, not in the Commissariat du Plan, not in the Ministry of Finance, not in the Bank of France—but in the war in Indochina, and after that the war in Algeria. The Fourth Republic survived the Indochina crisis, but it did not survive Algeria.

By the spring of 1954 the Indochina war was in its seventh year and the casualty total was approaching 150,000. A French expeditionary force of some 200,000 Foreign Legionnaires and French regulars was bogged down in the rice paddies and jungles of the Tongking Delta. (The French never did send conscripts to fight in Indochina, although they did to Algeria.) Another 200,000 Vietnamese natives had been armed and trained to fight alongside the French—not, however, with much evident enthusiasm. The cost of the war in 1954 was nearing $5 billion.

Here was the root of inflation and economic weakness which no government could solve without halting the war. Here too was another of the roots of political instability in France—for no premier was ever strong enough to muster either the means to win the war or, by overriding the "Indochina Lobby" in the National Assembly, the political power to end it. This was typical of the pattern of Fourth Republic politics, and for seven years the Indochina problem lurched from one government to the next, from one military commander to another, from bad to worse. Eventually France turned to the only really strong, historic figure among the nineteen different men who headed the twenty-three different governments of the Fourth Republic: Pierre Mendès-France.

Mendès-France's dynamic impact on the affairs of France, and his successful negotiation of an end to the Indochina war in 1954, represented far more than just a political drama of the Fourth Republic. The policies which he resolutely set out to pursue marked the first big diplomatic breach of the postwar era between Europe and the United States—the first decisive point at which Europe, rightly or wrongly, refused to follow policies and advice from Washington and rejected a course of action sought by the United States. France and Britain set out to liquidate by diplomatic means a situation in which Communism had gained an upper hand and in which the Western position, in the European view, was no longer tenable. The repercussions of the Indochina settlement are still a burning issue of the United States foreign policy a decade later. In 1954, Indochina produced the first of the great European clashes with that old diplomatic bullfighter and enigmatic moralist, John Foster Dulles.

On the heels of the Indochina partition and armistice which Dulles so resolutely opposed came the second of these affairs—the death of the State Department's beloved European Defense Community treaty, over which Mendès-France also presided. Two years later, the Suez affair erupted in a blaze of misunderstanding in the middle of the Atlantic Alliance. Then, beginning in January of 1963, Charles de Gaulle launched his determined campaign to end what he regards as an American political and military hegemony over Europe, with his thunderbolt veto of British entry into the European Common Market, and rejection of the "Kennedy Grand Design" concept for an Atlantic partnership.

In each of these complicated affairs the issues and the problems, the emotions and the personalities of the men involved differed widely. But there was one underlying theme. The United States was caught by surprise and had failed to assess fully the interests and actions of European governments. Inevitably it fell to one man to embody the breach with Washington: Mendès-France over Indochina and the death of the E.D.C. treaty; Eden over Suez; De Gaulle over Atlantic partnership and the future of the NATO alliance. There was therefore the easy tendency to dismiss what had happened with the remark that "one man's decision does not represent the interests of Europe." But this rationalization was really insufficient. There were plenty of other men in Europe, it is true, who objected to what was done on this or that occasion, and would have acted otherwise. But they were not in power and they did not have responsibility. Indeed, many of them failed when they did hold responsibility and power—in France in particular. History is made by the decisions of men, and the view of what should be done is never going to be the same in Paris or London or Bonn as it is in Washington. It is a great mistake, which Americans often seem to make when Europe fails to act as America would like, to take the attitude that European leaders do not know what they are doing or where their best interests lie.

Looking back across these diplomatic clashes between the United States and Europe, each of which I was covering at the time, there seems to have been a kind of historic inevitability about the events themselves. First would come an accumulation of small decisions and actions which were misinterpreted and misunderstood, after which wrong estimates of intentions were all too easily made. Then came the emergence of particular men in positions of high power, with strong personalities and commitments to their own consciences and their political supporters. Then followed a certain political opacity which can overtake the judgment of men in power when they have reached an inner conviction, producing a rationalization of decisions which were foreordained.

It was clear as events unfolded in those days of the Fourth Republic, and increasingly clear as the secret records and personal memoirs begin to emerge, that John Foster Dulles, by his own personality and character and above all by the fact that he held almost uninhibited freewheeling power at vital moments over the conduct of American foreign policy, contributed immeasurably to the frustrations and emotions, and ultimately to the bitter determination of men like Pierre Mendès-France and Sir Anthony Eden, Christian Pineau and Guy Mollet to assert their right to independent action. Charles de Gaulle harbored this same bitter frustration with Franklin D. Roosevelt and the United States, long before the days of Dulles, and De Gaulle waited more than twenty years before he found his ultimate moment to assert himself against the "Anglo-Saxon domination" of Europe.

On the Indochina question, Dulles was caught in an impossible "moral dilemma" of his own making. He was running a moral crusade against atheistic and abhorrent Communism, even though the Communists had clearly gained the upper hand in military power in the Tongking Delta. At the same time, Dulles had declared neutralism to be immoral, and took the attitude that colonialism was just short of immorality also—with the result that he was face to face with the problem of asking one of his allies to bolster its immoral colonial rule to fend off immoral Communism despite the feelings of immoral neutralists such as India without whose support or at least tacit blessing no policy was likely to work. Moralizing has always had its attractions for Americans in power, and in the 1950's Dulles carried it to Calvinist High Church extremes. But rendering unto God the things that are Caesar's can only lead to complications in the conduct of foreign policy. As Dulles's predecessor, Dean Acheson, has written:

> To characterize conduct between nations as moral or immoral will involve us in confusions of vocabulary and of thought with which, despite their importance, we need not struggle. The language of moral discourse—colored as it is apt to be at one end

> with fervor and, at the other, with self-righteousness—is more likely to obscure than to clarify. The substance of moral discussion, which concerns the conduct of individuals within a society toward one another, is more likely than not to be misleading if applied to the relations of one society to another. Undoubtedly the problems have something in common. Restraints upon the conduct of society as a whole may be adopted or imposed because of the effect of one society upon others. But they are not the same restraints. They deal with different situations; and it is best to state principles in terms of their purpose and effect without characterizing them as moral or immoral.*

The Indochina conference opened in Geneva on April 26, 1954—preceded by a feverish period of Dulles diplomacy which had as its main outcome a series of inter-Allied arguments and misunderstandings. The root of the problem lay in the fact that Dulles was pursuing one objective and the British and the French quite another. Dulles had laid down as a personal moral creed that he would never negotiate any kind of an agreement which involved the surrender of territory to Communism, no matter what the military facts might be, and he was therefore prepared to go to any length, including dropping the atomic bomb, in order to avoid "defeat at the conference table" over Indochina. But Sir Anthony Eden, Georges Bidault and finally Pierre Mendès-France were seeking to bring the fighting to an end on the best terms they could get. When Dulles's pre-conference moves to form a military alliance in the area and enlarge the war were rejected by Britain and France, the American Secretary of State withdrew from the Geneva scene in an extraordinary display of diplomatic pique. In the end, the British and French got far better terms in the 1954 Indochina settlement than Dulles ever believed possible—but it was no thanks to Dulles's diplomacy that they came out of the negotiation as well as they did.

Dulles's first move in advance of the Geneva conference was to try to form some kind of a "coalition front" in Southeast Asia on the NATO model, an alliance through which United States military power could be brought to bear, particularly against Red China. With this in mind, he flew to London on April 11 to meet Sir Anthony Eden for the first of many diplomatic misunderstandings which marked Indochina and after that the road to Suez.

Eden agreed that it would be wise to issue a diplomatic warning to

* Dean Acheson, *Power and Diplomacy*. Harvard University Press, 1959.

the Red Chinese of the dangers to peace if the Indochina conference were to fail. But he was firmly against any concrete action in advance of the conference which would enlarge the war. Above all, he emphasized to Dulles that nothing should be done without consulting India and Burma, whose support Eden felt to be essential to the West in obtaining a workable settlement. The two men then agreed on a London communiqué which stated that "we are ready to take part with other countries principally concerned in an examination of the possibility of establishing a collective defense" in Southeast Asia. This was as far as Eden intended or expected to go at that point. But Dulles flew home and suddenly announced four days later, without further consultation, that he was convening a "working group" of nine ambassadors in Washington to begin discussions on a new Southeast Asia Treaty Organization. India was not consulted, let alone invited. Dulles informed the British that if India were included he would have to invite Formosa too. Eden blew up. He instructed the British ambassador in Washington, Sir Roger Makins, to inform Dulles that Britain was not prepared to discuss any such treaty in advance of the Geneva meeting, and in a telegram to Makins he added:

> Americans may think the time past when they need consider the feelings or difficulties of their Allies. It is the conviction that this tendency becomes more pronounced every week that is creating mounting difficulties for anyone in this country who wants to maintain close Anglo-American relations. We, at least, have constantly to bear in mind all our Commonwealth partners, even if the United States does not like some of them; and I must ask you to keep close watch on this aspect of our affairs and not hesitate to press it on the United States.*

In the face of this blast from London, Dulles converted the Washington meeting into a "general briefing conference" on the forthcoming problems at Geneva—although Eden added that he was "still unhappy about the impression which this get-together might create." (Under the happiest of circumstances, Eden was a fussy and short-tempered diplomat).

In the meantime, with the opening of the Geneva conference now barely a week away, the French military posture in Indochina was rapidly deteriorating. Deep in the Tongking Delta, the French High Command had committed itself to a fortress "strong point" at a cross-

* Eden Memoirs, *Full Circle.*

road of jungle trails called Dienbienphu. The idea was to attract enemy forces to attack and thus meet their doom, on the model by which Marshal Leyautey had subdued Morocco for the French in the early 1900's. But the difference between Moroccan Berbers with 1870 rifles and Vietminh Communists backed by the Red Chinese was the difference of two worlds, vast resources and a whole epoch of ideological and revolutionary military thinking. Before the baffled French knew what hit them, the Dienbienphu defenders were suddenly faced with eight times the total enemy artillery which French intelligence had hitherto identified in the whole of North Vietnam. Dienbienphu was surrounded and cut off from reinforcements or supplies except by air. Instead of a strongpoint, the French had stuck their heads in a noose.

This was the situation when Dulles took off for Paris on April 22 for preliminary meetings with NATO, the British and the French before continuing to Geneva to confront Molotov and the Communist side. He found the French foreign minister, Georges Bidault, in a state of nerves which seemed to border on collapse. Bidault wanted help, but he wanted to end the war. He wanted to strengthen his position going into the conference, but not to a point of risking that the talks be broken off by the Communists before they even started. In fact, he did not know what to do.

Dulles now played his next card: an offer of United States military intervention in the form of an air strike from carriers, provided the French would formally request American help and the British agree to it. Then in private talks with Bidault, Dulles added the horrendous proposal of using the atom bomb. As far as is known, the atom bomb offer was never conveyed in writing. It appears in no formal records. It is not mentioned in either the Eden memoirs or those of President Eisenhower. But it is Bidault's stated recollection * that Dulles made the proposal not once but twice, in separate conversations in Paris on April 23. He first suggested an atomic strike against Chinese Communist territory north of Vietnam and the supply lines to the Vietminh forces. Next, according to Bidault, he talked about the possibility of using two tactical atom bombs against Vietminh troops surrounding Dienbienphu. Bidault, aghast at the implications of what Dulles was proposing, pointed out that it would be impossible to predict what Russia might do if a nuclear bomb fell on Red China. And as to its

* Bidault has recounted the story to the authors of *Duel at the Brink* (Doubleday, 1960), Roscoe Drummond and Gaston Coblentz, and to others.

use around Dienbienphu, the two sides were by now so closely engaged in trench-warfare conditions that it would be impossible to "atomize" the Communists without wiping out the French as well.

Meanwhile, Eden, who knew of the United States conditional offer of an air strike even if he did not know that Dulles had the atom bomb in mind, had been maneuvered into a "veto position." His indignation at Dulles's tactics was considerable, but there was no doubt in his mind about the answer. He flew posthaste to London for an emergency cabinet meeting on Sunday, April 24, and obtained from Sir Winston Churchill and the full cabinet immediate backing for a prompt and resolute "No": no intervention, no enlarging of the war until the outcome of the Geneva negotiations was known.

It is impossible to believe that a man of Dulles's experience and intelligence did not know or had not estimated the British and French reaction to his proposals. But presumably he had now safely satisfied his moral conscience. He had now made the maximum offer which any man on earth could make to fight the Communists—knowing that he was quite safe, that he could count on his Allies to haul him back from the brink. Since he had proved that they would not play his game, he would not play theirs. He stayed at Geneva only one week.

Dulles was nothing if not generous in his press background briefings, and he called us together the afternoon before his departure. At the end of a conference table he sat doodling on a long, yellow scratch-pad as he talked, his lean, strong, somewhat morose face an impassive mask except for an occasional nervous twitch in his left eye. Things might be done at Geneva which the United States "cannot accept," he said. What did he mean? How could you avoid the consequences of a defeat in arms? "Well, we just will not participate," was Dulles's answer. He had never signed a piece of paper ceding territory to the Communists, Dulles snapped at the correspondents, and you would never find his name on any such paper. And so, wrapping his morals around him, the Secretary of State of the free world's strongest power walked out, rebuffed in fighting the war, refusing to have anything to do with the peace.*

Eden labored on, possibly relieved that he no longer had to deal with Dulles face-to-face. United States Undersecretary of State Walter Bedell Smith, a no-nonsense soldier, was left behind to deal with the facts that Dulles refused to face, but eventually he too went home

* This crucial decision of Dulles's diplomacy is not even mentioned in President Eisenhower's memoirs.

and the American delegation was left in the hands of a career foreign service ambassador, U. Alexis Johnson. The immediate problem of the Western allies in those early days of May was to try to put a little cohesion and purpose into the French in the agony of the fall of Dienbienphu, whose heroic defenders, now fighting for a plot the size of a baseball field, surrendered on May 8, 1954, nine years to the day after the end of World War II in Europe. Gradually, and thanks largely to the presence in Geneva of some of those brilliant and hardheaded career diplomats who sustain French governments in crisis, a negotiation for an armistice began to take shape. There was a certain war weariness on the Communist side too, even though they had the upper hand locally in Tongking.

In Paris, the government of Joseph Laniel survived a confidence vote on Dienbienphu, and Bidault stumbled on at Geneva. But the end was only a matter of time. Laniel's was not a government which could take the hard decision necessary to concluding peace in Indochina. The Communists knew it and everybody in Paris knew it. At the end of May, the Foreign Ministers decided to take a one-month recess at Geneva and leave military experts and technical advisers behind to put together the outlines of draft agreements. In Indochina the military situation was temporarily quiet. Eden and Sir Winston Churchill flew to Washington for a meeting with Eisenhower and Dulles.

In the early hours of Monday, June 14, the sixteenth postwar government of France finally fell, and Pierre Mendès-France began consultations to form a new cabinet.

Pierre Mendès-France is a powerful example of the individualism of French politics. A member of that odd collection of political bedfellows, the French Radical Party (some collaborationists, some resistance leaders, some extreme Left, some to the Right), Mendès-France's own position is that of an unorthodox left-of-center liberal-nationalist. It attracted a great deal of intellectual admiration in Fourth Republic days, but little political following or support. He was not even the leader of his own party, and his political role in the National Assembly had been that of a kind of Cassandra of French affairs—particularly in regard to the war in Indochina—until France turned to him in June, 1954. Mendès-France had been a junior minister in one of the prewar governments, flew with the Free French Air Force during the war, and then joined De Gaulle's Committee of

National Liberation as a financial expert. He led the French delegation to the Bretton Woods negotiations which established the World Bank and International Monetary Fund in 1944, and on his return to Paris he became Minister of National Economy in the liberation government. In 1945 he resigned, to retire to the political sidelines for nine years, because De Gaulle would not back him in a rigorous program to call in the entire French currency issue, block all bank accounts and suppress war profiteering and inflation through complete currency reform. When De Gaulle pointed out to Mendès-France that all the experts of the day were against him, he coolly replied: "I know a Colonel de Gaulle who had all the experts against him," and quit. Now he was virtually the only strong figure in the National Assembly who had consistently and relentlessly pounded away on the theme that France had to liquidate its Indochina colonialism and end a war it could not win.

When the Assembly turned to him, he disdainfully announced that no matter how the Communists voted, he would not count their 93 members among his majority. He was endorsed in office by a vote of 419 to 47 in the early hours of June 18, with 143 deputies abstaining. His was a vast majority, and Communist support meant nothing in his bold accession to power. His first act was to declare publicly to the National Assembly that if he did not obtain an Indochina peace settlement within one month—he fixed the deadline as July 20—he would resign from office. His first diplomatic move was to fly to the Swiss capital of Berne to confer with Chou En-lai, then Chinese Communist foreign minister. Such conduct was anathema to Dulles and the established policies of the United States. There was no attempt in Washington to disguise official America's shock that France could have placed such a man in power and official America's feeling that complete sellout and total surrender would follow in Indochina. But Mendès-France was no Pétain. He was at last giving France the kind of clear and unequivocal leadership it so desperately needed. He took over the foreign ministry along with the premiership so that he personally would be conducting the Indochina negotiations, and for the first months in office he directed French affairs from the Quai d'Orsay instead of the prime minister's residence at the Hotel Matignon. He nailed one simple maxim to his office wall: *We must stop offering more than the French nation can perform and then we must perform what we offer.*

Along with his audacious self-imposed deadline for an armistice,

Mendès-France made two astute moves to bolster his bargaining position in Geneva and demonstrate to the Red Chinese and the Russians that he meant business. He announced to the National Assembly that if he did not get an armistice on honorable terms by July 20, then his last act before resigning as premier would be to ask the Assembly to authorize the sending of military conscripts to Indochina. He would demand a vote of confidence on such a measure, and then he would hand over to a successor the means to increase France's Indochina war effort. At the same time, at the urging of General Paul Ely, the Army Chief of Staff, and Ambassador Jean Chauvel who was in charge of the French delegation at Geneva, Mendès-France ordered small but significant regular Army reinforcements to Indochina immediately. The move was kept secret from the French public, but it was deliberately leaked to the Red Chinese.

Chauvel returned to Geneva in advance of Mendès-France and met Molotov for a preliminary review of the state of the negotiations before the two sides got down to work again. It was a conversation which marked a turning-point in the long and complicated affair. Chauvel talked for nearly half an hour, with Molotov listening impassively, interrupting only once. Chauvel told Molotov that the French had been moving ahead in a reasonably good atmosphere with the Vietminh political leaders, but that when it came to talking with the Vietminh military staff officers on such practical matters as drawing up map areas where one side or the other was agreed to be in local control, they were getting nowhere.

"Perhaps you can be of help to us in this," Chauvel said. "I am prepared to instruct the French military delegation to meet with the Russian military at any time."

Molotov grunted that this was a matter for the Vietminh and not one in which the Russians could interfere. Chauvel took the rebuff without comment and the conversation ended. Twenty minutes after Chauvel returned to the French villa, the Soviet delegation was on the telephone. The Russian military delegation would like a meeting with the French military at the earliest convenience of the French, a voice said. Chauvel's feeler had been picked up but, as often happens with the Russians, they made it *their* move and acted on *their* terms. Nevertheless, from that moment on the French were certain that they were going to get their Armistice.

Mendès-France returned to Geneva on July 10, with a bare ten days to go before his deadline.

Impossible as the situation seemed after months of dither and maneuver, behind the scenes a great deal of diplomatic spadework had been accomplished, so that the outcome now depended on hard policy decisions. But the first essential was the presence of the United States at the side of its Allies. Ambassador Johnson was the first to admit to correspondents who visited him that the absence of Dulles was all but inexplicable, and that it was essential for the United States to back the best chance the West had to obtaining a realistic settlement. Mendès-France, meanwhile, had conferred earnestly and at length with American ambassador, C. Douglas Dillon, in Paris on the problem, and on July 12 it was announced that Dulles would fly to the French capital to meet Eden and the French premier.

In Geneva that day, Mendès-France invited four or five Americans, who had been covering the negotiations from the early stages, to his lakeside villa for a talk. We gathered in chairs under the trees in the hot summer weather, and our first impression was of the relaxed, confident composure of the man, in sharp contrast to the bewildered and unhappy Bidault. Coolly and with no trace of irritation or anger, Mendès-France explained that while he could understand why Dulles might not want to be "associated" with an Indochina armistice, nevertheless, unless the Allies stood together and he had American support, anything could happen. There was a limit to what he would concede as an honorable peace settlement, and the Communist side knew that failure to agree meant that fighting would go on. With American support and backing, he thought he could obtain an honorable settlement.

The next morning we followed Mendès-France back to Paris for his confrontation with Dulles. They met alone for an hour first, and then were joined by Sir Anthony Eden for a "working dinner" at the Hotel Matignon. Dulles informed his Allies that, after discussions with President Eisenhower, it had been decided that he should not return to Geneva. American public opinion "would never tolerate the guaranteeing of the subjection of millions of Vietnamese to Communist rule," he told Eden and Mendès-France, and he said that he did not believe the French could get even minimally reasonable terms for a settlement. There then occurred one of those small illuminating incidents of men and history.

The Communists had been demanding partition of Indochina on the 14th or even 13th parallel as a basis for a settlement. Mendès-France produced a map of the country after dinner, and after reviewing the military situation, with Dulles at his side, he put his finger on the 18th parallel across the narrow waist of dumbbell-shaped Vietnam and declared that this was the partition line which he would demand. Dulles, peering with disbelief and thinking in terms of a line much farther south, thought the French premier had the map upside down. He turned it around and said: "You mean in this direction?" Mendès-France, startled and confused, turned the map back and said certainly not—he was talking about the 18th parallel and he was pointing to the 18th parallel. Dulles returned to the United States Embassy residence shortly before midnight—where twenty or so rather antagonistic American correspondents had been enjoying the hospitality of the Ambassador's cellar while waiting to interrogate him—and cabled President Eisenhower to the effect that his faith in French intention had been restored. He suggesting that Bedell Smith be sent back to Geneva. Still he would have nothing to do with the conference himself.

Back at Geneva, the Communist reduced their partition demands from the 14th parallel to the 15th and then the 16th while Mendès-France held out for the 18th—and finally settled on a river line just south of the 17th, which retained the ancient Annamite holy city of Hue in the territory of the South Vietnam state. All was virtually ready for final signature at 11 P.M. on the evening of July 20, with one hour to go to the Mendès-France deadline—but there was still one last drama to be played out.

The French delegation had been handling the drafting of the armistice agreements covering Vietnam and Laos, but the Cambodians—being an independent-minded people with a strong sense of national identity in the midst of Indochina—had insisted on doing their own drafting and negotiating within the framework of the big-power settlement. They were represented at Geneva by two remarkable little men, their foreign minister, Tep Phan, and their then ambassador to Washington, Nong Kimny. Each of them was only a little over five feet tall, and with their dark hair, smooth Oriental faces and slight bodies they looked almost adolescent. But they were to behave like giants in those final hours. I had seen Nong Kimny on numerous occasions during the absorbing eighty-six days of the Geneva conference, and he had made a deep impression on me—a man of strong emotions and humility masked by a cool intelligence and the controlled exterior of the Orient and the professional diplomat.

"Sometimes at night when I get back to my hotel from the conference sessions I become physically sick from the Communist twisting and distortions I have had to listen to all afternoon, and the terrible strain of knowing what could happen to my country if I miss a point or make a mistake out at the Palais des Nations," he had said to me quietly at lunch one day.

As the Mendès-France deadline neared, the Cambodians had been urgently pressing to get down to cases with the preoccupied and harassed principals—the French premier, Eden and Molotov. They found several points in the terms of the general settlement unacceptable for Cambodia and had quietly reinforced their position in a meeting with Bedell Smith, who had given them full American backing for their demands—in itself proof enough of the hollowness of Dulles's "absentee policy" and the extreme importance of strong American participation at the negotiations. Now as the clock ticked toward midnight, they waited to be summoned to the British lakeside villa where the "Big Three" were locked in negotiation.

At last the word came, and the Cambodians reached the villa at 11:20 P.M. They found Mendès-France near total exhaustion, slouched on a sofa and fighting to keep a tired body and an even more tired mind alert. Eden, notoriously short-tempered behind his diplomatic façade, was tense and edgy from the long strain. Molotov was Molotov—impassive and indestructible. The two Cambodians sat down and began with the utmost Oriental politeness.

"We explained to them," Nong Kimny recounted, "that while we understood the deadline of the Premier of France and its great importance, nevertheless we considered certain terms to be unacceptable to our country. We regretted that there had not been time to clear these points away, but we did not feel that it was our fault and so we had to insist on further discussions."

They then presented some remarkable demands which had the effect of changing the whole character of the Indochina settlement as it applied to Cambodia and of reinforcing the sovereignty and national integrity of that country—the only one of the three former Indochina states to have survived without Communist penetration.

First, the Big Three agreement had called for the organizing of "regroupment areas" in South Vietnam, Laos and Cambodia, into which the Communist forces would concentrate. They would then be disarmed and evacuated back to North Vietnam. The Cambodians calmly said that there was no such need for any such arrangements in their country. There should be a cease-fire and the Communists should simply get out, period. Mendès-France threw back his hands. The exasperated Eden controlled his temper. Molotov listened. Discussion began, and then, surprisingly, Molotov gave way and agreed to the Cambodian demand.

The two men now moved to their second point. The Big Three document would have forbidden the importation of arms or the establishment of foreign military bases in any of the three countries. The Cambodians looked at Molotov and said calmly that this was incompatible with true sovereignty. Cambodia had no intention of joining any foreign power blocs and would pursue a policy of strict neutrality, but if Cambodia wanted to import arms or seek foreign advisers to help preserve her indepedence and sovereignty, she must be free to do so. Such restrictions on national sovereignty just as a country was beginning its independent life were unacceptable, the Cambodians declared. Exasperation and tension again swept the room, and argument started all over. But again to the surprise of Eden and the exhausted Mendès-France, Molotov gave way. Possibly Old Iron Pants was so bemused by the courage of these men that he was impelled to be generous.

It was now well past midnight, but the Cambodians pressed relentlessly to yet a third demand. The Big Three had determined that the terms of the armistice were to be supervised by a commission consisting of India, Poland and Canada, and that the cost of the operations of the commission were to be borne by the Indochina states. Cambodia was a poor country with great economic problems to be faced, the Cambodian foreign minister said, and he did not think it right that the Great Powers impose an added burden on his government as a result of the peace settlement.

This time Molotov had had enough.

"We have agreed that the Communists forces will evacuate Cambodia without any regrouping," he said. "We have agreed that you will have the right to import arms and ask for foreign military advisers in your country if you wish. I think that Cambodia can pay for the jeeps for the armistice commission to supervise these arrangements."

Mendès-France and the exasperated Eden nodded their accord. Tep Phan and Nong Kimny expressed their thanks for the consideration they had received and, apologizing for the lateness of the hour, withdrew. It was just before 3 A.M. when their car pulled away from the British villa. The Geneva negotiations were over.

"We felt that our position was important to all the free nations of the world," Nong Kimny said very simply later that same day in recounting what had happened. It was more than that. His was a profound example of true "moral courage."

Pierre Mendès-France flew back to Paris and landed at Villacoublay military airfield near Versailles, closed off from the public. Relief in France at the end of the seven-year Indochina war was great, but as far as the French premier was concerned it was no occasion for national rejoicing or demonstrations. He had his driver follow a circuitous route into the city. All the same, a crowd of about 200 had gathered to cheer him when he arrived at the Quai d'Orsay. That afternoon in the National Assembly, he characterized the agreements as "sometimes cruel—but the best we could hope to get under the circumstances we faced." The next day the Assembly gave him a prodigious 471–14 vote of confidence.

Mendès-France was now in the strongest position of political power of any Frenchman since General de Gaulle at the liberation—the strongest enjoyed by any French premier until De Gaulle's return in 1958. It was a position not merely of votes in the Assembly, but the genuine substantive popular support of the French people. At last France had a leader who could and would lead. A wave of political exhilaration swept the nation. The initials "P.M.-F." took their place in newspaper headlines in an emulation of the style and impact of "F.D.R." There was, in fact, a deliberate cultivation by the "Mendèsistes" of the parallels between the New Deal and the political philosophy of Mendès-France. His once lonely position in the National Assembly now became a national political cult. Nor was Mendès-France shy about his political personality and public impact.

He did what no other Fourth Republic premier ever had bothered to do, and took to the radio regularly every Saturday night for "fireside chats" to discuss with the French people the problems of France. Every successful politican has to have his pleasant personal idiosyncracies about which people can poke fun and make jokes, and for a Frenchman, Mendès-France had two spendid ones. First of all he liked a big breakfast, English style: orange juice, cereal, bacon and eggs, toast, coffee and cold milk. Next, he urged the French people to drink milk instead of wine, even tried to get milk introduced into the French Army, and launched a national sobriety campaign. It was certainly a new idea for the French, and did wonders to fix the image of the new premier in people's minds and give him a "political identity." In national popularity as well as power and authority, Mendès-France was now rising like a balloon far above the heads of the dismayed deputies of the National Assembly who had launched him.

But Indochina was only the first and worst of an enormous accumulation of postponed decisions and avoided issues which he had inherited when he took office. His energy was a full match for both the problems and the power he now possessed, and he knew that he must strike fast and hard while the iron was hot. Ten days after the signature of the Indochina peace agreements, Mendès-France was on the move again.

He took off secretly at dawn from Villacoublay for Tunis in North Africa, where rioting had broken out while the Geneva conference was still in progress. With him as an act of political prudence he took two staunch Gaullists, Marshal Pierre Alphonse Juin and Christian Fouchet, later one of De Gaulle's cabinet ministers. From the airport they drove straight to the palace of the aging Bey of Tunis overlooking the sea at Carthage, and there Mendès-France made a startling offer: immediate home rule for the protectorate and discussions on a new treaty of association with France that would lead swiftly to Tunisian independence. Inevitably the end of the Indochina war and the independence which the former French colonies of Cambodia, Laos and divided Vietnam had now achieved would have repercussions in the rest of the French Empire and particularly in the Maghreb—the North African possessions of Morocco, Algeria and Tunisia. Once out of the Indochina fryingpan, France was about to find itself back in the North African fire. Mendès-France was determined to do what he could to head off a new conflagration, and Tunisia was a logical starting point, being the smallest and most sophisticated of the North African protectorates and the one where a change of policy was least likely to arouse a political eruption in Paris. The capital was amazed at the speed with which the premier, only six weeks in office, had moved, but at that point he was politically immune. And he now had set a whole new trend of French policy in motion—which was to reach its logical end when Algerian independence was finally proclaimed in 1962 and France shed the last of her colonial past.

Back in Paris, Mendès-France next rammed through two more remarkable votes of confidence in the National Assembly on a series of economic reforms which had long been recommended by the Commissariat du Plan, but which no government had been strong enough to bring to a vote. In substance they were aimed at striking off some of the shackles of protectionism which were checking French industrial expansion—the beginning of a fundamental shift in French economic policy which enabled the country to face competition in Europe and begin to realize its potential economic strength.

Indochina, Tunisia, economic reform in less than three months in office—and now Mendès-France was face to face with the central issue of French policy in Europe, and his next big clash with Dulles and the United States: the European Defense Community treaty.

The proposal to form a European Army had been hastily put together by the French in response to American demands for rearming the Germans after the outbreak of the Korean war. It was put forward in a speech to the National Assembly on October 24, 1950, by the Minister of Defense of that day, René Pleven. It was to be a neat military counterpart to the Schuman Plan, to pool European coal and steel industries under one supranational High Authority, which had been launched by Robert Schuman on May 9, 1950. Thus, the Pleven Plan for a European Army quickly attracted the same integrationist fervor, particularly from the United States. But at the outset there was one fundamental weakness. Coal and steel are inanimate raw materials. But armies are men, patriotism, sovereignty, life and death. Was a nation like France, with its vast military history and traditions, now to see its army merged into a polyglot force in order to permit the Germans to rearm? Skepticism and hostility to the scheme was deep-seated and widespread in France from the outset.

All the same, the United States grabbed the French proposal with more enthusiasm than the French. Those were the days in which America was deeply and directly involved in European affairs almost on a day-to-day basis, and held what amounted to make-or-break power of decision in all kinds of European questions. It was American policy to rearm Germany, and so—in a flurry of "European idealism" to cover that necessary but unpalatable fact—negotiations for the E.D.C. treaty got under way soon after work had begun on the Coal and Steel Community treaty. The French were cynically satisfied on at least one point—and their diplomats made no secret of it. They had gotten a postponement of German rearmament and gained time against the pressures of the United States. In fact it was to be nearly five years, in 1955, before the first German put on a uniform.

In the European mood of the early 1950's, the E.D.C. gained its converts and political supporters—eventually its passionate advocates and fierce propagandists. The Belgians, the Dutch, the Luxembourgers and the Italians all came in. It is no reflection either on the sincerity of Chancellor Konrad Adenauer's immediate support and endorsement to point out that in October 1950, Germany had everything to gain and nothing to lose by agreeing to the project. It was Adenauer's great aim of foreign policy not merely to align Germany with the West but to bind her with as many entangling and involving commitments as he could make. The old chancellor was constantly alive to the possibility that in the future, Germany might again be tempted to play diplomatic games in the middle of Europe or seek a power deal with Russia, as Germany did between the two wars and in Bismarck's time. Adenauer was therefore utterly dedicated to the cause of European unity, and was prepared to go as far down the road as anybody could travel.

The concept of a European Army was easy enough to put down on paper. The uniform could be designed and the tables of organization set up. But where was the political direction, the national will? Who would give the orders to fight. Where would spirit and pride come from, let alone command and control? Would a "higher European patriotism" really be enough? What about the simple differences in shade of meaning in issuing an order in French or German? It was enough to make the professional soldiers shake their heads in disbelief. True, in 1950, fourteen different nations were fighting together in the Korean war. But this was an example to prove the point. These were national forces—divisions, brigades, battalions, assigned to a higher command but fighting as national units on orders of their own governments. The European Army was to be one big polyglot integrated force with no national identity.

The British, quite predictably, were even less interested than they had been in the Coal and Steel Community. True, it was Winston Churchill who had first put forward the idea of "the immediate creation of a European army under unified command" in a speech at the Assembly of the Council of Europe in Strasbourg in August of 1950. But Churchill never had in mind an "integrated" force. Moreover, when the Conservatives returned to power in Britain in October of 1951, Anthony Eden, back at the Foreign Office, had obtained secret but powerful backing for the British "hands off" attitude from no less a person than General Eisenhower, then Supreme Allied Commander in Europe. At the semiannual meeting of NATO foreign ministers which was held in Rome that year, Eden sought out General Eisenhower for a discussion of the E.D.C. situation, after which he cabled to Churchill in London:

> The General volunteered his opinion on the question whether any offer on our part to participate in the European Army would be decisive for the success of the project. He said that he was convinced that such an offer now would be a mistake. Later I had an opportunity to probe this subject further with him. He confirmed that his was a definite conclusion which had not been lightly arrived at. He thought we should do all in our power to encourage the European Army, but, if we were to offer to enter it at this stage we should further complicate the budgetary and other technical arrangements and would delay rather than hasten a final solution. . . . As the European Army developed, it was his thought that we and the Americans could be drawn into reserve. We should be there and available if needed, but it might be no bad thing if the Europeans could stand on their own.*

Eden further comments that "this conversation was important; the United States Government had previously been inclined to favor our entry into the Defense Community; it was now clear that the policy which we preferred could be pursued in full accord with them." He wasted no time in acting. He called a press conference at the end of the NATO meeting in Rome, and on November 28, 1951, stated flatly that "British units and formations will not participate in the European Army, although there might be some other form of association."

When President Eisenhower and John Foster Dulles took office in the United States fourteen months later, they made European integration and French ratification of the E.D.C. treaty a first priority of American foreign policy. "Neither President Truman nor any one of his recent Secretaries of State has come out strongly and clearly on the subject of European integration," Dulles had said. "They have felt that it might appear to be unwarranted interference in the internal affairs of friendly nations. Also they have felt that pressure from the United States might be resented, and so react against the result we wanted."

Dulles promised quite a contrast to Dean Acheson's diplomatic technique. I remember putting a question to Acheson at a small gathering when he visited Europe in 1952, and ratification of the

* Eden Memoirs, *Full Circle.*

Schuman Plan seemed to be facing delays. "Mr. Secretary, isn't there some kind of pressure we can bring to bear to force the French to get on with this. After all, it's their idea and their future at stake, isn't it?"

Acheson smiled a somewhat pained smile.

"No, you just don't do it that way among allies," he said. "What you do is you go to Schuman and you say, 'Come on now, Uncle Robert, pull up your socks. What can we do to help?' "

One of Dulles's first acts was to "gag" every American ambassador in Europe on the question of whether or not there was any alternative if the treaty failed. His instructions were clear and unequivocal: In the American view there was no alternative. To discuss some substitute policy would be to admit that the treaty might not pass the French Assembly, and in Dulles's view would only weaken the pressure he was trying to build up for French passage.

On the face of it, nothing in politics or diplomacy is without alternate courses of action and anything can always happen—particularly with as fragmented and divided a body as the National Assembly of the Fourth Republic. But American policy would not hear of the possibility. I even recall one agitated State Department official in Paris calling me a "disloyal American" because I ventured to suggest in his office one day in the spring of 1954 that the Socialist deputies would split over an E.D.C. vote and could not be counted in solid support, even though the party leadership was backing the treaty. (Eventually when the vote finally was taken, half the Socialists voted against.) One American correspondent in Paris playfully suggested to the Embassy that the only way to get the treaty passed was to have C.I.A. go around and bet every one of the 695 French deputies $10,000 that it would fail.

In December of 1953, in baleful pursuit of his policy of pressure, Dulles dumped his threat of "agonizing reappraisal" on the annual gathering of the NATO foreign ministers in Paris. He delivered a long and compelling plea for European unity and the idealism of the European Army, and he appeared to be warning Europe that if France did not act soon to ratify the E.D.C. treaty, then the Republican administration might retreat into its traditional isolationism. But even to the Europeans the "threat" had a hollow ring. Where did Dulles's principles of foreign policy really lie? What kind of basic American interest was he really going to support? Was his policy isolationism or was it strong and forward American leadership? All he accomplished, in fact, was to prove that the Truman Administration had been right in its estimate of how such pressures might backfire in Europe.

In an instant, the French right-wing Gaullists were up in arms about "intolerable interference in French affairs," and Bidault was in a particularly incensed mood: "What a thing to say to me in front of all the other foreign ministers when I was doing everything conceivable to get the French parliament to ratify the treaty." Whether, indeed, Bidault was doing everything he could is another matter.* The Dulles threat may have produced a "strong" impression at home, but it produced only bitter resentment in France. Dulles had overbid his poker hand. In the end, he had to make an "agonizing reappraisal" of the two pairs. He was called, and he didn't have the cards.

However much the E.D.C. negotiators fiddled with formulas to mitigate these arguments and satisfy the conflicting demands of "integration" and "national sovereignty," the fundamental subsurface sense that "it won't ever work" not only remained but spread. Politically, it was much easier to "like" the Schuman Plan and support the idea of economic integration than to "like" and support the E.D.C. And yet after the Coal and Steel Community Treaty was signed in April of 1951, it still took the French until July of 1952 to ratify it. Meanwhile the E.D.C. treaty was finally signed in May of 1952, but no French government would bring it before the National Assembly for a vote. "First things first," they told their Allies, and the long drift and drag began. Early in 1953, Georges Bidault replaced Robert Schuman as French foreign minister, and French policy immediately began to veer away from the strongly European approach to a more nationalistic line. Insisting on various modifications and new interpretative protocols to the E.D.C. treaty, Bidault also demanded "one more round of talks with the Russians" before he could ask for an Assembly vote. Then came the Berlin Big Four Foreign Ministers' Conference in February of 1954, which had as its main result the arranging of the Indochina conference. Now Mendès-France was in power, well over two years since the E.D.C. treaty had been signed. Neither France nor its Allies could wait any longer.

Mendès-France had stayed aloof from the E.D.C. question in the long months before he took office. He now surveyed the situation not

* About this same time, Bidault had informed the British ambassador in Paris, Sir Gladwyn Jebb, that he did not see any chance of E.D.C. passing the National Assembly no matter how it was amended.

as an idealist but as a cool and practical political realist. Fresh from his successes over Indochina, Tunisia and economic policy, he was not going to risk the collapse of his government in three short months over a treaty which had been hanging fire for more than two years and looked increasingly foredoomed. In mid-August he announced his decision: He would seek sweeping revisions of the treaty, which would in effect change its entire supranational character and make it an amalgam of national armies. Only by such changes did he calculate passage in the National Assembly. But he was determined to end the long delay and if he could not get his European partners to agree to further changes, he would submit the treaty as it stood to a free vote of the Assembly and let the chips fall.

General Charles de Gaulle had already come out in thunderous opposition to the E.D.C. from his country retirement at Colombey-les-deux-Églises. Three of Mendès-France's cabinet ministers—all Gaullists—now resigned from the government because they wanted a straight "kill" for E.D.C. instead of one last effort at modification and passage. Mendès-France left on August 18 for Brussels and a meeting of the Foreign Ministers of the Six.

The argument at Brussels was bitter in the extreme—the first great tear in the European fabric which the Six had begun to weave. Neither the Belgians nor the Dutch were any more enthusiastic than the French about the necessity for German rearmament, but they had already ratified the treaty and were far more committed than Mendès-France to the "European principle." They refused to accept alterations which would change the supranational concept. Dulles dispatched the American Ambassador to the Coal and Steel Community, David K. E. Bruce, to Brussels and cabled a final appeal to save the situation. But the end was inevitable. A hoard of correspondents clustered on the sidewalk of the rue de la Loi outside the Belgian Foreign Ministry, for want of any place else to wait, while the argument continued into the late hours of Saturday night, August 21. Well past midnight a Dutch official stuck his head out of a window and passed the word: "It's all over." Mendès-France appeared at 2:45 A.M. and led a strange procession through the dark and deserted Brussels streets to the drawing room of the nearby French Embassy. There, in an oddly detached and self-satisfied mood, he briefly reported that his demands had been rejected.

In Washington, Dulles issued another call exhorting the French to "follow their great tradition of idealism." Mendès-France declared that it was up to the National Assembly to take a decision "which will be completely clear and will relieve French politics—internal and external—of the embarrassment of paralysis of these last years." He laid the treaty before the Assembly in the role of a referee rather than an advocate, setting forth the pros and cons but taking no position himself. He allowed a free vote, refusing to make the issue a question of confidence in the government, and his own cabinet split over the treaty while he abstained. Dulles, the State Department and the "Europeans" of French politics, who had dodged bringing it to the Assembly for two and a half years, never forgave him. On August 29 the treaty was defeated, 319–264.

Dulles, taking off from Washington for Manila the next day, bitterly declared that the United States "would now reappraise its foreign policies but not withdraw into isolation," and asked for an emergency meeting of the NATO powers. But in the immediate shock of the death of E.D.C. there was not much enthusiasm in Europe for another NATO meeting for the sake of a meeting—particularly since the United States, frozen in Dulles's "no alternative" policy, had no idea of what to propose next.

In what undoubtedly remains the most solid diplomatic achievement of his quarter-century of public life, Anthony Eden moved onto the scene. He struck upon the idea of converting the Brussels Treaty of 1948—which had joined Britain, France, Italy and the Benelux countries in a fifty-year military alliance which was the forerunner of the 1949 NATO treaty—into a wider pact to include West Germany and provide the treaty framework for controlled German rearmament, and German entry into NATO.

In his memoirs, Eden says that the idea occurred to him while in his bath one morning at his country home at Wiltshire. In November of 1954, however, after his formula had been adopted by the London Nine Power Conference, he told me that the idea came from one of the career diplomats of the Foreign Office, Sir Christopher Steel, then British Ambassador to NATO and later British Ambassador to Germany. Mendès-France also says that he circulated the idea through the French Foreign Office at about the same time—realizing, however, that feelings in Europe about France which had been generated by the death of E.D.C. made it best that the initiative come from elsewhere. But wherever the idea originated, it was Eden who translated it into action. On September 10, he took off for Brussels on the start of a swing around Europe to test the ground for the new plan. He was to continue on to Bonn and Rome with Paris his last stop.

In Manila on the other side of the globe, Dulles had received a curious cable from the State Department policy planning staff. Some of the top men around Dulles, passionately and idealistically devoted to the E.D.C., had convinced themselves that the treaty's failure in France was primarily the fault of the British. If Britain had joined E.D.C., they reasoned, or, failing that, had even been willing to go as far as assigning some troops to the European Army, the French Assembly would have passed the treaty. It is a moot point. Mendès-France does not believe that the Assembly votes were ever there, and almost all of the American correspondents working in Paris at that time would agree. But some State Department officials hold otherwise to this day. In any case, the policy planning staff now secretly advised Dulles that the United States should be very cautious in associating itself with Eden's new initiative.

Why? Because, they reasoned, his ideas did not contain the sacred principle of supranationalism. In addition, the Department planners believed that Britain was so discredited through failure to support E.D.C. that no Eden initiative was likely to be well received. This may have been what Dulles wanted to hear, but the State Department couldn't have been more wrong. By the time Eden had concluded his talks in Brussels and Bonn it was clear that his formula was taking hold. Eden had reached Rome when he suddenly received a surprising message that Dulles was flying to Bonn. He informed Eden that he intended to bypass Paris and Mendès-France completely, but would like a meeting in London. Eden noted in his diary that day:

> His reasons for visiting Bonn seemed to be singularly unconvincing. There is also a long rigmarole of criticism of the Brussels Treaty because it is not supranational. I was inclined to try to dissuade him from visiting Bonn without visiting Paris, but I contented myself with a short reply that I would be glad to see him in London, and a reply to his criticism.*

Eden had concluded that any further attempt for supranationalism would only result in another failure at the hands of the French, who were now veering away from the Schuman-Monnet influence and inspiration. Moreover, he felt that the success of the Brussels Treaty solution depended on building up a pattern of unanimity in Europe as

* Eden Memoirs, *Full Circle*.

he approached Paris and Mendès-France. Now, in Eden's view, Dulles was not only reopening the supranational issue but issuing a deliberate snub to Mendès-France. He was a great deal more irritated than his diary entry shows.

By the time the two men reached London—Eden from his Paris meeting and Dulles from Bonn—Eden's diplomacy was clearly dominating the situation. In Paris, Mendès-France had argued the difficulties for two days, and then in the end had given Eden a secret and personal commitment in principle to accept German rearmament under the Brussels Treaty, provided a whole series of controls could be elaborated as well. Most important of all, he agreed to immediate simultaneous admission of Germany into NATO. In London, Eden now faced Dulles on the supranationalism issue and the convening of the Nine Power Conference to work out the new agreements. But the argument really went by default to Eden. Dulles had no other alternative.

As a last gesture, Eden suggested that it might smooth things over if Dulles would at least telephone Mendès-France in Paris. Mendès-France later related to the author his version of the phone call.

"I was at La Celle Saint-Cloud [an official government château in the Paris suburbs] when the call was put through to me. It was a British Embassy operator saying that Mr. Dulles wished to speak to me over their tie line from London. Mr. Dulles came on the phone, but at that point the line was cut."

Mendès-France smiled meaningfully. In fact he had hung up, refusing to talk to the Secretary of State.

All the same, the Nine Power meeting which opened in London on September 26 was a sweeping success. On September 29, both Eden and Dulles gave decisive and historic pledges to keep their troops on the continent of Europe—to relieve France of the fear of being left alone in Europe with the new German Army. There was a crisis with Mendès-France over the arms control provisions in the revised treaty, but momentum was too strong to permit failure.

Yet the drama was not completely over. A formula for German rearmament and German admission to NATO had been found, but Mendès-France now insisted that the troublesome issue of the Saar should be resolved simultaneously between France and Germany. Konrad Adenauer journeyed to Paris in mid-October, and at that same villa at La Celle Saint-Cloud where Mendès-France had hung up on John Foster Dulles, the two men hammered out a compromise to remove yet another sore and irritation from the European body politic. A formula for "Europeanization" of the Saar cleared the last hurdle, and two years later that troublesome and ugly little industrial valley was quietly returned to Germany.

Just before Christmas, the last decisive debate opened in the National Assembly. It was a nightmare for Mendès-France and the Western Allies. After all the Alliance had been through, the Assembly suddenly rejected a first reading of the ratification bill. But this time Mendès-France was on his feet in an instant to demand a new Assembly vote on a question of confidence. He had now staked the life of his government on passage, and after the usual twenty-four-hour delay under parliamentary rules, the Assembly reassembled in a tense and angry mood. Mendès-France and the treaties scraped through by 287–260 votes—a far cry from that overwhelming backing which he had enjoyed in the Indochina crisis only six months before.

Such was the way of the French National Assembly and French politics. Mendès-France had done his work for France and his days as premier were clearly numbered. "That bear-pit," one enraged premier had once called the National Assembly when it had turned on him. Now the bears were ready for Mendès-France.

Fighting had broken out in the hills of Algeria on November 1, 1954—the start of another seven-year colonial war for France when the ink was scarcely dry on the Indochina peace settlement. Mendès-France had reacted instantly and rigorously to meet the situation—"the criminal designs of a few men will be broken by a repression without weakness," he had told the National Assembly a few days after the fighting began. Having just negotiated the end of the French Empire in Indochina and started Tunisia on the way to self-government and independence, it was politically impossible for him to respond to the Algerian situation in any other way. But by the end of the year, with the fighting spreading day by day, the powerful "Algerian Lobby" of the National Assembly was out for the premier's blood. To them, the case was quite clear: The settlement in Indochina, followed by the adoption of a liberal policy toward Tunisia, had inspired the Algerian nationalists to launch their rebellion against France—and Mendès-France was the cause of it all. On February 5, 1955, as he was in the final stages of secret negotiations with the imprisoned Tunisian nationalist leader Habib Bourguiba, the Assembly toppled him from power. He had lasted seven months and seventeen days.

In that one brief and dynamic period, Mendès-France accomplished more for the Fourth Republic than all its other premiers put together. He liquidated France's overextended and decaying imperial burdens in the Far East, and set French Africa on the road to independence. He rammed through a series of economic measures which enabled expansion to go forward. And in the name of France he took the crucial decisions by which Germany was restored to a position of full and equal partnership in the Atlantic Alliance.

Some Americans and some of his own countrymen never forgave him for the death of the European Defense Community treaty. They believe that he deliberately set out not to save it but to kill it, and that had he fought the battle the other way the treaty would have been ratified. Others found Mendès-France to be difficult, shifty and devious in his dealings. This was particularly true for the British when he made a last effort in January of 1955 to get their support for one more delay before final ratification of the new German accords while the Big Four held another meeting with the Russians. Sir Winston Churchill thwarted the attempt with a brutal personal letter to Mendès-France, telling him that "there shall be no meeting or invitation in any circumstances" to the Russians until the agreements were ratified "by all the signatories." He then warned Mendès-France that France's failure to act quickly and affirmatively on the Germany accords "may well lead to the adoption of other solutions." He concluded with massive Churchillian frankness:

> I should feel bound, whether as Prime Minister or as a private member, to support the policy known as the "empty chair," although this would involve large changes in the infrastructure of NATO, both military and political.

Under this threat, Mendès-France kept France's chair filled in the NATO Alliance, and whatever tears were shed over the death of the European Army and the defeat of supranationalism, the fact remains that the solution which Eden proposed and Mendès-France carried out was a far more straightforward answer to the German rearmament policy, far more in keeping with the principles of sovereignty, national dignity and mutual trust upon which any alliance worthy of the name must be based.

Back on the sidelines in the National Assembly, Mendès-France turned his dynamic energies to building a political following in the country. But he was a leader and an individualist and not a party man, and in the process he quarreled and split with one fellow Radical after another until his party was so fragmented as to be scarcely recognizable.

In his feelings about France and her place in the world, Mendès-France was not unlike Charles de Gaulle. He was fearless and merciless and he was the embodiment of strong leadership and strong government. He believed, too, in an essentially nationalistic French policy and wanted above all to see France restored and able to take a strong position for herself in the Atlantic Alliance. In seven short months in office, he gave the Fourth Republic a new lease on political life which perhaps it did not deserve.

But he was completely unlike De Gaulle in one fundamental respect. He was a believer in parliamentary democracy and parliamentary government in France. Where De Gaulle directed his scorn against the whole system of the Fourth Republic, Mendès-France's enemies were the weak and ineffective men who failed to make it work. He was the only premier of the Fourth Republic to march in the climactic Leftist rally at the Place de la République on May 28, 1958, to oppose General de Gaulle's return to power. He was the only premier of the Fourth Republic to fight openly and with all the political vigor at his command the De Gaulle constitution for the Fifth Republic which transferred power from parliament to the presidency. He was defeated for a National Assembly seat in the elections of 1958, and defeated again in 1962. Today he is in the political wilderness, but he remains the only true historic figure of the Fourth Republic—and thus the ultimate paradox of democracy in France.

3. France: The Fifth Republic

The death of the Fourth Republic began on February 6, 1956. It was to linger on for two years, five months and twenty-six days until the National Assembly, with a gun held at its head by the French Army, administered its own *coup de grâce* and voted General Charles de

Gaulle to power as its last premier on June 1, 1958. But the end had begun long before, on that February day in 1956 when Paris lost control over Algeria—more specifically over the French *colons* who dominated the Algerian scene and from then on dominated successive governments of the Fourth Republic as well, until they engineered its downfall.

Guy Mollet, the adroit and foxy secretary-general of the Socialist Party, became the nineteenth premier of the Fourth Republic on February 1, 1956. An English teacher and resistance leader from Arras, Mollet had long waited in the wings to choose his own moment for his turn at the Hotel Matignon, and he left his mark in three particulars. He quickly abandoned any Socialist or liberal ideas about solving the Algerian problem, and gave in to the *colon* "ultras" within a week after taking office. He masterminded the French arms deal with Israel and France's cat's-paw role in the Suez affair later that same year. And he lasted longer in office than any other Fourth Republic premier—just short of fifteen months. In the end he was instrumental in switching Socialist Party votes for the return of General de Gaulle.

Guy Mollet started out bravely and well. At the outset, he included Pierre Mendès-France in his cabinet and announced that he was naming one of France's most respected, experienced and liberal-minded soldiers, the aging but active General Georges Catroux, to a new post of Minister-Resident in Algeria. Both these moves promised a more liberal and understanding attitude by the French Government toward the Moslem community of Algeria—which was the last thing the French *colons* were prepared to tolerate. Even the new title of Minister-Resident for General Catroux was a significant change, implying that Paris intended to keep a tighter control over the direction of Algerian affairs instead of relying on a semiautonomous resident-general. When trouble broke out, as it did almost immediately, Mollet, in a typical maneuver, proposed changing Catroux's projected title to Minister, Resident in Algeria, but the substitution of a comma for a hyphen was scarcely enough appeasement for the *colons* of Algiers.

With liberal storm signals thus hoisted in Paris, angry antigovernment demonstrations broke out in the streets of Algiers. Mollet boldly announced that he would fly alone to Algeria to restore the authority of France, and on February 6, after five days in office, he landed at Maison Blanche Airport. His journey into the center of Algiers was a violent and savage nightmare. Tomatoes, eggs, potatoes, stones and even manure were rained on the car of the Premier of France by a howling, maddened mob of French Algerians. By the time he reached the safety of the Government-General Building on the heights overlooking the city, he was white and shaken with shock and fear.

General Catroux telephoned from Paris to offer his resignation from a post he had not yet assumed. Clearly his life would be in danger if he set foot in Algiers. Mollet, with relief, accepted. He was now able to placate the Algerian mob by naming in Catroux's place a fellow Socialist, Robert Lacoste, a big, hale, hearty and earthy man who had one policy for Algeria: pacification. He set out to bring as many troops into Algeria as he could find (including army conscripts which the Socialists had resolutely opposed using in Indochina), to fight the F.L.N. rebels until the war was won, and to support the French *colons* to the bitter end. He had no interest in liberalization of French policies toward the Moslems, no interest in seeking peace through negotiation. His sole objective was prosecution of the war. Mendès-France quit the cabinet after three months when Mollet refused to put through Moslem reform measures to accompany the stepped-up war effort.

Thus the Algerian mob successfully asserted its domination over the government in Paris, and the Fourth Republic never recovered. Lacoste lasted in office in Algiers to the eve of the end of the Fourth Republic and ingratiated himself so thoroughly with the French population that he was all but immune to instructions from Paris or removal by successive governments. The autonomous power of French colonial governors, and their ability to dominate weak and ever-changing regimes in Paris, was notorious throughout French imperial history. Much earlier, when Robert Schuman left the Ministry of Foreign Affairs (having been responsible for Morocco and Tunisia for four years), he described the difficulties of controlling the residents-general:

> They are on the spot, they receive and provide all the information, the scope of their initiative is vast and varied, and besides they have a tendency to widen it, especially if their views coincide with those of the French population. They interpret the instructions arriving from Paris and decide how they are put into effect. The *fait accompli* is the great and constant temptation which residents-general are to be commended for resisting *insofar as they do not succumb to it*. Above the residents-general, the Minister for Foreign Affairs is responsible for their administra-

tion, which is supposed to be in conformity with his own views. This is one of those fictions upon which the democratic regime rests.*

Robert Lacoste's tenure as the last resident-general of the Fourth Republic in Algiers provided a supreme example of the situation described by Schuman—the great temptation of the *fait accompli* which Lacoste not only did not resist, but happily exploited. Two nasty affairs stand out in the dismal history of the last days of the Fourth Republic in Algeria.

The first was the airplane kidnapping of the F.L.N. rebel leader Ahmed ben Bella, today the president of independent Algeria. In October, 1956, Ben Bella had flown secretly from rebel headquarters in Cairo to confer with the Sultan of Morocco in Rabat. He was then to continue back to Tunisia in the Sultan's private plane to meet Tunisia's president, Habib Bourguiba. But along the Algerian coast the French pilot, working on contract for the Sultan of Morocco, received radio orders from the French authorities to land at Algiers. He circled above the clouds for an hour and a half so that his unsuspecting passengers would think they were over Tunisia, and then swept down suddenly at Maison Blanche Airport. There police grabbed Ben Bella and hustled him off to Santé Prison in Paris where he spent the next five years.

The Ben Bella kidnapping was greeted with wild jubilation by the French *colons*—and their cup was overflowing when the news followed that Algiers had thumbed its nose at Paris and engineered the coup without the knowledge or consent of the French Government. But although Mollet would never have authorized the kidnapping, he now unashamedly rode out the storm among the Paris liberals, who realized that, with Ben Bella in prison, a negotiated peace in Algeria would never even be tried. Backing Lacoste's action, Mollet coolly sought to turn to his advantage the fact that he knew nothing about it in advance.

"I do not admit this in order to shirk the responsibility for the action, but rather because I do not want to take credit for it," the Premier told the National Assembly, with bland logic if without much principle.

Early in 1958, the Algerian authorities struck a second blow at the enfeebled authority of Paris, which led directly to the fall of the next-

* Writing in the magazine *La Nef* in March, 1953.

to-last government of the Fourth Republic and paved the way for the events that brought about the return of De Gaulle. On February 8, 1958, twenty-four bombers of the French Air Force took off from Algerian bases, crossed the Tunisian border and bombed the little Tunisian town of Sakhiet. It was a Saturday morning and the Arab marketplace was full. A Red Cross convoy happened to be in the town at the same time. Seventy-five people were killed, including thirty children in a school struck by French bombs, and more than a hundred others were wounded. There was no question that the town was being used as a "privileged sanctuary" by F.L.N. rebel leaders to train soldiers and smuggle arms and men across the border. But the French High Command attacked across an international border without informing or consulting Paris. In an instant the Arab world, Paris, and all of France's friends and allies were in an uproar.

Only great restraint by the commander of French forces at the Tunisian base of Bizerte and by President Bourguiba saved an open clash between the French and the Tunisians, which might indeed have been an excuse for the French High Command in Algiers to begin a "reconquest" of Tunisia. Again the French Government had been the victim of an incredibly dangerous *fait accompli* in Algiers—and it did not help France's standing in the world when Lacoste publicly denounced the "apologetic attitude" of the French Foreign Office toward the Tunisian Government.

The rot which had set in under Mollet was now complete, and the Fourth Republic was pathetically unable to control Algerian events any longer. Mollet and Lacoste, for example, had turned a blind eye to torture of Moslems by French paratroopers. In the end, the stories of the victims became too much to be ignored. Mollet established a "Commission to Safeguard Human Rights and Liberties," but three of its members soon resigned in protest over the impotence of the Commission. At another point, one of the French governments sought to make unofficial contacts with the F.L.N. through the imprisoned Ben Bella's Tunisian lawyer—who duly arrived in Paris on his secret mission, only to be expelled by the Ministry of the Interior before he could see anybody. Neofascism was rapidly pulling down French democracy. Wild-eyed mobs of young toughs roamed the streets of Paris in an endless succession of battles with the police and the C.R.S. security troops. Finally, on March 13, 1958, the police themselves—over 1,000 of them, some in uniform and some in civilian clothes—staged an anti-government demonstration outside the National Assembly, hooting and catcalling and insulting any unfortunate deputies who appeared on the steps, beating up one of the high police officials who tried to get them to disperse. The message to the government and the people of Paris was tragically clear: The Fourth Republic could no longer even count on the police to carry out its orders.

On Tuesday, April 15, 1958, one month after the police demonstrations, the government of Felix Gaillard was overthrown in a debate on the handling of relations with Tunisia in the wake of the Sakhiet bombing raid. The vote was 321–255. The death agony of the Fourth Republic now began.

As a symptom of the decay, it had become increasingly difficult to find a new candidate for the premiership when a government fell. New cabinets and new parliamentary majorities took increasingly longer to form. The "democratic processes" of the Fourth Republic had become exhausted. When Gaillard came to power, he received his investiture vote after an interregnum of five weeks, the longest of all. When he was toppled from power it took from April 15 to May 13—just short of one month—to find the last premier before De Gaulle. The delay was fatal to the Fourth Republic. While the dreary search dragged on, with both Paris and Algiers out of control, the Gaullist plotters worked feverishly to prepare the deathblow in the form of a "popular uprising" in Algeria against "surrender" in Paris, and with that, a revolt against the authority of the Fourth Republic by the French Army.

Oddly enough, when the crisis began, General de Gaulle's name and the possibility of his return to power did not figure very high in either public talk or political calculations—except, of course, among the secret plotters and his own political supporters. "Send for De Gaulle" had long been one of the standing jokes of the Fourth Republic. And the political situation in the last two weeks of April remained for De Gaulle much as it had been for thirteen years. There was no chance whatsoever of his gaining any investiture vote in the National Assembly—or so it seemed. The Communists and the Socialists would unite to oppose him, and there would be more than enough additional votes against him from the Center and the Left.

De Gaulle had written himself out of French politics and future French history. For years he had talked to visitors at his country home at Colombey-les-deux-Églises as a man who regarded his career to be over and ended. His political fortunes had waned after his abrupt walkout from the provisional government of France in January 1946.

He quit on a relatively minor point involving the defense budget, after getting his way in the argument in the National Assembly. But De Gaulle is no man to share power with anybody, and he really walked out in disgust at the political conditions under which he was trying to work. From his lofty heights, De Gaulle formed a political movement called the "Rally of the French People." It was typical of De Gaulle that he put his name at the head of a rally and not a political party. But those who flocked to the banner were an unsavory lot of right-wing coattail riders, and the party began to take on a distinct Fascist smell. After moderate electoral successes in 1947, the RPF won 120 seats in the National Assembly of 1951, to emerge as the strongest single right-wing bloc. But De Gaulle was not interested in making the Fourth Republic work. He was trying to break it up, which meant a policy of strict noncooperation. The result, however, was that his own following began to break up. In 1952 nearly a quarter of them refused to obey the General's instructions and voted in support of the right-wing government of Antoine Pinay. In 1953 came a severe defeat for the Gaullists in municipal elections, with the RPF dropping from 40 percent of the vote (in 1947) to barely 10 percent. After that, De Gaulle formally withdrew his official patronage of the Rally of the French People, and was out of politics completely.

> "Think by how many failures my public life has been marked!" he said to a visitor at his country home in those days. "First I tried to persuade the civil and military authorities to endow France with an armored force which would have spared us an invasion. I failed. I urged the Government to go to North Africa. In vain. I failed at Dakar. After our victory, I endeavored to maintain the unity I had formed around myself. But this unity was broken. Later, in grave circumstances, I tried again [by forming the RPF] and failed once more. If these failures had been mine they would have been of no importance—but they were also the failures of France. True, from time to time there were successes. And yet during the darkest moments of the war, I sometimes wondered: Perhaps it is my mission to represent the history of our country in its last upsurge toward the lofty heights. Perhaps it is my lot to have written the last pages in the book of our greatness." *

In this mood, De Gaulle had remained at Colombey-les-deux-Églises and watched disdainfully the mounting political chaos of the

* Quoted by Alexander Werth in *France 1940–55*.

Fourth Republic. He would visit Paris on the average of once a week, keeping an office and a small personal staff as a contact point in the capital. But although seldom commenting on affairs in public, De Gaulle kept in close touch behind the scenes with old friends and supporters and a few key officials among the senior civil servants of the government. In 1953 he had held a press conference to denounce the European Defense Community treaty, but then in July of 1955 he held another one which looked like his farewell to public life.

"It is my intention not to intervene again in what are conventionally called 'the public affairs of this country,' " he said on that occasion. "I say farewell to you, and perhaps for a long time to come. . . ."

Moreover, De Gaulle was by no means the favorite son of the French *colons,* the ultras on the Algerian question. They did not at all have De Gaulle's return to power in mind when they began pummeling the Fourth Republic to death in May of 1958. The reason was very simple. They did not know where De Gaulle stood on the Algerian question, or what his Algerian policy might ultimately prove to be. De Gaulle had never pronounced himself clearly or definitively on any "Algerian solution"—and in fact he was to conceal his ultimate aim of Algerian independence with great skill for three years after his return to power. In advance of the plot and the events of May 1958, one of the leaders of the Algerian ultras, Alain de Serigny, the editor of the newspaper *L'Echo d'Alger,* had arranged a secret conference with De Gaulle's political lieutenant, Jacques Soustelle, to warn that "Algerian opinion is very badly prepared for a return of De Gaulle," and to try to extract some firm definition of De Gaulle's Algerian policy from Soustelle. All he got from Soustelle was a vague discourse to the effect that "the General looks at it from a historian's and thinker's point of view rather than in terms of immediate action," and "he thinks that pacification ought to be conducted with the greatest energy but accompanied by a great social, educational, psychological and political effort." This was not exactly the ruthless militancy which the *colons* wanted from Paris. While they had no specific candidate for power of their own (except possibly Jacques Soustelle himself), they sought to end parliamentary democracy in Paris and to install a kind of fascist-minded semimilitary dictatorship to run France and Algeria with an iron hand.

The last government crisis of the Fourth Republic opened in rather typical euphoria, even though everyone realized that in the wake of the police demonstrations outside the National Assembly and the mounting turmoil of Algeria, this one was going to be very serious and difficult indeed. Municipal elections were coming up on April 20, and accordingly President René Coty (whose conduct throughout the extraordinary difficulties of the next six weeks was exemplary) delayed picking a first candidate for the premiership until the results were known. Felix Gaillard continued in nominal caretaker charge of government affairs. But the Socialist Party, which, now out of power, was veering toward being "liberal" once again on Algerian affairs, insisted that Robert Lacoste withdraw from Algiers after more than two years as resident-general. Lacoste came home, and thus there was a power vacuum in both Paris and Algeria.

Coty, in a customary first move to demonstrate what was not possible, began the search for a new premier with the veteran Georges Bidault, a member of the left-center Popular Republican Movement (MRP). Although Bidault might have been expected to draw strength from his party affiliation and his strong record of public service, in fact he had moved to a position of such nationalist extremism that he was now numbered among the ultras on the Algerian question. His was a course that was to lead to his miserable political exile to Brazil in 1963, just as the other ultra leader and Gaullist plotter of the day, Jacques Soustelle, is also now living outside France in secret, in Italy or perhaps in South America. As the first candidate for the last premiership of the Fourth Republic, Bidault proved too ultra on the Algerian question for his own party, and as he could not command any Socialist or moderate Left support, he gave up the attempt after two days.

From an MRP candidate, Coty next turned to the Right, and proposed André Morice, who was also among the extremists on the Algerian question, but Morice gave up before he ever began. With extremism thus checkmated, the President moved back to the Center and asked René Pleven, experienced and colorless, to see if he could patch together a government. Moving slowly and carefully, Pleven labored for ten days. It looked as if he was going to succeed until suddenly, at the last minute, the Radicals, who had been prepared to support him, reversed themselves and pulled out. As was customary, Coty then turned to the party which had blocked success, and asked two Radical leaders—Jean Berthoin and André Billières. Each of them in succession turned the offer down without even attempting to put together a cabinet.

Finally, on May 8, with the crisis entering its fourth week, Coty called on Pierre Pflimlin to form the twenty-second government of the Fourth Republic, the last before General de Gaulle. Pflimlin, an Alsatian Catholic and the respected mayor of the city of Strasbourg, is a somewhat cold and austere personality, but a man of great integrity and moral courage. Like Bidault, he is a member of the MRP, but he was a believer in a "liberal" solution in Algeria. He had been almost a cabinet fixture in the Fourth Republic, having served as a minister in fourteen previous governments, but this was his first time as Premier. He had failed to attain the Hotel Matignon on two previous invitations. President Coty's previous nominees having demonstrated that no candidate of the Algerian ultras could form a government, the choice of Pflimlin was now the signal for the Algerians to impose their will against a Paris "liberal" for the last time. As he began his consultations, the plotters were busily at work.

The French journalists, Serge and Merry Bromberger, have written of "the thirteen plots of the 13th of May." For all anybody knows or can establish, there may have been three or thirty plots in the chaotic conditions of those weeks in the spring of 1958. Moreover, it remains a mystery as to the extent to which General de Gaulle himself was working with the plotters—although the general impression is that he held to an "informed but aloof" position.

On the evening of May 9, General Raoul Salan, the French commander-in-chief in Algeria, dispatched a communication to President Coty through the Chief of the General Staff, General Paul Ely, warning that any weakness in Paris on the Algerian question, any hint of a policy of surrender, would produce a "reaction of despair" in the French Army. At the same time, one of the ultra organizations began distributing leaflets in Algeria declaring:

> Those advocating surrender have decided to eliminate once and for all the true defenders of French Algeria: Soustelle, Bidault, Lacoste, Morice. They want to give the key posts to those who intend to abandon Algeria. After Pleven, another notorious liquidator has been called in. His name is Pflimlin.

Pflimlin was thus the target of both the Army and the Algerian mob. On Saturday, May 10, news broke from the rebel side that three French prisoners had been executed by FLN—just the excuse which the ultras needed to mount an enormous demonstration against "surrender" in Paris. At this point, the shadowy figure of a man named Leon Delbecque enters the narrative.

Delbecque, self-made businessman and ardent Gaullist who had served as a reserve officer in Algeria, had entered the government of Felix Gaillard, at the suggestion of Jacques Soustelle, as a Ministry of Defense representative in Algiers. In this position, he had gone to work to create a network of "reliable officers" to act in support of an eventual uprising, although he carefully refrained from revealing that his aim, like Soustelle's, was to bring General de Gaulle to power. Instead he concentrated on preaching to the dissident officers the impotency of the Fourth Republic, the inevitability of its demise and the necessity of the Army's readiness to act to save France. Then on the civilian side, among the Algerian ultras, Delbecque secretly organized a "Committee of Vigilance," to which over twenty insurrectionist groups of students, ex-servicemen, secret political clubs and counter-terrorists had pledged support. When the Gaillard government fell in Paris, Delbecque's Committee of Vigilance emerged into the open.

At the news of the execution of the three French prisoners, the committee issued a call for a general strike and a mass demonstration at the Algiers War Memorial on Tuesday, May 13. This done Delbecque took off for Paris on May 10 to meet Jacques Soustelle. The gun was now loaded and pointed at Pflimlin, and the trigger ready to be pulled.

On May 13, Pflimlin had completed the construction of a cabinet and was ready to ask the National Assembly for a vote of investiture. The debate began at the Palais-Bourbon in midafternoon in somewhat desultory fashion, as steel shutters banged down over the shop-fronts of Algiers. The general strike had started, and the mob began to gather for the demonstration at the War Memorial.

The War Memorial stands at the foot of a vast flight of steps leading up a hill to an open square, The Forum, behind which stands the Government-General Building. By 6 o'clock in the evening a vast crowd had gathered at the Memorial, and senior Army officers arrived to pay formal tribute to the executed soldiers. When the brief ceremonies ended, a bearded, wild-eyed young leader of the ultras named Pierre Lagaillarde mounted the Memorial, wearing the uniform of a reserve lieutenant of the paratroopers, and, waving his arm in the direction of the Government-General Building, he harangued the crowd to follow him and "chuck all those rats into the sea." In an instant the mob began to surge up the steps with Lagaillarde in the lead. At The Forum they were met by companies of the Ministry of the Interior security troops, the CRS, specially trained in the handling of civil demonstrations and disorders.

It is almost an unwritten law of democracy in France that the Army is never used against the people, and the CRS companies had been established in the early postwar days by the Socialist Minister of the Interior of that time, Jules Moch, to give the government a reliable and disciplined paramilitary organization for internal security—in those days in particular to combat Communist-organized strikes and disorders.

The CRS now faced the Algerian mob streaming up the steps to The Forum and first responded with tear gas, falling back at the same time to the iron gates of the Government-General Building. There then occurred an odd and unexplained turning point in the whole affair. The CRS commander inside the building picked up the tie line telephone to Paris and was put through immediately to Felix Gaillard, still sitting in the Premier's office of the Hotel Matignon, still the acting head of the government until Pflimlin, waiting in the National Assembly, had won his vote of investiture.

The officer explained rapidly to Gaillard what was happening and asked for permission to order his men to open fire on the mob. The answer from Paris was a short, sharp "No." Gaillard undoubtedly had his eye on the problem of an Assembly majority for Pflimlin, and the news that French Algerians had been fired upon would not help his chances with the ultra vote. The CRS commander put down the phone and rejoined his men to face the howling and angry mob outside the building.

At that point, suddenly and mysteriously, truckloads of paratroopers rolled into The Forum with two of the ultra colonels of the Delbecque circle—Trinquier and Thomazo—in charge. Cheers went up from the crowd, for the paratroopers were popular with the Algerian *colons* for their ruthless work in suppressing the FLN in the city. At somebody's orders, the CRS withdrew to the rear of the building, leaving the paratroopers in charge. The demonstrators then helped themselves to a heavy army truck, and while the paratroopers stood by watching, they rammed the gates of the Government-General Building and swarmed inside—breaking windows, setting small fires, and incidentally, selectively looting the secret police files to eliminate some damaging security dossiers.

Shortly after 7 P.M., General Jacques Massu, commander of the paratroopers and city commandant of Algiers, appeared on the scene. Massu, an extremely tough and able combat officer who had commanded the French airborne landings at Suez, was not overly endowed with brains or political wisdom. He had a kind of fascist-liberal view of the Algerian scene, believing in ruthless military measures but at the same time critical of the difficulties which the attitude of the *colons* created with the Moslem population, and bitter about the vacillations of the Paris politicians. Before giving sanction to the torture of the Moslems in Algiers, he had himself tortured for a brief period to establish that it was not inhuman.

Massu's first orders were soldierly and correct: paratroopers were to clear the building and restore order. The general then called a conference inside the building with Lagaillarde and members of the Committee of Vigilance, the leaders of the mob.

At 7:35 P.M., General Salan arrived at the scene—"the Chinese General" as he was called in the French Army because of his predilection for opium, hashish and perversion, and with these stimulations, an Oriental ability to stay one short step away from events or decisions, close enough to cash his advantage, far enough back to disengage. Salan was at the scene at the crucial moment, but he left decisions to Massu.

At 9:10 P.M., General Massu appeared on the balcony of the Government-General Building and announced to the mob in The Forum below the creation of a "Committee of Public Safety" to take over the functions of government in Algiers, and the dispatch of a telegram to President Coty in Paris. Massu, judging from his statements at a press conference the next day, seems to have been only dimly aware that his was an act of insurrection.

"This has been done in view of the gravity of the situation and the absolute necessity to maintain order and avoid bloodshed," the telegram to Coty said. "We demand the creation in Paris of a government of public safety, alone capable of keeping Algeria as an integral part of metropolitan France."

There was not a mention of General de Gaulle. There was not a Gaullist on the Committee of Public Safety. Things had moved a little too rapidly for the ubiquitous Delbecque—who now galvanized into action, after returning earlier in the afternoon from his Paris meeting with Soustelle.

When the Committee of Vigilance called its general strike, it had been Delbecque's intention to stop with the War Memorial demonstration. A major assault on the Government-General Building and the authority of Paris would follow in a few days—by which time Soustelle was to have arrived in Algiers to take charge. As resident-general in Algiers for nearly two years before Lacoste, Soustelle was both a Gaullist and a hero of the Algerian ultras, whose interests he defended with such political ruthlessness in Paris that he was known as the *"tombeur,"* or chucker-out of governments which began to show the slightest inclination toward a peaceful solution to the Algerian problem. But Soustelle had decided to remain in Paris on May 13, believing that Pflimlin would not get a vote of investiture from the National Assembly—in which case he wanted to be on the scene in the capital to maneuver when the sacking of the Government-General Building began. Back from Paris, Delbecque rushed to The Forum and into the Government-General Building to the Committee of Public Safety, to be confronted by a grinning Lagaillarde who remarked: "I must admit we've gotten somewhat ahead of your script."

Delbecque then announced (wrongly) that Soustelle would be arriving in Algiers, probably the next day, and demanded in the meantime to be included on the Committee as Soustelle's prepresentative. This was quickly agreed.

In Paris, the National Assembly, with its typical sense of urgency, had recessed for a comfortable dinner before deciding on Pflimlin's bid for power. When the deputies reassembled at 9 P.M., Massu was about to make his insurrectionist announcement from the balcony in Algiers, and the news had been growing more menacing minute by minute. As debate resumed, the mood in the Assembly was one of feverish excitement.

Late in the evening, in the face of the Massu telegram from Algiers demanding a "government of public safety," several key Rightist leaders tried to get Pflimlin to step aside and allow Guy Mollet to form a national union government with broad support of the Socialists and the Right. But the austere Alsatian rejected yielding to the Algerian mob and declared that he would "accept his responsibilities." At 1:15 A.M. he was at the Assembly rostrum for a final appeal to the deputies, speaking with great firmness and force. When the Communists, who had sabotaged every Fourth Republic government except Pierre Mendès-France at the time of the Indochina investiture, suddenly cried for "immediate measures to save the Republic," jeers and protests broke out from the Right. But at 3:20 A.M. on Wednesday, May 14, Pflimlin became the last premier of the Fourth Republic before De Gaulle by a vote of 274–129, with the Communists abstaining.

Meanwhile, as the debate was in progress Gaillard, still the acting premier, sent a very secret message to General Salan in Algiers charging him with "all necessary measures for maintaining order and protecting life and property in Algeria." The "Chinese General" could now step forward and support, if not actually join, the revolt, armed with a *carte-blanche* from the legal government of Paris.

But on the heels of Gaillard's secret instructions to Salan, President Coty, a few hours after Pflimlin won his investiture vote, issued an order from the highest authority of France to the French Army to "follow the path of duty under the authority of the Government of the French Republic." The situation as dawn broke on the morning of May 14 was, therefore, that France now had a legally constituted government and the government was counting on Generals Salan and Massu to bring the Algerian revolt under control and respond to the authority of Paris.

This was not at all the situation which the plotters, the French *colons,* Delbecque, Soustelle or the French Army had planned or anticipated. Moreover, on that Wednesday morning after the investiture vote, other developments in Paris showed signs that the new government under Pflimlin might find its feet. Orders went out that Soustelle should be place under "the protection of the police"—ostensibly because of an assassination threat, but actually to prevent him from bolting for Algiers and taking charge of the revolt. Then three Rightist cabinet ministers quit the Pflimlin government even before taking office. The new premier moved immediately to strengthen his regime by including Guy Mollet as a vice-premier and the veteran Socialist Jules Moch as the Minister of the Interior—where he had rendered such powerful services to the Fourth Republic in the wave of Communist strikes and disorders in 1946 and 1947.

Throughout the day, uncertainty took hold of the higher Army officers in Algiers—particularly General Massu, who held an unusually apologetic press conference on the evening of May 14 to say that the Committee of Public Safety was a "provisional arrangement" pending the arrival of a new resident-general to replace Lacoste. The scheming Delbecque, however, told the senior officers in Algiers that they were now in the revolt up to their necks, and if the Fourth Republic did not fall, then their heads would roll. Their only hope, Delbecque kept preaching, was to see the revolt through and bring

General de Gaulle to power. Otherwise they and the cause of Algérie Française were finished.

In this atmosphere, the Algerian mob again swelled into The Forum on the morning of May 15, crying for Pflimlin's blood. This time General Salan appeared on the balcony of the Government-General Building with General Massu, Delbecque and other leaders of the Committee of Public Safety. Salan delivered an adroit speech in which he pledged his support and understanding of the wishes of the French *colons*. At the same time he alluded vaguely to his responsibilities for maintaining order. Thus avoiding any irretrievable pledges, Salan ended with the cry *"Vive l'Algérie Française, Vive la France!"* and turned to take his usual step backward. But there was Delbecque at his elbow, playing Iago to Othello. Salan glanced and hesitated, and then stepped forward again and cried to the mob below, *"Et vive De Gaulle!"* The French Algerians and the French Army, as Delbecque and Soustelle had plotted, were now committed to the otherthrow of the Fourth Republic and the return to power of General de Gaulle.

That afternoon in Paris, a few hours after Salan's balcony appearance, General de Gaulle at last broke his silence and responded to the cry from the Algiers Forum. He issued an oracular written statement in which he said:

> Faced with problems too difficult for a regime of parties to tackle, France has, for the last twelve years, been following a disastrous road. In the past, the country, from its very depths, entrusted me with the task of leading it to its salvation. Today, with the new ordeals facing it, let the country know that I am ready to assume the powers of the Republic.

With this direct bid for power, the struggle between General de Gaulle and the decayed and dying Fourth Republic was fully joined. But Premier Pflimlin was not ready to yield.

The next day, May 16, Pflimlin rose in the National Assembly to ask for passage of a bill establishing a three-month state of emergency in France. He disclosed that General Salan, in whom the Fourth Republic had placed its trust, had been using his enhanced authority to remove civil officials in Algeria without the consent of the government. A "grave problem of the loyalty of the Army to the nation" confronted France, Pflimlin declared. With Communist support, the emergency powers act passed by 461–114. The Army now knew that it had to move in for the kill. That evening the Army Chief of Staff,

General Paul Ely, resigned with a message so mutinous that it was censored.

Everywhere the foundations of authority were shaking. French Air Force planes began flying over Paris and Colombey-les-deux-Églises in the formation of a Cross of Lorraine—the Gaullist resistance symbol. More important, twenty-four troop-carrying transport planes were flown from bases in metropolitan France to Algiers without the authority of the Government, thus equipping the rebellious Army for a parachute lift to Paris. Four of the nine regional military commanders in France came out openly in support of the officers of Algiers. Jules Moch reported that he was beginning to doubt even the reliability of the CRS companies which he had created twelve years before.

On May 17, Jacques Soustelle, under police surveillance and ostensibly ill at his Paris home, received a visitor. He promptly stuffed himself in the trunk of the visitor's car, was driven past the police officers and off to Switzerland where he chartered a plane for Algiers. He was met at the airport by an indignant General Salan, worried that this might be going too far even for Paris, but news of his arrival quickly spread through the city. He and Salan had to patch up their argument, and made a triumphal joint balcony appearance at The Forum. It was one more step in committing the Army to De Gaulle and seeing the rebellion through.

On Monday, May 19, General de Gaulle called a press conference in Paris—his first appearance before the public in three years. He was skillful, aloof and utterly confident in the midst of tumultuous events. His chief aim was to woo the Socialists, who held the key to any leftist support for his return to power. De Gaulle first spoke of "my friend" Robert Lacoste, and then of Guy Mollet, "whom I esteem"—the ony two men to be so honored by direct mention that day. The General even recalled an "unforgettable" meeting with Mollet, the resistance leader, at Arras Town Hall after the liberation (although Mollet subsequently said that no such meeting had ever taken place). Otherwise De Gaulle had praise for his own past record in managing France's affairs, regrets for the political decline of the country, praise for the conduct of the French Army, sympathy for the French *colons* in Algeria, and a reiteration of his readiness to take power.

"Did I ever make any attempt on basic public liberties?" he replied scornfully to a question implying that he might want to be a dictator.

"On the contrary, I restored them. Why should I, at sixty-seven, begin a career as a dictator?"

With that he departed "to return to my village where I shall remain at the disposal of the country."

For the next several days there was a surface lull in the storm, but behind the scenes General Massu in Algiers was hard at work on a 32-page plan for an airborne invasion of Paris to prepare the way for seizure of power. General Salan, still keeping a step behind, decided instead to invade the island of Corsica, where he was certain resistance would be minimal and the result another safe blow to the tottering Fourth Republic.

On Saturday, May 24, Salan's operation was launched, and as he had anticipated, the government in Paris found itself powerless to respond. A CRS unit in Corsica prudently switched sides in the face of the strength of the invading paratroopers. The ubiquitous Delbecque went along for the ride from Algiers, and all went smoothly for the plotters—though not without musical comedy overtones. In the town of Bastia, a gallant Socialist mayor, loyal to the government of Paris, which paid his salary, demanded that he be ejected honorably from the Hotel de Ville by force—or at least a display of token force. But the script prepared in Algiers called for a peaceful and cooperative seizure of power, and the invaders demurred. The mayor then proposed that he head a procession leaving the Town Hall with everybody singing the "Marseillaise." This display of loyalty to Paris did not suit the plotters either. Eventually a compromise was reached, and the mayor marched down the steps draped in his tricolor sash of office, singing the "Marseillaise" by himself while his supporters followed silently behind.

All the same, Corsica fell to the revolt which was now fully led by the Army. At one of the last of Pflimlin's cabinet meetings, René Pleven summed up the state of the Fourth Republic bluntly and painfully: "We are the legal government. But what do we govern? The Minister for Algeria cannot enter Algeria. The Minister for the Sahara cannot go to the Sahara. The Minister of Information can do nothing but censor the press. The Minister of the Interior has no control over the police. The Minister of Defense is disobeyed by the Army."

That Sunday, Guy Mollet rose to the bait which General de Gaulle had dangled at his press conference, and addressed a long letter to Colombey-les-deux-Églises—couched in critical terms, but with the effect of sorrow rather than anger, and with an implied overture of possible support. This letter broke the unity of the existing government, and now Pflimlin began secret arrangements to meet De Gaulle.

Shortly before midnight on the night of Monday, May 26, Pflimlin's car dodged out of the Hotel Matignon, and while police vehicles blocked any pursuit, he made his way in circuitous secrecy to the government villa at La Celle Saint-Cloud. De Gaulle had driven by an equally roundabout method from Colombey-les-deux-Églises, and in strict security the two men talked for nearly two hours. Nothing was decided—but the fact that the meeting took place at all was sufficient to signal the end of the Pflimlin government. De Gaulle was back at Colombey shortly after 5 A.M. on Tuesday.

A few hours later, at the Ministry of the Interior, Jules Moch was handed secret intelligence that the Army in Algeria intended to launch its postponed invasion of the mainland and Paris that evening. Tanks from the Paris garrisons were to seize and hold Le Bourget and Villacoublay airfields for the paratroopers' arrival, and the uprising would be supported by a sudden call-up of paratroop reserve veterans in France. By now, Moch was certain that he could no longer count fully on the CRS units to resist such an action or to fight to prevent seizure of government buildings. The police had already demonstrated their dubious loyalties, even had they been trained or equipped to resist the Army.

The same intelligence appears to have reached General de Gaulle at about the same time—for at 12:30 P.M. that Tuesday, to the surprise and indignation of Pflimlin but to the relief of Jules Moch, De Gaulle issued a press statement that he had "embarked on the regular process necessary for establishing a Republican government." He coupled this with a determined declaration that "I cannot approve of any action" which might disturb public order, and a call to "land, sea and air forces to maintain the strictest discipline." He had moved to head off the invasion and the possible outbreak of civil war.

Pflimlin at once informed President Coty that he would resign the premiership at the end of an Assembly debate that evening, at which a vote was to be taken authorizing sweeping, although rather tardy, reforms in the Fourth Republic's constitution. In the early hours of Wednesday, May 28, the bill passed by 208–165. Pflimlin had won more crucial votes than most Fourth Republic premiers, but he resigned immediately. He had lasted just a few hours short of two weeks.

President Coty summoned party leaders to the Élysée Palace on

Wednesday afternoon and informed them that the choice for France was either General de Gaulle or a popular front led by Socialists and Communists—and that he would do everything in his power to install De Gaulle. That night the General made another midnight journey to Paris to state his terms for taking office to the party leaders, but the meeting broke up in angry disagreement.

On Thursday morning, word reached Paris that the Army had rescheduled its invasion once more and would be landing paratroopers to seize the government that very evening. Coty now sent a formal presidential message to the National Assembly—his first and last—declaring that if the deputies did not accept General de Gaulle as the only man to avert civil war, then he would resign the presidency. This would have meant that presidential powers would devolve on the Socialist president of the National Assembly, André le Troquer. An Army invasion of Paris and civil war would certainly have followed. The Assembly broke into an uproar at Coty's bludgeoning tactics, but that evening the President formally entrusted De Gaulle with the task of forming a government in accordance with the legal procedures of the Fourth Republic, and the Army invasion was again called off.

Throughout these tense events, the mood of the French public had been curiously apathetic. There had been a run on the shops for household staples such as sugar and flour, and the rate of the French franc had slumped on the black market. But Communist and Leftist efforts to call strikes in the nationalized industries, the coal fields, against the "Fascists" of Algiers and in support of the Fourth Republic had been dismally unsuccessful. The Left had managed to mass about 250,000 people at the Place de la République in an anti-De Gaulle rally the day Pflimlin resigned. But the Communist Jacques Duclos and Pierre Mendès-France were the only political leaders present in the front rank.

On Friday, May 30, the Socialist Party, under pressure from its own leaders—Mollet, Moch, Vincent Auriol, the ex-President of France, and others—decided to "negotiate" with De Gaulle, which in effect meant his acceptance. When the final vote came on June 1, the party in fact split almost down the middle, but the decision of the party leadership to switch from a position of entrenched opposition to acceptance of De Gaulle was crucial.

Sunday, June 1, 1958, was a dazzling day of late-spring beauty such as only Paris provides. The consultations were over, the terms had been argued and met, and above all, in curious contrast to the turbulence of the previous three weeks, legalities were being strictly preserved. The integrity of the constitution was being maintained. General Charles de Gaulle appeared before the National Assembly of the Fourth Republic to ask for the usual vote of investiture as its twenty-third premier. Police swarmed around the Palais-Bourbon and along the Quai d'Orsay, with reinforcements massed across the river in the Place de la Concorde where even the Metro stations had been closed to keep the people from gathering for this drama of French democracy.

At 3 o'clock, De Gaulle rose from his seat alone on the government bench and walked—as countless others had walked before him—to the high rostrum to ask the Assembly for power. He had not been inside the Palais-Bourbon, which he detested, for twelve years. A little nervously, he read a message, speaking of the "degradation" of the state and the Army as being "scandalized" by lack of authority. He asked for plenary powers for six months "to restore order and restore hope," after which he would submit a revised constitution to a people's referendum. It was one of the briefest investiture speeches on record. Georges Bidault remarked later that it could have been shorter still—simply: "Gentlemen, between you and the Seine is . . . . *moi*."

De Gaulle then withdrew from the Chamber, and a brief debate began. Mendès-France drew the most respectful attention, holding to his principles to the last. "This government is being imposed on us by those very people who have sabotaged every attempt at a human, reasonable settlement in North Africa," he told the Assembly. If the Fourth Republic was discredited, it was not the fault of democracy "but of anemic governments at the mercy of the very pressure groups represented in the new government of General de Gaulle." Whatever his personal feelings toward De Gaulle, Mendès-France concluded, "I cannot vote for him under the threat of violence and insurrection."

At 7:35 P.M., the voting began. De Gaulle, still absent from the Chamber, was approved by 329–224. The De Gaulle revolution was over. The De Gaulle Republic had begun.

"All my life," Charles de Gaulle wrote in his war memoirs, "I have thought of France in a certain way . . . as chosen for an exalted and exceptional destiny. Instinctively I have the feeling that Providence has created her either for complete successes or for exemplary misfortunes. If, in spite of this, mediocrity shows in her acts and deeds, it strikes me as an absurd anomaly, to be imputed to the faults of Frenchmen, not to the genius of the land. France is not really herself unless she is in the front rank. . . . Only vast enterprises are capable of counterbalancing the ferments of disintegration inherent in her people. In short, to my mind, France cannot be France without greatness. . . ."

France had passed through the ferment of disintegration, and now a Frenchman of true historic greatness was to set in motion the vast and counterbalancing enterprise of reconstruction of the state, renewal of the nation. Paralleling these tasks at home, General de Gaulle had two fundamental aims of foreign policy for France. The first was the restoration of France as an independent diplomatic and nuclear power in the world. The second was to break what he considered to be the Anglo-Saxon domination of postwar continental Europe. As these epochal Gaullist enterprises have unfolded, they have stirred in turn admiration, irritation, shock, amazement, envy, anger, bitterness, mistrust, enmity and honor for De Gaulle, both in France and throughout the world. But they have left no doubt that France had again turned abruptly, as she did in the time of Napoleon, from a period of chaos to a period of national greatness which already stands out in this century, and will gleam in the long pages of the history of the land.

Only rarely is there a convergence of the man, the task and the moment of historic opportunity—and such a convergence came for France and De Gaulle on June 1, 1958. All that had gone before—even the rallying of defeated France eighteen years ago that month—had been preparation. Late in life, having written himself off the political scene, De Gaulle returned with a towering self-confidence, a formidable intelligence, a profound sense of history, and an acute and highly personalized feel for the exercise of power. Power, its technique and use (or misuse), had been the fascination and frustration of his life, from his earliest days at the military academy at St.-Cyr and his earliest writings. At the same time, the "failures" about which he had brooded had given his life a lonely, rather bitter quality. Winston Churchill's great life bubbled over with adventure, gusto, humanity, humor and maganimity—but not De Gaulle's.

The chaos of his country for forty years, the behavior of Frenchmen, the attitude of his Allies, the weakness of his friends, the strength of his enemies, the character of his fellow Army officers, the satire of the cartoonists, the condemnations of the press, the wasting of French lives and genius, above all the shortcomings and contortions of French politicians—almost everything and everybody had, in De Gaulle's terms, contributed to the bitterness of his life. Yet paradoxically this, too, had played its part in molding and sustaining De Gaulle on a kind of lonely Pilgrim's Progress for France. It reinforced a self-confidence which transcended mere egotism. He had stood alone when France fell, storing up bitter memories of his countrymen and his Allies. He had stood alone through twelve years of political retirement, the locust years of the Fourth Republic, bitterly watching the self-destructive antics of those who were trying to govern France. Historically right so often, De Gaulle returned to power with a bitter indifference to those who might differ with him or oppose him, those who had been so wrong for France in the past.

He had long since developed in this lonely atmosphere a third-person detachment about "De Gaulle, the symbol of France."

"During the war I discovered that there existed in people's spirits someone named De Gaulle, having a personality separate from my own," he once said in a revealing conversation. "From that day forward I knew that I should have to take account of that man, of that General de Gaulle. I became almost his prisoner. Before every speech or decision, I questioned myself: Is this the way in which the people expect De Gaulle to act? There were many things I should like to have done but that I did not do, because they would not have been what was expected of General de Gaulle."

With this third-person approach to himself, De Gaulle brought great style, panache and *mystique* to the role of De Gaulle, ruler of France—a sense of grandeur, a revival of *la gloire*. A lesser man would have looked like someone dressing up in the ridiculous costumes of Molière's *Le Bourgeois Gentilhomme,* but in De Gaulle's hands this revival of nineteenth-century pomp and circumstance was far from playacting. It was a carefully calculated, long-cultivated and determined part of his own style, his own mechanism of power. As much as the votes of the people or the administration of justice and law, these ceremonies and honors were also instruments of the state, which had fallen into such a slovenly condition under the Fourth Republic that uniformed soldiers of the Garde Republicaine smoked cigarettes on duty in the sentry boxes outside the Élysée Palace.

"Is there not a connection between a man's inner strength and his outward appearance?" De Gaulle had written back in 1932 in a slim little volume called *The Edge of the Sword.* "Every page of Caesar's

Commentaries shows how carefully he measured his public gestures. And we also know how careful Napoleon was to produce the greatest effect with his public appearances."

Or, as Napoleon himself said when he created the Légion d'Honneur for France in 1802: "You can call these medals and ribbons baubles . . . but it is with such baubles that men are led." De Gaulle set out to restore these baubles, trappings and ceremonies into instruments of power and images of prestige—the power and prestige of France.

"Prestige arises from an elementary gift, from a certain natural aptitude which cannot be analyzed," De Gaulle also wrote in *The Edge of the Sword*. "The truth is that certain men carry with them almost from childhood a certain aura of authority. . . . Yet such a natural gift must, like any other natural talent, be developed. And in the first place, prestige cannot go without mystery, for people feel no reverence for anything with which they are too familiar."

In keeping with this rule of mystery, De Gaulle has no close friends, no confidants, and conceals himself and his political plans and objectives from everybody, allowing even his closest associates to know only exactly what he wants them to know. Often there are those who claim to know his mind or his plans (Jacques Soustelle's assumption about his aims for Algeria was a classic case), but in reality only De Gaulle speaks for De Gaulle. Even his own cabinet is never entirely certain what he might do until he announces a decision, and on occasion—such as his veto of British entry into the Common Market—the cabinet learns of it at the same time as he is informing the public.

Thus, De Gaulle uses mystery not to heighten his aura of prestige but also for the formidable advantages which secrecy and surprise give him in the management of French affairs, in the discomfiture of his political opponents, in dealings with other governments, in the control of his ministers and supporters and in the slow, often stealthful realization of concealed long-term aims.

"On the chessboard on which he plays, there can be no friendship between the knight that is moved and the hand that moves it," one of his ex-ministers once wrote.

When De Gaulle arrived at the Hotel Matignon on June 1, 1958, he faced a situation not unlike that which he had recorded in his memoirs on his arrival at the Ministry of War on the day of the liberation of Paris, August 25, 1944: "Nothing was missing except the state. It was my duty to restore it; I installed my staff at once and got down to work."

Since then, the De Gaulle era has fallen into three clear and distinct phases, almost military in character: buildup, attack and pursuit. The first phase, which lasted about two years, was a period of "renewal of the state," of consolidation of power, in which General de Gaulle concentrated primarily on setting France's internal house in order and transforming the French government into a "Gaullist apparat."

After the buildup, the attack. He then turned the full weight of his authority (and in particular his skill at concealing his ultimate aim) toward ending the war in Algeria. It took three years from his first offer of "self-determination" for the Algerians early in 1960 until the last Secret Army Organization terrorist had been executed by a firing squad against the walls of Fort d'Ivry outside Paris in March 1963. But in the end, Algeria had been given its independence and peace had been restored to France for the first time in a quarter of a century.

Then, with France stable, thriving and unencumbered by war or empire, Phase Three of the De Gaulle era began: Gaullist foreign policy. There had been many preliminary rumblings from the day De Gaulle took office, but this phase really was launched in earnest with his thunderbolt veto of British entry into the European Common Market at his famous press conference of January 14, 1963. It is the phase of independent French policy and diplomacy in the world which will go on as long as President de Gaulle remains in power, and probably for some time beyond.

De Gaulle had laid down the terms for his return to power. After his investiture, he moved immediately to see that they were carried out. First the National Assembly voted complete emergency powers to De Gaulle for six months. Next it passed an enabling act establishing a commission to draft a new constitution for submission to a people's referendum, in accordance with broad lines laid down by De Gaulle which had as the key principle: "Executive and legislative powers must be effectively separated. . . ." Then, on June 3, 1958, the last Assembly of the Fourth Republic recessed, never to return.

All the same, these last acts of the Fourth Republic deputies were seen through by De Gaulle in an unusual display of cordiality, charm and goodwill—like a host speeding parting guests. He went personally to the National Assembly to take part in the last debates. He even spoke, amid laughter and cheers, of "the pleasure and honor I feel at being in your midst." There was none of that scornful, sardonic bitterness which he was to heap on the politicians of the Fourth Republic in later years after his power was consolidated. He had enlisted three former premiers—Pflimlin, Mollet and Pinay—in his cabinet, and in this first stage he was manifestly concerned to symbolize unity in the nation, to heal the splits and wounds.

The drafting of a new constitution was begun by a commission headed by Michel Debré, Minister of Justice in the cabinet, one of De Gaulle's staunchest political supporters since the days of the resistance and later the first prime minister under De Gaulle's presidency.

Although starting with a clean sheet of paper and as open a mandate as any constitutional draftsmen ever were given, Debré and his team could not work in isolation from tradition, politics or French realities. The document which emerged in three months under high pressure has been called by René Capitant, a French professor of constitutional law, "the worst drafted text in our constitutional history . . . a source of permanent humiliation to those who held the pen."

Nevertheless, De Gaulle and Debré set out with one main determination: that the new constitution must establish where power and authority would lie in France. De Gaulle has spoken often of his experiences in 1940 where nowhere could power be identified—not in the hands of the President of the Republic, the Premier, the National Assembly, the Minister of War, the Generalissimo of the Armies, nowhere. In the Fourth Republic, power also was divided, resting basically with the National Assembly which in turn was so fragmented that no premier was able to govern for long.

Although much is left vague and unclear in the constitution of the Fifth Republic, the powers of the National Assembly were curbed and limited and have been separated from the powers of the executive branch of the government. Absent is the clarity of "separation of powers" which exists in the American constitution, or the equally clear "combination of powers" which exists in Britain where the Prime Minister and his government are responsible to Parliament. But the new French constitution did ordain that the President of the Republic would name the prime minister (a new title for France), approve his choice of ministers, and preside over cabinet meetings. It also requires ministers holding seats in the National Assembly or the Senate to resign upon taking a cabinet post. A government no longer has to obtain an "investiture vote" before taking office. Technically, the National Assembly cannot vote the government out of power either, although nobody knows what would happen if it repeatedly voted against a prime minister who chose to ignore its action. The president, but not the prime minister, holds power to dissolve the Assembly. The constitution at first appeared to provide for a president who would be a kind of "supreme arbiter" of French affairs. But De Gaulle has turned the office into one of supreme power, bending and indeed altering the constitution to suit his own concepts.

After an all-out political and propaganda campaign, in which government money was lavishly spent in support of government aims, the new constitution was overwhelmingly approved by the French people on September 28, 1958. It was, in fact, a far greater victory than the Gaullists expected. There were 17,666,828 "Yes" against only 4,624,475 "No" ballots. Nearly 80 percent of those voting, and 69 percent of the total electorate, had endorsed General de Gaulle's constitution for "renewal of the state."

The order which De Gaulle brought to the highest direction of French affairs was quickly communicated to lower echelons in the French Government. For example, a long-overdue reform and reorganization of the French court system was undertaken, with redistricting of the judiciary and simplification of court procedures. Similarly, the national defense regions were reorganized. Local community governments were given greater autonomy in administrative matters. The Government created a Paris Area Authority to undertake long-term regional planning for the capital, which has grown by 4,000,000 people in the last decade and is expected to reach a population of 10,000,000 by the 1970's.

On the economic front, the planners now had unprecedented governmental stability. A phased devaluation of the French franc was ordered—first the external rate was reduced, and then this new rate was applied to the internal rate as well. Symbolically more imporant, the Government clipped two zeros off the franc—so that 1,000 francs became 10 francs and 100 francs became 1 franc. It took three years and two new currency issues before the transition from the "old franc" to the "new franc" and finally to the "franc" was completed, and Parisians are still inclined to talk in terms of tens of thousands instead of hundreds. But a franc is a franc at last.

Even more symbolic of the "renewal of France" was the cleaning of the buildings of Paris—a simple matter of the enforcement of an old city ordinance which had long been allowed to lapse. The Government took the lead with public buildings, so that today the lovely façades of the Louvre and the Place de la Concorde glow in the soft cream tones of their natural stone, as they were when Napoleon ruled from the Tuileries and Benjamin Franklin signed the first international consular accord for the newly independent American states at the Hôtel du Crillon.

But politically, the De Gaulle honeymoon with the National Assembly scarcely lasted beyond its departure, and after the referendum approval of the Gaullist constitution the political atmosphere gave way to the more arrogant, strident and ruthless face of Gaullism. France went to the polls in November of 1958 to elect a new Fifth Republic National Assembly—and the result was another Gaullist sweep, with particularly staggering effects on the parties of the Left. The Gaullists marched into the new Assemby with a solid bloc of 188 seats. They could count on 132 Rightist members to give them firm parliamentary control. The Socialists, after all the maneuverings by Guy Mollet to identify the party with De Gaulle's return to power, came out miserably, their membership reduced by more than half, from 88 seats all the way down to 40. For the Communists, the election was a complete rout. Their 145 seats, which had represented the strongest parliamentary block in the last Fourth Republic Assembly, shrank to an almost undetectable 10. The Communists still, however, polled about 20 percent of the total vote.

The "old games" of the Fourth Republic were over, and De Gaulle was scarcely a man to show magnanimity in victory. He not only made no attempt to salve the wounded politicians, he set out to rub in political salt at every opportunity. Having done all he could to undermine the system of the Fourth Republic when he was in the political wilderness, he now heaped on scorn and ridicule. Steadily the regime lost its thin façade of national unity and became more and more Gaullist in character. Of the three former premiers in the cabinet, Guy Mollet resigned in December of 1958 in protest over economic policy. Antoine Pinay of the Conservatives lasted another year as Minister of Finance, disagreeing constantly and increasingly with General de Gaulle until he finally resigned by request in January of 1960. Pflimlin, the last of the trio, quit abruptly in May of 1962 after De Gaulle, at a press conference, engaged in a freewheeling denunciation of "European integration," which ran completely counter not only to Pflimlin's personal views but also to the traditional position of his

MRP party. With his departure, the French Government lost its last "political" figure and became a purely Gaullist instrument.

While this "Gaullization" of the French Government was taking place in Paris, the General was steadily at work asserting his control over the French Army in Algeria. He did this with an artful combination of promotions, awards and then reassignments. In the first year of his return to power, no fewer than 1,500 field-rank officers—lieutenant colonels and above—were shifted to new commands and reassigned in staff jobs in and out of Algeria. Plotters found themselves shifted to the Black Forest or Brazzaville or Madagascar, and officers loyal to De Gaulle moved steadily upward into the key commands. The Delbecque ring of ultra colonels was quickly dispersed. De Gaulle's treatment of General Salan was typical. When he returned to power, he congratulated Salan on his performance under difficulties, saluted him, decorated him and confirmed him as commander-in-chief in Algeria. But it was soon clear that De Gaulle and not Salan was going to give orders in the future. One year later, De Gaulle returned Salan to Paris, entertained him at a private lunch at the Élysée Palace on the anniversary of the May 13 uprising—and appointed him to the honorary and ceremonial post of Military Governor of Paris, where his main job would be to organize the parades on the Champs-Élysées. General Massu received a promotion, and then was ordered back to France for reassignment—languishing for nearly a year before he was finally put out of the way of trouble as Military Governor of Metz. It was perfectly clear to the French *colons* what was happening to their friends, the ultras of the Army, but they were powerless to do anything but sputter and grow more and more anti-Gaullist as the noose of authority closed around their necks. True, none of De Gaulle's moves stopped the abortive "Revolt of the Generals" in April of 1961, with Salan in the lead, but the revolt failed to a large degree because there were too many loyal Gaullist officers all over Algeria, refusing to cooperate with the generals.

From the outset, De Gaulle's technique in the explosive Algerian problem was to keep everybody off balance and uncertain, while concealing his real intentions, his ultimate policy. The shifting and promotion of Army officers was clearly aimed at restoring his authority over the Army, and he was laying the groundwork for something—but what? Nobody in the Army or in Algeria or in France itself could be quite sure. In Communist terms he was proceeding by "salami tactics," slicing away at the opposition one thin slice at a time. The tactics began on his first trip to Algiers on June 4, 1958, and his first appearance before a tumultuous if somewhat uncomprehending mob of French *colons* at The Forum, when he began his address with those wonderfully meaningless words: *"Je vous ai compris"* ("I have understood you")! The crowed roared its cheers to double-talk for two minutes. He had understood them, for certain, but had they understood him? How often were the *colons* and the ultras to spit out those words in bitter rage over the next four years.

Still De Gaulle left the central problem of ending the war almost completely alone for his first year in office. He turned first to the task of transforming the French colonies of Black Africa into independent states. On a series of whirlwind tours from Madagascar to Dakar, he visited each of the capitals in turn in the summer of 1958, while the new Fifth Republic constitution was being drafted. The constitution was to solve the colonial problems by giving France's possessions a free option to remain part of France, become independent but associated with France as part of the "French Community," or cut ties with France altogether.

The combination of De Gaulle's presence and economic and political persuasion proved irresistible to all the French-African colonies but one: Guinea, whose leader, Sekou Touré, opted for complete independence. The French gave it to him with a vengeance. They even took the telephones with them when they left Conakry, the capital—thereby opening the way for an invitation to Russia, Red China and the Eastern European Communist satellites to fill the vacuum. It was typical of the pettiness to which De Gaulle and France can sink on occasion, and it was only a combination of Sekou Touré's strong feelings about independence (feelings with which De Gaulle should certainly sympathize) and the ineptitude of the Communists who rushed to his assistance that prevented Guinea from becoming the first Communist bridgehead in Black Africa.

On January 29, 1960, De Gaulle was ready to tackle the Algerian problem in a concerted and determined way. He put on his old brigadier general's uniform and appeared over French television "in order to show that it is General de Gaulle who speaks as well as the Chief of State." He then declared that it was French policy to arrive at "peace that is peace" in Algeria and announced a turning-point decision: "The Algerians shall have free choice of their destiny." From then on—while Algeria seethed and sputtered and FLN fighting stepped-up and the terrorist attacks came and passed—De Gaulle moved like an inchworm, doubling up and then stretching forward with each press conference or public speech.

In September, at a press conference, he dumped the sacred cause of *Algerie Française*. "What solution will the Algerians choose? I shall refrain from prejudging. But I say to you that, as I see it, they will want Algeria to be Algerian," he said. Two months later, in a speech on November 4, 1960, he moved another step when he spoke of "the Algerian Republic, a republic which will one day exist."

In December, De Gaulle revealed his Algerian solution. Under the constitution of the Fifth Republic, Algeria was treated, as it had been for decades, as part of France. De Gaulle announced a national referendum in France and Algeria to confer extraconstitutional powers on the government to enable the Algerians to "choose their own destiny" —in other words, to secede from France. The president then took off on a flying visit to Algeria to "explain" his policy to the Army and campaign for its acceptance. He was greeted by rioting and anti-Gaullist demonstrations—almost the same kind of mob treatment which the *colons* had meted out to Guy Mollet four years before. But De Gaulle was no Mollet. On his return to Paris he found some of his ministers weakening and suggesting a postponement of the referendum, a cooling-off period. He stiffened, then instantly polled the cabinet individually and offered to accept the resignation of any minister who was not prepared to stand firm. The referendum was, of course, an overwhelming affirmative.

De Gaulle had now achieved two important breakthroughs in the situation. First, he had established a legal and constitutional position for ending the fiction that Algeria was French territory, so that the way was now clear to negotiate Algerian independence. Second, he had also succeeded through the referendum in isolating the French *colons* from their supposed backing by the French nation and the French people. France itself was sick of the "Algerian problem" and the Algerian war—having governments overthrown by distant events, policemen shot, plastic bombs in Paris cafés, street demonstrations raging in the capital to "keep Algeria French." When the French people finally were given a chance to express themselves, they voted overwhelmingly to get rid of Algeria. De Gaulle now had a legal and popular mandate to negotiate.

The French *colons* were nearing a state of panic-stricken desperation, compounded by the bitter anger of having themselves brought

De Gaulle to power. They were living in their own legacy of hatred, having rejected all reasonable approaches month after month, year after year, having contributed virtually nothing to any constructive efforts to find an Algerian solution, or even to improve relationships between themselves and the Moslem natives of Algeria. True, they had contributed much to the development of the land, and for many thousands of them, Algeria had been their homeland for generations. They ran the shops, the post offices, the schools, the public services, the country. Their one obsession was that they should go on running it forever, with the Moslems in a kind of perpetual state of bonded servitude and France providing an army to keep Algeria French. Moreover, despite the shifts and transfers of Army officers which De Gaulle had carried out—even because of it—there was plenty of anti-Gaullist sentiment and ultra support still to be found among the professional soldiers in Algeria. For them the De Gaulle policy was not a political solution but another defeat for the French Army—along with 1940, Indochina and Suez. The more De Gaulle increased the pressures for a solution, the more explosive the situation became. On April 22, 1961, a Saturday, it blew up with the Revolt of the Generals.

General Raoul Salan had resigned from his duties as Military Governor of Paris and become one of De Gaulle's most bitter critics. Late in 1960, he slipped out of France secretly and turned up in Madrid. There he was free of police surveillance and able to keep in constant contact with what was to become known as the Secret Army Organization—the extremists in and out of the French Army who were dedicated to keeping Algeria French. A new revolt against General de Gaulle and the authority of Paris was being plotted. Salan willingly placed himself at its head. This time the "Chinese General" was going to be one step in front. He arrived secretly in Algiers on April 20.

Three others joined him in the plot: General Maurice Challe, who had succeeded Salan for a year as commander in Algeria, and had resigned from his post as commander of Allied Forces on the NATO Central Front early in 1961 in protest against De Gaulle's policies; General Edmond Jouhaud, a former Air Force commander; and General Marie-André Zeller, a former Army Chief of Staff. On the morning of April 22, with the support of the paratroopers in Algiers and the Foreign Legion, the four generals seized the Government-General Building, placed the civilian delegate-general from Paris under house arrest, and announced that they were taking power to thwart General de Gaulle's "unconstitutional acts" and keep Algeria French.

But this time the plotters were up against De Gaulle and the Fifth Republic. Though virtually all of the French Army was either in Algeria or in Germany (even some of the Ministry of the Interior CRS companies had been moved to Algeria to insure government security during the referendum), there was an instant stiffening of government control throughout metropolitan France, and a movement of CRS reinforcements to Paris. Tension was high—but somehow the situation never had the "feel" of imminent collapse. Whatever the rebels might be doing in Algeria, there was a government in control in Paris which had the backing of the population.

Two personal incidents stand out in my recollections of that dramatic weekend.

On Sunday evening, Prime Minister Debré went on the French radio with an emotional warning that a paratroop invasion might be attempted by the leaders of the coup that very night. He announced that all airfields in France were being closed and runways blocked, and he exhorted the people to turn out in the streets to fight the Army if paratroopers did indeed land. Shortly after the speech, I got through by telephone to an acquaintance of mine on the intelligence and security liaison staff of the government.

I asked him about the situation, and he was crisp and categorical: "They have only sufficient airlift in Algeria for about two battalions, and none of the planes can make it to Paris non-stop. They would have to stop and refuel in southern France, which is why we are blocking all the runways in the country. We know that as of now nothing has taken off although they did try to load at one point but the air commander refused to accept the orders. So our main worry right now is whether other Army units in France or Germany might not defect and join. But the regular gasoline issue is such that nobody can move very far, and we have put in special security checks at every command for any signs of unauthorized movement."

All of this had a solid ring of truth and reality in the midst of rumor. A little while later that night, word came that civilians were being armed by the Ministry of the Interior, and I drove down to the rue Faubourg St. Honoré to see what was happening. True enough, on the pavement outside the Ministry courtyard, which was blocked off, little groups of men were gathered, looking serious, tough and determined, twenty or so to a group, almost like military units it seemed. I fell in with one such group which was calling out numbers to a Ministry official. When I reached the door I pulled out my French press card and mumbled, *"Presse américaine."* The official caught my arm and with a hard grin swung me back out the door. Talking with another group on the sidewalk, I learned that these units were a kind of Gaullist secret army—old resistance fighters from the war who had kept together and were evidently registered with the Ministry of the Interior as a secret civilian militia. I drove home in the early morning hours under a velvet night sky, quite certain that Paris would never be invaded. The revolt was bound to collapse. The power it sought to overthrow was too great.

On Monday night, De Gaulle appeared on television in his brigadier general's uniform in a performance of bull-like anger and authority that all but shattered the television screens. His voice powerful and tense with passion, his eyes blazing, he invoked—indeed epitomized—the supreme authority of the state, announced that he was taking full emergency powers under the constitution, and called upon French soldiers to shoot any officers in revolt against the state. "I order that all means—I say all means—be employed to bar these men until they are subjugated" were his words.

The next day the revolt collapsed. The Army commander at the city of Constantine had refused from the first to join the revolt. The commander at Oran had also stayed loyal while moving his command headquarters away from the city where it might have been surrounded or immobilized. Now he returned to reassert government control over the key port and military base. The Air Force, on orders from Paris, flew twenty-four troop transports back to French bases. Loyal units of the Ministry of the Interior CRS troops, along with a regiment of Zouaves which had refused to join the revolt, were ordered into Algiers from outside the city to reoccupy the government buildings. The paratroopers and the Foreign Legion units withdrew—later to be broken up and disbanded. General Challe alone of the four leaders had sufficient honor to "place himself at the disposal of French justice" and surrendered to French authorities immediately. Zeller gave himself up several days later. Jouhaud went underground until captured in September. Salan, running the Secret Army Organization and on the move constantly, was finally trapped one year almost to the day after the revolt—April 20, 1962. Today all four are in prison in a fortress in central France, on sentences ranging from fifteen years to life.

General de Gaulle emerged from this ordeal of power with his personal ascendancy over the French scene complete. The *colons* could no longer hope that the French Army would support their cause against the authority of Paris. The disciplining of the Army, which had been somewhat circumspect up to the Revolt of the Generals, became rigorous and ruthless. In addition, De Gaulle ordered the Army to start home, division by division, long before the Algerian cease-fire agreements had been concluded. The problem was now on the conference table, even though terrorism went on in Algeria and Paris with the aim of sabotaging any peace. It took a full year of on-again-off-again negotiations and contacts in secret and semisecret between the French and the rebel leaders until the end finally came in a hotel conference room in the French spa town of Evian, looking down on Lake Geneva. Daily for several weeks, a delegation of Algerian leaders had shuttled back and forth across the lake from Switzerland in helicopters provided by the Swiss Army. On March 19, 1962, all was ready. For two and a half hours the two delegations sat rereading and signing ninety-three pages of text which brought peace to Algeria and independence four months later.

Ahmed ben Bella was released from "château confinement," where he spent the last five months of his five years in the hands of the French, and driven across the border into Switzerland. Well recalling the circumstances of his capture in October of 1956, and not trusting another double cross, he asked for and received a United States Air Force transport plane to fly him back to Tunis on the first leg of his return to his native land.

Terrorism in Algeria and Paris reached a wanton, maddened state, the worse because all was over and it was now so utterly useless. But terrorism was to provide General de Gaulle, almost at the cost of his life, with the opportunity for a final stroke to mold the constitution of the Fifth Repubic and the office of President to his ultimate ideas of the proper political structure for France.

On the evening of August 23, 1962, President de Gaulle and his wife, with their son-in-law in the front seat, left the Élysée Palace in an official black Citroen sedan, with two motrocycle police riding in front, a security car behind, and more police following. They were on their way to Villacoublay airfield where the De Gaulles were to board a helicopter for a flight to Colombey-les-deux-Églises. Suddenly, as the little convoy sped through the suburban town of Petit-Clamart, it was caught in a hail of machine-gun bullets spraying from a parked truck, parked automobiles and a side street, in an ambush carefully prepared by at least a dozen men. One bullet passed through the rear of the presidential car and out the back window, missing De Gaulle's head by less than two inches. The driver jammed down the accelerator and sped to the airfield on puncture-proof tires which had also been pierced. Of eight known assassination plots or attempts on General de Gaulle's life in the four years he had been in power, this came by far the closest to succeeding. It was only by a providential reflex or accident that he was alive.

In the aftermath, one burning question stood out for all of France: Who would succeed De Gaulle? There was no obvious successor and there is no obvious successor today, but more than that, the machinery for choosing a successor was cumbersome and indirect—involving a national grand electorate of some 80,000 private citizens of special qualifications, such as mayors, prefects, members of local town councils. In the shock of the moment, De Gaulle seized the chance to ask the nation to change the constitution to provide for immediate direct election of a new president by universal sufferage at the expiration of the term, retirement or death of a president. It was yet another Gaullist move to increase the power and authority of the presidency at the expense of the National Assembly. And in addition, he stretched the provision of the constitution itself by going straight to the people with yet another referendum to approve the change, instead of asking the legislature first.

It was a furious and bitter referendum campaign, for direct election of the President of France meant a final end to the habits and concepts of the Fourth Republic. Moreover, the only time before in history when France had elected a president by popular vote had not been a great success for democracy. Louis Napoleon, was elected president in 1848 and he turned himself into an emperor three years later in 1851.

The De Gaulle amendment was approved—but it was the least impressive of the De Gaulle victories. It drew only 62 percent "Yes" votes, and by the time the abstentions and negative ballots were taken into account, this represented only about 46 percent of the electorate. De Gaulle was furious, and even talked impulsively of resigning. But instead he stayed on the political attack, dissolved the National Assembly and called new elections for deputies. In November of 1962 he was given a parliamentary victory as surprising as the narrowness of his near defeat in the referendum.

It was a Gaullist sweep from one end of France to the other. With 234 seats and a strong sprinkling of independent supporters, he won full control of the National Assembly—the first single-party control of parliament in French republican history.

The De Gaulle Republic was established and secure. De Gaulle foreign policy was about to begin.

4. Germany: The Adenauer Era

It was a simple, historic postwar necessity that Germany, or what could be saved of a truncated Germany for the West, should be restored and take her place in Europe once again. The "German miracle" had to happen. Germany had to come back. Nothing could ultimately stand in the way of that overriding demand of the times—no political hostility toward Germany, no wartime emotions, no fears of a Nazi revival, no anxieties about German competition, not even the grave and fundamental historic moral and psychological doubts about the honor and trustworthiness of the German nation.

Europe had to find a place for Germany, and Germany had to find her place in Europe. It was not a question of whether it would happen, but how it would happen and who would come to power in Germany to control and guide her. Here the chances and the risks were enormous.

At the same time, for the German people the idea of "belonging" in Europe—of having friends instead of enemies for the first time in this century—quickly became a new obsession. In the postwar post-Hitler atmosphere this was natural and understandable. Heaven knows that the Germans should have wanted to bury their debasing, guilt-ridden past and seek a new and positive future. All the same there was something irritating, even galling, about the blind way in which this schizophrenic people seemed to assume, when the poitical tide began to turn for them, that the crimes of history could be expatiated by a sort of "psychological whitewash"—by suddeny becoming not only "good" Europeans but better Europeans than anybody. It was a historical case of "If you can't lick 'em, join 'em." Moreover, when the Germans discover a cause they embrace it with suffocating enthusiasm. The heavy-handed *bestimmt* way in which they went at their new European faith recalled that classic wartime remark which the English novelist Evelyn Waugh, then serving in the Commandos, shouted to a fellow officer as they lay in a ditch in Crete being strafed by a Nazi dive-bomber: "Like most things the Germans do, this is far too noisy and is going on much too long."

It was easier to understand this sudden German conversion to the cause of Europe—and to be cynically amused by it—than it was to be very deeply convinced of the new German faith. After all, Germany had everything to gain and nothing to lose from the movement toward European unity.

The shareholders of I.G. Farben had no trouble persuading themselves that the old cartel ought to be allowed to stick together "in the interests of Europe." The Sudeten Germans who had been tossed out by Czechoslovakia and the East Prussians who had been driven west by the Russians trumpeted for restoration of their homelands "in the cause of European justice." Abolition of the limit on German steel production, the right to make synthetic rubber again, the return of the Saar which was then detached from Germany and firmly ruled by the French—all these demands were put forward in the name of Europe, not Germany. I recall touring an aluminum foundry at Bochum in the Ruhr in 1949 which had been heavily bombed and was lying idle, scheduled to be dismantled by the Allies for reparations. In fact, it was difficult to see what use this decaying, rusted, damaged machinery—which had not felt the heat of molten aluminum or the touch of a paintbrush or oil can for nearly five years—would have been to anybody, so I listened with double indifference to a well-fed plant manager discourse on the unemployment problem of the Ruhr, unrest among the workers, the inhumanity of dismantling, the injustice of Allied policy. Then his eyes lit up with the thought of a new appeal to my cold conscience: "And think, Herr Cook, this production is being denied to Europe."

In particular there remained the almost unbelievable wooden-headed inability of the German people to see themselves as others saw them. Introspection has never been a strongpoint of German character and under Hitler, blindness to the opinions or reactions of others had been transformed into a matter of national pride and principle. When

Allied travel restrictions began to ease for the Germans in 1952 and 1953, and the Bonn Government began to issue passports to its citizens, it had been twenty years since they had been able to travel freely in Europe and the world. Resolute tourists they are, and the urge to burst out and see Europe—to be European—was overwhelming, matched only by the obtuseness of the German mind. Up and down the highways and byways of France and Italy, Belgium and Holland, Norway and Denmark they charged, reinvading the scenes of their wartime exploits to show *mutti und die kinder* where *vati* had fought in 1940, impervious to their own past and the emotions they were arousing in others, undeterred by the stony hostility of natives who had for five years felt the jackboot of war and occupation. Nothing, it seemed, would stop the German photo fiends from debarking from cars and buses to snap pictures in front of houses they had requisitioned or bridges they had fought to capture. Even in the summer of 1963, German tourists were upsetting the placid Danes by gouging out huge sand fortifications on the smooth beaches of Jutland, lettering them with seashells, *Festung Frankfurt* or *Haus Essen,* and hanging up signs on them: *Occupied till further notice.*

More than once the old memories were far too strong to be quenched by the thought of European togetherness. The Norwegian Government refused to permit organized parties of German tourists to visit the country until the summer of 1961, sixteen years after the end of the war. They would allow German individuals to come with their families—but so concerned were they at the possible reactions of the Norwegian citizens that busloads or guided tours were ruled out.

As late as the spring of 1962, there was a nasty incident in Holland when four Germans crossed the border to visit a little town where they had served with an SS unit during the wartime occupation. As usual, the SS had given the townspeople a terrible time—the summary executions, the hostages, the roundup of Jews, the looting and shooting, the torture, the slave-labor shipments. The returning German veterans had a few friendly beers with the Dutch. Then they got carried away with the new times and announced that they had been there during the war, with the occupation forces. The pub where they were drinking grew quiet. One or two of the men and all of the women disappeared. The Germans drank blithely on without noticing the drop in temperature. But word of their presence was quickly spreading around the town, and suddenly they looked up to see what seemed like the entire adult male population converging on the pub. The drinking ex-SS men were beaten unmercifully and the next day shipped back across the border to Germany swathed in bandages. The Dutch and German authorities quickly consulted and agreed that the less said or done about the incident the better.

The bland expectation of the Germans about how simple and easy it would be for them to become acceptable as "good" Europeans always seemed to me to be epitomized by a conversation in a *beerstube* in Bonn one evening shortly after my assignment to Germany as a correspondent in May of 1949. I was sitting with a Norwegian friend when some Germans from an adjoining table leaned over and began mixing in the talk, clinking steins with us. Inevitably it turned out that one of them had been with the German occupation forces in Norway. After a few bleary reminiscences of how beautiful Norway was and how he had enjoyed his stay there—clearly seeking in ponderous and dim-witted Germanic fashion to put my Norwegian friend at ease—the German waved an arm and said grandly: *"Aber jetzt ist alles vorbei und vergessen."* To which the Norwegian retorted with icy civility: "All over—but not forgotten."

The Germans had to make their way back into Europe across mountains of prejudice and valleys of mistrust, further aggravated by the grating problems of national character and *herrenvolk* personality. Whatever the historical and political necessity for bringing Germany back into Europe, no red carpet was unrolled. It could scarcely have been otherwise after the tortures and tragedies which Germany had inflicted on its neighbors and the world. Every German action, word, deed, voice, mood and attitude has been watched inside Germany, and abroad, under the magnifying glass of public opinion. An alert and vigorous German press has made no small contribution to this process of self-policing and self-examination. No question has been more constantly in people's minds in postwar Europe than "Is it a new Germany or is it the same old Germany"—genuinely shed of its lusts and ambitions or sullenly waiting for another Hitler to satisfy the fuehrer-complex and present Europe with a new bill of nationalistic grievances? The Germans are confronted with this simple choice between their past and the future every time a young German tough smears a swastika on a rebuilt Jewish synagogue, every time another ex-Nazi turns up in high public office, every time the anniversary of the July 20, 1944, plot against Hitler rolls around and the debate starts up again whether the plotters were traitors or patriots.

Quite certainly there is strong German resentment at the fact that waves of suspicion rise so readily every time a headline recalls the past. Quite certainly there is bitterness among Germans that their easy formula of *"vorbei und vorgessen"* has not been so simple and acceptable to the rest of Europe. But the very fact that fears and hatreds had to be chipped and chipped and chipped away slowly in the 1950's was part of the positive process of building Europe—of insuring that Germany knew her place. And it was essential, too, that the German people not be allowed to forget all that quickly and easily. The Krupps and the Fricks have long since served their jail sentences (and are now vastly more prosperous than ever), but twenty years after the war Nazi criminals are still going into the dock to defend themselves. It may seem to be late to be trying them, but more important is the fact that the trials which are going on today reflect a moral sense that Germans support, a demand that the past continue to be exposed and punished.*

Today, doubts about Germany and the reluctance to award the German Federal Republic a new true bill of national character and historic trustworthiness have faded in Europe. The central fact of the postwar German scene is that Europe's worst fears and apprehensions have not materialized. Of course, there have been Nazi speeches, anti-Semitic eruptions and revanchist alarms from embittered refugees. But if the forces of decency, justice and the higher aspirations of life and democratic character have not triumphed over every creeping Nazi and latent anti-Semite in Germany, at least they have remained steadily in power and slowly have consolidated their control and moral domination over the country. Political stability has been achieved while a new generation has begun to emerge from the war. Democracy has not been threatened or engulfed.

Overwhelmingly the Germans owe their place in Europe, and this renewal or restoration of national character, to one man: Konrad Adenauer. For fourteen years, from 1949 to 1963, longer in power than any German chancellor since Bismarck, longer than the history of Hitler's Thousand-Year Reich, Adenauer was Germany. His as-

* An official Justice Ministry survey in late 1964 showed that West German courts have tried 12,960 Nazis since the war and convicted 5,482, of them 423 for murder or manslaughter. In all, about 10,500 Nazis served prison terms after the war, including those tried and sentenced by the Allies, and 489 were executed. The death penalty was abolished in Germany in the 1949 constitution.

cendancy and dominance over his nation was complete. It was Konrad Adenauer who was slowly and carefully taken back into the councils of Europe in the 1950's—not Germany. Europeans were able to forget or overlook the recurring disturbing headlines out of Hannover or Frankfurt or Munich or Düsseldorf about this or that demand from a rabble-rousing politician, or some fresh outburst of German national hysteria, because Adenauer was at the helm in Bonn, in full control, molding, solidifying and guiding his defeated, restive, strident nation.

Seldom in history has a statesman emerged so late in life, with so little evident preparation for a historic role, to win such respect and success as Konrad Adenauer. There was virtually nothing in the first seventy years of his life to point any finger of national or international destiny at the man. When he became the first Chancellor of the Federal Republic at the age of seventy-three, in September of 1949, the standard appraisal of the Military Government advisers of that day was "Best of the lot but a bit old for the job."

Adenauer was already thirty-eight years old when World War I broke out, married with three children, and a senior civil servant in the city administration of his beloved Cologne. Local government in Germany is run much more like a Wall Street law firm than a political machine and Adenauer, whose father was a secretary in the Cologne Law Courts and whose wife's family had strong political connections, moved steadily up the ladder. Then tragically, after a long illness and only ten years of marriage, his wife died in 1916. The following year he advanced to the post of Oberburgermeister of Cologne.

Adenauer was to hold the office continuously—though at one point he survived reelection by the Cologne City Council by only one vote—until 1933, when he was removed by Hermann Goering himself. In 1919 he married a second time, a neighborhood girl eighteen years younger than he who used to help with his children, Auguste "Gussi" Zinsser. She bore him five more children, but one died in infancy.

At one brief moment, Adenauer almost emerged on the German national political scene when, in 1926, the political leaders of the Weimar Republic summoned him to Berlin with a proposal that he become chancellor and form a "grand coalition" government of all the political parties. The negotiations fell through and offered a lesson in coalition politics which Adenauer never forgot. After four days of fruitless Berlin talks, he returned to Cologne.

Adenauer's downfall at the hands of the Nazis began in February,

1933. He ordered Cologne city workmen to take down Nazi flags and banners which had been put up by SS troopers without the lord mayor's permission on a bridge which Hitler was to cross for a triumphal entry into the city to address a Nazi Party rally. Democracy was then gasping its last in Germany, and Adenauer had taken a clear firm anti-Nazi political stand from the first. Six weeks after the flag incident he journeyed to Berlin, was summoned before Goering, and was summarily removed from office. He was even forbidden to reenter Cologne to visit his home and pack up his possessions. Returning to the Rhineland, he detoured around the city he had served for twenty-five years and took refuge in a Benedictine monastery at Maria Laach in the remote Eifel Mountains between the Rhine and Luxembourg. He remained there in semiseclusion for almost a year until the Nazi heat was off, and then, believing that he could live outside in peace, he joined Gussi and his children at a small suburban house on the outskirts of Berlin.

In 1934 came the Roehm Putsch and the Nazi "night of the long knives," and Adenauer was picked up by the Gestapo in Berlin for questioning. After two days of interrogation and threats he was released, and there followed another period of semifugitive life. Finally in 1936 some sympathetic old associates of Adenauer's in the Cologne city administration put through a small pension for the former lord mayor. He sold some of his property in Cologne and purchased a new home at the village of Rhöndorf, where he was to live the rest of his life—up a long steep flight of 56 stone steps which he still briskly climbed long after his retirement, on the heights overlooking the Rhine opposite Bad Godesberg, in the shadow of the Drachenfels where Siegfried slew the dragon. Here he settled quietly with his wife and some of his children as Hitler plunged on to war. On an adjoining mountaintop at the luxurious Hotel Petersberg, Neville Chamberlain came to stay for the first of his tragic "appeasement" conferences in 1938, to meet Hitler across the river at the Hotel Dreesen. Twelve years later the Dreesen was housing the French High Commission and the Petersberg became the headquarters of the combined Allied High Commission.

At the outbreak of the war, Adenauer deliberately slipped away to Switzerland, sensing that there might be an immediate Gestapo swoop against potential enemies of the Nazi regime. A month or so later, he returned quietly to Rhöndorf. But when the July 20 plot broke and failed in 1944, the Gestapo was at his door almost at once.

Adenauer had in fact been approached in great secrecy by the plotters on behalf of Carl Gordeler, the mayor of Leipzig who was to have become chancellor if the plot had succeeded. But he declined to have anything to do with the plot—because, he said in later years, he was convinced that an undertaking organized by Gordeler had no chance of success.

From Rhöndorf, Adenauer was taken to Cologne where a temporary detention center was already crammed with anti-Nazi suspects. Here he lodged until suddenly one evening a camp informer discovered Adenauer's name on a list for transport to Buchenwald the next day. A doctor-prisoner quickly arranged a simulated "heart attack" for the former lord mayor, and in a panic at the possibility of losing so prominent a political prisoner, the camp commandant had him transferred immediately to a prison hospital on the outskirts of Cologne. There Adenauer's wife had been lodged in another part of the prison, unbeknownst to her husband. They learned of each other's presence through the prison grapevine, and eventually they were allowed a brief visit. Then after four agonizing months of uncertainty, while the Gestapo went on and on devouring its lists of suspects in the bloodbath following the Hitler plot, the Adenauers were released and returned to Rhöndorf.

In March of 1945, the Allied Armies closed to the Rhine, and the Americans seized the Remagen Bridge in one of the most dramatic actions of the war—barely five miles south of Adenauer's village. Troops poured across the Rhine and the bridgehead was steadily enlarged. In the meantime, Adenauer was sheltering five escaped French prisoners-of-war, along with his family and neighbors—nineteen people in all—in a little garden dugout shelter. Below his home in the streets of Rhöndorf, a German tiger tank shelled American forces on the other side of the river, drawing counterfire in which the Adenauer home took two direct hits. Then suddenly on March 14, 1945, the guns grew quiet. The German forces pulled out of the village. The Americans moved in. The war was over for the Adenauers.

The next morning a jeep drew up in the street at the foot of the flight of 56 steps, and two American officers climbed briskly to Adenauer's door. In fluent German one of them announced to the sixty-nine-year-old head of the household: "We are calling at the request of the American Commander-in-Chief. We have orders to ask you, Dr. Adenauer, whether you would be prepared to resume the direction of the city administration of Cologne."

Adenauer hesitated. The officers urged that they were under orders to drive him immediately to the city. Finally he agreed with the stipulation that until Germany had concluded an armistice with the Allies, he would serve only as an "unofficial adviser" to the American forces.

"Three of my sons are still serving with the German Army," he explained simply. The American officers accepted his conditions at once, and half and hour later, Gussi with him, he was on his way back to Cologne. Fighting was still going on on the opposite bank of the Rhine when he reentered the city to begin his political life all over again.

Then six months later there occurred one of those ironic turns of history. When the permanent occupation zones were established after Germany's surrender, the British took over from the Americans in Cologne—and Mayor Adenauer was back in a familiar situation, for he had also had to deal with British occupation authorities in Cologne from 1919 until 1926. As the winter of 1945 approached, the British gave orders to Adenauer to have the trees in the city parks cut down to provide a fuel stockpile for the winter. He refused, and countered with a proposal—highly audacious for a German mayor in October of 1945—that the occupation authorities release their own stocks of requisitioned German coal to keep the Germans warm. In addition Adenauer received two visiting newspaper correspondents in his office and put his views on record in an interview.

That first Adenauer press interview ended on an oddly prophetic note. One of the two journalists remarked to Adenauer that General Charles de Gaulle had declared in a speech at Saarbrücken the day before that Germans and Frenchmen should cease all recriminations about the past and work together henceforth—remembering that they were all Western Europeans.

"I wish for a change some British statesman would speak of us as Western Europeans," the mayor remarked a little bitterly.

The next day Adenauer was summoned to British headquarters, and read a peremptory order removing him from office for having "failed in your duty toward the population," ordering him to leave Cologne as soon as possible and forbidding him "any political activity whatsoever" on pain of trial before a military court. Worst of all, as in Nazi times, he was barred from the city, and allowed only two visits a week to his wife who was in a Cologne hospital suffering from osteomyelitis contracted as a result of her stay in prison. The Military

Government order even dictated an exact route which Adenauer was to use driving in and out of town to the hospital. His wife made a partial recovery and returned to Rhöndorf, but died in March of 1948.

If Adenauer was bitter about his treatment at the hands of the British he never showed it openly, and in later years the incident was one of wry amusement for him. In fact, he undoubtedly gained by it politically—he had not been a tool of the Nazis and now he had proven to his countrymen that he was no tool of the Allies either. All the same, the incident happened, and who can know the subconscious reflections it left in Adenauer's thinking and reasoning in later years, when Britain was pressing to enter the European Common Market and he was working to align Germany solidly behind De Gaulle in Europe?

Back at Rhöndorf, Adenauer now turned to national politics. The British order forbidding him any political activity was virtually meaningless. In the first place it applied only in the state of North Rhine-Westphalia, and it was a simple matter for Adenauer to motor forty miles up the Rhine to meet his friends at Koblentz in the state of Rhineland-Pfalz. In any case, the order was never enforced, and soon Adenauer was traveling all over West Germany—Düsseldorf, Hannover, Hamburg, Frankfurt, Stuttgart, Munich—drawing together the organization of a new and predominantly Catholic political party, the Christian Democratic Union, which in Bavaria would be known as an allied but separate party, the Christian Socialist Union. It espoused the same political faith as the parties of De Gasperi in Italy and Georges Bidault and Robert Schuman in France, a Center Catholic part of liberal persuasion and orientation.

Early in 1949, the three Western Allies—with the Berlin blockade at its height and four-power rule of Germany irrevocably ended—authorized the formation of a parliamentary council for all of West Germany to draw up a constitution for a new German government. Adenauer, as leader of the strongest single political grouping in the country, became its chairman and guided its deliberations. And he also arranged that it should sit in Bonn, across the river from Rhöndorf—partly to get out from under the close wing of the Allies in Frankfurt, partly because of Adenauer's long antipathy toward "Prussianism" in Germany and his instinctive desire to see his native Rhineland play a key role in German political life.

On May 8, 1949, the fourth anniversary of Germany's surrender, the Parliamentary Council completed its work by approving a document of ponderous Germanic structure—147 articles meticulously defining many a right which other countries have long assumed as unwritten law. Article XVII, for example, provides that "every one shall have the right individually or jointly with others to address written requests or complaints to the competent authorities and to the popular representative bodies." But ponderous as it was the job was done, and Germany had a democratic constitution. Four days later the Berlin blockade was formally lifted by the Russians. In a week, General Lucius D. Clay retired as American Military Governor of Germany, and in mid-July, John J. McCloy arrived to take over as American High Commissioner. The transition of power had begun. The first free general elections in sixteen years in Germany were held on August 14, 1949, and Adenauer's CDU-CSU Party emerged in front with 31 percent of the votes and 139 out of 402 seats in the new Bundestag. Adenauer clearly would be the first chancellor of the new Federal Republic.

A few days after the election, correspondents trooped to Bonn from Frankfurt, Düsseldorf and elsewhere for Adenauer's first post-election press conference. It was a hot, hot August day. The little city of Bonn bore some sharp gashing scars of the war but, as a university town of no strategic or economic importance, had missed the worst. It lay sweltering in the heavy, humid Rhineland heat. We gathered in a white modernistic building, on the banks of the Rhine, which had been a teachers training college, part of Bonn University. The Parliamentary Council had been meeting there for the past eight months, and in another six weeks it was due to become the permanent home of the West German Bundestag.

Outside the windows, the schoolhouse lawn stretched down to the banks of the Rhine, where barges chugged slowly upstream against the current or briskly downstream to Düsseldorf and Rotterdam. In a big open field in front of the building, a German farmer on a tractor was cutting hay, and in that drowsy pastoral atmosphere it was impossible to visualize Bonn as a capital, the seat of power of a new German state. All that most of us wanted was to hear what the old man had to say and then hit the autobahn back to Frankfurt and the refreshments of the Press Club bar.

Adenauer entered the room, straight as a ramrod, with an easy, firm, dignified stride. He walked to a seat behind a table, with his back to the windows overlooking the Rhine. Nobody stood up. He smiled a cordial welcome, and then said with courtly hospitality, *"Meine*

Herren, as it is very warm I suggest we take off our coats." There was a murmur of appreciation and we shifted out of our jackets while Adenauer divested himself of his own dark, conservative, single-breasted suit-coat and stood before us in a white shirt with a detachable high stiff white collar, old-fashioned broad white suspenders, and stiff starched cuffs. I remember thinking instantly, "Those old photos of Calvin Collidge." And there was a touch, too, of my own grandfather who had been a Pittsburgh dandy in the 1890's.

We settled back for the press conference, and Adenauer made two remarkable declarations that day—though in the August heat nobody really cared much what an elderly German politician was saying, and the story never even made page one. Nevertheless, he went at his first press meeting with all the assurance and certainty of a man who had been in office for years.

First of all, he boldly declared that the German Federal Republic would seek to join the North Atlantic Treaty Organization as soon as it was permissible (NATO was then only four months old), and that West Germany would in the meantime seek to enter the Council of Europe at Strasbourg. We shifted in surprise at the audacity, indeed what almost seemed to be the silliness of the old man. The government had not even been formed. There had not even been a partial transfer of power. Military Government was still in full operation, and when it was dissolved, the Allied High Commission would continue to exercise control over German foreign affairs. Yet here was old Adenauer, already expecting to be treated as a NATO ally.

The questioning then shifted to the more practical problem of the formation of the new government. Although the CDU-CSU's 31 percent of the votes put it on top, the Social Democratic Party under the fiery Kurt Schumacher had been only 2 percentage points behind. Would there be a "grand coalition" of the parties of Left and Right—or would Adenauer form a Rightist coalition only, with his own followers and other right-wing groups in the Bundestag? The British in particular, with Labour Government in power in London, would have been happy to see a coalition of the two biggest parties, thus improving the fortunes of the Social Democrats and also getting the new German democracy off to a broadly based start.

There was an argument for it, but the old man in the high Coolidge collar never wavered for an instant when the question was put to him. Raising his hand in a gesture of grandfatherly admonition, with his head at a slight tilt, and nodding in emphasis to his words, Adenauer said in that slow, distinct, precise Rhenish German which was to become so familiar to German ears in the years ahead:

"Germans must acquaint themselves with the idea that one party must take responsibility and then, if it fails, it must pay. Then a strong opposition can take over. From 1918 to 1933 we did not develop correctly our democratic prerogatives. In the Weimar days we concerned ourselves too much with coalitions. When there is some great national crisis such as a war, a coalition may be necessary. But Germany is not in so critical a situation. We are the strongest faction. There is no doubt that the basic issue of the election campaign was economic policy, because there are no other big differences between us and the Social Democratic Party. But the SPD could not enter the government without affecting its economic policy. I personally think it is right that it should be that way."

We picked up our coats and walked to our cars, realizing that clearly here was a personality and a tough old boy to be reckoned with. Not even yet in office, he was laying down a foreign policy for West Germany and reading the Germans a necessary but forgotten lesson out of their dismal political past. He was going to give Germany a voice and a government. Three weeks later he was elected first Chancellor of the Federal Republic—by one vote, his own.

Konrad Adenauer's advanced age of seventy-three, which so worried the Military Government advisers of that day, gave him great advantages in postwar Germany when he became chancellor. To a large degree, his political ascendancy in Germany, as well as his international perspective and statesmanship, derived from the fact that he was rooted and matured in the most respectable of all periods of German history—the late 1800's and the turn of the century.

Adenauer was born at the high tide of the Bismarck era, in Cologne on January 5, 1876. It was a period in which Germany, after Bismarck's midcentury military adventures climaxed by the Franco-Prussian War and the annexation of Alsace-Lorraine, had established the international reputation of a powerful and dangerous but essentially right-minded member of the "concert of Europe." Bismarck, for all his aggressiveness, was nevertheless a statesman who knew how to keep the peace once he had unified Germany and achieved the power position he wanted in Europe. And from 1871 onward, the peace was kept. It was not until Kaiser Wilhelm dismissed the Iron Chancellor in 1890, after nineteen years in power, and then launched his own irresponsible diplomatic and power ventures after the turn of the century which led to World War I that the image of the bloodthirsty Hun replaced that of heavy-handed German respectability. Konrad Adenauer was, therefore, by education, upbringing, background and experience, a German "traditionalist" who belonged to a nostalgic, happy, prosperous, peaceful and almost forgotten German era. Thus, when he became chancellor, he was not just a "father figure" but a "grandfather figure" for the battered, confused, sick and muddled Germans. Their fathers had participated twice in the ruin of Germany—but their grandfathers! Ah! They were the Good Germans from a happy past.

The quality of grandfatherly traditionalism in Adenauer was well illustrated in his attitude toward student fraternities and dueling societies in German universities—which, to the Military Government "democratizers," were as abhorrent as the Nazi Party itself, synonymous with racism, fascism, militarism and the most craven impulses beating in Teutonic breasts. When the occupation began they were immediately outlawed, but gradually they revived, first in secret, then in defiance and finally in quasi-respectability.

As a young man in the 1890's, Adenauer had studied law at the universities of Freiburg, Munich and Bonn, transferring credits and studies from one university to another in the tradition of German students. While he never fought a student duel or acquired Eric von Stroheim scars on his high flat cheeks, he was nevertheless a lively and popular member of the Arminia Society at Bonn University, named, typically, after the Teutonic hero Arminius whose forces annihilated three Roman legions under General Varus in the year A.D. 9. Turning up one day at a reunion of his old society, the chancellor put a seal of "good traditionalism" on student fraternities in place of the old *diktat* of the occupation.

"When a student enters university, he or she is not a finished man or woman," he said. "A boy needs special atmosphere. I believe in student fraternities. I believe that they can give a young student a great deal. I look back at my student times and can only say that the atmosphere which I found in the fraternities has affected me for my whole life. A student can be raised only by the fellowship of his peers. After the terrible collapse at the end of the war, the rise of such a tradition is of very vital and great significance for all the German people."

It was typical Adenauer—leapfrogging back across the Hitler

times when the dueling societies were hothouses for young Nazi toughs, back even before World War I, to resuscitate for the Germans a past which almost none of them knew or could remember, and to identify the student fraternities with a tradition free of the guilt of modern times.

It would of course have been disastrous for Germany and for postwar European history if Adenauer had been a doddering and uncertain old man. But he was not. He was clear-headed, vigorous, autocratic, and he had a boundless mixture of patience and self-confidence. In the sickness and degradation, the myopia, megalomania and guilt complexes of postwar Germany, the old man out of the Bismarckian past, by his very presence in power, offered the German people a new sense of moral confidence and a restoration of traditional German values.

When he became chancellor, Adenauer had well perceived that Germany's opportunity for moral and political revival in Europe, as well as the road to economic recovery, lay in the interplay of the urge of the German people to "belong" in Europe and Europe's need for a healthy and reliable German partner. But the perception confronted Adenauer with a somewhat contradictory political problem.

On the one hand, Adenauer had to create confidence in the "new Germany" in Europe. He had to be the quiet, unassuming, trustworthy and moderate European statesman. But at home he had to be something of an autocratic German nationalist. Germans expect, respect and demand authority, and Adenauer knew it. It was the curse of history that the Weimar Republic never was able to satisfy this political need in Germany and instead found itself turning constantly to the German General Staff for support from the Army, until at last democracy had so fragmented that the country was ripe for the Hitler take-over. To be a strong chancellor, Adenauer launched at once into battle with the Allied High Commissioners for German interests.

Adenauer also had to do something else. He had to choose for his nation—the very deep and fundamental choice of Germany's role in the East-West struggle. Jean Monnet once said to me in later years that he considered Adenauer to be the true great man of postwar Europe, and that the measure of his greatness was this matter of making the historic choice.

"It may seem that his choice was an obvious one, and it may be difficult to recognize now how great a choice this was," Monnet said. "But remember Germany is divided. And it is a historic German temptation, indeed a policy, for Germany in the middle of Europe to play both ways. Adenauer had to choose between the possibility of a deal with the Communists, or staying completely with the West, and he chose the West. All we need to do is imagine what Europe would be like today if Adenauer had not made the choice and stuck to it. That is true greatness. De Gaulle—he did not really have any choice to make over giving Algeria its independence. He knew that France had to do it to end the Algerian war. It was not a choice—only a matter of method. But Adenauer had to choose."

It was not that easy a choice, politically, for Adenauer—even though he went straight on the record at that first press conference before he became chancellor and declared himself for German membership in NATO. True, Adenauer was an ardent Catholic and a thoroughly Western man. True, also, the Berlin blockade had just ended and the noose of Communism was tightening steadily around the necks of those haggard and starving Germans east of the Elbe. True, too, that Hitler himself and the memories of the Russian campaign had infected the German nation with the most virulent anti-Bolshevik passions. Just as the Germans were out to be better Europeans than any of their old enemies in the west, so they also seemed to be ready to prove themselves better anti-Communists than their new Allies. So there was, it seemed, plenty of emotion on which to base a completely pro-Western anti-Communist policy for the Federal Republic.

But there were other factors too. There were 18,000,000 Germans behind the Iron Curtain who could not be written off. There was the threat to Berlin. There was the traditional, Bismarckian policy of which Monnet spoke. And there were those classic examples of this policy in action in modern times—at Rapallo in 1923, and in the Hitler-Stalin pact of 1939.

To "sit in the middle" had strong nationalistic appeal in postwar Germany—not only among the ex-Nazis but, more important, with the respectable Social Democrats. Then too, sick of war and destruction, many Germans feared that a "choice" between East and West of the kind Adenauer was making would reduce the Fatherland once more to another and far more terrible battlefield. Pacificist and neutralist attitudes were widespread. Finally there was plenty of anti-occupation spirit to be manipulated by the politicans, so that cooperation with Allied foreign policy was neither an automatic nor an overwhelmingly popular reflex.

Adenauer did not by any means have a popular mandate behind his all-out pro-NATO policies in 1949. His own followers in the Christian Democratic Union were split as to how far to commit Germany to the Allied camp, most of them instinctively favoring a cautious, step-by-step line. They did not want the party accused of closing the door against East Germany, and they sensed the political unpopularity of appearing to be dancing to the tune of the occupying powers.

Moreover, that first West German Bundestag was almost—but not quite—as fragmented as the Reichstag of the Weimar Republic. The CDU-CSU with its 31 percent of the votes and 139 out of 402 Bundestag seats was in a strong but scarcely a dominant position in a parliament in which almost every type of German political screwball had found a front: Social Democrats, 131 seats; Free Democrats (the big business "liberals"), 52 seats; Deutsche Partei Rightists, 17; Bavarian Party right-wing Bavarian Nationalists, 17; Deutsche Rechts Partei neo-Nazis, 5; WAV refugee front, 13; Communists, 15; Zentrum Partei, 10; and finally 4 independents.

Fourteen years later, when Adenauer retired at the age of eighty-seven, Germany had a parliament of only three political parties, all supporting to the hilt the main lines of a pro-Western, NATO-based foreign policy. For the first time in German history, the country had achieved that vital and essential balance of democracy—a governing party and a responsible and strong opposition, the political objective at which Adenauer had aimed from that very first press conference before he took office. From nine political parties and four independent members in the elections of 1949, the Bundestag shook down to six political parties in the election of 1953, four in 1957, and three in the present parliament elected in 1961: The CDU-CSU with 242 seats; the Social Democrats with 190; and the Free Democrats whose 67 seats make the coalition government. The "Nazi vote" has slowly disappeared into the mainstream of German politics.

This is perhaps the greatest legacy of internal achievement which Adenauer leaves to his country. By his policies and his political strength and skill, he slowly extinguished the lunatic fringe of German splinter parties (with a large assist from the courts, the voters and the Socialists). And by winning one election after another on an uncompromising pro-NATO foreign policy, Adenauer finally drove the responsible Social Democratic leadership to a point at which it joined in a unanimous Bundestag vote after the 1961 elections to raise the compulsory military service period in Germany to eighteen months.

But this was a far, far distant hope when the Federal Republic was born in 1949. In those days, the rallying figure for the anti-Allied nationalistic forces in Germany was, disappointingly, the leader of the Social Democrats—that embittered, tortured human wreck, the fiery and indomitable Kurt Schumacher.

An arm gone and a leg gone—on opposite sides of his body, so that he had a kind of cruel physical balance—his teeth knocked out and his insides wracked and ruptured after twelve years in a Nazi concentration camp, Schumacher seemed to be living on nothing but the flames of a burning soul. He was a far more virulent and dynamic speaker than Adenauer, but compassion or understanding or magnanimity or humor had no part in his political makeup. Worst of all, carried away by the fact that he was a political leader at last, he never failed to resort to the nastiest postwar adaptations of German nationalistic rabble-rousing. Schumacher had no "policy" as such—only his own and his party's fine record of anti-Nazism and its traditions as the oldest political party in Germany, founded in 1863. But Schumacher thought that defeated Germany could and should extract a price for every act of postwar cooperation with the Allies or with Europe.

I first heard Schumacher speak during the 1949 election campaign at an SPD rally at the Odeonsplatz in Munich, almost within shouting distance of that old Nazi shrine, the Brown Haus, where Hitler organized the ill-fated beer hall putsche of 1932. Schumacher's voice, the sounds, the stridency, the ravings about Germany's rightful place in the world and the inequities of the Allies—it could have been 1923 or 1933 all over again. He evoked a strange and disturbing mixture of feelings—anguish at what he had gone through physically for his Social Democratic principles, but frightened dismay at his political blindness. I turned away from the election rally disgusted by the noise and the dim-witted fascination of the Bavarian crowd. Four months later, Schumacher was opposing German entry into the Assembly of the Council of Europe at Strasbourg unless France first returned the Saar.

When Secretary of State Dean Acheson made his first visit to Bonn in November 1949—the first visit of any senior minister of any country to the little capital—he arranged a meeting with Schumacher and his lieutenants in the Social Democratic Party, and his reaction was, unhappily, typical. Acheson recorded later:

> Schumacher at once launched into a unrestrained and bitter attack against Adenauer, whom he apparently hated, on the strange ground that Adenauer was working smoothly with the British, American and French occupation authorities. I pointed out what immense benefits this had brought to the German people, and wondered what sensible alternative he thought possible. Apparently the Russians were to be induced to reunite Eastern and Western Germany by a German policy of aloofness to the West, which almost ten years later became known as "disengagement"—the removal of all foreign troops from the soil of a "neutralized" Germany. The clear demonstration that the Soviet Union was not prepared to make any agreement about Germany which would weaken Soviet control in the Eastern Zone was immaterial to him. I broke off this futile interview as soon as politeness permitted.*

This was the man with whom Adenauer was competing in 1949 for the leadership of Germany—and they were separated by only 2 percentage points in the total electoral vote. It was inevitable that the old chancellor should develop his own techniques of German nationalism in order to stay out in front.

One tumultuous parliamentary eruption stands out in those early days. After weeks of argument with the High Commissioners, Adenauer came down the hill from the mountaintop headquarters at the Petersberg with his first package success: a new and comprehensive agreement to wind up the plant dismantling and Allied reparations program and prepare the way for West Germany to reenter international life and the European Community, beginning with some secondary but important organizations such as the International Labor Office, the Food and Agricultural Organization, and the International Monetary Fund. Considering that the Federal Republic had only been established for two and a half months, it was a remarkable achievement for Adenauer. But when he laid the agreement before the Bundestag on November 24, 1949, Schumacher attacked in a fury—nobody could follow his logic but basically his case was that Adenauer hadn't gotten enough. At 3 A.M. this stormy debate climaxed when Schumacher, his eyes blazing and his one arm flailing the air, called Adenauer the *"Bundeskanzler der Allierten"* (Chancellor of the Allies), and pandemonium broke out. Vainly the president of the Bundestag clanged that school bell, which was the only

* In *Sketches from Life.* Harper & Brothers, 1960.

way his call to order could be heard above the incredible cacophony of Germans shouting at each other, and finally he walked off the rostrum and suspended the session. The Rules Committee then met for two hours, and at 5:30 A.M. they announced that unless Schumacher withdrew his remark he would be barred from attending the next twenty Bundestag sittings. Schumacher promptly refused to withdraw, and his Social Democratic followers voted unanimously to stay out with him. It was a thoroughly nasty and chaotic parliamentary scene. Were we heading back into another Weimar? Fortunately we were not, but the outcome was far from clear at the moment.

In the prevailing situation, Adenauer had the Allies in a corner. Schumacher as an alternative was a frightening prospect. With a persistence and staying power and energy that left men half his age wilted in exhaustion and amazement, Adenauer used his political advantage to argue with the Allies relentlessly and endlessly about almost anything and everything. They are long forgotten, passing arguments of almost forgotten days, but they dominated the atmosphere of Bonn completely when Adenauer formed his government. Plant dismantling had been the first big issue, and then came the devaluation of the deutsche mark; the fate of the last twenty-eight Nazi war criminals under death sentence at Landsberg (seven were finally hanged); the removal of shipbuilding restrictions; permission to end gasoline rationing in Germany; Allied decartelization policy; the Allied limit on German steel production; membership in the hated Ruhr Authority; a long-forgotten law against remilitarization of Germany; de-Nazification; occupation costs. And when there was nothing else there was always the Saar problem.

To accompany these demands and match his nationalistic political opponents, Adenauer developed his own particular brand of strong-sounding political rhetoric—phrases which made good headlines but had an essential meaningless quality, such as, "West Germany will never sign the Schuman Plan treaty until the Bundestag has had a chance to discuss the Saar question." The papers headlined the "never sign" part, and forgot about the rest.

Another time Adenauer wailed to a meeting of his Christian Democratic followers, "Is it worth going on if we are to be treated like this?" after the Allies had used their veto power for the one and only time: to halt an income tax law of dubious wisdom. Naturally it was worth going on. The Allied veto was soon withdrawn, and meanwhile

Adenauer's political audience had been thoroughly captivated by the image of a "strong chancellor" fighting every step of the way with Germany's masters.

It was, of course, Allied policy to see Germany restored to the ranks of a sovereign and independent European state. Then, with the outbreak of the Korean war in June 1950, Allied policy changed almost overnight on the question of German rearmament. Once the supplicant, trekking endlessly up to the Petersberg to fight for concessions and favors for his defeated nation, Adenauer suddenly found the balance changing and his role transformed. Germany was now being asked to take up arms at the side of the Allies. Although the first German soldier did not put on a uniform until 1955—sufficient evidence in itself of the political complications of rearmament both inside and outside Germany—the central fact so far as Adenauer and the Allies were concerned was that once Allied policy changed on rearmament, so did the power relationship between the conquerors and the defeated.

The pace of the "return of Germany" could no longer be slowed. It had to be speeded up. And everything now depended on Adenauer. There could be no turning back, and if Adenauer failed the West, failed his nation, failed himself, nobody had the faintest idea what would happen or who would pick up the pieces.

And there were often times when Allied officials, nervously watching from the sidelines as the pace of the transition of power quickened, were distressed, doubtful and unhappy about Adenauer in one particular essential. He never was as outspoken or as vigorous as people hoped he would be in the political battle against latent and erupting Nazism in Germany.

Constantly, often virulently, Nazism would break through the thin crust of German political respectability—as it continues to today, though with much less effect or danger—and time after time, Adenauer responded with a tentative, hesitant, almost indifferent attitude. His own record, his moral courage and his feelings about Nazism and what it had done to Germany were never in doubt for an instant. Nor was he indifferent to the Nazi danger. But he was indifferent to the political battle. He left "Nazi fighting" to others, applauding and encouraging them from the sidelines. The trade unions, the Social Democratic Party, the press which continues to serve as an admirable public watchdog in Germany, some courageous public prosecutors who were not afraid to put an anti-Semite or an ex-SS man in the dock in the various state capitals, and ultimately the German voters and German public opinion—these did the fighting, not the old chancellor.

Two small examples illustrate the way in which Adenauer continually sidestepped the challenges. In May 1951, his CDU party faced an election battle in the state of Lower Saxony, a hotbed of neo-Nazi political sentiment which had coalesced in an organization called the "Socialistische Reichs Partei." The activities of this open Nazi front organization had become so virulent, so antistate, that the Federal Interior Minister in Bonn declared that if the local authorities did not act soon to curb it, the Federal Government would step in. A few days after this forceful declaration, however, Adenauer visited Hannover for an election rally and calmly told a press conference that while he deplored the SRP, control of political parties was a matter for the state authorities and not the federal government.

There were hoots of joy in the Nazi circles—for in effect they had been made to look too strong and tough for Adenauer to tackle. In the end the Federal Government had to act, and a suit was brought against the SRP in the Constitutional Court in Karlsruhe. In October 1952, the party was declared anticonstitutional and outlawed. The Communist Party was similarly extinguished in West Germany at about the same time.

Then there is the eternal German debate over the July 20 plotters —were they patriots or traitors? When the Bonn government began forming an embryo defense ministry around officers who had been involved in the plot, the debate grew intensely bitter. The SRP and various neo-Nazi veterans organizations led the attack, declaiming that Germans could never serve in uniform with those who had "betrayed" the Fatherland in war. At the time, the High Commissioners were increasingly worried about Germany's political trend, and finally Adenauer gave them a private assurance that on the anniversary of the July 20 plot in 1951 he would issue a public statement. Instead he slipped off to Switzerland on a vacation and said nothing. Five weeks later he inserted the most backhanded and minimal of tributes to the plotters in the middle of a radio address on other topics. All he would say was that July 20 "was the day when the democratic elements in Germany were willing to free the German people from National Socialism." The statement was scarcely a ringing cry of praise.

In fact, Adenauer's tactics in dealing with the Nazi question in

Germany were motivated by simple political expendiency. Shrewd politician that he was, Adenauer knew that the Germans were fed up with being preached at about guilt and the Nazi past. While it would be untrue and unfair to say that Adenauer deliberately went after the Nazi vote in Germany, he did avoid the kind of public political battle with the neo-Nazis which would have led their sympathizers to vote against him.

An old man who had lived through so much violent history, Adenauer adopted a philosophical view: the Nazi problem would be solved by the erosion of time. He could not allow indifference to open the way to a Nazi revival in Germany, but neither did he choose to continue opening up old wounds. Thus, rather than expending his political strength in leading the attack, he sought to play the grandfatherly role by offering rehabilitation and a revival of German morals to all those who sought them (including former Nazis). Adenauer certainly achieved this stability for the Federal Republic, but it remains for history to assess how well, how effectively, Germany rid itself of the Nazi spirit under his relatively lenient guidance and leadership.

Nothing caused more continuous debate and controversy, or more disturbing thought, during Adenauer's fourteen years in power than the presence of Dr. Hans Globke as his constant right-hand man, as State Secretary of the Federal Chancellery and the No. 1 civil servant of the Bonn Government. Globke was straight out of the Nazi past. The story of his appointment by Adenauer, and its effects, in fact epitomized the whole national problem of the German civil service. Globke never joined the Nazi Party, but his record included one central act on behalf of the Hitler regime more damning than if he had been a "little Nazi" and nothing else.

As one of the top civil servants of the Nazi Ministry of the Interior, Globke drew up the commentaries and judicial interpretations of the infamous Nazi race laws. His defense in postwar years was that as a civil servant he had been handed a job to do and, disagreeing with the whole philosophy of the race laws, he contrived to draft as liberal and open a commentary as possible on their implementation. He also had a record of personal assistance to Jewish friends and families in Nazi times. (In Carl Zuchmayer's play *The Devil's General* there is a bitter self-indicting remark in which a sympathetic German general muses: *"Ja—jeder Deutsche hat seinen Juden"* ("Yes, every German has his Jew").

When the Bonn Government was formed in 1949, very few trained and competent civil servants were ready to come forward to serve the new regime. Reestablishing a civil service therefore became an enormous problem for the new government, and still is one of Germany's governmental headaches. Nobody in his right mind could pretend that Germany could have a government without a competent civil service —yet the simple fact was that virtually all men with government experience had served the Nazi regime. The problem was even worse in the judiciary. The law can only be administered by men trained and qualified in the law. No new crop of post-Nazi lawyers could be produced between 1945 and 1949, and barely a handful of qualified men of legal training were completely "clean" of the Nazi regime. So the Federal Republic and the state governments had to turn to those who had been judges or civil servants in Hitler's time. It was this that made across-the-board de-Nazification of Germany such an impossible task.

Globke was one of the few top experienced men who offered to work in Bonn. As he had never joined the Nazi Party, he was superficially "clean," and like Adenauer he was a Catholic and a Rhinelander. But his record in the Nazi race law affair was well known, and the three High Commissioners all protested privately but strongly to Adenauer when it became known that the Chancellor intended to make him State Secretary and place him in charge of the entire Chancellery. Adenauer went ahead with the appointment anyway—possibly even spurred on by the Allied opposition. Disregarding the past, he took Globke at face value: a loyal, tireless, trained, intelligent, capable and effective civil servant. And in fact Globke was not by any stretch of the imagination a sinister or evil man. Not one diplomat in Bonn over the fourteen years in which he served at Adenauer's side found him anything but straightforward and intelligent. Was he to be denied public service because he had been a public servant under the Nazis? On five different occasions, as his name again and again leaped into headlines embarrassing to the government, Globke tried to resign. But Adenauer would never hear of it. In the end he retired at the civil service age limit of sixty-five, only a few weeks before Adenauer's own long tenure of office ended. A few months earlier, in July of 1963, an East German Communist court held a "show trial" of Globke in East Berlin, at which he was charged in absentia with war crimes and crimes against humanity, and "sentenced" to life imprisonment.

Such was the Globke story. The trouble was not that Globke himself constituted a menace, but that he became a kind of cover and excuse for the return of Nazis in other places. With Globke running the Federal Chancellery in Bonn, it was difficult to pass moral or political judgment against ex-Nazis in the state or city administrations of Munich, Stuttgart, Würzburg and elsewhere.

To Adenauer, the relevant issue was who held political power in Germany—not who the civil servants or the judges were. But efficiency and personal loyalty were insufficient arguments for placing a man of Globke's record in such a key spot. It remains a fault and a failure of the Adenauer era that the old chancellor, with so much wisdom and statesmanship and political courage in other directions, did not rigorously insure that his countrymen always knew that there was one small all-powerful office in the land—the Federal Chancellery—where loyal servants of the Third Reich could never get to the top.

At breakfast time on the morning of Saturday, May 6, 1950, the Night Express train from Paris to Cologne lurched to a special stop at the little Rhineland town of Remagen where, five years before, the American Army had captured the famous bridge and crossed the Rhine into the heart of Germany. French High Commissioner André François-Poncet now lived above the town in a magnificent schloss with a sweeping view of a bend of the river, and the Paris night train was specially routed along the Rhine in those days so that it could be halted in one direction or the other at the convenience of the French occupation authorities.

One lone passenger stepped down from the wagon-lit car onto the Remagen station platform that morning—briefcase in hand, unobtrusive, quietly dressed and unmistakably French among the thick-necked Rhinelanders smoking after-breakfast cigars and waiting for the local commuter train to Cologne and the Ruhr. His name is still secret, but let us say that it was Pierre Lisson. He was a close personal friend of the French foreign minister, Robert Schuman, a businessman and a private citizen. He had arrived in Germany on a secret official mission of historic importance to Europe and the entire world. Another Frenchman quickly stepped forward to greet him on the station platform, and the two swept past the ticket-taker and into a waiting French High Commission limousine to be whisked up the hill to François-Poncet's residence. An hour or so later the French Liaison Office in Bonn was on the phone to the Federal Chancellery.

It was an unusual Saturday request, but would the Chancellor receive as soon as possible a special emissary who had arrived from Paris with a personal and private communication from M. Schuman?

An appointment was speedily arranged, and late that Saturday morning, Lisson was ushered into Adenauer's spacious, pleasant but unpretentious office, with its modernistic Germano-Danish furniture, on a rear corner of the second floor of the Palais Schaumburg, a graceful white eighteenth-century mansion set in a large park of trees and gardens sloping down to the Rhine. Only an interpreter was present with the two men. Lisson explained his mission briefly. The French foreign minister was considering launching a very far-reaching proposal to pool the coal and steel industries of France and Germany and place them under a single supranational High Authority with wide political powers. Although built around heavy industry, the plan's primary effect was to be political rather than economic. It was to become the nucleus of a truly federated Europe. Other states would be invited to join as well, but it was essential that the French Government know in advance what attitude the Federal Republic might take toward such a proposal.

At the same time, secrecy was of the utmost importance. Schuman was endeavoring to enlist as much secret support as possible before confronting the full French cabinet and arranging the formal backing of his own government. (Such was the style in the Fourth Republic.) Lisson had been sent in person to insure that there would be no leakage of the scheme as a result of telegrams going back and forth through regular diplomatic channels. In Germany, only the French High Commissioner and his personal staff were aware of the secret. Lisson handed Adenauer two communications: one a formal document outlining the proposal which was to be known as the Schuman Plan, and the other a personal letter from Schuman expressing his hopes and feelings about the plan and future political cooperation between France and Germany. The Frenchman then told Adenauer that he would be available to carry any private message back to Paris, and withdrew.

At that time, the Bonn Government had no foreign office. West Germany, in early 1950, had only recently been allowed to establish consular missions in Paris, London, Washington and a few other Allied capitals, and was far from being recognized as a sovereign state. It had diplomatic relations with nobody but the Allied High Commission. In the Federal Chancellery, however, Adenauer had organized a small foreign affairs advisory section headed by Dr. Herbert Blankenhorn, an old Wilhelmstrasse man who had served in the German Embassy in Washington before the war (and had also joined the Nazi Party at the same time in 1938). With the historic letter from Schuman on his desk, Adenauer now called in Blankenhorn. Alone and in secrecy they discussed the French plan for more than two hours. There were many tricky political and economic problems for Germany in the French offer—the Saar question, for example—but one central fact stood out clearly: Here was a breakthrough for the German Federal Republic, here was the beginning of a German foreign policy, here was a way back into Europe and the family of Western nations.

Adenauer consulted nobody else in his cabinet or entourage. He acted immediately and without hesitation. Like Ernest Bevin when the Marshall Plan was offered from the steps of Harvard University almost exactly three years before, he "grasped it with both his hands." The Chancellor drafted an immediate warm response and assurances of endorsement and support to Schuman, which was sent by courier to Lisson at the High Commissioner's residence late in the afternoon. Schuman's secret emissary then boarded the Night Express back to Paris that evening, delivered the reply to the foreign minister at the Quai d'Orsay on Sunday morning, and disappeared from the scene of history as unobtrusively as he had arrived.

In Paris that same Sunday morning, Secretary of State Dean Acheson arrived from Washington for preliminary consultations with the French before continuing to London for the semiannual NATO Foreign Ministers' gathering. Acheson was met at Orly Airport by David K. E. Bruce, then Ambassador to France, who told him as they drove into Paris to the Embassy Residence that Schuman had requested an unusual private meeting that afternoon, instead of awaiting the customary first call of a visitor at the Quai d'Orsay. At 4 o'clock the French foreign minister arrived at the residence, accompanied only by an aide-interpreter. The four men settled down in the paneled library, and there Schuman unfolded his plan. He explained to Acheson that only a few top ministers were yet aware of the proposal, and that it was essential to know what the reaction of the United States might be. For Acheson, the first red light that went on (along with the green lights) could be summarized in one word: cartel. For many Americans, World War II was fought against I. G. Farben, Krupps and the German steel cartel as well as Hitler, and at first glance the Schuman Plan would look like a bigger cartel than ever to the United States.

Acheson has since written:

> I put the danger to Schuman. The question surprised rather than offended him. Of course a cartel in coal and steel could be created, he answered. But his purpose, which he had tried to make clear, was very different. It was basically a political conception—to move toward the unification of Western Europe by economic means. He treated my fear almost as an irrelevance, as back he went to the central theme, the unity of Europe, the end of national rivalries in a new, spacious and vastly productive Europe. As he talked, we caught his enthusiasm and the breadth of his thought, the rebirth of Europe, which, as an entity had been in eclipse since the Reformation.*

Acheson's first problem was to maintain control of the official American reaction when the announcement came, so that the "cartel conscience" of the Justice or Commerce departments in Washington would not suddenly swamp the entire project. President Truman was on his way west by train to dedicate a new dam, so Acheson and Bruce first sent off a brief "for the President's eyes only" cable to the White House train in which they informed the President that an imminent French move was under discussion which they felt should have United States support. They added that they would elaborate as soon as possible, but in the meantime they urged Mr. Truman to impose a "no comment" attitude on the government in the event of any advance leak from Europe.

The next day, Monday, John J. McCloy, the American High Commissioner in Germany, arrived in Paris and a conference was arranged for the top Americans with Jean Monnet, the originator of the plan. Meanwhile, that afternoon, Schuman unveiled the plan to the full French cabinet for the first time. He had the secret backing of the Germans and the Americans, the support in advance of several top ministers, and he quickly obtained full government approval. At the end of the day, Acheson was able to advise President Truman, again in an "eyes only" cable, the full details which would be announced the next day.

On Tuesday morning, May 9, Acheson flew to London with the French secret, but he could not tell his great friend Ernest Bevin. He had pledged his word to the French and he kept it. First he had a

* Dean Acheson, *Sketches from Life*. Harper & Brothers, 1961.

morning meeting with Bevin, and then as they were lunching together a message arrived that the French ambassador wished to see the British foreign secretary right after lunch at the urgent instructions of the Quai d'Orsay, and would like an appointment with the American Secretary of State one hour later. Acheson of course knew what was coming. He arranged to see Bevin again at 4 P.M. and he returned, he wrote, "with dragging feet" to find Bevin "in a towering rage."

Ernest Bevin, when he was in full flight of anger, was a sight to be seen. (He once vented his wrath on me over a question I asked in a discussion of Palestine, and his bellows filled his vast office and his fist smashed again and again on his desk. But it was Bevin's saving grace that he turned it off as quickly as he turned it on, and as we left the room, he threw his great arm around my shoulder and said, "Well, now, that was the price of admission.") Sitting beneath the huge portrait of King George III which hangs behind the foreign secretary's desk, he turned on Acheson and accused the United States of being in a conspiracy with the French to create a European trade combination behind Britain's back. He stormed that this was no way for Allies to behave to each other and declaimed that it was clearly a put-up job from the first: Acheson stopping off in Paris for secret consultations, and then this announcement being sprung on him. Acheson finally found a chance to begin a determined counterattack, and little by little Bevin calmed down. Schuman was announcing the plan at a press conference at the Quai d'Orsay at that very hour, and some kind of reaction would be expected in London from the American and British foreign secretaries.

Britain would have no part of the Schuman Plan—and it was for precisely this reason that the French did not consult the British in advance. They reasoned that the British reaction would be negative, and therefore any preliminary discussions with the Foreign Office would only weaken the plan, weaken Schuman's quick salesmanship to his own cabinet, and delay and weaken the dramatic impact on the European scene which Schuman, Monnet and company were seeking.*

On Wednesday, May 10, with the French proposal in headlines

* As far as the author can learn, the French never did reveal to either the United States or Britain the fact of Schuman's secret contact with Adenauer. Diplomatically, this would have offended Bevin even more than the fact that Britain was not consulted, for it amounted to France consulting an enemy but not an ally.

all over Europe, Schuman arrived in London for the NATO meeting. Bevin, still smarting under the treatment Britain had been given, asked for a Big Three session before the NATO opening. In a private room at Lancaster House he went after Schuman and Acheson together. This was no way for allies to act, he bluntly said, and now Britain was faced with a *fait accompli*. He wanted to know where he stood—what the rules of the Alliance were going to be. Before Schuman could reply, Acheson spoke first. He agreed that the workings of an Alliance required full and frank discussions, but he added that necessities of national considerations sometimes warped the ideal. As an example, he pointed out that in Washington only a few months before the British had informed the United States secretly of their plans to devalue pound sterling, and asked that it be kept secret from everybody, including the French who would be deeply concerned and whose finance and foreign ministers were just then in Washington. The United States had acceded to Britain's wishes.

By now, Bevin had had enough. "Oh hell. Let's join the others. We're keeping them waiting," he said. And as they marched into the NATO meeting together, Schuman murmured to Acheson: "My friend, you have a large deposit in my bank. You may draw on it whenever you please." *

As the NATO meeting opened in London, Adenauer went before the Bundestag in Bonn to hail the Schuman Plan as "a magnanimous step of the greatest possible significance—not empty talk but a concrete proposal." He then seized the moment to announce West Germany's first independent foreign policy decision: It would accept a six-week-old invitation to join the Strasburg Council of Europe as an associate member.

German reaction to the Strasbourg invitation had been negative and the answer long delayed because the Saar had simultaneously been handed a similar associate membership invitation. But Adenauer now declared that the Schuman Plan proposal had changed the atmosphere and a positive decision from Germany was necessary and desirable. Schumacher, with predictable irascibility, denounced both steps as "undemocratic, nationalistic and un-European because the Saar continues to be separated from Germany." But in the Ruhr two days later, the big guns of German heavy industry lined up immediately behind Adenauer. He dispatched the vice-chancellor, Franz

* Dean Acheson, *Sketches from Life*.

Blucher, to meet the Association of German Iron and Steel Manufacturers, and the Ruhr barons wasted no time in sending their endorsement to Adenauer.

Two weeks later, Jean Monnet arrived in Bonn for the first consultations with Adenauer on organizing the negotiations and the framework of the treaty. After Britain's anticipated rejection, Italy and the Benelux nations announced that they would join, so that the new Europe would be built around the Continental Six. Adenauer, casting around for somebody to handle this first vital, historic postwar diplomatic venture for the new Germany, turned to an obscure and untainted professor of law at Frankfurt University—Dr. Walter Hallstein, who had been a prisoner-of-war in the United States, never a Nazi, and spoke fluent French and English. Today he is president of the High Commission of the European Common Market.

The Schuman Plan negotiations opened in Paris in June of 1950 and marched steadily and carefully to a successful conclusion in March of 1951—not without snags and difficulties, because a great deal of new legal and economic terrain was being explored, but never with any threat of breakdown or failure. Hallstein and the German delegation played a quiet but effective low-key legalistic role, with Adenauer making the vital decisions and agreeing at almost every step with Monnet's ideas and suggestions.

When the great work was concluded and the treaty embossed in bound volumes and ready for signature, Konrad Adenauer boarded that same Night Express to Paris on Thursday, April 12, 1951 for his first official visit to the French capital—the first in a twelve-year series of twenty-eight journeys of reconciliation. In 1951, the appearance of a German chancellor in Paris was as rare as infidels at the Kaaba in Mecca. In fact, it was a good measure of the historic state of Franco-German relations up to 1951 that there had been only three peacetime visits of either German chancellors or foreign ministers to Paris in almost 100 years. Bismarck had come with his armies and so had Hitler, but only three had come peacefully by invitation. To avoid protocol problems, Adenauer made that first visit in his capacity as Foreign Minister of West Germany. From the outset he was to display that tact and delicacy of manner so lacking in his fellow countrymen and so essential to his long and steady labors to build trust in the new Germany. He strolled along the Champs-Élysées quietly with Blankenhorn and Hallstein, scarcely recognized by anybody but photographers assigned to cover him. That odd, flat, almost Mongol face with the high cheeks and the wise, penetrating eyes was not yet so familiar in Europe.

He paid a simple tribute at the Eternal Flame and the Tomb of the Unknown Soldier under the Arc de Triomphe—a personal wreath of flowers, no bands or marching ceremonial which might stimulate counter-demonstrations from the Parisians. At his suite in the Hotel Crillon he received a little French girl from Alsace who presented him with a Croix de Guerre which her father had won fighting the Germans in the first World War, as her personal contribution to Franco-German understanding. When the protocol officials came to discuss the ceremonies for the signing of the Schuman Plan treaty at the Quai d'Orsay, they told the Chancellor that he would be expected to speak after the French foreign minister, since Germany was the second largest steel-producing country among the treaty powers. The old face changed expression only slightly, and Adenauer mused quietly to his delegation: "No, we Germans had too much to say and were heard from too often from 1933 onwards. I think I will just keep quiet. There's that young fellow Sforza. [Count Sforza, then Foreign Minister of Italy, eighty-two years old.] I think he should speak next. If I have anything to say I'll wait till last."

And so the Schuman Plan treaty was signed in April, 1951. Ratifications were completed by the six countries in July, 1952. The High Authority of the Coal and Steel Community was established under the presidency of Jean Monnet in Luxembourg in January, 1953. And on April 30, 1953, Monnet put "integrated Europe" in business when he tapped that first blast furnace of European pigiron in Esch.

The signing ceremonies over at the Quai d'Orsay, Adenauer boarded the Night Express back to his little capital. It was relatively immaterial that sovereignty and NATO membership for Germany was still more than four years away. With Adenauer's signature on the Schuman Plan treaty, de facto sovereignty had already been achieved, and the niggling arguments with the High Commissioners about German tax laws and gasoline rationing and plant dismantling would soon be over. When Adenauer returned to Bonn, the problem was how to close the books on the occupation.

The Allies had agreed that this would be achieved on a basis of "contractual agreements," under which West Germany would accept certain basic obligations to continue policies laid down by the occupying powers in such fields as de-Nazification, decartelization, and the maintenance of certain occupation rights for Allied forces in Germany.

In return, the three Western powers would relinquish to the Federal Republic the powers which they held by right of Germany's unconditional surrender. These long and complicated contractual documents took two years to negotiate, and German sovereignty was scheduled to come into force simultaneously with passage of the European Defense Community treaty and the start of German rearmament inside the European Army.

But suddenly at the end of August, 1954, the EDC treaty was killed in the French National Assembly—and for a few brief weeks it looked as if the whole political edifice of postward Europe would collapse as well. Then Anthony Eden moved onto the scene, and successfully found the treaty formula for new arrangements to provide for German national rearmament under controls written into the revised Brussels Treaty, with full West German membership in NATO. Of course the contractual agreements to establish German sovereignty were incorporated as part of the package. Adenauer again journeyed to Paris, and made some essential last-minute concessions to Pierre Mendès-France on the Saar question as his contribution to agreement. On May 5, 1955, the new treaties came into force. In an amazingly short span of less than six years, Konrad Adenauer had arrived at the goal of sovereign membership in NATO which he had fixed for his defeated nation at that first press conference after his election victory in 1949.

Out of the events of 1954—beginning with the Berlin Big Four conference in February of that year and continuing through the demise of EDC and Germany's eventual entry into NATO—there emerged that unusual Cold War friendship between Konrad Adenauer and John Foster Dulles. It was a friendship borne primarily of events and the forces of international affairs. It was a situation in which each could give and gain. On the surface, two more opposite personalities could scarcely have been drawn together. Dulles was a cold, detached, rigid Calvinist, a man to whom everything in public and private life was a means to an end, to be used without compunction or compassion in the pursuit of his personal goals of politics and diplomacy. Adenauer, on the other hand, is a Roman Catholic of great warmth, conviviality and humor, who enjoys friendship for friendship's sake and not for reasons of politics. Nonetheless, over the years, the Dulles-Adenauer relationship deepened into genuine trust, mutual reliance and accord.

There was another less noble but nonetheless real element in their growing closeness. Neither Dulles nor Adenauer trusted the way in which Britain directed its diplomacy almost unceasingly toward the possibility of accommodation with the Soviet Union. They stood wholeheartedly, automatically, instinctively in accord on a policy of utter Cold War rigidity—give nothing, stand firm, make agreement even to talk with the Russians a matter of major diplomatic concession. Dulles saw it as a moral as well as a political and diplomatic attitude. For Adenauer accommodation with Russia could only be achieved at the expense of Berlin or West Germany. Thus, while the British were constantly complaining about the "inflexibility" of Adenauer and Dulles, and talking about trying another four-power meeting or a summit conference or a new effort to seek understanding, the two men looked to each other for mutual support. It is debatable whether British policy was right, and Dulles and Adenauer were wrong. But there is no question that British policy had a negative effect on British relations with West Germany, and Britain was to pay a price.

Dulles, moreover, arrived at the State Department with a long-held conviction that American policy had been too strongly centered on the Anglo-American "special relationship." He was determined to redress the imbalance and direct American policy toward closer alignment with continental Europe. With the death of EDC he found France to be less than a strong and stable working partner, and so he turned to Adenauer and Germany. In the meantime, Adenauer had lost his closest personal associate in the French Government when Robert Schuman left the political scene in 1953, and it was highly useful for him to make emerging Germany the closest friend and strongest supporter of the United States.

Thus, a combination of ideals, events and prejudices brought Dulles and Adenauer together. Dulles neither spoke nor understood German, and Adenauer's understanding of English remained rudimentary. But across those peregrinating years, Dulles developed the habit of "the Bonn stopover," and cables and correspondence between the two men flowed back and forth unceasingly. Once Dulles flew to the little West German capital for only five hours, to explain to the Chancellor personally why it had been necessary to pull American air units out of Germany in support of the Lebanon landings of 1958. There had been no time to consult the German Government in advance, and Dulles sought to allay the obsessive German fear that the United States would one day leave Germany defenseless before the Red Army.

With Dulles at the State Department, Adenauer never had any doubts as to how the United States would play the diplomatic hand with Russia and never any doubts that West Germany's interests were to be rigorously safeguarded. But when Dulles began to fade from the scene in 1958, lingering on until his death by cancer in 1959, Nikita Khrushchev launched a new offensive against Berlin and Germany with his threat to sign a separate East German peace treaty and turn control of the access routes to Berlin over to the East German puppet regime. Macmillan, in a burst of diplomatic initiative, flew to Moscow in February of 1959, and as a result of his trip the Big Three foreign ministers spent three desultory and fruitless months discussing the Berlin question at Geneva. Christian Herter succeeded Dulles, who died in Washington in late May, two weeks after the Geneva Conference began.

"You cannot know how the Chancellor fretted about Washington after Dulles was gone," one of his long-time close associates related to me after Adenauer left office. "He would seize upon the slightest little lapses of evidence that Washington was keeping him in the dark —things which would never have bothered him in Dulles's day when he would pick up the newspaper and read something that he hadn't been informed about in a government cable. All we could do was to try to persuade him that it wasn't that important, but he felt the gap acutely and of course that increased his suspicions of United States policy when big issues arose."

Into this gap stepped Charles de Gaulle—the second of Adenauer's great historic friendships. As was the case with Dulles, the association with De Gaulle was borne of events, of common interests and the fact that each could give and gain with the other. That same attitude of rigidity toward the Russians prevailed (although for De Gaulle the rationale was cold political pragmatism rather than moral fervor) as did the same suspicion of the British. But the Adenauer-De Gaulle friendship had something much greater behind it than the Adenauer-Dulles friendship ever could have offered—the community of interests which France and Germany share as neighbors. Thus, slowly and steadily, almost naturally, De Gaulle succeeded Dulles as the greatest influence, friend and partner of the aging West German chancellor.

The two men first met at De Gaulle's country home at Colombey-les-deux-Églises, 120 miles east of Paris, in September of 1958, five months after De Gaulle's return to power. De Gaulle chose the country meeting place so that he would not have to receive Adenauer formally in official Paris surroundings until he had first satisfied himself that he would want to work with Adenauer.

The Chancellor drove from Bonn across the war-scarred countryside of Verdun and eastern France. He and De Gaulle had a morning talk, a luncheon, and a long conversation in the afternoon. He drove back to Bonn the same evening. Each man had sized up the other accurately. Here at last was the greatest Frenchman of the age building a strong and stable France, and able to offer his hand to a German of respect and authority seeking to mold his country to an entirely new European future.

"Old men do not make new friends easily and they want to keep things simple and comfortable," Adenauer's associate also recounted to me. "Adenauer was getting too old to deal with the diplomatic complications of a broad European policy—keeping up harmony of relations between Britain and France at the same time, and the subtle but important issues which were cropping up in the Common Market all the time. With Dulles gone, he felt that uncertainty about the United States. And so he had an instinctive wish to simplify things in his later years. The straight Franco-German line which De Gaulle offered him was not only simple and straightforward, but a very great historic goal for Adenauer and for our two countries. That is how he gradually came to turn away from the complications of seeing Britain into the Common Market, or keeping up the momentum of European unity, and concentrate his policy entirely on relations with De Gaulle and France."

In the days of Robert Schuman and Jean Monnet, Adenauer had followed the strong European federalist line. But when De Gaulle returned to power, the eclipse of the federalists in France was almost complete. It was De Gaulle's concept that Europe could only organize itself as a confederation of independent nation-states, and he set out from the first to expunge federalism from French policy. But the Belgians, the Dutch, and to a lesser extent the Italians continued to fight a rearguard action to keep the cause of federation alive.

In August of 1960, De Gaulle made his first concrete move to bring Adenauer to his side. At a meeting at Rambouillet, he proposed that France and Germany sponsor a European political treaty based on confederation and cooperation—as opposed to the type of political unity treaty which the federalists were seeking. Adenauer at first accepted, but when he returned to Bonn his advisers succeeded in convincing him that he could not abandon his support for federated Europe so abruptly or easily. De Gaulle then convened a meeting of the other premiers of the Six and by a process of not making himself entirely clear, reached agreement to go ahead with the outlines of a treaty for a European Political Community. De Gaulle's partners saw in it a first step toward federation. Drafting began, and some essential concessions were made by the French negotiators which did indeed keep the door to federation open. Then suddenly in January of 1962, the draft, known as the Fouchet Plan, reached De Gaulle personally for final approval as official French policy, whereupon he repudiated the concessions which had been made and reduced the document to an unyielding formula of "confederation or nothing." The other European partners threw up their hands, and work on political unity came to an end.

In this atmosphere, Adenauer made a formal official state visit to Paris in July, 1962—to be received at De Gaulle's invitation as no other German chancellor in history, with full honors and flags flying. De Gaulle had now maneuvered the European political scene so that he was able to confront Adenauer with the situation: "Where is Europe heading? A dead end has been reached. The others will not cooperate. Europe must move forward. What can we do?"

In a final conversation in a private sitting room at the Élysée Palace, the French president put it bluntly to the West German chancellor: "Monsieur le Chancellier, we have reviewed the European situation together, and we are agreed in our assessment of the outlook for Europe and the state of opinion among the other European governments. Are you now prepared to move forward with France alone?"

It was a question which had been discussed earnestly with Adenauer by his ministers and advisers, and some of the strongest and closest wanted Germany to stick to a policy of unity of the Six rather than bilateralism with France. But now De Gaulle was putting the question, and aides and interpreters tensely waited for the answer. *"Ja wohl,"* he replied very simply. A corner of history had been turned. The focus of Adenauer's policy had shifted, and the way was open for the Franco-German Treaty of Cooperation.

Two months later, in September of 1962, De Gaulle made a state visit to Germany—a fabulously successful tour of Düsseldorf, Hamburg, Munich and other cities in which the French president evoked the wildest enthusiasm, speaking in excellent German, which he had learned in a German prison camp during the first World War. In one tremendous moment before thousands packed into the Town Hall square at Bonn, De Gaulle, his arms outstretched, proclaimed France's friendship and confidence in *"das grosse volk Sie sind—ja, das grosse Deutsche volk."* Germans who for seventeen years had been nurtured on national guilt complexes and national degradation, went wild to hear themselves called "the great people you are—yes, the great German people" by their neighbor, Charles de Gaulle. It was one of those climactic emotional moments of national reconciliation, long awaited, long anticipated, long prepared, and suddenly a reality.

When Adenauer bade good-bye to De Gaulle in September of 1962, the crowning act of their friendship was still ahead. They had instructed their foreign offices to begin work on a formal agreement of cooperation, and they scheduled a return visit by Adenauer to Paris in January of 1963 for a signing ceremony. But in the meantime, Adenauer was confronted with a steadily deteriorating political situation at home. For all his great achievements, for all his monumental work in bringing the German nation back into the European family, the years had taken their toll of his power and his political popularity, as well as his hold over his cabinet and the government. Adenauer was on the eve of his eighty-seventh birthday at the end of 1962. A new generation had arrived, and as "Der Alte" held on and on in power, political restlessness grew sharper and stronger. The Free Democrats in his coalition were increasing their political pressures against him, and outside the government the Social Democrats were showing election gains which were causing uneasiness among the Christian Democrats. Insistence on a change reached a climax when the government ordered the arrest on treason charges of the editor and five senior executives and editorial staff members of the popular weekly news magazine *Der Spiegel.*

For months and months the magazine had been pursuing a personal vendetta against the German defense minister, the burly and combative Bavarian, Franz Josef Strauss. Without a doubt it had been laying its hands on defense documents and information which constituted dangerous and potentially harmful security leaks not only for Germany but for the NATO Alliance. All the same, Strauss moved to "get" the editors of *Der Spiegel* in a dangerously extra-legal manner, and it was typical of an autocratic weakness and blind spot in Adenauer, who had little use for the magazine himself, that he did not sense the backfire which the freedom of the press issue would cause in Germany. Moreover, the government case was weak, and after long periods in prison, the accused were finally let out, one by one.

On the heels of the arrests, the Free Democrats walked out of Adenauer's government and said they would not come back until Strauss was fired. Adenauer and Strauss tried to stand firm, but in the end Strauss resigned. The Free Democrats, feeling their strength, then put a new price on their support. They demanded that the old man pledge his own resignation. Adenauer maneuvered, fought and argued, but he was cornered. He could not command a Bundestag majority without the FDP votes. In December, 1962, in order to hold his government together and realize his dream of the Franco-German treaty, he pledged that he would retire at the end of the parliamentary year, in the late summer of 1963. The government was re-formed, and the scene was set for his January journey to Paris.

The Adenauer era was nearing its end. He was the first truly great man that Germany had produced in more than a century. Now it would be for his nation to live up to the opportunities of his achievements.

5. Germany: Berlin and Beyond

In winter when snow covers the flat expanse of the Brandenburg Plain and the northern sun casts a pale glow through the hazy frosty air, the city and the countryside around it are one. As the aircraft settles slowly out of the west, the first landmarks are the lakes and the woods—the Wannsee, the Havel, the river Spree and then the Grünewald, with the straight line of the Avus motor raceway cutting through the trees, and in the midst of the snow-covered woodland, the bare patch of the American garrison's firing range. The plane swings north and east to begin a wide circle for its landing at Templehof in the center of the city. On the left in the open countryside below, invisible in the snow, is a double line of cement posts and barbed wire. In spring and summer it stands out quite clearly from the air—a concentration camp fence that slashes across farms and gardens, fields and woods, country roads and streams, plunging relentlessly over little hills and down shallow valleys, complete with watchtowers, searchlights, patrol dogs and a "death strip" of plowed fields and felled trees to a depth of twenty yards on the other side, sown with land mines and swept with gunfire. When the fields are soft with the delicate green of early spring or ripe with harvest grain and the trees give life and color to the countryside, then from the air the fence and death-strip look like a running blight of scabrous gray-brown, cutting the city off from its natural hinterland. But under a mantle of winter whiteness, the landscape stretches northward clean and unmarred.

The aircraft tilts to the south and west, and beyond the wing on the right the garish lights of Kurfuerstendamm flicker in the fading winter afternoon, like a piece of cheap costume jewelry on a shabbily dressed woman. Then the Tiergarten spreads below in what used to be the heart of the city, bisected by the long wide "victory parade" central axis of old Berlin, the Charlottenburger Chaussee, stretching across the city from west to east like a column of goose-stepping Prussian Grenadiers. But it is dead-ended now, at the wall in front of the Brandenburger Tor. In the snow below, the arches and columns of the Brandenburger Tor, shorn of its prewar topping of triumphal chariots and statuary, stand out clearly, and beyond it Unter den Linden stretches into East Berlin with its line of saplings growing up to replace the fine old linden trees which were cut down for firewood after the war. So also does that massive old pile of Prussian baroque, the Reichstag Building, stand out at the edge of the Tiergarten just inside West Berlin. But the wall itself, which divides the city across the middle, is as difficult to trace in the winter whiteness as the fence that surrounds West Berlin in the countryside to the north. The plane swings a little to the east in the free airspace over the city to complete the landing circuit, and down below, the snow masks the rubble and grime and aging decay of the buildings of East Berlin just as it masks the bright new roofs, the gaily colored balconies, the clean little parks and gardens and the modern architecture of West Berlin.

The red lights of the Tempelhof glide-path begin flickering by beneath the wings. The pilot needs every foot of runway he can get, and, as he eases down, the wings almost seem to brush the balconies of the apartment buildings that crowd up to the very edge of the airport. The wheels crunch on the snow. The aircraft turns and taxis for the vast semicircular cantilevered overhang of the airport building.

All around the brightly lit Tempelhof waiting room are WELCOME TO BERLIN posters and advertisements and information booths, telephone extensions to downtown hotels, car-rental counters, stacks of "what to do in Berlin" literature, billboards for theater and music performances, and beckoning bids for the lonely businessman from the endless erotica of the city's nightclubs, bars and cabarets. West Berlin lives on its arrivals and departures. You do not go *through* Berlin or *to* Berlin; you go *into* Berlin and *out of* Berlin. For other cities the process of arrival-and-departure is a natural, almost insignificant routine, like breathing out and breathing in. But for West Berlin there is always a Communist finger on the windpipe. To be sure it is a productive city of 2,200,000 inhabitants, making electrical equipment, optics, chemicals, dresses, machine tools, engineering equipment, food products, books, furniture, and so on. But the raw materials all have to be brought into the city, and the products have to be taken away, most of them, to be sold. The food Berlin eats, the milk it drinks, the coal it burns, all have to be delivered as if the city were an oasis in a desert or an island in the sea. Other cities live on industry and manufacturing, commerce and business, finance and banking; on culture, art, antiquities or history; on universities and libraries; on government and power—or on combinations of these. But West Berlin lives on the drone of aircraft engines, the whine of jets, the roar of diesel trucks, the chug of barges on its canals and the distant hoot of train whistles, taking goods and people in and out of the city. Berliners watch the traffic reports on the autobahn to West Germany as closely as other citizens watch the weather reports or the stock market, for it is arrivals and departures that give West Berlin its life and its existence.

This is an enormous historic and psychological change for the citadel of Prussian militarism, of Bismarck, the Kaisers and Hitler. No longer does power radiate from Berlin. No one is governed from the city except the people of West Berlin by their mayor, and he governs with the consent of the Allies. Berlin is no longer the focus of German national life, the magnet of national feeling. People arrive in Berlin on visits to teach, to study, to sing, to conduct, to act, to lecture, to consult, to do business, to show the flag and have a good time. But seldom any longer do people move to Berlin to stay and live and work, except in journeyman jobs in industry that are going begging, despite big tax and social security advantages which workers gain by moving to West Berlin instead of staying in West Germany.

To keep visitors coming and keep the city alive with a sense of activity and enterprise, West Berlin spends more money subsidizing its opera, theater and music, more on city propaganda and literature, more on tours, tourist facilities and public amenities, more on publicity, than any other city in Germany. The money comes in the form of generous government grants from the Federal Republic in Bonn, to the tune of $450,000,000 every year. Among other things, the airline fare between West Germany and West Berlin is subsidized, making it the cheapest air trip in Europe—an average of about $15 one way from any city in Germany. Berlin is the most "welcome-minded" city in Europe. In such matters as interpreters, guides, secretarial services, car rentals, staffs to organize conventions and meetings, exhibition halls and conference rooms, West Berlin spends and spends with remarkable results—more than 500 conventions, exhibitions, conferences, business meetings and cultural festivals in the city every year.

In fact, the real victory of Berlin twenty years after the war is not merely that it remains as a free world fortress in the midst of Communist territory, not its survival of the Stalin blockade of 1948–49 and the Communist wall of 1961, not that its people across these dramatic years have refused to lose heart or yield to intimidations or threats. The real triumph is the fact that despite all the bizarre abnormalcy of its hand-to-mouth dependence on airplanes, trucks and trains, West Berlin has nevertheless managed to become a normal, healthy city, with production booming and more jobs than people to fill them. West Berlin is beginning to find a creative life of its own and a vitality of its own, and is even beginning to grow again.

This triumph of normalcy is of enormous importance not only from the standpoint of the daily life of the Berliners, but in the long-range political calculations which govern the thinking of the Kremlin. For fourteen years, from the airlift days of 1948 until the big

East-West test of the Cuban crisis in 1962, West Berlin lived under almost unremitting Communist pressures. Their sole aim was: to whittle away the position of the Western Allies and absorb the city into the satellite East German Communist state. But each succeeding test of strength has invariably ended with Communist retreat. Far from achieving their objective, the Communists have succeeded in demonstrating that there was and remains a fundamental Western situation of strength in Berlin which threats and pressures cannot eliminate. Today, surrounded by the Communist wall, West Berlin is living in confidence and security, expanding its economic and cultural life, stronger than ever—which is just the opposite of what the Kremlin intended.

Berlin's subconscious fear across those years was that the city might become a forgotten, stagnant, abandoned backwater. There used to be an old Berlin saying: "The worst crisis will come when there is no crisis." But the Russians never let that happen either. For years the city lived on a kind of "crisis Benzedrine." Crisis was both exhilarating and reassuring to the West Berliners. The 1950's were days of grave unemployment and hardship in the city, which lagged well behind the pace of recovery in West Germany and the rest of Europe. Meanwhile the West Germans, preoccupied with their own economic problems, showed indifference to Berlin's fate. Businessmen preferred to invest in the west. Few wanted to take the risks of tying up capital and production facilities in a city surrounded by the Russians. Autobahn slowdowns and harassment of truck traffic meant delays in the delivery of raw materials and orders. And from a political standpoint, there was considerable inertia in the Bonn Government over Berlin's plight. Chancellor Adenauer was a Rhinelander, a Catholic and a Christian Democrat, while Berlin was Prussian, Protestant and dominated by the Social Democrats. The United States, pouring Marshall Plan money into Berlin, pleaded constantly for Bonn to pick up more of the burden. Crisis was therefore always oddly welcomed in West Berlin. It brought journalists rushing to the city, churned up fresh reassurances of Allied firmness, and often spurred the Federal Government into new subsidies. Allied military planners would go to work all over again dusting off contingency plans and Berlin would be back at the center of world affairs. Seldom did six months go by without some kind of crisis, major or minor.

If there wasn't a crisis involving Allied rights in the city, or German traffic on the autobahns, then just as often there was trouble in the wretched Communist state of East Germany—beginning with the short-lived heroism of the uprising of June 17, 1953. For a few brief hours on that fateful day, East Germany teetered on the brink of revolution, in a preview of what was to happen in Poland and Hungary three years later. But the demonstrators never really had a chance.

Barely three months after Stalin's death, at a moment when a feeling of uncertainty and change was rising all over Eastern Europe, the uprising began as a demonstration of construction workers on the huge and hideous Stalin Allee housing project in East Berlin. There was no real leadership, no undercover group or movement. It was triggered by an announcement of new increases in Communist work norms, but it was really a reflection of mass frustration. Soon after reporting for the morning shift, the men put down their tools and streamed down from the building scaffolds to gather in angry groups. Spontaneously they merged into one huge swelling mob and started to march across the center of East Berlin toward the Communist government office buildings in Friedrichstrasse and Leipzigerstrasse, not far from the West Berlin border.

Word of the demonstration swept the city like wildfire. In those days there was free movement back and forth between East and West Berlin with only cursory police controls. In no time, the big radio station in the American sector of the city, RIAS, was broadcasting the news all across East Germany, and within another hour demonstrations were starting in the factories of Leipzig, Dresden, Cottbus, Madgeburg, Halle, Rostock, Chemnitz, and other cities in the Soviet zone.

As the Stalin Allee construction men pushed across the city, they were joined by other Berlin workers, and in the face of the swelling mob the East German Volkspolizei fell back in confusion. Many of them waved the demonstrators on. In the discussions before they started their march, the men had formulated some blunt, spontaneous demands which they intended to present at the government offices: lowering of work targets, taxes and prices; resignation of the Government; free elections; abolition of the state security service; abolition of zonal borders; withdrawal of all occupation troops from Germany; abolition of the People's Police; freedom of speech and the press; complete safety for the strike leaders. The leaders came from nowhere, and nobody today knows who they were.

The demonstrators reached the government buildings and for a while they milled about, shouting angrily. Then about noon the first shots were fired by East German police reinforcements. Meanwhile all over East Germany workers were smashing local meeting halls of the Communist-front Socialist Unity Party, beating up Communist shop stewards in the factories, setting fire to propaganda billboards and posters, and stoning police headquarters. At 1:30 P.M. came swift and ruthless action by the commandant of the Soviet sector of Berlin, General Dibrova. A state of emergency was declared, marshal law was invoked, a curfew was imposed and all public gatherings of more than three people were banned. The Red Army was ordered out of its barracks, and tanks and troops poured into the cities of East Germany to crush the uprising. Youths with tears streaming down their faces pelted the tanks with bricks and stones as they rolled straight to the sector borders of East Berlin. In a matter of hours the Red Army sealed off every street crossing between East and West—just as the Communists were to seal it off with a wall of concrete blocks and barbed wire eight years later. For five days, East Berlin was cut off from the West as the hated Volkspolizei slowly regained control under watchful Russian eyes.

When the sector borders reopened, East Germans who had taken part in the demonstrations and managed to hide out from the police began streaming to the safety of West Berlin. A total of 297,040 fled to West Berlin that year—by far the highest one-year total in the long refugee parade that ended when the wall was built. But East Germany's one brief moment of heroism had been snuffed out.

In the Kremlin, the abortive revolt came at a time of grave political argument among Stalin's heirs and left a footnote to history that has never been forgotten by political strategists in the West. On July 10, 1953, came the Kremlin announcement of the arrest of Lavrenti Beria, the Stalinist head of the Soviet secret police and the boss of the vast slave-labor system. The charges against Beria were couched in the customary Soviet style for such occasions: "exposed enemy of the people . . . carefully concealed criminal activity . . . revealed at last in his true colors . . . vicious enemy of the Party . . . foul machinations for the purpose of seizing power." But buried in all this was one sentence which in later years took on fresh significance: "This adventurer and hireling of foreign imperialist forces was planning to seize the leadership of the Party and the country with the object of destroying the Communist Party *and of substi-*

tuting, in place of the Party's policy worked out over many years, a policy of capitulation which, in the final analysis, would have led to the restoration of capitalism." Capitulation to whom? What kind of capitulation? Beria was tried and executed on December 23, 1953. Years later the secret was disclosed by Nikita Khrushschev.

At the time of Beria's downfall, all of the evidence pointed to a power struggle in the Kremlin in which the other heirs of Stalin were determined to break the power of Beria's secret police—and the only way to do that was to get rid of Beria. The business of charging Beria with "substituting a policy of capitulation" did not then seem to have much special meaning. Then Gregori Malenkov was toppled as Soviet premier and banished to a Siberian electricity works, and after that Nicolai Bulganin departed and Khrushchev's control over the Kremlin was supreme. In 1959, Khrushchev, who was always letting skeletons out of the Kremlin closet, disclosed in a speech to a party meeting in Moscow that, after Stalin's death, Beria had proposed that Russia withdraw from East Germany, and that Malenkov had supported him. The argument was apparently in progress when the East German uprising broke out. Khrushchev never said what the arguments were which Beria and Malenkov used to press their case, but the belief among Western experts is that Beria foresaw trouble in the satellites, was concerned that it might spread to Russia itself, and as Soviet police chief wanted to cut losses outside Russia and strengthen his control over the home front. Malenkov apparently had a parallel interest in seeking to curtail the Stalinist military policies which had overextended the Russian economy and made it impossible to offer much improvement in the living standards of the Soviet people. It was in fact a dismal time for the Kremlin, the spring of 1953: The Berlin blockade had failed. Pressures against the West in Europe had only resulted in the creation of NATO and consolidation of American power. The satellites were proving more of an economic burden than an asset. The Korean war had ended in stalemate. The Red Army was extended all over Poland, Czechoslovakia, Hungary, Rumania and Bulgaria as well as East Germany, and in the post-Stalin era there was plenty of home-front discontent to worry the MVD secret police.

Such were the elements which presumably figured in the Kremlin argument after Stalin's death—although nothing concrete is known except Khrushchev's brief disclosure that withdrawal from East

Germany had been proposed by Beria. But when the June 17 uprising broke in the middle of it all—as Beria had feared—instead of justifying a policy of withdrawal, the Russian reaction had to be the opposite. The demonstration had to be crushed. And at the same time, the uprising was just what the anti-Beria faction in the Kremlin needed to give the police chief a final shove from power.

Some American experts on Soviet affairs—among them Charles E. Bohlen, former Ambassador to Moscow—have long held that the Russians will eventually withdraw from East Germany, when they see that it has become impossible to run it as a satellite state any longer. The real importance of the Beria story is the fact that such a complete reversal of Russian policy was in fact once proposed and seriously discussed at the top level of the Soviet Government. The Russians crushed the June 17 uprising, and they went on to crush the much more serious revolution in Budapest in October, 1956. But today, were they to use the Red Army in such an operation, they would risk far more serious repercussions, far greater bloodshed, and even possible defeat. Russia's dwindling power to dictate policy to its satellites and control their actions is openly visible in Warsaw, Budapest and even Prague. In East Germany, no threat of an uprising challenges the Red Army, but only the Red Army keeps the Communist regime in power. The conditions for a Soviet policy of withdrawal, or disengagement, are in fact more apparent and logical today in the mid-1960's than they were when Beria and Malenkov argued the case in 1953. And Soviet withdrawal remains Europe's most dramatic and best hope of peace and prosperity for all its divergent peoples.

But in the aftermath of the 1953 uprising, with Beria in prison awaiting trial and execution, the Stalinist hard line over Berlin and Germany remained unchanged. In February, 1954, at the urging of the French and the British, John Foster Dulles agreed to a meeting of the Big Four Foreign Ministers in Berlin itself. Anthony Eden had long been pressing for a meeting to probe for some possible post-Stalin change in Russian policy. Georges Bidault said he needed "one more try" with the Russians before he could ask the French National Assembly to vote for the European Defense Community treaty and West German rearmament. Dulles had little enthusiasm for any meeting at all, but he decided that it was best to get it over with. Molotov came along to complete the party, and he was at his stone-faced iron-pants worst. Not only that; it was the coldest postwar winter on record in Berlin, with the temperatures ranging down to 10 degrees below zero (Fahrenheit) almost every night, and seldom rising above 20 degrees during the day. The wind whipping through the city from the east was so fierce and penetrating that military police on duty around the conference building were rotated every half hour instead of the normal two hours. Inside, the conference temperature was not much better. The Cold War reached an all-time diplomatic low when Dulles and Eden, pleading with Molotov to agree to a state treaty at last for little Austria, announced that they were ready to accept every one of the amendments to the proposed treaty which the Russian negotiators had been demanding. But Molotov never batted an eye. He would not even accept his own demands! "In present circumstances we must recognize that agreement is not possible," he said coldly. Barely a year later in one of those remarkable Kremlin switches, the Russians decided that they were at last ready to pull out of Austria, and in no time at all the Austrian State Treaty was concluded and signed in joyous Vienna in May of 1955.

Across the years from the 1953 uprising to the beginning of the "Khrushchev Offensive" against Berlin in 1958, the Russians concentrated on the relentless consolidation of East Germany into a Communist puppet state, while keeping up the pinpricks and constant harassment of West Berlin and its traffic. In the wake of the uprising, "justice" in the Soviet zone was accelerated to a Stalinist frenzy. Sentences of ten to fifteen years in prison for "collaboration with Western espionage agencies" or "distribution of fascist propaganda" became routine. Collectivization of the once-productive East German farms began, with predictable results, in crop failures and the flight of farmers to West Germany. Alongside the Volkspolizei, the Communist regime organized a paramilitary barracks police, which then officially became the East German Army after rearmament of West Germany began in 1955. Absorption of small businesses, small industrial plants and factories into state ownership advanced inexorably. Food shops, department stores, hotels and the "luxury" restaurants were swept into one big state trade organization. Moscow-dictated economic plans for industry were laid down (and seldom fulfilled). East Germany was reorganized along administrative lines to suit the new Communist mold, and the old state and county borders were completely redrawn. Party recruiting and propaganda were turned up to a shrill, screeching pitch in endless red-and-black Communist posters. BAN THE ATOM BOMB and AMI GO HOME and FREEDOM AND UNITY slogans smeared every bridge and billboard along the autobahn between West Germany and West Berlin. The youth of East Germany were herded into the Freie Deutsche Jugend and quickly taught that if they could not learn to be good Communists, they would not be given the opportunity to learn anything else.

As for West Berlin, the process of physically isolating the city moved steadily forward. Electricity and water supply systems which served both sides of Berlin had been cut and separated during the days of the airlift. Then abruptly, the telephone cable connections between West Berlin and West Germany were pulled out. The city was ready with a microwave-radio relay system, so that the breakdown was only minimal. It took longer for the Russians to engineer the cut of the internal phone system in the city, but direct communication between East and West Berlin went out in 1956. (Today, West Berlin is connected by direct-dial telephone and telex with every city in West Germany and many cities of Europe; but to make a phone call from West Berlin to East Berlin involves routing via Frankfurt and back through Leipzig, or often through Stockholm!)

In the harassment of road traffic to Berlin, the East German authorities suddenly clamped an autobahn tax on all cars and trucks making the 110-mile journey. They began by demanding 150 deutsche marks per truck—or about $37 in the currency value of the time. For some days an immense backlog of traffic mounted while the West German authorities countered by refusing to sign a pending East German trade agreement. Finally a compromise road toll figure was reached, and today cars pay from 5 to 15 marks for the journey while trucks are assessed on size and weight. It is a highly lucrative toll business for the East German regime—which collected nearly $10 million in 1964 from West German cars, buses and trucks.

Around West Berlin, streets and crossing-points between the two halves of the city were blocked one after another. Originally there were 277 road and street crossings from West Berlin to East Berlin, and to the Soviet occupation zone of East Germany surrounding Berlin to the north. But by the end of 1954, barricades had been placed across all but sixty of these streets.

These barricades did not prevent pedestrians from walking across the sector borders, but they did halt all automobile and truck traffic, and they made it easier for the police to control and observe movement between the two sides of the city. Streetcar tracks were also ripped up at the sector borders, and of course city buses between the two halves had long since been halted. Slowly the Soviet authorities were channeling traffic into a few main arteries—which made it much simpler, physically, to cut the whole city in half abruptly, overnight, as they were to do on the night the wall went up, August 12–13, 1961.

Escape to West Berlin became more difficult, but still required care, patience and prudence rather than courage. The only risk was that a would-be escapee might be stopped at the last moment and asked for his identity papers. If they showed that he was from some distant city in East Germany, then he might be hauled off for questioning, possibly charged and jailed as an "enemy of the people," or lodged on a police suspect list. But on the whole the East German police checks were a matter of spot control rather than any systematic action to halt the refugees. An East German wishing to make his way out would first have to find a reason to ask police permission to travel to Berlin. This could usually be arranged and a pass produced on the train to Berlin which would satisfy the Volkspolizei. Once in the city, he had only to walk across one of the many barricaded streets when the police were not around, or board the U-Bahn subway in East Berlin with the regular city traffic and get off in West Berlin. Some 50,000 East Berliners were crossing every day to work or study in West Berlin, and in addition there was constant casual back-and-forth traffic among neighbors and friends along the sector border, housewives who would shop in West Berlin, boys dating girls, and families visiting. This made it easy for refugees to slip in with the Berliners.

And so they kept coming—297,000 in 1953; 95,000 in 1954; 134,000 in 1955; 140,000 in 1956; 110,000 in 1957; 104,000 in 1958; 79,000 in 1959; 103,000 in 1960; and 73,000 in 1961—to the time the wall went up in August. Many thousands more made their way directly to West Germany. In all since the end of the war, 3.6 million people have fled from the Soviet occupation zone. The drain on the East German economy has been enormous, because it was primarily the professional people—the doctors, engineers and teachers, along with young people and skilled workers—who fled. People of intelligence, ingenuity and energy who could not stand the Communist system and well knew they could start a new life in West Germany. They were the people East Germany could least afford to lose.

When Berlin was divided into British, French, American and Soviet sectors in 1945, the occupation borders were fixed on a basis of the borough boundaries of the city. The building of blockades and street barriers and the marking of borders therefore went on to the accompaniment of endless arguments over precise map locations and city surveyor records. Was the border in the middle of the street? Or was it on the left sidewalk or the right sidewalk or along the property building line? Was it on one side of a fence or the other? Then there were the cases of the "exclaves"—little communities just outside the West Berlin borders, but legally part of the western sectors of the city. The village of Steinstucken, for example, consists of barely 100 people who pay their taxes and get their mail and public utilities from the West Berlin borough of Zehlendorf. But it is cut off from Zehlendorf by a strip of about 400 yards of Russian territory and frequently, when the Russians have been in a harassing mood, has been subject to a "baby blockade" all alone. These border arguments and incidents might have seemed ridiculously funny had they not been a matter of freedom or slavery for the Berliners. Even so, the situation did occasionally produce its humor.

When the British Army moved into Berlin in 1945, it took over an old Wehrmacht barracks in the Spandau section of the city which was built along a street that turned out to mark the border between West Berlin and Soviet East Germany. The border ran down the middle of the street, which was patrolled occasionally by the Red Army. When the Cold War temperature was low, the Russians would drive along shouting at the British troops to get on the sidewalk on their own side of the border and quit wandering into Russian territory. Eventually, a battalion of the famous Scottish regiment, the Black Watch, was assigned to the Spandau barracks, under the command of a colorful soldier with bristling moustaches, a monocle and a string of war medals acquired as a Chindit column commander in the jungles of Burma. His name was Bernard Fergusson, and later he became British High Commissioner in New Zealand.

Colonel Fergusson finally decided that he had had enough of the barracking of his men by the Russians, and he ordered that a white line be painted down the middle of the street—so that it would be clear who was on which side of the border. A detail was duly formed consisting of a couple of privates with paintbrushes and paint cans, a corporal, a lieutenant to oversee the work, and a military engineer to survey the line in accordance with the official ordnance maps.

As soons as the painting operation began, great activity broke out among the Russians on the other side of the street. It was a Russian rule of the Russian game in Berlin that they could do anything they wanted any time in the way of marking borders or tearing up streets without consulting anybody—but nobody on the Western side could mark a border without consulting them. Jeeps began tearing around, and senior Russian officers arrived. Consultations were held and more Russians arrived. Meanwhile the Black Watch soldiers were stolidly painting their line down the middle of the road as ordered, paying no attention to the commotion they were causing on the other side.

Suddenly orders were barked by a Russian officer, and a Red Army soldier strode forward in shiny boots and came to a stop with his feet planted squarely in the middle of the street, in the path of the oncoming white line. At this point the Black Watch lieutenant sent for Colonel Fergusson, regretfully disturbing his lunch. Fergusson arrived to find the painting detail nearing the Russian soldier's feet, while Russian officers watched from their side of the street.

"Sir, what shall we do?" the Black Watch lieutenant said, saluting. Fergusson strode up and down briefly, swagger stick under his arm, surveying the scene through his monocle.

"Tell him to paint over his damned boots," he ordered.

The lieutenant repeated the colonel's order to the corporal who repeated it to the private kneeling in the street. The private dipped his brush heavily into the white paint, and with one delicious swipe smeared across the Russian soldier's shiny boots and resumed carefully working the white line on down the center of the street. Russian officers rushed forward in a rage. Fergusson stepped up to the white line and stopped them with a stiffly British military salute. He turned to a British interpreter who had been hovering in the background, and said:

"Tell the Russian colonel that I propose leaving our line just as it is, with two footmarkes showing, as evidence of the friendly relations between the British Army and the Soviet Army."

The Russian colonel grunted. Fergusson threw another salute and returned to his lunch.

The Khrushchev offensive against Berlin began on November 10, 1958, and lasted almost exactly four years—until the Cuban crisis died away and the Berlin crisis with it, in November of 1962. The opening gun was fired by Khrushchev in a speech at the Moscow Sports Palace in which he ranted an railed at the "subversive activities of the Western powers against the Warsaw Treaty countries" from

West Berlin. Two weeks later, the Russian Government dispatched a formal diplomatic note to each of the three Western powers in which it declared the Potsdam Agreements to be "null and void," and all four-power occupation arrangements including those covering Berlin to be ended.

"The Soviet Government would consider it possible to solve the West Berlin question by the conversion of West Berlin into an independent political unit—a free city, without any state, including both existing German states, interfering in its life," the note said. Then the Russians threatened:

> In view of this, the Soviet Government proposes to make no changes in the present procedure for military traffic of the U.S.A., Great Britain and France from West Berlin to West Germany for half a year. . . . If the above-mentioned period is not utilized to reach an adequate agreement, the Soviet Union will then carry out the planned measures through an agreement with the German Democratic Republic [East Germany]. It is envisaged that the G.D.R., like any other independent state, must fully deal with questions concerning its space—that is, exercise its sovereignty on land, on water and in the air. At the same time, there will terminate all contacts still maintained between representatives of the armed forces and other officials of the Soviet Union in Germany, and corresponding representatives of the armed forces and other officials of the U.S.A., Great Britain and France on questions pertaining to Berlin. . . .

It was a massive frontal attack—no less than a threat to extinguish the Allied presence in Berlin completely. For the next four years, Berlin was scarcely ever out of the headlines.

Four months later, on February 17, 1959, Khrushchev added an additional threat: to sign a separate peace treaty with East Germany. Would the Western Allies start a war over a peace treaty? he was asking rhetorically. "Soviet troops are not in East Germany to play games," he said menacingly. "If anybody should start shooting this would mean the beginning of war." Again and again Khrushchev hammered on this theme in the months and years that followed. Walter Ulbricht, the bearded, Moscow-trained East German puppet leader, added his menaces along the way. He announced, for example, that as soon as East Germany got control over the air corridors to Berlin, the West Berlin airfields—Templehof, Tegel and Gatow—all would be closed down and all air traffic to the city routed through Schoenfeld Airdrome just outside East Berlin.

For the Western powers, the Russian threat boiled down to one fundamental question: What do we do if they stop the traffic?

Despite all the Russian propaganda bombast, the Berlin problem for the West was really quite simple in its final analysis. It did not, in the end, matter very much who claimed sovereignty over the territory around Berlin. As long as Soviet troops remain in occupation of East Germany, the sovereignty of any East German Government will be a political fiction anyway. All that really counted was whether or not people and goods kept moving in and out of the city. As long as arrivals and departures were not halted, the city could be kept alive. The West had proved this in 1948 and 1949. And for the next four years, in the most extreme moments of diplomatic tension, the traffic never stopped. The Russians never went to the brink of war over Berlin.

The Russians never shot down an aircraft in the air corridors—although they buzzed quite a few and threw plenty of headline scares into pilots and passengers. They never halted the trains, barges or road traffic—although they delayed traffic many times and did all that they could by tactics of harassment and fear to reduce traffic into the city.

The response of the Allies to the challenge over Berlin was simple: keep cool, keep firm, keep reasonable and keep talking. But in the meantime, in the deep secrecy of the military staffs, the United States, Britain and France went to work on the grim question of what military action they would take if a Russian land blockade of Berlin again materialized. In 1959, the planners were asked to make recommendations for joint Allied military action in the event that either the Russians, or East Germans acting for the Russians, stopped Allied military convoys at the Helmstedt checkpoint on the East German border and refused to let them clear for West Berlin. The Allied governments had already said publicly that they would accept East Germans as Russian agents. They would not, in other words, argue over whether a Russian checked the convoy orders or an East German. The only question was what to do if the convoys were halted.

The military planners examined the problem from every conceivable angle, in particular in the light of the experience with the Berlin blockade of 1949. In the end, they recommended an extreme course of action: a limited military operation by Allied forces to invade East Germany and seize and hold the Helmstedt checkpoint.

The planners proposed that if the Russians turned control over to the East Germans, a British-French-American military task force be formed opposite Helmstedt immediately, and reinforcements to the extent of two divisions moved into the border area in support. Then if the East Germans began a blockade of Berlin, this force was to be ordered to cross the border north of Helmstedt, swing around behind the checkpoint to the east, cut the autobahn to Berlin, and occupy a salient of East German territory.

The action would have been limited in scope, and would have been accompanied by government declarations from the Allied powers to the effect that Western forces would be withdrawn from East German territory as soon as freedom of access to Berlin was guaranteed. There was no plan to "shoot through to Berlin" on the autobahn. This would have been more hazardous in any case. But the Allies were preparing to mount a limited operation with plenty of force in reserve, to seize and hold a sizable chunk of East German territory. The Russian choice would then have been to escalate the Allied action into a full-scale war in the middle of Europe; to let the Allies sit in control of a piece of East German territory while a Berlin blockade continued; or to call the blockade off in return for Allied withdrawal.

Such was the military recommendation which the British, French and United States staffs submitted to their governments. It never became necessary for the governments to decide whether or not to put it into operation, and it therefore remained a staff agreement rather than a government agreement. The contingency for which it was prepared never arose. More important, the plan reached the Russians through one of their spies in the West. By 1961, United States counterintelligence was aware that the Helmstedt plan, along with other Berlin contingency plans, was known in Moscow. It was not until 1963 that the Russian spy was finally trapped: a Frenchman named Georges Pacques who for several years worked in the private office of French Defense Minister Pierre Messmer and then became deputy press director of the North Atlantic Treaty Organization, with what is called a "Cosmic" security clearance, giving him access to virtually every document passing through the NATO machine. He is now serving a sentence of life imprisonment.

The Russians were therefore aware that they ran a war risk if they attempted another Berlin blockade, and tense as things became, they always stopped short of cutting Berlin traffic.

The first diplomatic move in response to Khrushchev's Berlin threat came from the British. In December, 1958, Prime Minister

Macmillan put out a discreet and entirely secret feeler to Moscow, asking whether he might return the official visit which Khrushchev and Bulganin had made to Britain in 1955. The Russians, always probing for a weak link in Allied armor, sent back an immediate invitation. Macmillan flew to Moscow in February, 1959, accompanied by every British and American news correspondent who requested a visa, with a promise of censorship-free filing facilities from the Soviet Union for the first time since the Moscow Foreign Ministers Conference of 1947. It was a fascinating odyssey, from Moscow to Kiev to Leningrad and back to Moscow, with Macmillan's hosts alternately warm and cold. First exchanges, on a Sunday at Khrushchev's country dacha outside Moscow, were full of conviviality, and included a clay pigeon shoot in the snow-covered park. But two days later, as it became evident that Macmillan was prepared to talk a great deal but not to give, Khrushchev turned nasty.

"You are not ready to negotiate seriously," he stormed at Macmillan. "We saw this with you British in 1939. If Sir Stafford Cripps had come here to negotiate seriously in 1939 there would have been no war. Six million Russians would never have died."

Macmillan in a cold fury stood up and replied that if the Russians wanted to debate the origins of the second World War there was no point in going on with the talks. He walked out of the room. In an antichamber of the Kremlin, he turned to Selwyn Lloyd, the foreign secretary, and said: "Shall we send for the Comet [the aircraft which had brought him to Moscow]?"

The British party was due to take off that afternoon for the tour of Kiev and Leningrad. In the security of the Rolls Royce driving back to the British Embassy, Macmillan's advisers pressed upon him that he still had another week in which to make direct contact with the Russian people, including a promised television broadcast at the end of his visit, and that this was worth overlooking the diplomatic snub. Back at the Embassy a phone call came saying that Khrushchev, who had intended to accompany Macmillan to Kiev, now had a toothache which had to be taken care of. Khrushchev would not be making the journey.

Macmillan looked drawn and exhausted when he stepped out of the aircraft at Kiev, but none of the citizens or officials was aware of the drama which had taken place in the Kremlin that morning, and he was accorded an enthusiastic welcome. He strode to a microphone, wearing a cream-colored fur hat, and resolutely delivered a few words of greeting. "We want peace and you want peace," he said. "But if you want peace you must negotiate." Thirty-six hours later, we all flew on to Leningrad, and there the atmosphere changed. Khrushchev still did not turn up, but he sent Andre Gromyko, the foreign minister, and Anastas Mikoyan, the deputy first secretary, to put the official seal of good will back on the Macmillan visit.

By the evening of our departure from Leningrad, word was out that the Russians had agreed to a British proposal to convene a conference of the Big Four Foreign Ministers at Geneva in May to discuss Germany and the Berlin question. Time had been bought in the Berlin crisis—and although there was not much enthusiasm for the British move in Paris or Bonn, at least nothing had been given away and nobody could think of anything better to take the heat out of the crisis.

We all boarded a special overnight train from Leningrad to Moscow—correspondents and Russian and British diplomats—and late in the evening I found myself sitting talking alone with a Russian at a table in the dining car. He was a government official, but I do not know what his job was and it is better to forget his name.

"Meester Cook," he said as we sipped some insufferably sweet Russian champagne, "what do you think of the Soviet Union?"

I said quite genuinely that I had been tremendously impressed by the amount of building going on everywhere and the obvious strides the people of Kiev and Leningrad had made in repairing the destruction of the war. And, I went on, both sincerely and pointedly, I was also now much more aware than I had been before coming to the Soviet Union how deeply the Russian people wanted and needed peace.

"Meester Cook," the Russian opposite me said quietly, "there will be no war over Berlin. The Russian people will not support the Soviet Government if it tries to go to war over Berlin."

The train swayed gently and the gleaming linen tablecloth and Tzarist crystal glasses reflected in the windowpane as I glanced out into the darkness. I turned and looked at the Russian, trying not to show my astonishment at the fact that a Russian official would even suggest to an American newspaper correspondent that the Russian people might not be behind the government in the Berlin crisis. I said as matter-of-factly as I could, "Well, I'm glad to hear you say that, because you know that we don't want a war over Berlin."

As the Berlin crisis wore on through 1959, 1960, 1961 and 1962 my mind went back constantly to that strange and unexpected moment on the train to Moscow. Khrushchev was using the threat of an East German peace treaty to whip up a war crisis to force the West out of Berlin. But in so doing, he was preaching peace so hard to the Russians that, it seemed, he had passed the point where he could now turn around and tell them they had to go to war. Peace had become a matter of deep Russian yearning. It was one thing to have formed such an impression traveling around Russia, but it was quite another to have a Soviet official say to you, quietly and alone, that it was true.

The Geneva Conference opened in May, 1959, and, with recesses, lasted into August. The Western powers made a series of offers to the Russians for interim arrangements pending a final Berlin settlement. But Christian Herter, who had replaced Dulles as Secretary of State, estimated that he spent thirty-one hours trying to get an answer out of Gromyko to the question, "What happens if there is no final settlement after the interim period?" As the Geneva Conference faded into frustration and oblivion, President Eisenhower moved to keep the dialogue going by inviting Khrushchev to visit the United States. This produced the famous Camp David meeting of September, 1959, when it was agreed to hold a Big Four Summit Conference.

But Eisenhower and Macmillan had not taken the trouble to find out what the attitude of President de Gaulle might be, and the imperious Frenchman immediately let it be known that there would be no Summit Conference until he, too, had first had his personal talk with Khrushchev. The British bit their diplomatic fingernails with worry that "Khrushchev's mood might wear off," but instead the Russian leader came, all smiles, on a visit to France in February, 1960. At last came the Summit in May, 1960—only to crash before it ever got off the ground with the U-2 spy plane affair. Khrushchev stormed out of Paris to the noise of the most terrible threats. United States military forces were on a seven-hour strategic alert as he started for home. Would he now sign his East German peace treaty? Would East Germans take over control of the autobahn and the air corridors? Was a blockade about to begin? Was the world approaching the brink of war? When Khrushchev returned to Moscow, he coolly called off the dogs again, and made it known that he would now wait for his showdown until after the United States elections. And so the Berlin crisis rocked into its third year.

By the time President Kennedy and Khrushchev met at Vienna in May, 1961, the heat was being turned up everywhere. The Laos situation had worsened. Disarmament and nuclear test ban treaty talks in Geneva were getting nowhere. The Russians had announced a 28-percent boost in their arms budget. Harassment of autobahn and air corridor traffic in and out of Berlin was increasing. The Russians had even scattered "window"—strips of metal foil, designed to confuse radar screens—in the path of aircraft flying up the Berlin air corridors.

"It looks like a cold winter," President Kennedy remarked grimly as he left Vienna, knowing that he was now heading into a major test of nerve and strength which would not be met or mastered simply by sitting it out. The President returned to Washington and announced an increase in the American defense budget, the calling up of some military reservists, the dispatch of two more American Army divisions and a flock of nuclear air squadrons to Europe.

By June, 1961, the tension over Berlin had produced one grim result. Refugees were pouring out of East Germany into West Berlin in a panic rush for freedom. In June the average had been 500 to 600 every day. In July it began to climb rapidly, soon passed the 1,000-a-day figure, and totaled more than 30,000 for the month. The rate was now higher than at any time since the 1953 East German uprising. In August, refugees were streaming into West Berlin in a near frenzy. After another war-breathing speech by Khrushchev on August 7, more than 5,000 crossed into West Berlin in the next two days. On August 11, an all-time one-day record of nearly 4,000 East Germans registered in West Berlin. They were almost the last.

On the night of August 12–13, the East German Army moved across the city and as the early northern dawn began on a clear hot day, every street and crossing-point between East Berlin and West Berlin was closed. A few unfortunate waitresses, bar girls from the nightclubs and East Berlin night-shift workers with jobs in West Berlin, not realizing what was taking place, made a last one-way trip home that morning. Then throughout the day under the hot sun of August 13, Communist troops busily unrolled miles and miles of barbed wire all the way across the 27-mile center of Berlin from west to east. The same thing began to happen on the Soviet Zone borders of Berlin to the north. West Berliners streamed to the center of the city to watch, jeer and weep in disbelief. Indeed nothing more unbelievable, more unreal, nothing so mad had ever happened in the long history of mankind. In Jerusalem, a war had ended with barbed wire dividing the city between Arabs and Jews. But here were Germans putting up a fence against other Germans across the middle of their great city of Berlin. It seemed so utterly ludicrous, so insane, that Berliners, with tears streaming down their faces, shouting derisive insults and raging oaths at the sullen East German soldiers, could not grasp what was really happening. Ten days later, on August 23, began the real horror—the building of the wall. A cry of anguish and indignation went up from Berlin and was heard around the world.

A week later, the Russians resumed nuclear testing, unilaterally breaking a three-year moratorium without a word of warning to anybody, and climaxing their test series with a monster city-killer of something like 80 kilotons.

But when the wall went up, the Russians lost what slight hope they might ever have had of taking over West Berlin. If Berlin had seemed like an irritant and dangerous problem of peace to people and nations not directly involved, the Communist wall transformed it overnight into a dramatic citadel of liberty for all the world. A surge of support for Berlin followed among neutrals, among the uncommitted, such as the city had never known before.

And with this, the squalid and nauseous Communist puppet government of East Germany lost any shred of claim to being a state or a government deserving of recognition in the world. The Communists did not know they had lost—they were jeering and cheering triumphantly and predicting the early collapse of the West Berlin economy. But they could not conceal the fact that the wall, above all, was a confession of the weakness and the miserable failure of the Communist system in East Germany. Its only purpose was to stop that flow of refugees which was draining the life out of the Soviet occupation zone. And in building the wall, the Communists had also shot down one of their own propaganda arguments for liquidating West Berlin—the charge that it was a danger to peace because it was a hotbed of spies, saboteurs and troublemakers for East Germany and a "slave market" for refugees.

The Russians and the East Germans apparently were convinced that West Berlin was so dependent on workers from East Berlin that its economy would wither and die with the building of the wall. They counted next on slow strangulation of Allied traffic, first by introducing controls over Allied vehicles crossing through the wall to East Berlin, and then by transferring those controls to East Germans, and after that—once the pattern had been established in Berlin—applying the new control system to Allied traffic between West Berlin and West Germany. At that point they expected West Berlin to drop into Communist hands like a dead fruit from a tree. That this did not happen might have seemed a miracle. But it was less a matter of heroism or wonder than it was a triumph of simple common sense, and a refusal of the Western Allies, the Berlin officials, the West Berlin police—in fact the whole city—to be rattled or frightened.

Ironically leaving aside the human element and the personal tragedies it has created, the wall has been the best political and propaganda break West Berlin has had since the war.

General Lucius D. Clay, organizer of the airlift and symbol of Berlin's resistance and victory in the blockade of 1948–49, arrived in the city a month after the wall went up as President Kennedy's special representative and immediately embarked on a policy of action. He stepped up the military convoys moving on the autobahn in and out of West Berlin. He increased helicopter flights over East Berlin, despite constant protests and threats that they would be shot down. He ordered constant patrolling of East Berlin by American military sedans. He kept busloads of American soldiers going through the wall to tour East Berlin. He brought noncommissioned officers from all over West Germany to see the wall and return to brief their troops on the Berlin situation. He pleaded with business friends in the United States and West Germany to establish branches in Berlin, invest in Berlin, build in Berlin, move to Berlin, produce in Berlin.

The climactic point of General Clay's second "Battle of Berlin" came when he sent United States Army tanks to Checkpoint Charlie, the main crossing-point through the wall, to enforce the right of official American vehicles to drive into East Berlin without interference or inspection by either the Russians or the East Germans. Under the guns of the American tanks, two army jeeps escorted an official State Department car across the checkpoint, turned around, and slowly drove back out again—the point having been forcefully made. As the American vehicles returned, Russian tanks rumbled to the checkpoint on the other side, and for twelve hours the U. S. and Russia were gun barrel to gun barrel in Berlin. But the American vehicles kept moving without interference. General Clay had made his point, and he then ordered the tanks withdrawn. After that the Russian tanks rumbled off, and since then there has been no effort to impose controls over official American vehicles driving through the wall. To have given way would have been to give up Western rights in East

Berlin. By such action over such trivia have the Allies remained in Berlin for twenty years.

In fact, there was always a kind of frightening banality about a Berlin crisis. Invariably the point at issue—the point of confrontation between the Western powers and the Communists—involved some argument which in any other circumstances would have been dismissed as utterly childish and superficial. The Russians were always at their Byzantine best in constructing a crisis out of nothing.

The business of ordering American soldiers to dismount from convoy vehicles to be counted was a classic case in point. For sixteen years, from 1945 to 1961, American military convoys moved up the autobahn to Berlin on a fixed procedure, under which the convoy commander would hand the Russian control officer a set of military orders specifying the number of vehicles and the number of men in his convoy. The Russians would then count the vehicles, and usually they would peer into the trucks and count the men. The thoroughness of the check depended on the Cold War mood of the moment.

When the Berlin wall went up, President Kennedy ordered a full American Army Battle Group, 1,500 men, to move to Berlin immediately by road convoy. Vice-President Lyndon Johnson was in the city waiting to greet the reinforcements. An officer named Colonel Glovers John was in command. He reached Helmstedt, and to avoid any delay in clearing for Berlin, he ordered his men to disembark from their vehicles so the Russians could count them. They were counted, all right, and quickly waved on to Berlin—but for the next two years there were constant arguments with the Russians over whether U.S. soldiers had to disembark to be counted or not. Finally, after one convoy had been held outside Berlin for nearly three days while messages flashed between Moscow and Washington, the Western Allies stated that they would disembark to be counted if the convoys totaled more than fifty men, and if the weather was good. But in bad weather, or with less than fifty men, they would stay in their vehicles. One small slip by an American officer—which could not possibly have seemed to be a slip or a mistake at the time—took two years to straighten out and ended in another of those small diminutions of Allied freedom of action moving in and out of Berlin.

General Clay returned to the United States after eight months in Berlin. The wall was now nearly one year old, and the crisis wearing to the end of its fourth year. But things were stabilizing in a grim way. The pinpricks against Berlin were drawing less and less blood, and had less real thrust behind them. More than that, by the summer of 1962 the Russians were fishing in much bigger waters—the Caribbean. In October, 1962, came the Cuban crisis. When it was over, Berliners woke up to find that the four-year ordeal of the Berlin crisis was over too.

It simply faded out like a radio station going off the air at midnight. The threats and the harassments, the pressures and the pinpricks, the slowdown of autobahn clearances and the buzzing of air corridor traffic, the talk of a separate peace treaty with East Germany and the Russian promises to hand over controls to the odious Walter Ulbricht, the ultimatums that the Allies get out of the city, and the proposals to turn West Berlin into a "demilitarized free city"—these four years of headlines were suddenly as dead as yesterday's newspaper.

All the same, what would West Berlin be like now? What of the old adage: "The worst crisis will be when there's no crisis"? For four years the city had been an almost unceasing center of world news and world attention. "Crisis Benzedrine" had kept the world and Berlin itself awake day and night to the vital importance of the city in the East-West struggle, and to the urgency of little things like whether soldiers had to get out of vehicles to be counted, or whether American officials had to show passes to East German guards in the center of Berlin. The city faced a psychological letdown. But when the crisis faded and West Berliners looked around, they found their city in remarkably good shape. And more than that, the wall, adding hideous and sinister drama to the plight of West Berlin, had become one of the big tourist attractions of Europe, visited and photographed by thousands.

Official visitors to West Germany, trade delegations, cultural missions and visiting newspapermen and diplomats were flown to Berlin as a matter of fixed routine to see the wall. They walked the grim blocks of Bernauerstrasse, with its apartment windows and doors all bricked up and its wooden crosses planted in the sidewalk in West Berlin where grandmothers, mothers, fathers and youngsters had jumped to escape the Volkspolizei and died. The escape stories multiplied into a separate anthology of Cold War legend.

There were the tunnels—one dug by gravediggers from an open grave in an East Berlin cemetery close to the wall; others dug from the West to East Berlin by students and young people, sometimes running for 100 yards or more to cellars of buildings far beyond the wall. There were the escapes through the sewers until the East Berlin police sealed them off with heavy iron bars. There were the forgery operations with identity cards and passports. Then there was the epidemic of trucks and cars crashing through the wall until the Communists countered by putting up tank barriers and reinforcing the wall with heavy concrete blocks.

There were comedy escapes, like the young man who got out in a homemade American Army uniform, and the East Berlin photographer who backed across the border while focusing his camera on a group of Communist VIPs at the wall, and the interpreter who was lecturing a party of Communist tourists from a platform looking across the wall and ended his remarks with one mighty leap to freedom. There were the happy boaters on the River Spree who got the captain of an East Berlin pleasure steamer drunk, locked him in a cabin and headed for the West Berlin side of the river in a hail of machine-gun fire. There was the railroad engineer and his crew who loosened a rusty old switch that had not been thrown for sixteen years, and ran their train into the West with their families in a car behind.

There was the young man with a tiny sports car who carefully measured the height of the checkpoint barrier, and worked it out that by removing his windshield and deflating his tires and crouching down in his car, he could just make it under the barrier with his fiancee curled up in the luggage compartment. (After that, the Communists attached vertical metal strips to the horizontal crossing barriers.) And there was the young couple who solemnly arrived at Checkpoint Charlie with a large wreath of flowers on the top of their car at the same time that parties of Russians were being waved through by the Communist guards to pay their tributes at the Russian War Memorial in West Berlin on Red Army day. The couple were waved through too, and leaped joyously out of their car to embrace the West Berlin police on the other side.

As long as the wall remains, these stories will grow and multiply—in part because the escapes have to be more ingenious, more carefully prepared and more daringly executed all the time. As 1962 gave way to 1963, the East Germans completed a wall within the wall on their side of the city, and made it practically impossible for any citizen of the Communist state to come within sight of the wall except on a guided tour, let alone tunnel or climb over it. But still the escapees come. On the third anniversary of the building of the wall in August, 1964, the West German Ministry of All German Affairs reported that 19,700 East Germans had made it to the West since the wall went up, either through Berlin or across the East-West German border. Of these, more than 1,600 were East German Volkspolizei or border guards. Despite all of the barriers and all of the risks of failure (prison at best and death at the worst), an average of eighteen people still get out every day. In that three years, at least 100 East Germans are known to have been shot trying to get over the wall or across the borders—how many killed, only the East German authorities know.

Actually the building of the wall affected the economic life of the city very little. Before the wall went up, about 50,000 to 60,000 people had crossed the sector borders every day from East Berlin to jobs in West Berlin. Another 4,000 East German students were attending West Berlin's universities and grammar schools. The flow of refugees into West Berlin had also given the city a much-needed floating labor market, a pool of readily employable workers, most of them skilled. The refugees also kept the Berlin population more or less stable at about 2.2 million people, for Berlin is still an "old" city in which the death rate is higher than the birth rate. This is because so many thousands of young people elected to move to West Germany in years past, leaving parents and grandparents behind.

When the wall first went up, Berlin's productivity sagged, and the population began falling steadily. While there was not any panic rush to move out of Berlin, the population nevertheless dropped in late 1961 and 1962 by about 1,000 to 1,500 every month. The 50,000 workers who used to cross the border to jobs in West Berlin had been employed mainly in building trades and construction work, in service trades such as waitresses, hotel porters and maids, as bar girls in the endless seedy nightclubs of West Berlin, in private homes as daily help, and also in the ready-to-wear dress manufacturing trade as seamstresses. The loss of 50,000 workers was a blow, but not nearly as heavy as Allied authorities and West Berlin city officials feared. Employers in West Berlin had been generous in featherbedding their payrolls with East Germans, and when the labor no longer turned up, productivity per worker increased. The Berlin production index therefore barely faltered. It stood at 167 in August of 1961, had moved to 172 in August of 1962, and went up to 175 in August of 1963.

To a large degree, Berlin met the crisis because West German business never panicked. In the 1950's, a crisis in Berlin almost invariably produced a falling off of orders for the city's industries, a curtailment or suspension of plans for investment, a drop in savings deposits, a general financial uneasiness. But by 1961, West German business had a big investment in Berlin—and more, the West German *political* attitude toward Berlin had changed. Indifference and pre-occupation with its own problems which used to mark West Germany's attitude toward Berlin had given way to a more dynamic appreciation of the political importance of the city in determining the fate of Germany as a whole. West Germany had recovered from the war and was strong again, and this brought new strength of attitude in meeting the crisis when the wall went up. Not only did the order books for Berlin industry remain full, but West German business went out of its way to place new orders in the city and push ahead with plant expansion plans. Savings deposits in the Berlin banks were $100,000,000 *higher* in August, 1962, than they were when the wall went up a year earlier. The West German Government not only contributed an enormous new subsidy grant to expand Berlin's cultural and civic activities, but also went to work figuring out some effective practical inducements to get Germans to move to Berlin. To West German students, the Bonn Government proposed, "Spend a year studying in Berlin." And any young man moving to Berlin automatically avoids being conscripted into the West German Army.

Tax advantages of life in Berlin are considerable. First of all, Berliners receive an automatic 30-percent cut on income taxes. Business gets a 4-percent reduction on production taxes, and a new building in Berlin can be depreciated by 75 percent in three years. From the day the wall went up, the Berlin city government began paying a 4,000 deutsche mark ($1,000) "family founding loan" to every couple marrying in Berlin, to be paid back within ten years, or written off by 25 percent for each child born in Berlin. In 1962, this marriage grant was paid out to nearly 25,000 Berlin newlyweds.

Each worker moving to Berlin receives up to 500 deutsche marks to cover his transportation and moving costs, and another grant of 200 to 300 marks to help him get settled. A married man who leaves his family behind in West Germany to work in Berlin gets a free air trip home after three months in the city, and a single person gets a home trip after six months. As a result, the population which had fallen by 1,000 a month during late 1961 and 1962 has been rising by about 1,000 a month since early 1963. And at the end of 1964, out of a population of almost exactly 2.2 million, Berlin had only 8,000 unemployed.

In the meantime, real estate values in the city have shot up by more than 25 percent since the crisis ended, and for the first time since the war, private house building (as apart from city-subsidized apartment building) has resumed in Berlin's pleasant and fashionable western suburbs. The rise in property values dates, curiously, from the Berlin visit of President Kennedy in June, 1963, which for psychological and political reasons appears to have marked the turn of the Berlin scene from crisis to normalcy.

But the biggest change in Berlin in the years since the wall went up has been in the mood and atmosphere of the city. It has become a young people's city. Statistically it is still an "old" city, with the great majority of the population in their fifties or sixties. But this is slowly changing, and the atmosphere is changing more rapidly than the statistics. It used to be that young Berliners moved to West Germany to jobs and opportunity. Now with the marriage grants and tax advantages and the certainty of job security in Germany's greatest city—cut in half as it is—young people are not only staying but are moving back to Berlin. In addition, money is being poured into increased university facilities and the expansion of specialized schools teaching stage design, music, conducting, dance, acting, art, architecture.

The West German Government is making the city the center of Germany's student exchange program. From Africa, Latin America, Asia and all over Europe, students on cultural grants are sent to West Berlin not only for the educational opportunities of the city but also to give them a firsthand experience of the Communist wall and the contrast between its two sides. University enrollments are nearly 7,000 higher in West Berlin today than they were before the wall went up. Berlin may no longer be in the headlines, but it has begun to live a life of its own again, with its own momentum and its own vitality.

Nikita Khrushchev wrote "finish" to his own crisis when he summoned Walter Ulbricht to Moscow in June, 1964, to sign a twenty-year "Treaty of Friendship and Mutual Assistance." It was a far cry from the East German peace treaty which he had threatened for nearly four years, and Khrushchev even took the unusual step of advising the three Western powers in advance of what he was about to do, and assuring them that it would not in any way affect Russian control over Allied access to West Berlin.

A few months before, while on a visit to Berlin, I took advantage of the semiannual Leipzig Fair to slip off to East Germany for a brief look at life beyond the wall. I had made the trip frequently since a first visit in 1949. On one journey, a group of us which included Joseph Wechsberg of *The New Yorker,* Joseph Alsop, the columnist, and William Attwood, then a magazine writer and now United States Ambassador to Kenya, were held for three hours in the Leipzig police headquarters because of some pictures Attwood had innocently taken of parading Freie Deutsche Jugend. The Leipzig Fair was never much of an exhibition under the Communists, but it was always a chance to penetrate forbidden territory.

Things were both better and worse than they had been on my last visit to Leipzig, before the wall went up. Of the kind of police surveillance to be encountered in the 1950's, there was little—at least nothing visible. The wall which sealed off the escape route to West Berlin had permitted the police to relax their grip on the daily life of the East German population. A great deal of new building had gone on in Leipzig, but the center of the city, two decades after the war, still remained a mess of bombed-out mud holes and rubble heaps. The food had improved in variety. There was much more in the shops and the people were better dressed. Yet it was worse in ways which were difficult to capture and define.

A decade of Communist leveling had done its work on Leipzig life and society. There was a subdued almost conspiratorial hush about conversation and voices. Faces were expressionless, smiles and laughter absent—except for one young man who lurched up to me outside the Bahnhof late in the evening, full of beer, to ask the way to a train and tell me with a derisive chuckle that he was due to report to the East German Army. Otherwise, Leipzig seemed to be peopled by shuffling silent bodies. Once one of the centers of German music, art, literature, publishing, theater and culture, it had become a disembodied city without life and without soul. There was more character and vitality in the ruins of Leipzig in the early 1950's than there was in the rebuilt city of 1963. Gone, now, were the last of the little artisan shops which had formed such a rich and varied part of Leipzig's tradition and past. The city had also been a center of the fur trade and fur tailoring in Germany, of baroque silver design, of jewelry manufacture, pottery and fine handwork and craftsmanship in dozens of trades. A decade ago in the ruins you would still find the occasional shop run by an elderly man and wife with a few pieces of exquisite handwork to offer—a violin maker or a jeweler or a tailor.

But these were all gone now, either swept up in the vacuum cleaner of state ownership, or simply closed down with the death of the owner.

Gone, too, were the fine pieces of antiques which had filled the occasional display window in the early 1950's. I browsed in a secondhand bookstore briefly to see what books might still be found—but apart from old sets of Schiller and Goethe and the collected works of Karl Marx for the Communist who has Everything, there was nothing. As a gesture to Leipzig's great cultural past, the state had just completed a new theater in the center of the city—a monstrous square pile of granite rising to a peaked slate roof, topped at the corners by those gingerbread minarets so beloved by Comrade Stalin. The East Germans have been late all along the way in catching up with de-Stalinization.

There was something else that was depressing about the city—and that was the slow Balkanization of its appearance and character. It was ceasing to be German, and becoming more and more Slavic. The Stalin-style theater was part of it, and so was the drab and barren architecture of a curving sweep of apartment buildings not far from the center of town. They reminded me of Kiev. The shopwindows were filled with Slavic goods, since the only trade which East Germany does in consumer lines is with the Communist bloc. There were bottles and bottles of Hungarian, Bulgarian and Russian wines, Polish and Russian vodka. There were cans of Russian fish, Czechoslovakian shoes, and an occasional pathetic effort at sophistication and smartness in the form of the latest dresses from Budapest. For a special treat in diet, there were bean sprouts and water chestnuts and preserved ginger and canned pork from Red China. It was a saddening demise for a city which for five centuries was the traditional crossroads trading center of Europe, with its semiannual Trade Fair almost in the dead center of the old continent between the great cities and cultures of East and West.

Worst of all, to me, was the peculiar and unmistakeable *smell* of Russia and the Communist world which pervaded Leipzig. Anyone who has ever set foot in the Soviet Union knows that smell. It hits you as soon as you board a Russian airplane, however far from Moscow, and it never leaves you all the time you are traveling in Eastern Europe. It is a stale, heavy, unwashed smell, like a room slept in but never aired, ashtrays and beer glasses unemptied the morning after a party, clothes which are never dry-cleaned, streetcars and buses which are never taken out of service to be reconditioned. It is a smell of Turkish tobacco, old coffee grounds, bay leaves, paprika, fish oil, stale cabbage, cooking fat used over and over again, peeling paint, old lavatories, carbolic soap, unwashed bodies. It is a prison smell of hopelessness and despair and indifference, a morgue smell of formaldehyde and the cleanliness of death. It is a smell that closes in as soon as you enter a building, a smell that nobody can do anything about, a smell that goes with the system.

On a Sunday morning, before heading back to Berlin, I drove to St. Thomas's Church in the center of Leipzig and parked in a space behind its damaged altar windows—the same spot, in fact, where Alsop, Wechsberg, Attwood and I had fallen into the hands of the police in 1950. This time I was in an unobtrusive Volkswagen which I had rented in West Berlin. I walked to the front door of the church, and a small party of Freie Deutsche Jugend boys in blue shorts and shirts went striding by, carrying a red, gold, and black banner emblazoned with the hammer and sickle. The Lutheran rector was on the steps of the church in deep and earnest conversation with a couple of elderly German ladies with complexions of parchment and wearing hats that looked like inverted flowerpots. I slipped inside and took a seat in a rear pew, wondering how many would turn up for the service which was due to start in about twenty minutes.

Johann Sebastian Bach conducted the choir at St. Thomas's, and lies buried in a side aisle of the church. The great organ on which Bach used to play was giving forth quiet prologue music, and people were coming in slowly, almost all of them in their fifties, sixties or seventies. Then just before the service was due to start, they began arriving in a rush, younger and younger—teen-age grandsons and granddaughters with their grandmothers, young couples with small children and babies in arms, many young mothers without their husbands bringing scrubbed and pigtailed youngsters of ten or eleven years. The organ swelled into a mighty Bach fugue and the choir which Bach used to conduct took up a determined anthem. The rector strode vigorously up the steps to the pulpit and the call to worship and the responses rang out in loud clear tones. The church was almost full as the service began. I slipped out, and the air was clean and the smell was gone and Bach's music was echoing around the empty church square as I drove away for Berlin.

6. Britain: From Socialism to Suez

Winston was back. England's brief, necessary and not very profound or painful experience of Socialism had come to an end after barely six years. In October, 1951, the Labour Party lost a general election and the Conservatives returned to power to remain for exactly thirteen years—the longest period of continuous rule by one party in Britain since the reign of King George III. England had been through the exhaustions of war, the strains of economic recovery, the irritations of austerity, the heat of political battle over nationalization of industry and the socialistic measures of Labour's rule, the transition of India to independence, the upheavals of Greece and Palestine, the Berlin airlift, the Cold War, and in 1951 the jungle war in Malaya and the Korean war still being fought. But a euphoria now settled over the land. It was the Indian Summer of British power and the British Empire in the world, and the Indian Summer of a great man's life. The pink cherubic face, the bowler hat and walking stick, the V-for-Victory sign, the cigar and the irrepressible grin were again reassuringly framed in the Georgian doorway of No. 10 Downing Street.

The erosion of British power had begun, but an amazing amount of that "pink area" was still intact on schoolboy maps of the world. Nearly 80,000 British troops were stationed in the Suez Canal base, guarding the lifeline of the Empire to the East. King Farouk was still on the throne of Egypt. The Union Jack flew over Khartoum, and Britain controlled the headwaters of the Nile. In the Caribbean, in West Africa, Central Africa, East Africa, in the Arabian Peninsula, the Persian Gulf, the Malay Straits, the China Sea and the Central Pacific, British colonial governors ruled more than 100,000,000 people with gentle despotism and Victorian manners and customs. Countless sultans, sheiks, maharajahs, naizams, rajahs, kings, princes, rulers and tribal leaders were still glad to pay homage to the British Crown, for they, too, were part of the old order. And the Royal Navy was still never very far away from Aden, Kuwait, Basara, Baharein, Malta, Trincomalee, Trinidad, Singapore, Simmonstown, Hamilton, Hongkong, Mombassa, Muscat, Gibraltar or the North Cape.

The transition of the old empire into a multiracial commonwealth was underway in an atmosphere more reassuring than disturbing to the British. The Labour Government's astute and courageous handling of the India problem was paying off brilliantly, and the word "British" had been discreetly dropped from the phrase "British Commonwealth of Nations." India, although taking a Republican form of government with a president as its sovereign head, had recognized the King of England as "Head of the Commonwealth." Thus, by semantical threads, the Commonwealth was held together even while great changes took place in the status and relationship of its members. Burma had elected to cut all ties with Britain, but few tears and no blood had been shed. India, Ceylon, Pakistan, were all remaining Commonwealth members. (They were, after all, run by Oxford, Cambridge and Sandhurst men.) Ahead of all other colonial powers, the British with the greatest empire of all had recognized the need for change and had initiated a peaceful evolution of their possessions.

Closer to home, Britain looked across the channel in 1951 to a Europe where economic recovery was only just beginning to show momentum. The British had taken the lead in organizing the economic cooperation machinery for the Marshall Plan in Europe. On the Continent, European political leadership was still immobilized in the problems of postwar recovery. France floundered in the continuous instability of the Fourth Republic. Germany had taken only the first steps back in to the community of nations. No country in Europe even approached the prestige and power of Great Britain. In addition, there was the "special relationship" between Britain and the United States. For all their troubles, the British still stood uniquely poised in world politics, power and diplomacy.

To most Britons, to the traditional and dominant British instincts and emotions, it was soothing and reassuring to have Winston Churchill back at Downing Street. The Conservatives were voted back into power on a promise that postwar austerity would at last disappear from daily life (althought it was not, in fact, until July, 1954, that the British at last threw away their meat ration books). There was a yearning for normalcy and for the comforts of Churchillian prestige.

If the sun was setting on the Union Jack, at least it could still give a warm and mellow glow to Britain and the world.

Churchill was seventy-seven years old when he formed his last government, and while of course he was not as active as he once had been, his health was good, his mind vigorous and wide-ranging, and his mastery of the House of Commons was an unfailing excitement and delight. Churchill by merely entering the Commons Chamber evoked a sense of anticipation. His sonorous oratory would roll forth like the swelling of the sea. But then he would impishly and hesitatingly fumble and search for a word, holding everybody with him until out it would come, and he would beam like a boy who had found the prize in a box of Cracker Jack.

Humor enlivened every day of his great life. It took a brave and confident member to rise to challenge him. Once one of his fellow Conservatives sought to tax Churchill at the pace with which he was carrying out the party election promise to "Set the People Free" from rationing and restrictions. The Prime Minister growled at the unfortunate man: "The speed with which we can set the people free depends, of course, upon the weight of the shackles which must be struck from them." The House of Commons, in those days, was still enriched by dozens of members schooled in the old-fashioned traditions of debate, and scarred in many a battle of parliamentary wit and oratory. But Churchill, like a conductor who pulls a performance out of an orchestra or a leading actor who raises the standard of the rest of the cast, gave to the whole House, which he loved beyond any human institution, a particular sense of vitality, of history and greatness.

Europe looked with anticipation and reassurance to Churchill's return. Here was the man who had cried "Europe Unite" in his first great postwar speech at Zurich in September, 1946—and then had gone on to do something about it. Churchill launched the United Europe movement with a rally at London's Albert Hall in June, 1947. A year later, the movement held its second international congress at The Hague, again with Churchill as the principal sponsor, with political notables, parliamentarians and private citizens from every country and political faith in Europe (except the Communists and the British Labour Party). The Hague Congress passed a unanimous resolution demanding government action in the cause of European unity, and as a result, the Council of Europe was born in 1949. Although lacking the supranational effectiveness and political importance of the European Coal and Steel Community and the European Common Market which were to follow, the Council of Europe was the first postwar effort to organize a united Europe, and it is still the largest of the European organizations and remains the principal European forum of international parliamentary debate.

The Assembly of the Council of Europe first met at Strasbourg in August, 1949, with Churchill leading the British Conservative Party delegation. A year later, at the Strasbourg Assembly in August, 1950, a few weeks after the outbreak of the Korean war, Churchill rose with a dramatic speech proposing "the immediate creation of a European Army under a united command in which we should all bear a worthy and honorable part." Churchill offered no blueprint that day. But when René Pleven, the French Minister of Defense, announced French proposals for a European Defense Community treaty three months later, he acknowledged his debt to the Churchill initiative at Strasbourg.

Would Churchill and the Conservatives, back in power, reverse the sour Labour Party attitude toward Europe, and follow the trail which Churchill himself had so clearly blazed? Labour had refused to have anything to do with the European Coal and Steel Community project, but the treaty was still not yet ratified and there was time for Britain to join. Labour had refused to have anything to do with the European Defense Community, but it was still being negotiated. When Churchill came back, Jean Monnet sought out a member of the new government and told him that "no power on earth can keep Britain out of Europe if it wants to come in," and in this mood Europe waited for Churchill's first moves.

Could Churchill have taken Britain into Europe? Many imponderables enmesh the long, awkward, unhappy and still unfinished chronicle of Britain's postwar relations with Europe. There will never be any full or definitive answer from Churchill himself because, so far as is known, he never wrote on the acts and policies of his years in office from 1951 to 1955. All of the evidence of his speeches and political activity before he returned to power was in the direction of a flexible approach to find ways and means of joining Britain to Europe. But it was not to be. The hopes and promises were never fulfilled.

Years later, Harold Macmillan, after he had retired as Prime Minister, reminisced: "Churchill could have taken Britain into Europe. He had the prestige and the vision and the power with the Conservative Party. But he was too old when he came back to office.

He was perfectly sound in health and mind—I don't mean that. But he was too old to undertake the long and concentrated political and diplomatic effort that it would have required to reverse all of our traditional policies and outlook. Look at the problems I had trying to do it ten years later!"

In part, hopes were excessively high because Europeans never fully realized that Churchill was far ahead of his party in his "Europeanism." In fact, this was not at all an expression of the traditions or idealism of British Conservatism. True, the Conservatives appeared to be enthusiastically following Churchill's lead in the days when they were in opposition. But this was for reasons of domestic British politics, and had little to do with any constructive efforts to build Europe. As one prominent Conservative who had been a leading delegate at Strasbourg said to me with blithe candor in later years, "All we were really doing at Strasbourg was using the Council of Europe to beat the Labour Party over the head." In this endeavor, the Conservatives succeeded admirably. They made the harassed but able Labour Foreign Secretary, Ernest Bevin, look like an embittered and backward man who understood neither Europe nor his job. Bevin came to hate Strasbourg, and dug in his heels at any proposals to see the Council of Europe's powers enlarged or its machinery made more effective.

Moreover, Churchill had his differences over European policy with his long-time friend and chosen heir apparent, Anthony Eden. Eden had studiously avoided associating himself too prominently with Churchill's "Europe Unite" campaign. He believed—and not without good reason—that the theme was being overplayed and would give false hopes on the Continent as to exactly how far Britain was prepared to go with its European policy.

At the time of The Hague Congress in 1948, Eden clashed directly with Churchill on the Europe issue. A dinner-party meeting of Conservative leaders was arranged the night before the opening of the Congress, and Churchill presented the outlines of the new "Europe Unite" appeal which he intended to deliver next day. Eden tried to get him to pull back, arguing that he should not go beyond policies which a Conservative Government would carry out when returned to power. Churchill's son-in-law, Duncan Sandys, took the lead in arguing the other way, and as polite Tory discussions go, it was a major row. Churchill decided to stick to his text, and Eden ostentatiously packed his bags the next day and flew home to London, boycotting the Congress in a manner which made it clear that Churchill did not have his backing for the big speech.

When Churchill returned to power, Eden of course automatically returned to the Foreign Office. No matter how Churchill might have felt about wanting to begin the process of entering Europe, he was not going to clash with his heir apparent about long-term British policy. Eden was a complete traditionalist by training and outlook in the conduct of British foreign affairs. He was not out to break any new ground or launch any new European ventures. Sitting in the Foreign Secretary's splendid room with its vast windows looking out across St. James's Park and the Horse Guard's Parade, beneath that huge portrait of King George III which American visitors wryly regard as a gentle British effort at psychological warfare, reading telegrams pouring in and drafting instructions going out to Cairo, Delhi, Paris, Baghdad, Bonn, Rome, Moscow, Athens, Washington and beyond, it would in fact be difficult for any man to be other than traditional in directing British foreign policy.

These traditions have been admirably enshrined in a classic Foreign Office memorandum written in 1907 by Sir Eyre Crowe. Two wars and half a century later, the times have altered enormously. But the instinctive pattern of British diplomacy and the broad approach of the British to the rest of the world has changed surprisingly little.

The memorandum opens with an empirical description of England: "An island state with vast overseas colonies and dependencies whose existence and survival as an independent community are inseparably bound up with the possession of preponderant sea power." In such a position, Sir Eyre Crowe reasoned, Britain could not risk, or resist, any general hostility on the part of other countries, and therefore it must direct its policy to being "closely identified with the primary and vital interests of a majority, or as many as possible, of the other nations." The most vital interest of any nation is its independence, the memorandum said, and accordingly "England more than any other non-insular power has a direct and positive interest in the maintenance of the independence of nations and therefore must be the natural enemy of any country threatening the independence of others." Then came the succinct and classic summation of how Britain should direct its foreign relations:

> The most efficacious system for maintaining national independence is the balance of power. It has become almost a his-

> torical truism to identify England's secular policy with the maintenance of this balance by throwing her weight now in this scale, now in that, but ever on the side opposed to the dictatorship of the strongest single state or group at a given time.

Of course this classic 1907 exposition did not always work out so neatly in practice. Eden recognized as clearly as any statesman that the world had changed. The balance of power in postwar Europe was no longer a game to be played by maneuvering and manipulating the independence and alignment of a number of little states. Two great power blocs headed by two great superpowers now faced each other in the middle of Europe, and there was no room to play diplomatic games. Nevertheless, the Eyre Crowe memorandum left its legacy in the instinctive, ingrained mistrust it had implanted in British thought of having Britain tied too closely to any one grouping, most of all to any continental bloc, or entangling itself in treaties which would involve loss of British independence.

This attitude had been reinforced by the prestige and honor of having stood alone in the war while the Continent had been overrun—the very opposite of the political emotions which the war left among the continental nations, where the common experience of destruction had produced a common determination to reach some kind of unity. The British "special relationship" with the United States might seem to be an exception to the Eyre Crowe rule of maintaining independence and avoiding close alignment in world affairs, but in fact it was not. In the first place, it was an alignment of understanding and mutual interest which had grown up in the war, and was not based on any treaty obligations. In the second place, it was an Anglo-Saxon understanding of tongue and traditions. It placed Britain alongside the strongest power in the world, opposed to dictatorship of the Communist power bloc. And in British minds, there was always the subconscious psychological feeling that Britain was really guiding Anglo-American policies instead of following the American lead.

In place of the old balance of power, Eden liked to describe Britain's postwar policy in the world as based on three interlocking circles with the British at the center. Sometimes he would use the illustration of a stool standing on three legs, each of which must be given equal care and attention: the Commonwealth relationship, the special Anglo-American relationship, and finally relations with Europe. The only trouble was that all through the 1950's, two of those three legs were being warped or whittled away. The Commonwealth was waning as a symbol of British power in the world, and was no longer even much of an instrument of British foreign policy. Its main function was to serve as a vehicle for the peaceful liquidation of British colonies. Meanwhile in Europe the growing unity of the continental Six, the successful development of the Coal and Steel Community and the Common Market, along with Europe's rapidly improving economic health, were slowly freezing Britain out of her old role of independent influence in continental affairs.

Perhaps Eden's greatest mistake in this period was to misjudge the mood and strength of the movement toward European unity. His instinctive feeling—never openly expressed but always inherent in his policy toward Europe—was that treaties based on the supranational concept would fail, and that loose arrangements along cooperative lines of the kind always favored by Britain would in the end prevail. In 1951, not a great deal had yet actually been achieved in the direction of supranationalism. The Coal and Steel Community Treaty was not finally ratified until July of 1952. The European Defense Community treaty was still being negotiated and running into difficulties. And it was the British experience of the E.D.C. affair which more than anything confirmed Eden in his instinctive view that Europe was really fed up with supranationalism and that there was not sufficient political strength or will to pass another supranational treaty.

But the death of E.D.C. was a great personal blow to John Foster Dulles, who had staked his policy on the cause of European integration and had threatened "agonizing reappraisal" of American foreign policy if the E.D.C. did not pass. To this day, there are State Department officials who blame Eden and the British as much as Pierre Mendès-France for the failure of the E.D.C. treaty. Had the British been willing to join the E.D.C., they argue, or even if Eden had been willing to assign a few British divisions to E.D.C. or pledge the permanent stationing of British forces on the Continent of Europe, the outcome would have been different. It is a very doubtful contention. But the fact remains that the failure of Dulles's policy and the success of Eden's diplomacy in picking up the pieces in 1954 did little to enhance the personal relations or the understanding between the two men.

Dulles and Eden disliked each other intensely. Eden had even gone so far as to try to prevent Dulles's appointment as Secretary of State by President Eisenhower. He had crossed to Paris for a conversation with Eisenhower at Supreme Allied Headquarters just before Eisenhower's return to the United States in 1952 to accept the Republican nomination for the Presidency. He spoke quite bluntly of his feelings about Dulles, and said that he hoped if Eisenhower became President he would not make Dulles his Secretary of State.

"From anyone else I would have resented such a suggestion as an unwarranted intrusion in America's affairs," Eisenhower says in his memoirs. "But my long association and friendship with him during war and peace, involving the frankest kind of exchanges between us, made such a remark understandable. So I made no reply accept to say that I knew of no other American so well qualified as Foster to take over the duties of that particular office." *

Dulles and Eden of course maintained all of the surface cordialities, rather ostentatiously covering up a fundamental clash of temperament, personality, outlook and approach to common problems. Eden called Dulles "Foster" and Dulles called Eden "Anthony." But Anthony couldn't stand Foster's moral vanity, particularly on the question of colonialism, and he hated the legalistic circumlocution with which Dulles dealt with problems and adjusted facts to his own vision. And Foster had a lofty disdain (some thought it a latent inferiority complex) for the Eden "style," the old-school European approach to diplomacy and foreign policy. They disagreed about European integration. They disagreed about colonialism. They disagreed about probing the Russians and holding four-power conferences. They disagreed over liquidating the Indochina war in 1954. They disagreed about the Baghdad Pact and Britain's role in the Middle East. They disagreed about neutralism. And above all they disagreed over Suez.

Dulles at times seemed to go out of his way deliberately to irritate Eden and the British—for example, when he visted Cairo in 1953, on his first trip abroad after taking office, and ceremoniously handed a pair of pearl-handled pistols to General Mohammed Neguib, then front-man for Colonel Nasser and the Egyptian Officer's Revolution. At that point, Eden and the British were deeply involved in the complicated and emotional negotiations over ending the Anglo-Egyptian Condominium in the Sudan and evacuating the Suez Canal base. They never forgot or forgave Dulles for what looked to them like symbolic backing of Egyptian nationalism. Viewed from London, Dulles had handed the Egyptian leader a pair of pistols to point at the head of America's closest ally.

All the same, despite difficulties with Dulles and a misjudgment of

* Eisenhower, *Mandate for Change,* Chapter VI.

the tide of unity in Europe, the years from 1951 to 1955 were years of intensive and on the whole successful diplomacy for Eden. At the crest of these successes, he became Prime Minister of Great Britain in April, 1955.

Sir Winston Churchill retired at last at the age of eighty-one, a mellow figure, honored, respected and revered in the world as no other man of political life in this century. He went off with his paints and his collection of hats-for-every-occasion, his budgerigars and his cigars, to the warmth of the Mediterranean sun, at Sicily, at Monte Carlo, at Marrakesh where he had recovered from a bout of pneumonia during the war, on cruises to the Greek Isles and across the Atlantic to the West Indies. The stories kept emerging of his endless humor. When he suffered a stroke in 1953, and the doctors explained to him gently that a circulation blockage had developed, he thought a minute and said: "Well, let's do what we used to do during the war. If the Piccadilly Line was blocked we went round another way." At his last Big Three conference in Bermuda in December, 1953, he was apprised on a Sunday morning that President Eisenhower would be attending church and the French premier, Joseph Laniel, was going to Mass. Churchill nodded sympathetically and remarked: "I shall be meeting my Maker soon enough." But he still had well over a decade to go.

At his last cabinet meeting at No. 10 Downing Street, tributes were paid and valedictory speeches delivered. There was a long pause in that room where Pitt ordered Nelson to Trafalgar, where Churchill succeeded Chamberlain in 1940, where so much history has been made.

"No one trusted himself to speak another word," one of the ministers present has recorded. "The Prime Minister looked slowly round at his friends. His last remark at his last cabinet was: 'Sir Norman Brook (the cabinet secretary), with his customary foresight, has arranged for a photographer to take our picture upstairs. Let us go. We are not a bad-looking lot.' " *

After Churchill retired, his voice was not heard again in the House of Commons until he rose to thank members for their tributes to him when he appeared in the Chamber on his eighty-eighth birthday, November 30, 1962. But he was at the House constantly until he gave up his seat at the time of the General Election of 1964, and he could attract more attention blowing his nose or adjusting his hearing aid

* Viscount Eccles, Minister of Works at the time.

than most members could by asking questions. He had political opponents, but no enemies. Enmity could not live in the presence of his magnanimity and humor. When he died in January, 1965, there were few alive in the world whose life he had not spanned—from the cavalry charge with the 21st Lancers at Omdurman in 1898 to the atom bomb on Hiroshima and the withdrawal of British troops from Suez. His great life reached out and touched almost all mankind, and for another half-century and more, men will be recalling what it was like to be alive in Winston Churchill's time.

Eden decided to go to the country immediately, and led the Conservative Party to a sweeping election victory in May of 1955. The Tories picked up an additional 24 seats in the House of Commons and controlled the new Parliament by an easy majority of 62 over Labour and Liberal combined. For twenty years, Eden had been destined for the highest office in the land, ever since he became Foreign Secretary in 1935 at the age of thirty-eight. Now he was secure in his own right with his own election victory. And as Lord Melbourne was told by a friend when he was debating whether to accept King William IV's invitation to form a government in 1834: "Why damn it all, such a position was never held by any Greek or Roman. And if it lasts only three months it will be worthwhile to have been Prime Minister of England."

Eden's tenure, which started out so positively, with such a strong election victory, was to last less than two years. The time was full of action, frustrations and eruptions, and ended in that tragic complex of political, emotional, military and diplomatic disaster, the Suez affair. It was as if, with Churchill's departure, a dam had burst for the British and a sea of troubles loosed upon them. By 1955, the process of withdrawal of British power in the world, on the whole skillfully managed (though little applauded in the United States), was reaching a point where the more the British gave up around the globe, the more vociferous and unreasonable the demands against them seemed to become. Eden, as Foreign Secretary, had already forced his party to accept two major withdrawals in the Middle East: the end of British rule over the Sudan, and evacuation of the Suez Canal base. Over the Sudan, Eden had been through painful arguments with Churchill, who had accompanied Kitchener's Army up the Nile in 1898 to avenge General Gordon's death at Khartoum and bring the Sudan under the British flag. "One of the rare occasions when we differed on a matter of foreign policy," Eden said in his memoirs. Now he had inherited the Churchillian mantle, the Churchillian watchwords: "I did not become the King's First Minister to preside over liquidation of the British Empire." Deep political and patriotic emotions were involved for Eden and the Conservative Party in maintaining British power in the world and checking the pace at which the Union Jack was being hauled down around the globe and in the Middle East especially.

But in the meantime, in the summer of 1955, the Big Four Summit Conference offered a brief interlude of pallid diplomacy and speech-making for Eden while Europe went on about its business. It also produced a deceptive lowering of tensions on the banks of Lake Geneva. Seldom in history have so few gathered in the presence of so many to say so little at such effort and expense. But at least it was mercifully brief, and the meeting of Eisenhower, Eden, Edgar Faure, and Bulganin and Khrushchev had finally quenched the British thirst for Summitry. Eden exercised his taste for reasoned diplomatic analysis and used the opportunity to invite the Russians to visit Britain. He went home satisfied, reporting to the House of Commons: "Geneva has given this simple message to the whole world. It has reduced the dangers of war." Neither Eden nor any other statesman anticipated the rapid downhill plunge of events in the Middle East.

Two months after the Summit Conference, on September 27, 1955, Colonel Nasser announced in Cairo that Egypt had concluded a deal with Czechoslovakia for arms and military equipment. Although he gave no details, clearly the deal could not have been made without Russian consent. And when British Intelligence began picking up further information a few weeks later, it learned that the agreement included much more than could ever be built at the Skoda Works in Czechoslovakia: MIG fighters, Ilyushin jet bombers, Josef Stalin Mark III heavy tanks, in addition to Czech T-34 light tanks, artillery, antitank weapons, heavy trucks and other hardware. Until that point, arms going into the Middle East—either to the Arabs or to Israel—had been fairly carefully controlled and balanced by the Big Three Western powers, who notified and consulted constantly on every machine gun or tank which they allowed to be shipped. Of course there was smuggling and there had been smaller deals outside the control of the West. But in the main, the arms balance had been kept.

The Czech arms deal with Egypt not only marked the end of effective Western control over the situation, but the beginning of the Middle East phase of Russian expansionist pressures in the world.

Since the end of World War II, the Communist thrust has shifted in distinct operations from one part of the globe to another. The first was pressure against Europe, which began as soon as the guns were stilled and continued until Stalin called off the Berlin blockade. By that time, the Marshall Plan had turned the tide of recovery in Europe, the NATO Alliance had been born, and although Czechoslovakia was absorbed in the Soviet bloc, the rest of Western Europe had held firm and Communist expansion had been checked.

From Europe, Stalin switched the pressure almost immediately to the Far East—launching the Korean war in June, 1950, and subsequently stepping up the campaign against the French in Indochina. Stalin's death in 1953, and Dulles's threat to use atomic weapons in Korea if hostilities did not end, combined to produce, at long last, the Korean armistice. After that came the Indochina settlement of 1954. But the Far Eastern phase of Communist pressure did not finally die away until after Dulles and the United States stood firm behind Chiang Kai-shek and the Nationalist Chinese at Quemoy and Matsu, the offshore islands of China, when the Red Chinese made their big challenge to seize the islands in 1955.

In the Middle East in 1955, when Anthony Eden came to power, the Russians found fertile ground for a new campaign of pressure on the West. First of all, the lifelines of commerce, trade and military power between Europe and the Orient run through the Middle East. In the Middle East lay the oil on which Europe, and Britain in particular, depended for its very economic life. The old order of British imperialism and colonial mandates was rapidly breaking down in the face of the new Arab nationalism of Colonel Nasser. For the Russians, the Middle East offered a perfect strategic flanking operation against Europe. There were plenty of young Arabs looking for support and sympathy, ripe for revolutionary propaganda, ready to charge into the streets against Britain, the West and anybody who supported Israel. To arouse and inflame Arab nationalism, and set it against British imperialism, was an obvious move for the Communists. Moreover, the Russians stood to gain a considerable subsidiary benefit out of trouble in the Middle East. They could exploit the split over Middle East policy which existed between the United States and Britain.

From the time Dulles took office—from his first Cairo visit when he presented those pearl-handled pistols to General Neguib—he set out to avoid aligning the United States in the Arab world too closely with the British. Dulles sought to shift the American diplomatic position away from the pro-Israeli posture which he inherited from the Truman administration and present the United States as sympathetic to the aspirations of Arab nationalism, anti-imperialist and anti-colonialist. As the months unfolded and trouble erupted from one Middle East country to another—in Jordan, Syria, Saudi Arabia, Lebanon, Iraq, the Persian Gulf, Egypt—this split between the United States and Britain was exposed and exploited again and again, until it culminated in the ultimate disaster of Suez. With the Czech arms deal for Egypt, Russia thrust herself directly into the embroilment, and the Middle East phase of Soviet pressure against the West did not die away until after the United States and Britain joined in the military landings in Jordan and Lebanon in July, 1958—their policies again aligned at last. At the end of 1958, a new Russian campaign began. Khrushchev switched the pressures back to Berlin, and then eventually to Cuba. In the meantime, the Middle East slipped back to its normal condition of endless internal Arab squabbles and revolts, with the Great Powers watching from the sidelines.

Although the Czech arms deal marked Russia's direct entry into the Middle East, storm signals had in fact been set much earlier. Britain's answer to the oncoming Communist offensive was the Baghdad Pact. This in turn involved Eden and Dulles in one long running argument, for the British had fully expected to find the United States in equal support of the Baghdad Pact. Instead, Dulles temporized endlessly and would never say "Yes" but never would quite say "No." Eden comments bitterly in his memoirs:

> In recent years, the United States sometimes failed to put its weight behind its friends in the hope of being popular with their foes. Having played a leading part to inspire the Baghdad Pact, the United States held back while Britain joined it, alone of the Western powers. Worse still, they tried to take credit for this attitude in capitals like Cairo. Then by a series of hesitant steps, they drew nearer the pact, sending an observer and spending money, but still not joining it. An ounce of membership would have been worth all the wavering and saved a ton of trouble later on. A devious course is disastrous. It is a borrower and lender in diplomacy and loses both itself and friend. The repeated hesitations perplexed and harassed our friends in Turkey, Iraq, Iran and Pakistan. They strengthened the Russian and Egyptian will

> to destroy the pact and overthrow the governments which supported it.*

The Baghdad Pact was signed originally in January, 1955, by those two tough anti-Communists, Adnan Menderes, then Premier of Turkey, and Nuri es-Said, Premier of Iraq. Nuri, who was slaughtered in the Iraq revolution of July, 1958, was one of Britain's closest friends and strongest supporters in the Middle East. In proposing the Baghdad Pact to the Turks, he had the full backing, if not the direct inspiration, of Eden. And he had also been given preliminary endorsement for the concept by Dulles and the United States. Strategically, the Baghdad Pact was in the Dulles mold—a kind of Middle East NATO, which, along with the Southeast Asia Treaty Organization, would complete the treaty encirclement and containment of the Communist perimeter from the North Cape to the China Sea. It would link the northern tier of Middle East states on the Russian border, and for the British offered a convenient means by which they could end their special military rights in Iraq, and place them under the new collective defense treaty before being forced to abandon them entirely.

Pakistan and Iran quickly accepted membership in the Baghdad Pact, and in April, 1955, Eden announced Britain's decision to join. Behind the scenes, Britain and its Middle East allies were urging the United States to come in too, but Dulles stuck to a position of "moral support." In the meantime, the British ceremoniously handed over their big Royal Air Force base at Habbaniya, in the middle of Iraq, to the Iraqi government, designating it a Baghdad Pact base with an R.A.F. detachment remaining there for common Middle East defense. The Union Jack had again come down in the Middle East, but British power had remained.

The first meeting of the Baghdad Pact powers took place in the capital of Iraq in November, 1955, six weeks after the Czech arms deal had been announced. My *Herald Tribune* assignment took me frequently to the Middle East during that period, and on this occasion I had even managed to make my way to Baghdad direct from Israel —out through the Mandelbaum Gate in Jerusalem into Jordan (although in theory the Arabs would not admit any travelers who had been in Israel). I drove from Jerusalem across the Dead Sea Valley to the Jordanian capital of Amman, and then flew to Baghdad, where the pact meeting was held in a charming royal palace decorated with

* Eden Memoirs, *Full Circle.*

endless mosaics and set in the center of a cool and colorful park of trees and gardens on the outskirts of the city—the Palace of Flowers it was called. Harold Macmillan was then British foreign secretary, and he flew from London along with General Sir Gerald Templer, the Chief of the Imperial General Staff. It was very much a Sandhurst and Whitehall affair, businesslike and determined, with the British showing their best stiff upper lip. But the absence of the United States was almost painful. America was all for checking Communism in the Middle East, was suitably alarmed by the Czech arms deal with Egypt, but the best Dulles could offer was to instruct the American Ambassador to sit in as an observer.

At the end of the first day's discussions at the Palace of Flowers, the Pakistan prime minister turned to the unhappy American, Ambassador Waldemar Gallman (who had continuously relayed to Dulles the urgings of the Iraq Government to join the pact), and said with a cool smile: "I think it is time we had some observations from the American observer." A few months later, Dulles inched forward to the extent of an offer of military equipment for individual members of the pact. After Suez, in 1957, the United States assigned staff officers to pact headquarters and began to participate at top level in the meetings. With the Iraqi revolution and the grizzly murder of Nuri es-Said and King Feisal, the Iraq Government swung to the left and renounced its membership in the Baghdad Pact. Files and headquarters were removed to Ankara, and the pact label changed to CENTO —Central Treaty Organization. Today, to all intents and purposes, the United States is a full and functioning CENTO member even though it still has not signed the actual treaty. But American failure to join in 1955, whatever Dulles's reasoning or logic, must be put down as another of those Eden-Dulles differences and divergencies which continuously ate away at mutual trust and understanding in the months before Suez.

At this same time, moreover—the fall of 1955—fresh trouble and additional Anglo-American differences broke out in Saudi Arabia. The Saudis suddenly occupied and laid claim to the oasis of Buraimi, a watering hole with a few coconut trees at a desert crossroads in the northeastern corner of the Arabian Peninsula. Buraimi had never been Saudi territory on any modern map, and was claimed equally by two of the British protectorate rulers of the Persian Gulf—the Sultan of Muscat and Oman, and the Sheikh of Abu Dhabi. Buraimi's importance, if any, lay in the possibility of oil in the area, but for years it had slept in the searing desert heat, an uncontested backwater and resting-place for desert caravans crossing to the Persian Gulf.

Eden promptly ordered the British-led Trucial Oman Scouts—the little peace-keeping police force on the Persian Gulf—to cross the desert and throw the Saudis out of Buraimi. At the same time, he appealed to Washington for support. In particular Eden wanted the United States to require the Arabian-American Oil Company to curtail its royalty advances to the Saudi Government, which the British were convinced were being spent to foment anti-British troubles among the tribes of the Persian Gulf. The little military operation by the Trucial Oman Scouts was carried out with suitable Lawrence of Arabia dash, and Buraimi was restored to its status as a desert oasis which three rulers claimed and nobody contested. But Saudi Arabia broke diplomatic relations with Britain, and the United States declined to offer any open support for the British action. A considerable technical problem faced the American Government if it asked the Arabian-American Oil Company to cut its advances to the Saudi Government. But more important, Dulles had his eye on the big United States airbase in Saudi territory at Daharan, and among his other ventures into Middle East diplomacy he had begun a friendship campaign with King Iban Saud in an effort to offset some of the activities of Colonel Nasser. Britain and the United States were thus at cross-purposes in yet another Middle East trouble spot.

In the wake of the November, 1955, gathering of Baghdad Pact ministers, Nasser's attack on the pact and his Arab neighbors who supported it reached that particular pitch of Arab hysteria which is turned on and turned off for so many issues and occasions in the Middle East. Receiving arms from the Communist world, Nasser was opposed to a defense arrangement designed to protect the Middle East against Communism. But more than that, he saw the pact as a British device to continue British hegemony over the area and thwart his own dreams of Arab independence and Arab unity.

Nasser lashed out with particular violence against old Nuri es-Said and young King Hussein of Jordan. Nuri, tough and scarred in many an Arab political squabble, with considerable oil revenues and the most viable nation in the Middle East, was secure—at least until he was toppled by revolution in 1958. But Jordan was fertile soil for Nasser's propaganda—a political as well as a geographical creation of British policy, a poverty-stricken little country, one-third of its population unemployed refugees from Israel, ready to put their faith and support behind anybody who promised to restore their old homes. King Hussein depended for his precarious hold on the country on his popularity with the Bedouin Arabs who inhabited the eastern deserts of his domain beyond the river Jordan. From these tribes were drawn most of the officers and men of his fine little army, the Arab Legion. But the Legion was commanded by a British lieutenant general, Sir John Bagot Glubb, the legendary Glubb Pasha who had spent twenty-five years in Jordan. In Cairo, Hussein was constantly portrayed as a puppet dangling on Glubb's strings, and it did not much help either the King's position or his personal feelings to have the British press often conveying the same picture of the Jordan Government.

King Hussein had stayed out of the Baghdad Pact despite strong British hints that he would be welcome. But in December, 1955, following the pact meeting in Baghdad, General Glubb sent a message to London advising that Hussein was now ready to consider membership. Almost immediately, General Templer, the Chief of the Imperial General Staff, was sent to Amman with an offer of additional British arms and military equipment if Jordan would join. Hussein was on the verge of signing when violent street demonstrations erupted in his capital, fomented and financed by Egyptian agents. Much British and American property was damaged or destroyed, including one of those favorite targets of mobs in the Arab world and beyond, the United States Information Service library. Eden ordered three extra battalions of paratroops flown to Cyprus, earmarked for assistance to Jordan if Hussein should ask for it. Instead, Hussein quickly abandoned plans to join the Baghdad Pact. Nasser had won the round. And for Eden and the British, worse was yet to come.

The Egyptian propaganda campaign against Hussein continued with unabated nastiness and violence. Propaganda in the Middle East is conducted with the most venomous invention and falsehood, and Nasser's was taking effect. The nationalist pressures against Hussein in his little kingdom were mounting. On March 2, 1956, the King suddenly dismissed General Glubb as head of the Arab Legion. He acted without a word of warning to Glubb, with whom he had conferred on routine Legion matters only a few hours before removing him from command. He ordered him bundled out of the country with an escort of tanks to the Amman Airport, without even allowing him time to organize his possessions of twenty-five years. In London, the news threw Eden into a state of anger which his close associates had seldom seen. He stayed up until 4 A.M. the night Glubb flew out of

Jordan, raging around the cabinet room and then later with several of his inner circle in an upstairs sitting room of No. 10 Downing Street, coming back again and again to one theme: This was the last straw, he was not going to be pushed around by Nasser any longer. Months later, after the Suez affair was over and Eden had left office, one of his former ministers who spent most of that day and evening with him told me that from that moment on, Eden was determined on a showdown with Nasser. He turned British policy firmly away from any further efforts to come to terms with Arab nationalism.

Diplomatic coincidence added insult to the British injury. As it happened, the Foreign Secretary, Selwyn Lloyd, had left London on a long-arranged trip to the Middle East and Karachi, and was having dinner with Nasser in Cairo the evening that Glubb's dismissal was ordered in Amman. Nasser was as surprised by the news of Glubb's firing as Lloyd, though certainly not upset or displeased at this show of his effectiveness in the Middle East. For the British, the humiliation continued. Lloyd flew on across the Arabian Peninsula to Bahrein, one of Britain's crown jewels on the Persian Gulf. During his stopover to confer with the ruler of Bahrein, pro-Nasser demonstrations broke out with such violence that his departure for Karachi had to be delayed for two hours while British troops were called out to join the police in clearing the road to the airport. At Karachi, yet another disappointment awaited the British. The Baghdad Pact powers were holding their second semiannual meeting, and again they appealed for more solid American support, and again they were turned down. All of this constant, cumulative twisting of the British lion's tail was driving Eden into a mood of angry frustration which was quickly conveyed through the Government.

"General Glubb was a symbol of British power and influence—almost the last visible evidence that Britain is not yet finished in the Middle East—and if weak and helpless Jordan can do this to us, how is it going to look to the rest of the Arabs?" a senior Foreign Office official exploded to me the day Glubb was fired. But at the same time, there were others in London who, while just as alarmed and upset by the downward plunge of events for Britain, were even more disturbed by the mood and attitude which was beginning to dominate the Prime Minister's actions and responses. General Glubb himself was one of these.

When he arrived in London on a cold and rainy evening in early March, with his two adopted Arab children, he took a much more temperate and calm view of his dismissal by King Hussein than was being voiced by Eden and the British press. Glubb was invited to lunch with Eden at the Prime Minister's official country residence at Chequers the next day, and at once he counseled against too rash a judgment of the young king, or too harsh a reaction. Glubb had been the close friend and confidant of Hussein's father, who was assassinated in Jerusalem in the aftermath of the Israeli war. Glubb had recognized clearly that the son, sooner or later, would want to rule in his own right. Running his own army with his own appointed commanding officer was inevitably going to be part of this aim. The fact was that Glubb himself had made pointed inquiries in London some months before his dismissal as to whether it was not time that he be withdrawn from the Arab Legion command. Eden had assured him that the British Government wanted him to stay on. Now Glubb was out, and his parting words at lunch to the harassed Prime Minister were: Keep the long-term interests of Anglo-Jordan friendship uppermost in mind; this incident will pass away. Glubb retired to the country to write several excellent books on his personal experiences in the Middle East and military studies of its past history, including a very temperate account of his career with the Arab Legion and his dismissal.

Others at the Foreign Office, as well as British ambassadors in the Middle East, were urging caution and restraint on Eden, pointing out that precipitous action against Hussein—such as the ending of British economic aid which Eden was considering—might only drive him straight into Nasser's arms. In the end, the Prime Minister held himself in check, but only barely. He himself describes his speech to the House of Commons on the dismissal of Glubb as one of the poorest performances of his parliamentary career.

By the spring of 1956, one year after taking office, Eden was also in political trouble at home. The internal economic situation in Britain had worsened to a point where the Government had to introduce an emergency budget and impose additional sales taxes to check inflation and bring the balance-of-payments situation under control. Eden had also dilly-dallied for weeks over plans to reorganize the cabinet. First it was rumored that cabinet changes were coming. Then word was passed that the changes had been called off. Finally, at the end of 1955, Eden did shuffle the cabinet, but the main result was the shifting of Selwyn Lloyd to the Foreign Office in place of

Harold Macmillan, giving the impression that Eden intended to take a much closer hold over foreign policy himself. As one who had often felt too much interference by Churchill in running foreign policy, Eden might have been expected to handle things differently when he reached Downing Street. He did not. Moreover, he was fussy and short-tempered in the conduct of government business. Outwardly he gave the impression of a cool, self-assured and even languid figure, but in his dealings with his staff and with individual ministers he was the opposite. As Prime Minister, he paid far too much attention to the London newspapers, which specialize in needling snippets of governmental gossip and leaks of news usually designed more to irritate than inform. Spotting these, morning and afternoon, Eden would be on the telephone personally to ministers often before they had seen the papers themselves, demanding to know the truth about this item or that, and an investigation as to who leaked it. Once he personally ordered the disciplining of an official in the News Department at the Foreign Office for a press conference statement which both the press and the Foreign Office found entirely justified and unexceptional, but which Eden did not like.

Eden had waited in the wings for fifteen years in the shadow of a great prime minister before acceding to power himself, and when he arrived at Downing Street his handling of government affairs never did show the coolness and the detachment which a chief mininster needs. His fussiness and temper began to inhibit the whole government machine. From every quarter in early 1956, dissatisfaction with Eden was rising and there was open talk of "Eden must go" in the Conservative Party.

"There is a favorite gesture of the Prime Minister's," said the ultra-Conservative London *Daily Telegraph* at this period. "To emphasize a point he will clench one fist to smack the open palm of his other hand—but the smack is seldom heard. The country is waiting to feel the smack of a firm government." This kind of comment, to which Eden was inordinately sensitive, was driving him, along with events in the Middle East which he could not control, to the mood of Suez.

Such was the state of Eden's political health when Nikita Khrushchev and Nicolai Bulganin checked into fashionable Claridge's Hotel in the heart of Mayfair in April, 1956. The management dutifully hung the Red hammer and sickle over the front door but surrounded it on each side with the Union Jack out of deference to its regular guests. The two Russian leaders received an absolutely correct, cold welcome during their ten days in Britain. Sizable crowds of silent citizens watched them wherever they went. The visit had one important highlight for Eden. The Prime Minister spent more than twelve hours in formal political talks with the Russians at No. 10 Downing Street. Reviewing the situation in the Middle East, Eden told the Russians that uninterrupted oil supplies were vital to the British economy. "I said I thought I must be absolutely blunt about the oil because we would fight for it," Eden records in his memoirs.*

Khrushchev responded that if this was a threat to fight a war close to the Soviet frontiers, Russia must reject it. Russia, he said, would only fight if she or the Warsaw Pact nations were attacked. What was Britain's policy? What was Eden talking about? Eden answered that he was not threatening anybody; he was simply stating a British position. Britain had no intention of being strangled to death. He spoke carefully and deliberately, and he had now issued a sober and determined war warning to the Russians in defense of British interests and British oil in the Middle East.

Eden had already talked to the United States in terms of the use of force. On his last official visit to Washington in February, 1956, the Prime Minister had proposed to President Eisenhower and Dulles that the United States join Britain and France in putting teeth, and a pledge of readiness to use force, into the 1950 Tripartite Declaration guaranteeing the existing Arab-Israeli armistice frontiers. Under the Tripartite Declaration, the three Western powers had worked to control arms in the Middle East and maintain a semblance of military balance between Israel and the Arabs. Now, with Russian arms flowing to Egypt in such large quantities, Eden argued that the *status quo* could only be maintained if the three powers declared that they were ready to intervene with force if either side attacked the other. Dulles had no enthusiasm for such a declaration for diplomatic reasons. Eisenhower declined for constitutional reasons. He could not commit the United States in advance to use of force without the sanction of Congress, and he did not think much of Eden's proposal anyway. Thus another Anglo-American divergency developed.

In all of Eden's actions concerning the Middle East, there was one common denominator: He was searching for traditional devices of power with which to shore up a declining British position. The earlier moves of withdrawal had brought neither peace nor security to British

* Eden Memoirs, *Full Circle.*

interests, and so far as Eden was concerned, Britain's back was to the wall. In May, 1955, the last British soldiers boarded troop transports at Port Said and sailed from the Suez Canal base—a battalion of the Grenadier Guards, who had fought at the Battle of Tell El Kebir in 1882 when Britain's suzerainty over Egypt had begun. The Union Jack was lowered at the mouth of the Suez Canal amid fervent and remarkably friendly Anglo-Egyptian farewells. Though much imperial spirit was still alive in London, though bits and pieces of British territory remained scattered around the globe, at that moment Britain's imperial epoch had come to an end.

As the flag came down, Eden had the satisfaction of one area of improved understanding with the United States, and that concerned the handling of Egypt's request for financial aid and technical assistance to build the Nile High Dam. The High Dam scheme was much more than a superirrigation and hydroelectric project. For Egypt it was a matter of national existence. The Egyptian population, growing at a phenomenal rate of 5 to 6 percent every year, could not, in the long run, be sustained on the existing water resources of the country. Billions of gallons of precious fresh water flood down the Nile every year and out into the Mediterranean. The High Dam project would check the Nile floods, create an enormous lake 160 miles back into the Sudan, and provide Egypt with a mighty reservoir from which to expand its irrigated land and raise its industrial and economic level to provide jobs for its expanding population.

Britain and the United States had taken a sympathetic interest in an early Egyptian request for help, and the project was turned over to the World Bank for detailed economic study. Russia, in the wake of the Czech arms deal, then threw out hints that it was ready to help on easier terms than the West might offer.

Britain and the United States, meanwhile, had agreed that the High Dam loan could be organized only if it were proven to be financially sound, if Egypt would accept financial self-discipline, and if Nasser showed a little more political cooperation with the West. In early July, 1956, the World Bank study reached the two Governments. Sufficient doubts were raised about the financial aspects of the loan to bring the British cabinet to a secret decision to turn Nasser down. By now there was certainly not much political enthusiasm for helping Nasser anyway. Consultations back and forth with Washington began, and the United States came to the same decision. But both the Foreign Office and the State Department agreed to keep the decision secret and make no hasty or precipitous moves.

But this was not to be. The Egyptians forced the hand. After the events, some Western diplomats concluded that Egypt probably had received secret intelligence that the loan was going to be turned down and saw in this decision a trap and an excuse for nationalizing the Suez Canal as a retaliation. If it was such a trap, Dulles walked straight into it, despite a warning from Maurice Couve de Murville, then French Ambassador to Washington and a former ambassador in Cairo, that blunt action by the West against Nasser would almost certainly produce nationalization of the canal.

On July 19, 1956, the Egyptian Ambassador to Washington, Dr. Ahmed Hussein, returned from consultations in Cairo with instructions to seek a point-blank American answer on the High Dam loan. An appointment with Dulles was quickly arranged. At first the conversation went in circles, with Dulles temporizing and avoiding a direct answer. But gradually an increasingly negative attitude emerged from what the Secretary of State was saying.

Finally Dr. Hussein issued a direct challenge. Egypt already had a counter-offer from the Russians, he said. (In fact, they had no such offer at that time, only hints of Russian readiness to talk about financing the High Dam.) Was the United States now saying No to the Egyptian request? Dr. Hussein demanded. Dulles, incensed by what he regarded as an attempt at blackmail, waved the Ambassador from his office, bluntly retorting that if Egypt already had the money there was no need to be talking to the United States. The possibility of American help, Dulles said flatly, was now withdrawn.

A cable went to the Foreign Office in London immediately, detailing Dulles's conversation and action. To the British, Dulles added the explanation that the Senate Appropriations Committee was about to insert a rider in an appropriation bill which would deny the use of American funds for the High Dam. This, Dulles said, would be tantamount to allowing Congress to legislate foreign policy, and this he could not permit. Therefore, he told the British, he had to act along lines agreed and cancel participation in the project. A State Department announcement of Dulles's action was issued shortly after the Ambassador had returned to the Egyptian Embassy. In London, the Foreign Office followed with a similar statement aligning Britain with the United States.

In the swirl of misunderstandings and diplomatic confusion which surround the Suez affair, it has been said or assumed that Dulles acted against British wishes in turning down the High Dam loan. This was not true—as Eden's own memoirs show. The British were taken by surprise by Dulles's abrupt timing, but there was complete Anglo-American agreement in advance on the policy. Dulles might better have left it to Congress to deny the funds in an appropriation bill, which would have created a different diplomatic climate. But it was only Dulles's method, and not the action itself, which is open to Anglo-American dispute.

One week later, on July 26, 1956, to the shock of the western world and the delirious joy of a vast Egyptian mob, Nasser announced in a speech at a political rally in Alexandria that Egypt had seized the Suez Canal that morning. Egyptian troops had surrounded the offices and installations of the French-administered company which ran the French-built canal, and had taken over all Suez Canal Company property in Egypt. An Egyptian administrator had been named to operate the waterway. All pilots had been asked to stay on the job, but the French administrative staff was being bundled out of the country. From the profits of the canal, Nasser exulted, Egypt would now build the Nile High Dam.

When the news broke, the peripatetic Dulles was in Lima, Peru, representing the United States at the inauguration of the new Peruvian president. The news reached Sir Anthony Eden in London in particularly dramatic circumstances. He was host at a formal white-tie dinner party at No. 10 Downing Street in honor of King Feisal of Iraq, then on a state visit to England accompanied by Prime Minister Nuri es-Said. Shortly after 9 P.M. a private secretary entered the dining room where the guests were all chatting amiably and handed Eden a press association bulletin from Cairo. He interrupted the conversation to read it aloud to the dinner party then instructed the private secretary, to summon several senior cabinet ministers and the Chiefs of Staff to join him later that night. The social atmosphere quickly evaporated. Everyone knew that a grave turning point in the Middle East, if not world history, was at hand.

The dinner broke up early.

The Suez crisis was on.

The Suez affair is an inglorious catalog of national misunderstandings, misjudgments and mistakes. John Foster Dulles failed to maintain solidarity and confidence with Britain and France. He did not assess fully the extent to which they believed their national rights and security imperiled. He failed at decisive moments to give them the diplomatic backing which they expected to secure their legitimate interests by peaceful means. And so, Britain and France turned to secret collaboration with Israel behind America's back and launched a small war against Egypt in the hope of toppling Nasser from power and restoring the canal to international control. They, in turn, failed to assess the wrath of Dulles's reaction. Israel alone emerged from this lamentable affair with national gain. The Egyptian Army on her borders was routed and vast stocks of Russian and Czech war booty were seized in the Sinai Desert. Israel's back-door port of Eilat on the Gulf of Aqaba was freed at last from Egyptian blockade, opening the country's sea route to the Far East.

A decade after, it is impossible to render any clear or simple judgment on who was right and who was wrong over Suez. Everybody was guilty of concealments and deceptions, little ones and big ones. Everybody made mistakes. Mistrust piled on mistrust. Nor is it clear if the use of force could at some point have been avoided. Once Nasser nationalized the canal, once Israel found her very existence in mortal danger, once Eden and the British felt their backs to the wall in the Middle East, once France was involved and aroused, and once Dulles's tortured and legalistic diplomacy not only failed to produce any positive results but in fact aggravated the frustrations of his Allies, then force became inevitable. Other men, dealing with nationalization of the Suez in other circumstances, might have avoided force. But not the men in power in 1956, acting in the temper of the times.

In Britain, seizure of the canal produced an immediate upsurge of patriotic emotion. Eden had been under heavy fire not only from the Labour Party but from many of his own supporters for his handling of Middle East affairs. His critics had argued that Britain must accept the rise of Arab nationalism and must adjust its old imperial role in the Middle East to come to terms with the political forces of the future. This, they charged, Eden failed to realize and was failing to do. But Nasser's action in nationalizing the Suez Canal shocked and stunned Eden's most outspoken critics, and he had a united House of Commons behind him as he faced the most decisive challenge to confront a British prime minister since the days of World War II. Hugh Gaitskell called the action "high-handed and totally unjustified" and urged immediate blocking of Egyptian funds and other economic sanctions. Differences over the use of force against Nasser, and above all the secret collaboration and the way in which Eden resorted to use of force, were to come later. At the outset, Britain was united. Meanwhile, in Eden's mind a parallel had formed between Nasser and Hitler. Eden had been foreign secretary in the prewar days when Britain had failed to act to halt Hitler's seizure of territory in Europe. He had resigned from the Chamberlain government in protest. Now he was Prime Minister and he would not let Nasser repeat the experience.

Across the Channel, the French reacted to nationalization of the canal almost more personally than the British. The British owned the majority of the shares in the canal; it was identified with British power, not French. But the British shares were largely in the hands of the government. They were bought by Disraeli from the bankrupt Khedive of Egypt in 1875. On the other hand, thousands of individual Frenchmen held small investments in the original De Lesseps company which built the canal, and held a concession which had been negotiated in 1888 and was valid until 1968. Although majority ownership had passed to the British, the French continued to operate the canal, which remained a symbol of French genius and French national pride.*

France's relations with Egypt were already at a low point for another reason. Cairo was the headquarters of the FLN Algerian rebel leaders, who had set up a government-in-exile, with Egypt as the main supplier of arms, money, propaganda and support for the Algerian war. Guy Mollet's government had been in office for five months when the canal was nationalized; it was already under heavy pressure from the French Army for action against Egypt. The seizure of the canal, therefore, simply reinforced existing feelings against Nasser and gave the French a better excuse for a policy of force.

In Jerusalem, David Ben-Gurion was probably the only national leader who could make a clear, straightforward, uninhibited analysis and plan of action. Israel was confronted with a very direct and simple problem: national security. No overtones of political frustra-

* The sensitivity of the Suez Canal Company's French managers to any criticism had been extreme. On a trip to the Middle East in 1955, I visited the Canal Zone and wrote a story about how few Egyptians the company was employing as canal pilots, and the likelihood that the canal would be the next target for Nasser's ambitions after the British completed their evacuation of the Suez base. When the story appeared in the European Edition of the *Herald Tribune* in Paris, the Suez Canal Company threatened to withdraw its semi-annual advertisement of its financial statement.

tion or problems of declining imperialism hindered Ben-Gurion. No debate about "understanding Arab nationalism" split the Israeli parliament. No qualms about the morality of using military force troubled the Israeli nation. No sense of big power responsibility for "maintaining peace in the world" clouded the view from Jerusalem. The very existence of the State of Israel was at stake, and increasingly the Israelis saw only one answer: remove the threat to their security by military force. Ben-Gurion had returned to power in Israel early in 1955, and as Communist arms poured into Egypt and Fedayeen saboteurs crept across the border to terrorize the Israeli countryside by night, he had stepped up retaliation raids against Jordan, Egypt and Syria. These had been limited set-piece battles, short and sharp. But they had not halted the Fedayeen raids, and the Western powers had done little to protect Israel or even to help Israel protect herself against Communist arms and the changing military balance.

But now, by nationalizing the Suez Canal, Nasser and Egypt were also threatening the vital interests of France and Britain. In this situation, was there not a natural alliance for Israel? Did not Israel, France and Britain all have a common interest in bringing Nasser to heel? In utter secrecy, while maintaining an outward appearance of composure and calm along with a plaintive hopefulness that her interests were not being overlooked, Israel began actively seeking the political and diplomatic support and above all the military equipment which she needed to attack and destroy the Egyptian forces in the Sinai Desert.

Across the Atlantic, John Foster Dulles, as he flew hastily back to Washington from Peru, was faced with a maze of conflicting considerations. He had tried to accommodate his policies to Arab nationalism, while still maintaining working relationships with Britain. But the Communists were outbidding him in support of the Arabs. He thought colonialism immoral, and he had contrived that the United States should not be identified with colonial interests. But nationalization of the canal, and the threat to the old imperialist order, was a direct challenge to the security and the peace of the world. It was a blatant violation of international law, and Dulles believed above all else in the rule of law. The 1888 concession had recognized that the canal would one day revert to Egypt, but a legal violation of an international agreement had taken place. Suppose Panama decided to follow Nasser's lead and seize the Panama Canal regardless of the legal fact that the United States has a permanent concession across

Panamaian territory? Dulles was faced with contradictions from every side. In the end, sifting through the cross-currents to determine what American policy should be, Dulles did not find any compelling or strong United States identity of interest with Britain over the Suez. The canal was a vital British lifeline, but it was not directly vital to American commerce or the American economy. It was part of the imperial past. There was the general interest of maintaining Anglo-American understanding and the unity of the West in the face of Communism. But for Dulles, this general interest certainly did not extend to fighting the Egyptians. Above all, President Eisenhower was about to run for a second term, and the overriding theme of the election campaign was to be Peace. Peace, then, must dominate Dulles's policy —peace at any price, even the price of misunderstanding and indicting one's closest allies.

As the crisis opened, all eyes were on London. What would British reaction be? After bidding good night to King Feisal and Nuri es-Said—Arab leaders of the old order who felt as much threatened by Nasser as the British themselves—Eden and a few of his ministers and the Chiefs of Staff gathered in the cabinet room for a first survey of the situation. Eden asked the French Ambassador to London, Jean Chauvel, and the American chargé d'affaires, A. B. Foster, to join in the discussion so they could report directly on British reaction to their governments. Action to block Egyptian sterling balances in London was ordered prepared that night, along with a survey of British domestic oil reserves. British military dispositions were reviewed, and first diplomatic moves were discussed.

The next day, Eden dispatched a personal cable to President Eisenhower. It said in part:

> We are all agreed that we cannot afford to allow Nasser to seize control of the canal in this way, in defiance of international agreements. If we take a firm stand over this now, we shall have the support of all the maritime powers. If we do not, our influence and yours throughout the Middle East will, we are convinced, be finally destroyed. . . .
>
> We should not allow ourselves to become involved in legal quibbles about the rights of the Egyptian Government to nationalize what is technically an Egyptian company, or in financial arguments about their capacity to pay the compensation they have offered. I feel sure that we should take issue with Nasser on the broader international grounds. As we see it, we are unlikely to attain our objective by economic pressures alone. . . . We

> ought in the first instance to bring maximum political pressure to bear on Egypt. . . . My colleagues and I are convinced that we must be ready, in the last resort, to use force to bring Nasser to his senses. For our part we are prepared to do so. I have this morning instructed our Chiefs of Staff to prepare a military plan accordingly. . . .*

With Dulles still away in Peru, Eisenhower decided to send Robert Murphy, the veteran career diplomat and Deputy Undersecretary of State, to London immediately with simple instructions to "hold the fort" and report what the British were doing and saying. On his second night in London, Murphy sat down to dinner with two old friends from wartime days, Harold Macmillan and Field Marshal Lord Alexander. Macmillan was Chancellor of the Exchequer in the Eden Government, and the dinner took place at his official residence at No. 11 Downing Street. Murphy, in his memoirs, records that Macmillan was categorical and explicit on British readiness to use force against Nasser. Alexander elaborated on details of the military plans which were being prepared. Troop movements would start soon in August, he said to Murphy, and it "would not take much to chase Nasser out of Egypt"—at the most two divisions. Murphy returned to the American Embassy after dinner and cabled a summary of the conversation to Eisenhower. The next morning the President answered that Dulles would fly to London. Meanwhile, Murphy continued his rounds with a luncheon meeting with Eden, at which he found much less candor about plans to use force, but "a confident assumption that the United States would go along with anything Britain and France did." Eden told Murphy: "We do hope that you will take care of the Bear"—meaning Russia, if Russia sought to step in. Murphy comments in his memoirs: "I gave no encouragement to the idea." **

From the outset of the Suez affair right through to the climax, Eden never apparently could accept or realize that the United States was bluntly opposed to force against Nasser and would not support Britain if she restorted to its use. Eden consistently acted on a different assumption. Either the American attitude was never made sufficiently clear to him, or he chose to interpret American statements to suit his own ideas. Wherever the fault lay, this was one of the basic misunderstandings on the road to Suez.

When Dulles arrived in London he brought a message from Eisen-

* Eden Memoirs, *Full Circle*.
** Robert Murphy, *Diplomat Among Warriors*.

hower which, Eden says, "was emphatic upon the importance of negotiation" but "did not rule out the use of force." Murphy, on the other hand, gives quite a different account of Eisenhower's attitude. The President, he says, held "a strong personal conviction that fundamental principles were involved—that the United States could not be a party to this type of military operation in view of its support of the rule of law and the United Nations Charter, and in view of what Eisenhower considered the injustice of insisting on these principles in the case of smaller powers if we were to wink at violations by greater powers."

During the first round of the London talks, Eden took Dulles aside for a private conversation. He told him that the United States naval attaché had been inquiring about British fleet movements and military plans, and said that Britain was quite prepared to give this information if the United States really wanted to have it. Dulles responded that the United States well understood the purpose of British preparations. But he thought it preferable, he told Eden, that the United States should not seek detailed information.

Dulles made similar comments on British military preparations at a background news conference which he gave before leaving London. He said that he thought a buildup of force could have a useful effect on the situation. To add to Eden's subconscious feeling that he had American approval, if not outright support, Dulles asserted that seizure of the canal was intolerable and Nasser must be made "to disgorge." In Eden's comment, these were "forthright words; they rang in my ears for months." All the same, Eden, after his long experience with Dulles, should have allowed for the fact that the Secretary of State always covered all possibilities, and always left himself plenty of room for maneuver.

Christian Pineau, the French foreign minister, flew from Paris to join the discussions with Murphy and Dulles, and he quickly proved himself to be a great deal more waspish, aggressive, and determined on action against Egypt and Nasser than even the British. Barely concealing his attitude in diplomatic language, he as much as told the Americans that they were simply naïve about the Middle East. He pointed to what Egypt was doing to support the war in Algeria (which failed to arouse Dulles's fighting instincts) and was impatient of legalistic or diplomatic formulas to deal with the situation. France wanted action. In separate talks with the British, they were getting it.

On August 2, Eden announced the call-up of some 20,000 reservists. The Royal Navy began de-cocooning four tank-landing ships. Sixty Canberra jet bombers and several squadrons of Valiant heavy bombers were alerted for transfer to military airfields in Malta, Cyprus, Libya and Aden. On August 5, as Macmillan had predicted to Murphy, 1,000 men of the British Paratroop Brigade loaded full equipment on the aircraft carrier *Thesus* and sailed for the Middle East. Britain would soon have three divisions in the area.

But Dulles had succeeded in those first talks in London in his first diplomatic aim—which was to get the canal problem onto a legal basis. This was just what Eden had sought to avoid in his first cable to Eisenhower. Nevertheless, the British and French agreed with Dulles to issue invitations to twenty-two powers to attend a conference in London on August 16 to discuss a joint policy of all interested nations for future control of Suez. The Big Three agreed that there was nothing to be done to stop Nasser from nationalizing the canal. But there was an international treaty covering the Suez waterway, and the aim of the Western powers was to continue international supervision and control over the canal, regardless of who owned the property.

Egypt, as was expected, declined to have anything to do with the meeting. In the end, eighteen nations accepted, including Russia. The conference lasted one week, and from Dulles's standpoint it was a considerable diplomatic success. Seventeen of the eighteen nations—with only Russia opposing—agreed on a set of principles to be put before the Egyptians as the basis for negotiating a new international treaty to establish an international control. Egyptian sovereignty, ownership and rights to revenues were respected. But how to get Egypt to agree?

Australian Prime Minister Robert Menzies flew to Cairo on August 31 as head of an international delegation to present the plan to Nasser. First he had an informal private meeting with Nasser, of which he wrote: "I said to Nasser that I was not making threats. But frankness as between two heads of government required me to offer my personal opinion that he was not facing a bluff but a stark condition of fact which his country ought not to ignore." Nasser thanked him, acknowledged his national responsibility, and said he did not regard British preparations as a bluff. But by the time formal talks with the Menzies mission began, he had stiffened.

Menzies says: "He had, like the rest of us, read in the morning newspapers a statement of policy of the United States Government which said in headlines, 'There Must Be No Use of Force,' and if the proposals of the London conference were rejected, others must be considered. From that time on, Nasser felt he was through the period of danger."

President Eisenhower had held a press conference in Washington at which he had said: "We are determined to exhaust every possible, every feasible, method of a peaceful settlement. I am still very hopeful that the London proposals will be accepted; but the position of the United States is not to give up, even if we do run into obstacles. We are committed to a peaceful settlement of this dispute, nothing else."

It is debatable whether these comments from Eisenhower were really decisive in stiffening Nasser's attitude. In any event Egypt rejected the London proposals, and there is no debate about the fact that both Menzies and Eden believed that the American statements and the American attitude were working against British interests. Three days after the London proposals were killed in Cairo, Eisenhower sent a personal message to Eden stating flatly that American public opinion rejected the use of force. But Eden's reply leaves the impression that he did not regard this as an expression of what Eisenhower and the American Government would actually do if force was employed as a last resort. The Prime Minister drafted a long telegram reiterating that his first objective was a peaceful settlement. He then compared Nasser's actions to those of Hitler and the Russians in the Berlin blockade. After citing the penalties of failure to head off past dictators and the success that had flowed from standing up to the Berlin blockade, he concluded with Churchillian rhetoric:

> I can assure you that we are conscious of the burdens and perils attending military intervention. But if our assessment is correct, and if the only alternative is to allow Nasser's plans quietly to develop until this country and all Western Europe are held to ransom by Egypt acting at Russia's behest, it seems to us that our duty is plain. We have many times led Europe in the fight for freedom. It would be an ignoble end to our long history if we accepted to perish by degrees.

By the time this cable had been sent from London on September 6, secret military plans were already well advanced. A joint Franco-British planning staff had been established in London, and a joint headquarters for operations against Egypt was being set up on the island of Cyprus. At the end of August, first elements of French forces arrived in Cyprus from Algeria to join British reinforcements which continued to pour into the Middle East. British liaison officers had been assigned to French headquarters in Algiers for coordination of troop movements and military operations.

The planners proposed two possible lines of action. The first plan called for landings at the Mediterranean port of Alexandria (in Napoleonic style) and an advance up the Nile Delta to seize Cairo, with the simple aim of removing Nasser from power. The second plan was aimed directly at the Suez Canal—paratroop drops at Port Said and Port Fuad on either side of the mouth of the canal, to be followed by infantry and tank landings, and then an infantry and armored car advance up the length of the waterway.

Neither plan was particularly imaginative, and in the midst of preparations Field Marshal Lord Montgomery, then still deputy Supreme Allied Commander in Europe, got wind of what was being proposed and hastened to London. He saw Eden, and told him in typical Monty style that "it's all wrong—the planners have got it wrong, quite wrong." Monty urged that the operation be based on four paratroop drops—one at Port Said, two others to seize old British base installations along the middle of the canal, and a fourth at Port Suez at the end of the canal. This, he said, should be supported by the Royal Navy in the Red Sea. Monty argued that it was a mistake to undertake a World War II type landing and a lateral advance along the canal which would be subject to constant flank attacks and street-fighting harassments. He believed that four strong paratroop drops would throw the Egyptians into complete confusion, that they would not be able to organize sufficient counterattack strength to wipe out the paratroops, and that seaborne forces could then be put into Port Said and Port Suez to link up with the units in the center of the canal. Meanwhile, the whole length of the canal would be in British and French hands in one operation.

In view of what finally happened, Monty's recommendations made a lot more sense than the plan which was adopted. But the Field Marshal's advice was not taken for one very simple reason. The British did not have a sufficient airlift capacity to launch a paratroop operation on the scale Monty was suggesting. More than that, they were having to call up paratroop reservists for a crash program of jump-training to get ready for even the limited plans. The French were in much better shape for paratroops, but not sufficiently to do it Monty's way. In the end, the "Alexandria plan" was deliberately leaked as a cover, to entice Nasser to draw forces away from the canal and back to the delta to protect Cairo, while the operation at Port Said and the mouth of the canal was adopted.

But while these discussions and arguments were going on, secret contacts of far greater significance were taking place between France and Israel. Not even the British knew of these until later in the game, for the simple reason that the French, determined to provoke military action in the Middle East, wanted no interference from anybody. Complete secrecy was even more important to the Israelis.

In early August, some ten days after Nasser seized the canal, the Israeli Government, having surveyed the changed outlook in cold calculation, sent the senior civil service head of its Ministry of Defense, Simon Peres, to Paris with instructions to seek French agreement for the purchase of a large order of additional military equipment for the Israeli forces. The Israelis did not approach the British for two reasons. First, the British had a treaty of alliance with Jordan. Second, the Israelis did not trust British reaction to their proposal and foresaw endless consultations with the United States, newspaper leaks, questions in Parliament. On the other hand they reasoned that this was just the kind of politico-military coup which would stimulate the French sense of intrigue and power diplomacy.

The French took one look at the Israeli shopping list and readily realized what the Israelis had in mind. Among the items was a request for 125 AMX-13 tank destroyers—an extremely mobile French-designed desert weapon, a high-velocity 75-millimeter gun mounted on a lightly armored chassis which rode on four huge wheels at speeds of up to thirty-five miles an hour. The Israelis had already obtained a small order of these weapons after the Czech arms deal with the Egyptians. Accordingly they had plenty of trained crews. All that was needed was one big order to fill out the equipment tables and turn the Israeli Army from an essentially defensive posture into one of offensive readiness. The implication was perfectly clear to the French, who wasted no time in concurring.

It would take time to acquire, manufacture and ship the arms, and elaborate cover plans were worked out by the French and the Israelis to conceal what was underway. The Israelis had acquired considerable experience since 1947 in the art of obtaining arms in secret. The French, for their part, simply ceased to notify Britain and the United States of arms sales to the Middle East. This drying up of French information under the Tripartite Agreement passed unnoticed in

Washington for some weeks. Meanwhile false destinations and bill-of-lading descriptions were assigned to arms cargoes, and ships rerouted at sea after clearing French harbors. Aircraft which the Israelis ordered took off with false markings for secret delivery. It was an old game to both sides. After I arrived in Israel during the Suez fighting, the United States military attaché in Tel Aviv told me that the deliveries had been so skillfully concealed that the American Embassy had only begun to get first reports of the arrival of the big order of AMX-13s at Haifa about ten days before the Israeli attack. Even then, all that the Embassy knew was that unusually heavy arms cargoes were being unloaded. The United States never did get the full details until it was all over.

Of these secret preparations by France and Israel the United States Government was completely unaware during August, September and October, almost to the eve of the Israeli attack. The possibility that Israel might strike at Egypt does not even appear to have entered into Dulles's calculations—probably because he assumed that the Israelis did not have sufficient arms. And certainly the United States did not believe its Allies to be capable of secret collusion with Israel to start a war. All the same, on September 23, David Ben-Gurion told a rally of his political followers in Tel Aviv: "Israel at last has one true Ally." And after Suez was over, Pineau told the French National Assembly: "We knew the intentions of Israel. Was it not natural that our two Governments should consult?"

Meanwhile, with the failure of the Menzies mission and the Egyptian rejection of the London proposals, Britain informed the United States on September 7 that it wished to take the dispute to the United Nations Security Council. Dulles, for a complex variety of reasons, not only objected to going to the U.N., but informed the British that "it would be very difficult to go along with the operation" in the form which Britain planned. Instead, the ever-fertile legal brain came up with a new scheme—to organize the Suez Canal Users Association as a kind of holding operation against Nasser. A second conference was called in London, and SCUA was duly formed. If SCUA had any usefulness at all, it was to collect canal tolls and withhold them from Egypt until the Egyptians agreed to new international control arrangements for the waterway. But Dulles, after thinking up the scheme and getting the canal users to join, had to inform the British and the French that he saw no way of compelling American users to pay canal dues to the association instead of to the Egyptians. Of the SCUA plan,

Robert Murphy says: "If Dulles ever actually was convinced of the possibility of a Canal Users Association to operate the Suez Canal, I was not aware of it. It seemed to me that he was skillfully working for time in the hope that public opinion in Western Europe would harden against a military adventure."

When Dulles returned to Washington after the SCUA conference in London, he told a press conference on October 2: "There is talk about teeth being pulled out of the SCUA plan, but I know of no teeth; there were no teeth in it, so far as I am aware." In short, Nasser did not need to worry that Dulles's SCUA plan would have any real effect on the situation. The Secretary of State then went on to divest himself once again of his views on colonialism.

"The United States cannot be expected to identify itself one hundred percent either with the colonial powers or the powers uniquely concerned with the problem of getting independence as rapidly and as fully as possible," he said. "There were, I admit, differences of approach by the three nations to the Suez dispute. . . . For while we stand together, and I hope we shall always stand together in treaty relations covering the North Atlantic, any area encroaching in some form or manner on the problem of so-called colonialism finds the United States playing a somewhat independent role."

Dulles had now told Nasser—and Britain and France—that the United States would support its Allies in the North Atlantic, but not, necessarily, anywhere else in the world. The failure of the Menzies mission was already laid at Dulles's door by Eden. Dulles had declined to support a British appeal to the Security Council. Dulles had invented SCUA and then declined to give it any real backing. Dulles was trotting out the old colonialism bogey at an extremely difficult time for the Atlantic Alliance. He may have been playing for time, as Murphy says, but the effect on Eden, Mollet and Pineau—as well as Ben-Gurion in Israel—was to harden them in just the opposite direction. Force loomed as the only recourse.

Eden and Selwyn Lloyd flew to Paris on September 26 for another bilateral meeting with Mollet and Pineau. In his memoirs, Eden is circumspect on all aspects of British-French-Israeli "collusion." He deals in vague hints and allusions, leaving more questions asked than answered, and the September 26 meeting remains veiled in generalities.

Much else of course has been written about Suez, some accounts bitterly biased against Eden, fiercely pro-Egyptian, and anti-Israeli.

Other accounts throw the blame for Suez just as heavily on John Foster Dulles. Much also has been recounted in private conversations which cannot be directly quoted, involving matters of what was said in cabinet discussions and state secrets. Today the basic pattern of events is clear, but details are still missing, important details, and it is in fact questionable whether it will ever be possible for anyone to put together a fully documented, detailed history of the Suez affair. Key decisions were taken at secret meetings where no records were kept. Possibly one day private notes on these meetings will emerge.* At the time of Suez, I was London correspondent for the New York *Herald Tribune,* and I spent three weeks in Israel during and after the fighting. In the years since, I have had numberless talks with British, French, Israeil and American diplomats, civil servants, military officers, cabinet ministers and ex-ministers who were involved in the events in varying degrees. But in the end, one is still left with a portrait in which the focus and color of the eyes, or the shape of the mouth, is still ultimately to be filled in.

Of the September 26 meeting in Paris, Eden records that "the French favored [military] action at an early date." Britain, on the other hand, thwarted by Dulles from going to the United Nations earlier in the month, pressed this as the next step. The French reluctantly agreed, on the explicit understanding, in Eden's words, that "we must not allow our case to be submerged or maneuvered into some backwater." Meanwhile all evidence points to the fact that the French still did not disclose to the British how far their secret collaboration with Israel had gone. In terms of cold, calculating power diplomacy, the French played by far the cleverest hand over Suez.

Blame, analysis and judgment over Suez always turns on Dulles and Eden—but without French collaboration with Israel, kept secret until the very hour of the attack, the Suez war could not have happened. And on September 26, the French still held their secret from the British. Eden knew in a general way that the French were holding talks with Israel. But Eden was not yet "at the brink" on the use of force. He was still talking in terms of going to the U.N., and he had refused to go along with French urgings for action at an early date. The French, being as astute as they are calculating, were not going to let Eden in on the full picture of the Israeli

* At least one member of the Eden Government has committed everything he knows about Suez—which is a great deal—to a manuscript which lies in a London bank vault.

operation until he was ready to commit himself to a policy of force.

As Aneurin Bevan said in the House of Commons after it was all over, in one of his telling and memorable debating classics: "Did Marianne take John Bull to an unknown rendezvous? And on the way was there a forest fire, and did John Bull say, 'We ought to put it out'? And did Marianne then say, 'No, we ought to warm our hands by it'? Did Marianne deceive John Bull, or seduce him?"

While Dulles played for time, he did not realize or did not appreciate that there were no inhibitions of public opinion whatsoever operating against the French and Israeli Governments. The French were already fighting the Arabs in Algeria, and the Israelis were fighting them almost every night outside their own homes. Neither France nor Israel gave a damn about the "larger moral issues" which preoccupied Dulles, or about "the same rules for great powers as we apply to small powers when it comes to using force" which preoccupied Eisenhower, or the provisions of the United Nations Charter which were supposed to preoccupy everybody. As often happens in international affairs, this was not a question of moral right or wrong, but of stark political fact. And the fact was that both Israel and France were determined to use force against Egypt.

In early October, Selwyn Lloyd and Christian Pineau flew to New York to direct the Franco-British appeal to the Security Council of the United Nations. The French, meanwhile, got down to serious and detailed military talks with the Israelis. Up to this point, they had talked military supplies and equipment. Now they turned to specific discussions of how, where and when the Israelis planned to attack Egypt, and what kind of additional military support they needed from France. In a new whirl of secret visits, Major General Moshe Dayan, the Israeli Chief of Staff, Colonel Yehashafat Harkabi, Director of Intelligence, and Simon Peres, who had negotiated the original arms deal, all visited Paris. At these meetings, Israel unveiled its plans for the Sinai attack and the help which it needed beyond its own resources: high-level air cover for Tel Aviv, Haifa and the skies over Israel while the Israeli Air Force was committed to action in the Sinai Desert; naval screening of the Israeli coast against heavier units of the Egyptian fleet; and additional transport and supply aircraft to drop supplies for Israeli forces as they moved into Egyptian territory.

On October 15, General Maurice Challe, then French Air Chief of Staff (who later was one of the leaders of the Revolt of the Generals in Algeria and is now in jail), flew to London to disclose the full details of Franco-Israeli plans to the British. By this time the last diplomatic operation at the United Nations had ended in another victorious stalemate for Dulles, producing no change and no breakthrough toward any political solution. Eden and the British were now at the brink on the question of force. What was needed was a *reason,* an *excuse* for military intervention. An Israeli attack against Egypt and the Suez Canal would certainly provide one.

On that same day, Selwyn Lloyd returned to London and Pineau to Paris from the discussions in New York. Before leaving they had gathered with Dulles in his suite at the Waldorf-Astoria for a last conversation. The Security Council had accepted a resolution of six principles to govern future operation of the canal, but the Russians had vetoed an accompanying part of the resolution which called upon Egypt to negotiate. Thus things were very much as they had been after the eighteen-power conference in London. Everybody had agreed on principles for new international arrangements for control of the canal. But nobody was applying any pressure to force Egypt to cooperate. Lloyd that evening pleaded with Dulles for the last time to withhold American shipping tolls from Egypt through SCUA, or at least make the gesture of stopping Americans from accepting jobs in Egypt as Suez Canal pilots. Dulles, however, continued to play his waiting game and chaffed Pineau and Lloyd about the military buildup on Cyprus. He even waved an admonishing finger at Pineau and said, "I know that you think if you use force after our elections we will take no action, but let me tell you now, we will!"

Dulles, according to one of his close associates, had begun to feel that something was being concealed from him by the British and the French, and that he was not really getting frank speaking and a meeting of minds. The United Nations operation was over and a dead end had been reached. But neither Pineau nor Lloyd had anything to say to Dulles on "where do we go from here." Dulles was quite right to feel as he did. The British and the French had given up following Dulles's diplomacy.

But the Secretary of State was satisfied with the outcome in New York, and President Eisenhower even proclaimed in an election speech that "it looks like here is a very great crisis that is behind us." The real crisis was only two weeks away.

When Selwyn Lloyd returned to London on October 15, Eden and the British Chiefs of Staff were at last in possession of full information on Israel's preparations, with French support, to attack Egypt. Eden had been scheduled to see Mollet and Pineau in Paris on October 18, but he hastily made arrangements to fly to the French capital with Lloyd the next day. For the better part of five hours on October 16, the four men were closeted alone without advisers or interpreters. Of this crucial meeting, no details have ever been disclosed. Eden's account in his memoirs is delightfully disingenuous:

> We asked the French ministers to do everything they could to make clear to Israel that an attack on Jordan would have to be resisted by us. This they undertook to do. It was not only our own treaty engagements which concerned us, but the effect upon Iraq of events in Jordan. . . . If Israel were to break out against Egypt and not against Jordan, this dilemma would not arise. For this reason, if there were to be a break out, it was far better from our point of view that it should be against Egypt. On the other hand, if the break out were against Egypt, then there were other worries, for example the safety of the canal. . . . In common prudence, we had to consider what our action should be, for our two countries were, as we knew, the only powers to have effective military forces at our command in the area. . . .*

It does not take much retrospective reading between the lines to amplify the implications of these words. Eden could not have worried for long about Israel attacking Jordan. The Israelis were well aware of Britain's treaty arrangements with Jordan. The Israelis were quite clear that Egypt was the strategic enemy—not Jordan. It was Egypt which had made the big arms deal with the Communist bloc, and it was Egypt which at that very moment was putting together a joint military command, linking Syria, Jordan and Egypt under an Egyptian field marshal.

True, the Israelis had been engaged in increasingly heavy retaliation raids across the Jordanian frontier, climaxed by a particularly big assault in mid-October on the town of Qalqilya. When Israeli mobilization began on October 25, all of the troop movements appeared to be in the direction of the Jordan frontier—but in fact these menaces at Jordan were the Israeli cover plan to conceal the main operation in the Sinai.

Often the speck-on-the-map geography of Israel is cited as a besetting military weakness, and it certainly is a weakness in many respects—particularly air defense. But the Israelis fight on very short

* Eden Memoirs, *Full Circle.*

lines of interior supply and communication. They can shift forces with great rapidity from the Syrian frontier in the north to the Egyptian frontier in the south, or from the Lebanese border to the Jordanian border. On the other hand, the Arab armies which face Israel are at the end of long supply lines, and above all they are uncoordinated. Jordan, in 1956, had no decent supply port or harbor. Egypt's massive stocks of Communist equipment were strung out in storage along desert roads. Syrian forces facing Israel are miles from any port or railroad. As for the joint command which the Egyptians organized on the eve of the Suez attack, the only order which it is known to have issued was a declaration in Cairo releasing Syria and Jordan from any obligation to attack Israel in support of Egypt.

At the Paris meeting of October 16, the next-to-the-last piece in the jigsaw of collaboration was put in place. Israel would attack Egypt, probably in two weeks, and this would provide the excuse for Britain and France to intervene, in Eden's words, to secure "the safety of the canal." Eden's main discussion with the French was over the terms of the intervention. The French were in a "damn the torpedoes" mood and would happily have gone into Suez in direct support of Israel against Nasser, without any political double-talk. But Eden needed a formula.

The British could not be as uninhibited as the French. First they had their treaty relations with Jordan and Iraq to consider. Reaction of the Commonwealth was always on Eden's mind. He wanted to satisfy his own moral doubts about the use of force, and he knew that there would be strong Parliamentary opposition from the Labour Party. Finally he was looking for a formula for intervention to satisfy his misplaced hope that the United States would adopt an attitude of understanding, if not support. The formula which the British and the French agreed upon was, therefore, that after the Israelis attacked, they would "act to separate the belligerents," and occupy the Suez Canal to stop the war from spreading!

One more secret conference—the most secret of all—was needed. On October 23, David Ben-Gurion arrived at Villacoublay airfield from Tel Aviv and was whisked to the luxurious security of a French government villa at Sèvres, about halfway between the center of Paris and Versailles. For the next thirty-six hours, Ben-Gurion was locked in final conferences with Mollet, Pineau and French and Israeli military staffs. On the evening of October 23, Pineau flew suddenly to London for dinner conversations with Selwyn Lloyd, using Northolt

Military Airfield. Lloyd then returned secretly to Paris that night in Pineau's plane to join the talks at Sèvres with Ben-Gurion on the morning of October 24. He was back in London in time to answer questions at the House of Commons at 3 o'clock that afternoon.

Ben-Gurion flew back to Tel Aviv during the night of October 24–25, and from his desk that afternoon he pressed the mobilization button. On the morning of October 26, Israelis began flocking to mobilization stations. The Suez war was now only a matters of hours away.

Of the military side of the Suez story, the most intriguing unanswered question concerns the timing of the Israeli attack—specifically, did the Israelis jump the gun on their Allies and launch the war in advance of the original timetable with the French and the British? Nobody has ever disclosed exactly *what* was agreed at Sèvres and in earlier Franco-Israeli staff talks, and it is therefore impossible to give a conclusive answer. But all of the circumstantial evidence indicates that the Israelis did jump the gun.

The Israelis attacked on October 29. Britain and France served their joint ultimatum on Egypt and Israel ("pull back ten miles from the canal on each side") on October 30. The first British and French paratroops did not land at the mouth of the canal until November 5, and the seaborne British Commando force did not hit the beaches at Port Said until November 6. By that time, the Israeli campaign in the Sinai was effectively over. Despite all the collaboration and collusion, the actual military operations turned out to be scarcely coordinated at all. Why such a long gap between the start of the Israeli operations and the landings by the British and French?

The circumstantial explanation is that it was all *supposed* to be closely dovetailed and coordinated, but the Israelis kicked off in advance of the starting date by about three days. The British and French were unable to speed their somewhat ponderous military timetable for one simple reason: the time it takes to sail a tank-landing ship from Malta across the Mediterranean to Port Said—five to six days.

This was the straitjacket which controlled the Franco-British military plan. The paratroops and infantry were all on Cyprus, ready to go. But Cyprus had no hard loading facilities, so the tanks to back up the landings after the paratroops had been dropped had to be loaded at Malta. Orders to load the tank-landing ships were flashed to Malta on October 28. Assuming that the original Israeli D-day was supposed to have been November 1 or November 2, the tank-landing ships would already have been at sea, and after a twenty-four-hour interval for the ultimatum to the Egyptians and the Israelis, the Franco-British landings in the canal would have come while the Israelis were still pushing across the Sinai. But instead of a tightly coordinated military and political timetable across five or six days, events sprawled across ten days.

There are a number of plausible reasons for assuming that Israel jumped the gun. The first is that the United States had begun to sense that something was definitely in the wind. By the time Ben-Gurion returned to Tel Aviv from the Sèvres meeting, the U.S. had definite intelligence of the delivery of additional aircraft to Israel by the French and the arrival of heavy arms shipments at Haifa including the AMX-13 tank destroyers. Since the U.S. had received no official notification of these arms sales through the Tripartite machinery, it would not take much guesswork to suspect that something big was going on in secret. The United States radio relay center and monitoring station on Cyprus, surrounded by French and British troops and military staffs, had noted a marked increase in coded traffic between Paris and Tel Aviv. Ever since Dulles's last conversation with Selwyn Lloyd and Pineau at the Waldorf-Astoria in mid-October, messages to the State Department from the French and British had dwindled down to a point where Dulles was now convinced that he was being kept in the dark about something. Ben-Gurion had begun to receive messages from President Eisenhower, in the final stages of his election campaign, urging restraint and moderation.

Not only were American suspicions rising. The fact that the British were now actively involved in a three-way collaboration was not all that reassuring to Israel. If the United States did manage to piece together what was going on, it would bring heavy pressure to stop it first of all on Britain. Eden was much more susceptible to political pressure from the United States, the Commonwealth and elsewhere than the French. (When the operation was finally underway, Eden did, in fact, signal the British commander-in-chief at Cyprus, Lt. Gen. Sir Charles Keightley, on November 4, and ask if military movements which had begun could be suspended or held up. Keightley refused, saying that the choice was either to call off the whole operation or to go forward.) In a sense, the fate of the enterprise was in the hands of the British. The Israelis, by launching their operations against Egypt at once, on their own, eliminated the possibility of any last-minute doubts or changes of heart in London. It did not matter to Ben-Gurion that the Allies still had to load their tanks at Malta. All that Israel required was the shifting of a few French air squadrons to fields in Israel and support of the French fleet and French air transport, all of which was easy to put into operation. To sit too long on an agreed military plan, with everybody ready to go, would in any case have been a considerable security risk.

Finally, the Israelis wanted the Sinai victory over the Egyptians for themselves. If their operations against Egypt coincided too closely with the British-French landings, then the outcome might look more like a victory which depended on Allied help. Israel wanted to make it absolutely clear to all the Arab states on her borders that she had established a military superiority which could not be challenged. The Israelis wanted their five-day Sinai campaign to stand out by itself, as a separate victory from whatever happened when the British and French landed on the canal. And so, on October 25, Ben-Gurion pressed the button.

A few hours before news of the Israeli mobilization reached London, Eden summoned a full meeting of the cabinet to discuss, in his words, "the specific possibility of conflict between Israel and Egypt and decide in principle how it would react if this occurred." This was, in fact, the first time that the full British cabinet had been confronted with the state of affairs in Suez. At the outset of the crisis when the canal was nationalized, Eden had formed a small inner cabinet of six ministers, functioning on the war cabinet model, and all of the policy-making decisions had been confined to this group. At the Foreign Office, ony two senior officials knew of the Eden-Lloyd discussions with the French in Paris on October 16 and the extent to which plans and preparations for action over Suez had gone. Even at the cabinet meeting of October 25, it was still possible for Eden to conceal from the rest of his ministers the extent to which Britain was a party to collusion. In a narrow sense, Eden had contrived to keep the British one step removed from the actual dealings with Israel. He had left direct collusion to the French. But he was aware of what was going on, and he concurred in joining in military action. Now all he had to do was present the cabinet with a "hypothetical possibility." The inner secrets of Suez, and how Britain went to war, were concealed in the British Government to the very end.

Eden says that "I have been a member of many governments in times of nominal peace; I have not known one more united on an issue of first importance." But two junior ministers resigned over Suez—

Anthony Nutting from the Foreign Office and Sir Edward Boyle from the Treasury. Six career diplomats and three senior officials of other departments considered resigning. One key department head was persuaded to stick to his job only as a result of a conversation with a close friend at the American Embassy. Cabinet ministers who remained loyal to the Government throughout the ensuing weeks were nonetheless shocked and deeply incensed at the way the Prime Minister confronted the Government with the Suez war.

On October 25, there was little that the cabinet could do but break up in protest or follow Eden's lead. The senior ministers stuck together. The bitterness was to come later, when the wreckage of Britain's position in the Middle East was complete, and the extent of Eden's secret dealings became known to the rest of the Government. Meanwhile, the cabinet agreed, Eden says, that in the event of war between Israel and Egypt, "the Governments of France and the United Kingdom should at once call on both parties to stop hostilities and withdraw their forces to a distance from either bank of the canal. If one or both failed to comply within a definite period, then British and French forces would intervene as a temporary measure to separate the combatants. To ensure this being effective, they would have to occupy key positions at Port Said, Ismailia and Suez." *

Throughout history, governments have usually drafted ultimatums for the purpose of enabling leaders to do what they intend to do anyway, while seeking to shift blame and responsibility to the opponent. No British minister worthy of holding the seals of office could possibly have believed that the Egyptian Government would docilely withdraw its own armies from the banks of the Suez Canal, its own national territory, and peacefully admit the military forces of Britain and France. When a copy of the ultimatum was handed to American Ambassador Winthrop Aldrich for the information of the United States Government five days later, Aldrich could scarcely believe that it was a serious document. Its only purpose was to provide Eden with a fig-leaf excuse for military action and his showdown with Nasser.

While these last secret decisions launching the Suez war were being made in London, Paris and Tel Aviv, the eyes of the world were on Budapest. The Hungarian revolt against Communist rule began on October 23—the day David Ben-Gurion flew to Paris—and events were gathering speed every day. For five days, stories of the agonizing heroism of the Hungarian Freedom Fighters filled the headlines, and

* Eden Memoirs, *Full Circle.*

then Khrushchev and the Russians moved with brutal and overwhelming force to extinguish the rebellion. Russia was in deep political trouble in Eastern Europe, and in no position to make any very rapid or pronounced response to the outbreak of fighting in the Middle East. This may well have been another of the calculations of Ben-Gurion in his decision to order mobilization as soon as he returned to Israel.

The Israeli attack on Egypt began at approximately 4 P.M. on Monday, October 29, with a paratroop drop on Egyptian fortifications in the Mitla Mountains, forty miles east of the Suez Canal, and about 130 miles west of the Israeli frontier with Egypt in the Sinai Desert. The Israelis deliberately chose an objective deep in Egyptian territory for two reasons. First, they wanted it known at once in Cairo that this was the real thing and not just another retaliation raid. They hoped for a panic reaction. Second, they believed that by striking well behind the main Egyptian forces in the Sinai with a paratroop drop, they would throw Egyptian defense plans into confusion. It would mean that part of the Egyptian Army, at least, would have to turn around and face the other way. Late afternoon was chosen for the timing of the paratroop drop on the assumption that the Mitla fortifications could be overrun and secured before nightfall, leaving no time for the Egyptians to organize any air support or counterattack before dark. By the time a counterattack could take place the next day, the Israeli forces would be dug in and relatively secure. All these assumptions worked out as planned.

It was shortly after 9 A.M. Washington time on Monday when news of the Israeli attack reached the State Department—just as John Foster Dulles was exulting over the appalling display of Communist brutality which had reached its climax in Hungary. Now his mood turned to bull anger—according to his associates, the maddest he ever got in his four years at the State Department. Dulles turned at once to organizing a counteroffensive against Israel in the United Nations. He did not yet know that Britain and France had already decided to intervene with force against Egypt.

On Tuesday morning, as Israeli infantry columns began spreading out across the Sinai Peninsula in various encirclement movements against the Egyptian Army, Pineau and Mollet rushed to London to have lunch with Eden and press for the immediate launching of the British and French paratroop drop at Port Said. The French had been impatient all along with the rather ponderous British staff plans and had been prepared to send their paratroops into action against the Egyptians without waiting for a tank buildup from Malta. Had all been going according to the original plans, the French desire for dash and the British desire for tanks would have been combined in one operation. But now the Israeli attack was underway, the tanks were still five days from Suez, and the French wanted to go into action as soon as the planned ultimatum expired. But Eden insisted on sticking to the military plans as agreed. Pineau and Mollet flew back to Paris immediately after lunch.

At 4 P.M., Eden rose in the House of Commons to announce the terms of the ultimatum to Egypt and Israel. It was greeted on the Labour side with derisive incredulousness. A debate "on a matter of urgent public interest" was arranged to begin at 7 P.M. During the evening, Eisenhower cabled a personal appeal to Eden to call off the ultimatum and the threat of force. In New York that same night, Dulles and Henry Cabot Lodge rushed a resolution condemning Israeli aggression to the Security Council—where it got far speedier handling than similar resolutions over Hungary, and in the end was vetoed shortly before midnight by the British, using their veto in the United Nations for the first and only time.

At the end of a tumultuous House of Commons debate, the Conservative majority held solidly behind Eden and his policy of intervention on a vote taken at 11 P.M. Eden returned to No. 10 Downing Street and convened a midnight cabinet meeting to discuss Eisenhower's appeal to call off the ultimatum. But the decision was confirmed and orders went to Cyprus to proceed with military operations as planned from 4 P.M. on Wednesday, November 1.

On Wednesday morning, I had gotten the last available seat on an Israeli Airlines flight to Tel Aviv, but at Rome in midafternoon came word that the flight would be held overnight. It was at this point that the veil of secrecy which had clouded even the possibility of collusion between Israel, France and Britain began to lift. The El Al pilot, wearing two rows of ribbons from the Battle of Britain and the wings of the Royal Air Force on his airline tunic, joined the table where I was enjoying a plate of spaghetti with an old acquaintance who was on the flight, Harry Zinder, director of Radio Israel, and a dark-eyed and rather dramatic young lady named Yael Dayan, the daughter of Major General Dayan, the Israeli Chief of Staff. Miss Dayan was rushing home from New York to volunteer for two years' military service, required of all young Israelis, men and women.

"From here on we will be flying under wartime conditions, under R.A.F. control from Cyprus," the pilot said casually. "The bombings of Egypt are beginning, and they have a lot of military traffic moving north-south from the Cyprus control area. We have to get clearance to cross that, more or less east-west. Also in Israel they have stopped all day time flying except for military sorties. We've been instructed to land at Tel Aviv blacked out just after dark for security reasons. So we will be here overnight, leave late in the morning, stop in Athens during the afternoon and then get to Tel Aviv around 10 o'clock tomorrow night."

The kind of detailed operational arrangements which the El Al pilot described to us could not have been put together in the hours since Eden had announced his ultimatum to Egypt. Clearly there had been some kind of advance joint preparations by Israel, France and Britain for this moment—and evidently pretty thorough preparations at that. But this was still a matter of mystery and speculation.

We flew on to Tel Aviv on Thursday, landing shortly after 10 P.M. in a blackout at Lydda airport. I took a taxi straight to the Government Information Office, where the latest news was that an artillery bombardment of the Gaza Strip had begun that afternoon and was being followed up by a night infantry attack. Meanwhile, in the thirty-six hours since I had left London, an Israeli desert column had struck straight across the center of the Sinai to join up with the paratroop force that had been dropped 130 miles inside Egyptian territory at Mitla. Once these forces were linked, the Israelis turned south along the coast of the Gulf of Suez, in a rough overland trek across trackless desert with supplies and gasoline dropped from aircraft. With complete surprise, they descended on the little Egyptian fort of Sharm-el-Sheikh at the southern tip of the Sinai Peninsula where the Gulf of Aqaba empties into the Red Sea. While this was going on, an Israeli Navy motor patrol boat had been transported by truck overland through the Dead Sea Valley and launched in the Gulf of Aqaba at the Israeli port of Eilat. Egyptian guns at Sharm-el-Sheikh had been silenced, the Gulf of Aqaba was being patrolled by the Israeli Navy, and Israel's back door on the sea was now freed of Egyptian blockade.

In the north, Israeli brigades hooked around behind the Egyptians to seize the towns of Abu Aweigia, Rafa and El Arish, with sizable military supply dumps falling to the invaders intact. The Gaza Strip was thus cut off from reinforcements and left to the last.

The Gaza Strip, approximately ten miles wide and thirty miles long, contained the biggest concentration of Arab refugees on the Israeli borders, some 250,000, and was the operational center of the fedayeen raids. Often on previous trips to Israel I had visited the little Israeli kibbutz settlement of Nahal-Oz, right on the border of the Gaza Strip, and peered through binoculars across the flat and fertile ten miles sloping down to the seacoast. Napoleon marched through Gaza on his way to the Siege of Acre in 1799. The railway from Cairo to Jerusalem runs through the town, now cut at the Israeli border. The terrain was dominated by an old Turkish fort where the British, under Allenby, fought a bloody battle with the Ottoman forces on their way to the capture of Jerusalem in 1917. By the afternoon of Friday, November 3, Israeli troops had secured the town of Gaza, although there was still some sporadic shooting going on, and the Army had thoughtfully kept a bus standing by at Nahal-Oz to take waiting correspondents on a tour of the town before dusk fell. The Sinai campaign was over.

Israel was now suddenly the dead center of the cyclone which it had loosed on the Middle East, calm and quiet as events swirled with such emotion, force and repercussions. Eight French Air Force pilots who had been turning up in uniform to drink in the evening at the Dan Hotel bar in Tel Aviv flew away. Major General Dayan held a press briefing to review the campaign, and acknowledged that the British-French air strikes against Egypt "had a major effect" in enabling the Israeli forces to move without fear of air attack. All the same, the Israelis had their victory over the Egyptian Army, clean and fast, and the big problem which General Dayan now faced was moving vast stocks of captured Egyptian, Russian and Czech war booty back to Israel.

While the Israelis were winning their lightning victory, tank-landing ships of the Royal Navy were steaming with agonizing slowness across the Mediterranean toward Suez. Bombing of Egyptian military targets by the Royal Air Force began on the evening of October 31.* The Russian Ilyushin bombers which the Egyptians had received prudently took off for Khartoum and Saudi Arabia, far from the scene of action. But a disastrous five-day hiatus now ensued for the British and the French. Only the swiftest and most effective possible military action

* One RAF pilot refused orders to take off on a bombing mission. He pulled the landing gear of his Canberra and wrecked the aircraft in the middle of a runway of Nicosia Airfield, putting the runway out of use for nearly an hour at a particularly tense time. He was later court-martialed.

by the British and the French could have made a success of Suez—if success, indeed, was possible. Instead, the Israelis had now won their victory and almost all military purpose or surprise had gone from the operation when British and French paratroops at last dropped out of the skies on Port Said and Port Fuad at 8 A.M. on Sunday, November 5. In the early hours of Monday, the first Royal Marine Commandos arrived at last with the tanks from Malta and went ashore to begin the advance down the canal. They had moved twenty-three miles along the waterway when Britain bowed to the United Nations cease-fire order and called a halt at midnight. During the afternoon of November 6, Guy Mollet telephoned Eden from Paris and pleaded with him to keep going. But Eden had had enough.

Political pressure against Britain in particular had become enormous—but there was one very simple reason for not going on. By the night of November 6, the fighting *had* stopped. The Egyptians had given up. It would have been indefensible for British and French soldiers to go on walking up the canal, guns at the ready, with the avowed purpose of ending fighting which had already ceased.

Britain was feeling much more than political pressure. The Treasury informed Eden that a massive run on sterling had begun. British reserves dropped by $37 million in September and $84 million in October—but with the Suez ultimatum, Britain's gold and dollars began melting away at a fearful rate, totaling a whopping $279 million before the month was out, about 15 percent of the total currency resources. Harold Macmillan, preparing to go to the International Monetary fund, was told flatly by the United States Treasury that America would not agree to any IMF borrowing until Britain complied with United Nations resolutions for a cease-fire and withdrawal from Suez. The Commonwealth was nearing a state of political collapse, with India openly threatening to withdraw from membership if Britain did not order the fighting stopped.

In the United Nations, Henry Cabot Lodge had the bit in his teeth. A Republican election victory was still to be won on November 7, and Lodge relentlessly pressed for the arraignment of Britain, France and Israel. He had the enthusiastic support of the Soviet Union, anxious to distract attention from its own brutality in Budapest, and America's Allies were allowed none of the delays for discussion, none of the procedural twists and blockings, which had brought U.N. action over Hungary to a halt.

Behind the gunfire of Hungary, the Russians, after first reacting cautiously, now sent a letter to Eden which in effect threatened nuclear war against England in defense of Egypt. Eden considered returning the letter as unacceptable. Although nobody in Washington, London or Paris took the Russian threat very seriously, Russia has claimed credit ever since for forcing acceptance of the cease-fire in the Suez.

Richard Nixon gleefully inserted in a wind-up election campaign speech: "For the first time in history we have shown independence of Anglo-French policies toward Asia and Africa which seemed to us to reflect the colonial tradition. This declaration of independence has had an electrifying effect throughout the world."

President Eisenhower telephoned his old friend Anthony Eden over the new transatlantic cable circuit which had just come into operation the week of Suez. Britain had by then agreed to the cease-fire, the election was over, and Eisenhower sought in a personal way to take some of the bitterness out of the situation. Eden suggested an early meeting, and Ike agreed. Eden hung up in elation, and telephoned Mollet at once to arrange that they should fly to Washington that very evening. But an hour later, Eisenhower was on the phone again. He had thought it over, he said, and as he would be busy with Congressional affairs in the next few weeks, the meeting should wait until there had been Anglo-French compliance with the various United Nations resolutions.

At the height of the crisis Dulles, who was pouring all of his relentless energy and legalistic know-how into bringing Britain and France to heel, suddenly developed intense abdominal pains and entered Walter Reed Hospital for an emergency operation. Robert Murphy says in his memoirs:

> Many British newspapers blamed the American Secretary of State for the Suez fiasco, but their bitter comments did not bother Dulles. In fact, he seemed to enjoy their attitude. If they wanted to assign to him, rather than to Eisenhower, the dominant role in our Suez policy, that did not displease Dulles. And gradually, largely as reaction to this Suez criticism, Dulles's reputation grew in stature.*

And so the cease-fire was ordered, and next the arguments began about withdrawal of British, French and Israeli troops from Egyptian territory and their replacement by a U.N. peace keeping force. In fact, it was March 7, 1957, before the last Israeli troops pulled out of

* Robert Murphy, *Diplomat Among Warriors.*

the Gaza Strip, leaving a U.N. force to insure that the fadayeen raids into Israel were over forever.

On November 22, Eden's health broke under the strain. He had never been in completely sound physical condition since a series of bile duct operations in 1952 and 1953. Now, under the strain of long hours and unremitting pressures, the bile duct troubles had returned, and he suddenly was seized with feverish exhaustion. His physician, Lord Evans, ordered an immediate, complete rest for a period of at least three weeks.

Eden called in his senior ministers and gave them the news that he must take immediate leave. They nodded in sympathetic agreement. Then Eden said, "I am going to Jamaica."

There was an uncomfortable silence.

"Prime Minister, of course we understand and agree to the need for an immediate rest, but why Jamaica? Why not the south coast, or Cornwall?"

Eden snapped that he needed to get away completely, and he needed warmth and sunshine.

"But, Prime Minister, you have taken the country into war. You cannot leave England under these circumstances."

"Clarissa has arranged it and we are going to Jamaica," Eden retorted. The ministers left the room. Eden and his wife flew off the next day to the Jamaica home of novelist Ian Fleming while the cabinet wrestled on in the November and December gloom with the political, economic, military and moral wreckage of Suez. Even had Eden's health recovered, he could not have recovered his ascendancy over his own ministers.

The most eloquent, the simplest summation of the Suez affair came from Aneurin Bevan, speaking in a House of Commons debate in early December, just after Britain had agreed, one month after the Suez landings, to pull her troops out:

> "The social furniture of modern society is so complicated and fragile that it cannot tolerate the jackboot. You cannot run the processes of modern society by attempting to impose your will upon nations by armed force. We must not believe that because Eden is wrong, Nasser is right. That is not the view taken on the Labour side of the House and never has been. What has deeply offended us is that such wrongs that Nasser has done, such faults as he has, have been covered up by the bigger blunders of the British Government."

The same could well have been said of the Suez diplomacy of John Foster Dulles.

Sir Anthony and Lady Eden returned from Jamaica on December 13. The bile duct fever kept recurring. On January 8, 1957, he traveled to Sandringham where Queen Elizabeth II was spending the New Year's season and told her of the advice which three doctors had given him. He must retire. The Queen returned to London, and Eden turned in his seals of office in a formal audience at Buckingham Palace on January 9. He and his wife sailed ten days later for a long recuperative rest in New Zealand on the other side of the globe.

Eden had shot the last bolt of Britain's imperial history, and finished himself with it.

7. Britain: From Suez to Europe

When Sir Anthony Eden left office, he did not give the usual advice of a retiring prime minister to the Sovereign as to who should be summoned to form a new government. If a prime minister's party is defeated in a general election, he automatically recommends that the Sovereign send for the victorious Leader of the Opposition. If he retires for health or other reasons, while his party is secure in power, he almost always suggests a successor from his own cabinet. Only twice before in more than a century and a half has a new prime minister of England been named by the Sovereign without the formal advice of his predecessor. In 1894, Queen Victoria deliberately snubbed the retiring William Ewart Gladstone and did not ask for his advice. She had already made up her mind to send for Lord Rosebery, in preference to Lord Spencer whom she knew Gladstone wished to recommend. In 1922, Bonar Law resigned from office in the advance stages of throat cancer, and was physically unable to advise King George V on a successor. The King was faced with a difficult and delicate choice between Lord Curzon and Stanley Baldwin, and after seeking the opinions of a number of Conservative leaders, he decided to send for Baldwin.

Until Eden's private papers are available, or an official historian has access to the records of the reign of Queen Elizabeth II, it will probably not be known whether Eden decided not to offer the traditional advice to the Queen, or whether the Queen, following the Victorian precedent, deliberately avoided asking him to recommend a successor. In his memoirs, Eden gives no explanation and in fact does not even refer to the matter at all. His personal choice almost certainly would have been Richard Austen Butler, his deputy in the cabinet. But both Eden and the Queen were probably aware that there was considerable opposition to Butler. As one of his fellow cabinet ministers later wrote: "His habit of hedging his political bets was too great a weakness, and this had damaged his position both in the Conservative hierarchy and in the Parliamentary party." * To have advised the Queen formally to send for Butler would have created a very difficult constitutional and political situation, and the Conservatives were already in difficulties enough in the aftermath of Suez. It was therefore better that Eden gave no advice, whether credit for this prudence lies with the Queen or the outgoing prime minister himself.

There now ensued one of those obscure oligarchical rituals by which the Conservatives of England choose a man from their hierarchy to lead the party and govern the country. The Labour Party always names its leader and potential prime minister by a secret ballot of party members in the House of Commons and the House of Lords—a straightforward and democratic method which establishes the Party's choice clearly and without any mysticism. But the Conservatives use a system which is euphemistically called "the usual processes of consultation"—and this can mean anything from a weekend houseparty at some stately home to a conversation over a glass of port at the Carlton Club or a judiciously timed editorial in *The Times*.

When Eden left office, public speculation and expectation about his successor centered almost entirely on "Rab" Butler, who was known to be his favorite, but behind the scenes a very different atmosphere prevailed. Shortly before 3 o'clock on the afternoon of Wednesday, January 9, 1957, the Marquess of Salisbury, leader of the House of

* Lord Kilmuir, the former Sir David Maxwell-Fyfe, chief British prosecutor at the Nurenberg War Crimes trial, who has told the full story of how Macmillan was chosen over Butler in his autobiography *Political Aventure*.

Lords and Lord President of the Council in the Eden cabinet, called on the Earl of Kilmuir, the Lord Chancellor, in Kilmuir's private apartment in the House of Lords overlooking the Thames. Salisbury, a member of the Cecil family which had served England since the reign of Queen Elizabeth I and a close personal friend of Eden's, brought the news that Eden would inform the cabinet of his decision to retire at 4 P.M. and go to Buckingham Palace immediately after to turn in his seals of office. The news came as no great surprise to Kilmuir, as Eden has discussed the possibility with him only the week before. Salisbury and Kilmuir were the two senior ministers in the cabinet who, as members of the House of Lords, were automatically out of the running to succeed Eden. Salisbury, moreover, was evidently also aware that there would be no "advice to the Queen" on a successor. He and Kilmuir decided that the choice would lie between Butler and Harold Macmillan, Chancellor of the Exchequer in the cabinet, and that the quickest and best way to organize the "usual consultations" on this occasion would be to poll the rest of the cabinet individually and in secret as soon as Eden left for the Palace.

They drove together to the cabinet meeting, and after a brief session at which Butler, Macmillan and Salisbury all paid tributes to Eden, the Prime Minister left No. 10 Downing Street fighting back tears. Meanwhile, Kilmuir and Salisbury asked the other ministers to remain behind and come one by one through a private passage from Downing Street to Salisbury's Privy Council office in the Old Treasury Building a hundred yards away. Complete secrecy was preserved, and the story of the Cabinet poll and how Macmillan was selected over Butler did not leak out until months later.

The interviews were brief and to the point. As each minister entered the room, Salisbury, who has a slight lisp, simply said with a smile, "Well, which is it, Wab or Hawold?" The vote was never disclosed, but it was overwhelmingly for Macmillan by a margin of something like 19–4. Thus was a new prime minister chosen in the oldest parliamentary democracy in the world! Next morning, after further soundings among Conservative back-benchers in the House of Commons, Lord Salisbury visited Buckingham Palace to inform the Queen of the results of "the usual consultations." The Queen then sent for Sir Winston Churchill to ask the opinion of the Tory's elder statesman. Churchill also endorsed the choice, and on the afternoon of January 10, the Queen summoned Harold Macmillan to Buckingham Palace. When the telephone call came, Macmillan's wife was distracted with the problems of a sick grandchild. Macmillan walked into the room and said, "I've been called to the Palace." His wife replied, "What on earth do *they* want?" He explained to her gently that he was about to become Prime Minister of England.

Harold Macmillan held office for six years and nine months until illness forced his retirement in October of 1963, just short of the modern record of seven years and one month set by Asquith from 1908 to 1915. Most of his time in office, Macmillan dominated the British political scene. He was Britain's strongest peacetime prime minister in this century. He was not a great prime minister, but he ran his government with extraordinary effectiveness and political skill and he controlled the country completely. No member or faction of his own party challenged his leadership, and he administered a sharp election defeat to the Labour Party in 1959. Had he succeeded in his bid to take Britain into Europe, Macmillan might have gone down with greatness, as a prime minister who had indeed made history for his nation. But the prize was dashed from him by President Charles de Gaulle, and Macmillan's last year in office was a dismal and at times farcical tragicomedy.

Next to Winston Churchill himself, Macmillan had a wider variety of ministerial experience when he arrived at Downing Street than any other prime minister in modern times. He had entered Parliament in 1924, and he waited long years on the back benches before receiving his first government post in 1940. But then he moved from one department to another in the wartime government and when the Conservatives returned to power in 1951: Ministry of Supply, the Colonial Office, the Air Ministry, the Ministry of Housing and Local Government, Minister of Defense, Foreign Secretary and Chancellor of the Exchequer. From a personal standpoint, perhaps the most valuable period of office for Macmillan was outside the country from 1942 to 1945, when Churchill sent him to Algiers and later Italy to serve as British minister-resident at Allied Force Headquarters. In this post he functioned as British political adviser to General Dwight D. Eisenhower, and was also in close and constant contact with General Charles de Gaulle. He made much of these old comradeships when he became prime minister.

In ministerial experience as well as personality and temperament, Macmillan was a marked contrast to Eden, who had spent almost his entire career dealing with foreign policy. Macmillan not only knew a great deal more about mundane problems of economics and domestic affairs, he had none of Eden's fussiness or nervous temper, and although he was a tough and ruthless politician who could make harsh decisions, he was a very calm, urbane and relaxed chief minister. His calm quickly communicated itself down through the government after the disaster of Suez. He left ministers alone to work out their own problems and run their own departments. He liked brevity in paper work and cabinet discussions, and he presided over a very efficient and smooth-running government machine. He knew how to stick to essentials of high policy and let others get on with the job of carrying out day-to-day business. Where Eden was excessively sensitive, Macmillan was practically impervious to criticism. He paid little or no attention to the newspapers except to glance at them and find out what was going on.

Macmillan was a politician to his fingertips. Like President Johnson, he looked for political effect in practically everything he did, every move he made. He had great political style—so much so, in fact, that it was difficult to tell where style stopped and sincerity started. His style centered on a cultivated Edwardian image of slightly foppish, old-fashioned appearance and manners. The Eden image had been that of the confident statesman, bareheaded or wearing a black Homburg, mounting the steps of the League of Nations at Geneva. With Macmillan, it was baggy tweeds, gumboots and a shotgun on the grouse moors of Yorkshire when the shooting season opened every August 12, floppy cardigan sweaters, plus-fours and a tweed cap on the golf course, or the gray topper and morning dress at the Ascot Races or the Derby—all with a faint odor of mothballs which served to establish his particular political personality and identity. In keeping with this Edwardian image, Macmillan was a devoted London clubman. He belonged to five clubs in London, and he liked to turn up casually at Pratts or the Beefsteak or occasionally that citadel of Toryism, the Carlton, when he had no official engagements for lunch or dinner. One evening he walked out of Downing Street and climbed into his limousine without telling anyone where he was going, and an hour or so later, the White House was on the "Red Line" telephone which connects the Prime Minister's residence with Washington. President Eisenhower wanted to speak with the Prime Minister. Frantic calls went out around London until Macmillan was finally located having dinner with some fellow members at Buck's Club. He took the call in the phone booth in the hall. The Macmillan image was a godsend to the London cartoonists. Unflappable Mac, Mr. Mac-wonder, Super-Mac, Mac-the-Knife, all blossomed in the London papers from the cartoonists' pens. Sometimes the drawings were savage cariacatures of bewilderment or dissipation. But Macmillan was too shrewd a politician not to realize that even these were indirect tributes to his political domination.

Macmillan was no great orator, and in fact most of his speeches were banal beyond belief. "We have not done badly. We have done quite well even. But we have not done quite well enough. We have just got to make an extra effort," was a typical Macmillan passage. Or again: "Some things are not so good. We must strive to improve them. And what is bad must be eradicated." He could occasionally make a speech of vision and vigor, as when he courageously told the South African parliament that "the winds of change are blowing" in Africa, and when he smoothly sold the Conservative Party on the cause of joining Europe in a speech to the annual Party conference in October 1961 without the Conservatives quite knowing what was happening. But in the main, Macmillan was remembered for catchphrases rather than speeches, quotable lines such as "You never had it so good" which became the campaign slogan of the 1959 election, or his "There ain't gonna be no war" when he returned to London from a session of the United Nations General Assembly.

Nevertheless, he was a political master of the House of Commons, not in the Churchillian style of massive domination and pungent wit, but with a technique of elusive deftness. Macmillan had humor, but he was no great wit. Clement Attlee, when he was Labour Prime Minister and used to have to answer Macmillan's debating attacks, once described him as "an elephant who thinks he's a flea." But by the time Macmillan became prime minister, he knew all of the Parliamentary tricks of both asking and answering questions, and he knew how to use the advantages which the man at the dispatch box holds when he is doing the answering. He was exasperatingly difficult for the opposition to corner. He kept his statements in Parliament and his answers to questions short and perfunctory, leaving it to his opponents to chase him round and round trying to pin him down. And he then usually contrived to convey the greatest respect and courtesy —even an irritating sympathy—for his interrogators while evading them.

Behind this elusive, urbane, Edwardian exterior, Macmillan had a ruthlessness which often shook his closest cabinet colleagues. He had dozens of associates and acquaintances, but few friends. His personality was scarcely winning, and he was too much the complete politician for trusted friendships. He ran the cabinet and the government very much on the English public school model. He was headmaster, and beneath him at a distance there was always a head boy and after that there were senior prefects and prefects jockeying for position and hoping to catch a nod of approval. The relationship and the distance were always kept. Moreover, when one head boy in the cabinet seemed to be getting too far out in front, Macmillan would shuffle the government to put everybody off balance and start the game of "who is head boy now?" all over again. In July, 1962, he fired Lord Kilmuir on barely four hours' notice, after eight years as Lord Chancellor, and dropped the faithful Selwyn Lloyd from the cabinet at the same time in a shake-up which caused much bitterness in the Conservative Party.* Much earlier, Lord Salisbury, who with Kilmuir had arranged the cabinet poll which brought Macmillan to power, quit the government in protest over Macmillan's decision to bring Archbishop Makarios back from exile in order to start solving the Cyprus question. Macmillan paid scarcely any attention at all to this defection of one of the high priests of the Conservative Party. He called it "a little local difficulty" and flew off next day to visit Australia. At the end of his premiership, from his hospital bed after undergoing an emergency prostate operation, Macmillan devoted a last burst of political energy to blocking the unfortunate Rab Butler from No. 10 Downing Street once more, maneuvering the "usual consultations" in the Conservative Party so that he could advise Queen Elizabeth to name Sir Alec Douglas-Home as his successor.

Macmillan's skill and effectiveness as a prime minister lay in his technique of leading without getting too far out in front of his own party or the country. After Eden's disastrous political misjudgments in every direction over Suez, Macmillan contrived a smooth, soft approach to Britain's problems, never overexposing himself to attack. He liked to get things done while pretending that nothing very important was really happening. For example, he completely reversed the Eden approach to Britain's colonial problems—beginning with his decision to bring Makarios back from exile and end the EOKA war in Cyprus. Under Macmillian's premiership, almost every one of the remaining British colonies was either given self-government and independence or a timetable for eventual independence. This was per-

* "Sacked like a pregnant chambermaid," was the sardonic comment of another minister who was dropped in the same shuffle.

haps the most solid achievement of his era. It was an obvious and necessary policy which did not involve any particular political courage or choice, but it did involve political skill. Macmillan brought it off with such success that the Conservative Party, which had cheered Eden and the Suez operation to the rafters, turned around and developed a positive enthusiasm for bidding good-bye to the old Empire and presenting new parliaments with a carved chair for the Speaker, a mace, and leather-bound volumes of the *Rules of Parliamentary Order*.

At the same time, under Macmillan, Britain settled down to a period of comfortable if somewhat deceptive prosperity. There was a job for almost everybody who wanted one, money to spend, plenty to buy, easy credit terms and a little bit of inflation. In fact, beneath the surface Britain was steadily being outpaced in economic growth by most of the rest of Europe, Britain's share of world trade was falling, and the British were constantly running into problems of trade deficit and balance of payments. But these uncomfortable realities were not allowed to worry the public, or for that matter, the Government. Along with the aura of prosperity, the Conservatives ushered in new laws to ease restrictions on life and living—a new gambling act, lottery bonds, longer pub hours, late closing hours for nightclubs.

Macmillan thus produced the image of a modern and forward-looking government presided over by a skillful old Edwardian. He could be irritatingly disappointing for an intelligent and experienced political leader. I recall going to see him for a talk alone in the fall of 1960. I asked him how he saw the future developing for Britain—in particular, relations with France, Europe and the Common Market. If the question was not particularly original or profound, it was a subject which seemed worth discussing with the British prime minister. "Oh," said Macmillan with a wave of his whisky glass, "there's no time to think of the future in my job. It's enough to keep up with the problems that cross the desk every day." I know that the Prime Minister must have thought about the future, but that was that. He was not a man to focus national issues, define the realities or stir up public discussion or launch any "great debate" about the state of Britain. He never forced the country to take a hard look at the problem of Britain's long-term economic stability and strength. He never questioned the declining competitive state of British industry and the problem of lagging economic growth. He never defined a consistent British defense policy. The same was true of British agriculture, of the archaic state of British trade unionism, of the realities of the Commonwealth and its declining importance for British trade and foreign policy. Macmillan preferred to watch from a safe distance and allow problems to emerge, and then step in, hopefully, in time to be out in front without being overtaken. This was particularly true in the case of Britain's relationship with Europe. From 1959 onward, British entry into the Common Market was a matter of intense debate and discussion among industrial, political and intellectual leaders and in the press. But Macmillan stayed aloof, gave no impetus or lead. He waited until the summer of 1961 before deciding that it was time to get out in front—by which time Europe was far stronger economically and the negotiation much tougher than he had anticipated.

With all of his political skill, there was a large streak of the thespian in Macmillan's actions, words and gestures. Months after he left office, he remarked in a reminiscent conversation: "The great thing in politics and government is to be able to play the game—and watch at the same time. Winston had that ability to a wonderful degree, and so did your President Kennedy. . . ." Plainly, he thought that Harold Macmillan did also. Macmillan did play the game and watch at the same time, but with attitudes of self-satisfaction, smugness and a shallowness that betrayed the rest of the image. Hugh Gaitskell, the Labour opposition leader during most of the Macmillan era, had a dislike and mistrust of the Prime Minister which far exceeded the usual antipathies of politics. Gaitskell's private opinion of Macmillan was that he was "an actor, and a bad actor at that." And one of Macmillan's senior cabinet minister echoed the same assessment with different emphasis after the Prime Minister retired. "The trouble with Harold was that you could never really tell when he was acting and when he was being genuine and real, even in a cabinet meeting," he said to me.

In the end, events overtook Macmillan, and it was impossible for him to play the game effectively and enjoy watching at the same time. His old comrade General Charles de Gaulle showed how little he cared for style and friendship in matters of national interest when he slammed the door on British entry into the Common Market. Then came the Profumo scandal—the war minister who lied to the House of Commons about an affair he was having with a call girl, who was also having an affair at the same time with the Russian naval attaché in London. Macmillan was not a man to run away from disaster, but illness forced him out. When photographers went to take his picture as he was recuperating at his country home from his prostate operation, they asked if he had any comment on public affairs. He waved them away in the grand manner with the curtain line from Pagliacci.

"La commedia è finita!" the former Prime Minister said.

The Conservatives of England are a political party unlike any other in the rest of Europe or the modern world. They are the repository of the aristocracy, wealth, land and capital of Britain to an overwhelming degree, and the rank and file of the Conservatives are possessed of a simple faith in the superiority of their own patriotism and the divine right of their party to govern England. The Party attracts the essential floating vote partly through a kind of inverted snobbism, and more positively because of the ability of the Conservatives to govern intelligently and well. All the same, the dyed-in-the-wool Conservative regards possession of the Government as part of the Conservative heritage and tradition—snatched away from the Party occasionally by lesser men, but always returned when the country comes to its senses. Nowhere in the West does a political party identify itself so synonomously and possessively with national destiny as Britain's Conservatives. As long as they are in power, the Conservatives never lose faith in Britain. That is why it scarcely even occurred to the Conservatives to quit or ask the country for a new vote of confidence after the disaster of Suez.

British power, prestige and political influence in the Middle East were in ruins. The Commonwealth had almost broken up completely. The precious gold and dollar reserves of the sterling area had plummeted by nearly 15 percent. Relations with the United States were at the lowest ebb in half a century. The Suez Canal was unusable for another four months, blocked by dozens of sunken ships, and still firmly under Nasser's control. The United Nations had been defied. The price of gasoline had gone up and rationing had been imposed, as oil tankers plied the long haul around Africa. The national budget had been thrown completely out of calculation by the cost of the Suez operation. Some 40,000 British troops had been dispatched to the Middle East in an enterprise which had turned out to be useless and wasteful. As for those abstract assets on which Britain prided itself—moral leadership, political wisdom, diplomatic skill, foresight, prudence, sound judgment—these could scarcely be mentioned in the same sentence with Suez.

Such was the wreckage which Eden left behind for the Conservatives when he sailed off to New Zealand. But the Party still had a 60-vote majority in the House of Commons and three years to go before it would be constitutionally necessary to call another general election. The Conservatives are also intensely conformist and always close ranks in the most cloying and unquestioning fashion when disaster threatens or a new leader is chosen. Harold Macmillan therefore moved into Downing Street as imperturbably as if his predecessor had only suffered an unfortunate case of influenza. But he took over a stricken government and a demoralized party, and nobody would have given tuppence for Conservative chances if he had decided that the country deserved a chance to vote.

Macmillan's first political task was to bury the Suez disaster and restore his party's spirit and morale. He had gained the premiership over Butler in part because the cabinet knew that he had been more forthright than Butler in his support of Eden and the Suez operation. With the Tories, loyalty to the leader counts enormously at the top as well as in the ranks. When Macmillan became Prime Minister he was of course badgered endlessly from the Labour benches in the House of Commons with demands for an official inquiry into Suez, information about the secret conferences between Britain and France, questions about his own role in promoting the affair, bits of evidence of collusion with Israel, accusations of double-dealing and bad judgment, cries of "Get out" and "Resign." But his questioners, seeking to keep the disaster alive, could get neither apology nor satisfaction from him. Macmillan never retreated from his position of public support for Eden over Suez, but he drew a veil of obscurity across what had happened and refused to be drawn into any discussion, argument or debate. He treated his questioners with weary indulgence or lofty indifference, as men who were insisting on living in the past while he was trying to get on with building Britain's future.

Macmillan's unyielding stand over Suez thus staved off the Labour opposition and put heart back into his Conservative supporters. But at the same time—much more important—Macmillan also accepted the fact that Suez marked the end of Britain's days as a great power, able to act independently in the world. He did not announce this conclusion or pronounce upon it, but he set out adjusting British foreign policy and the British image accordingly. In an anomalous and contradictory way, only a "man of Suez" could have worked such a reversal for the Conservative Party. Macmillan had the political skill to turn away from Suez without bitterness or rancor and without ever ceasing to defend and support his predecessor.

Suez was an acute spiritual crisis in English life—and not merely for the Tory Party. British power had declined a great deal in the world by 1956, and every Briton knew it. But Britain was still the strongest nation in Europe and the most stable. The British were playing an active role all around the globe. Britain stood for a great deal in the world, her prestige was high, and the British cherished a fundamental belief that morality and the interests of the free world still coincided with British interests as they did in 1940, and that Britain could act accordingly. Suez laid bare how much things had changed, how little any of this remained true.

Nor should it be overlooked how much of a shock Suez was to the pride of ordinary Englishmen, far removed from considerations of national morality or high policy. Tens of thousands of Britons had served in Egypt. They shared a dislike and contempt for the Egyptians, resentment at the way Britain was being pushed around, and were all for having a bash at the wogs.* Eden launched the Suez operation to a strong wave of jingo popular support, and there was plenty of bitterness at the pubs and the firesides when Britain was humbled into calling a halt and humiliated by its strongest and closest Ally. For those who opposed Suez and were proven right, there remained the bitter chagrin that a British government could have so misjudged events, and been proven so tragically wrong.

For any prime minister to have taken hold of a nation in such a state of division, bewilderment, confusion and even shock, and re-create a sense of unity and national purpose, would have been a very considerable feat. In fact, Harold Macmillan provided more imagery than reality, more shadow than substance. He made his first task the restoration of Anglo-American relations, but this presented no particular difficulties as there was equal anxiety on the other side of the Atlantic to get back to understanding and common sense. Next Macmillan sought the role of go-between and "honest broker" with Moscow, but the best that could be said for this effort was that he kept a dialogue going when nobody else had any other ideas about what to do. This role for Britain ended with the crash of the Summit Conference in Paris in 1960. The third and final phase of the Macmillan era centered on his effort, at last, to take Britain into Europe. If he made his move too late and did not accurately judge the issues

* The imperial abbreviation for "wily Oriental gentlemen."

and the difficulties, it was still not his fault that the effort ultimately failed. He had made a correct and courageous choice for Britain, and he almost made history. In the meantime, Macmillan had skillfully presided over liquidation of most of the remainder of the British Empire (or to put it more popularly and palatably, its transformation into the multiracial Commonwealth), and he had given Britain an Edwardian glow of prosperity, comfort and self-satisfaction once again.

The "special relationship" with the United States was an obvious starting point for Macmillan in his post-Suez reconstruction, for it has a political meaning and importance in Britain out of all proportion to its importance in Washington. The British go through waves of anti-Americanism, resentment and exasperation at American leadership, and Suez certainly started one such wave. But like it or not, every British prime minister since Churchill in World War II has been measured in part in domestic politics by the strength of his influence and the soundness of his relations with the American President.

The flight to Washington, the handshake on the White House steps, the Presidential arm around the shoulder and the long talk in the oval office, the confident communiqué, the press conference or the address to the National Press Club, and then the stop-off in Ottawa before returning to London with those tranquilizing words "the President and I . . ." This is as much a part of British politics today as the Irish vote is for the Kennedys in Boston or the farm vote in Iowa. Macmillan got down to work on the problem on his first full day as Prime Minister, before he had even completed forming his cabinet. He called in a small group of American correspondents for a drink at No. 10 Downing Street and a background talk, duly reported in the American papers next day. With utter calm, as if Suez had never happened, he sketched his plans for a prosperous Britain, the need to face the future, and the importance which he attached to Anglo-American understanding in maintaining peace in the world.

Macmillan had a number of special advantages in his first task of getting Anglo-American relations back to common sense. First of all, his wartime relationship with President Eisenhower had been close, intimate and personal—a great deal closer than Anthony Eden's ever was. Eden had operated on the cabinet level, with Eisenhower as a subordinate with whom matters were discussed and to whom instructions were then given. Macmillan and Eisenhower had sat down to lunch and dinner in each other's company countless times at Allied Headquarters in Algiers, and had spent endless hours discussing instructions from their superiors in London and Washington, and how to reconcile them and carry them out. Macmillan, like Eden, had his sense of intellectual superiority over Eisenhower. But there was no personality clash and he knew how to be successfully self-effacing, as Churchill was able to be with Roosevelt. Moreover, unlike Eden, Macmillan had never tangled personally with John Foster Dulles, let alone gone as far as Eden did when he urged Eisenhower privately before he became President not to make Dulles his Secretary of State.

Five short weeks after taking office, Macmillan was able to announce that the pilgrimage of restoration had been arranged. He would shortly meet President Eisenhower and Secretary Dulles at Bermuda, where he could play the host. He met at least twice yearly with President Eisenhower, and after that President Kennedy, from then on until he retired.

From the Washington side, there were different but equally impelling reasons to seek a restoration of Anglo-American relations. Disastrous as Eden's handling of Suez had been, there was not all that much pleasure or satisfaction among Americans at the ruthless fashion in which Dulles had arraigned Britain and Israel in the United Nations and wound up siding with the Russians in the midst of the Hungarian affair. Nor did everybody share the glee with which Vice-President Nixon had proclaimed American independence at last of the actions of colonial powers in the world. Eisenhower had maintained an attitude of pained aloofness throughout, but now the fact that his old comrade from Algiers had taken over in London made reconciliation easy.

Moreover, there was a practical matter of military strategy in which the United States needed Britain's help. The Soviet Union had made considerable headway in the development of intercontinental missiles by 1957, and John Foster Dulles's "massive retaliation" thesis did not have the same validity, either politically or militarily, that it seemed to have when the Eisenhower administration came to power in 1953. The United States was now threatened, or about to be threatened, by Russian missiles to which it could not respond. The U.S. had developed medium-range missiles—the Thor and the Jupiter—but its intercontinental arsenal was still some years away. The "missile gap" had arrived. Would Britain consent that the American medium-range missiles be moved where they could be targeted against Russia, and installed on British soil under joint U.S.-British control?

On this and other matters of military collaboration, Macmillan of course responded handsomely. Britain undertook to build the missile sites and provide Royal Air Force crews. The U.S. agreed to pay a major share of the cost. A double-key system was worked out so that British and American officers had to act together to fire a missile. Other projects followed. A huge early-warning radar search installation was built in Yorkshire as part of the missile defense system for the North American continent. Royal Air Force officers were assigned to U.S. Strategic Air Force Headquarters, and joint targeting against the Soviet Union was organized. Exchange of intelligence and technical information, cooperation between the U.S. and British secret services, and coordination of military staff planning in every area of the world began again in greater depth than at any time since the days of the war. With the new transatlantic undersea telephone cable, a special circuit with supersecret scrambler equipment was set aside to link the White House with Downing Street. Finally, Congress at last amended the Atomic Energy Act in 1958 to permit resumption of full Anglo-American cooperation in the field of nuclear weapons.

But for the British Conservatives, the real climax came when the United States decided to land troops in Lebanon in July, 1958, and Britain joined the operation immediately by dispatching troops to Jordan. The action was taken in the wake of a revolt in Iraq—a bloody military coup in which young King Feisal and his family were hacked to death and the body of old Nuri es-Said was dragged through the streets of Baghdad behind an army jeep. The revolution broke out at a time when civil war had been dragging on for weeks in Lebanon. Colonel Nasser was indulging in a new wave of threats against the West, and, as usual, tiny Jordan was again teetering on the edge of a coup against its king. Behind all this lay evidence of Communist intrigue—particularly in the events in Baghdad. Macmillan was ready to intervene to assist King Hussein of Jordan, but he was determined that this time Britain would not go it alone in the Middle East.

When President Eisenhower and Dulles gave the order to the United States Marines to land in Beirut, the Tories of England who had so fervently supported the Suez operation found self-vindication at last. Macmillan, in the eyes of his followers, had succeeded where Eden had failed. He had persuaded the United States of the necessity of using force to protect Western interests in the Middle East. At the same time, the operation restored for the Conservatives the "great power" image which had been so demolished by Suez. When the British troops flew into Jordan, I spent ten days in Amman amid an odd mixture of local tensions and old-home-week. Arab-speaking British officers who had served under General Glubb in the Arab Legion arrived back in platoons, many to stay on after the British troops were withdrawn. But the city was under curfew, censorship was severe, and rigorous security restrictions were in force everywhere. All the same, the Anglo-American intervention worked. Jordan kept its king and its independence, and five years later Hussein married a British officer's daughter! The Lebanon ended its civil war and elected a new president. Nasser's expansionist aims were checked. Iraq descended into savage confusion, but stopped short of going Communist. After seven weeks, withdrawal of the British and American troops began. Above all, a period of calm then settled over the Middle East after four turbulent years in which its problems had dominated the world scene. Macmillan had restored the prestige of the Conservative Government, his relations with the United States were secure, and he was now ready to move carefully out in front of Washington.

The Berlin crisis, launched by Khrushchev in November, 1958, gave him his chance.

The role of "honest broker" between Washington and Moscow has often attracted British foreign secretaries since the end of World War II, with the exception of Ernest Bevin, who spent too many years fighting the Communists in the British trade union movement to have any illusions about how Communism does its business. Bevin, of course, was directing British foreign policy through the worst of the Stalin period, when Hungary and Czechoslovakia were taken over completely by the Communists, Berlin was blockaded, and the Korean war broke out. There was little room for any honest brokerage in these transactions. But with Stalin's death, Churchill set the pattern for British thinking with his call for "a parley at the Summit," and his famous remark that "jaw-jaw is better than war-war." This approach was almost the antithesis of Dulles's Cold War diplomacy. Still, Churchill and Eden managed to jog the United States to the Summit Conference at Geneva in 1955, and with Khrushchev's renewed threat to Berlin, Macmillan decided that the time had come to start up the slope once again.

Macmillan felt that the renewed Russian threat to Berlin was a much more serious affair which somehow had to be de-fused. He believed that to handle the matter with usual Cold War tactics, without sitting down with the Russians, could lead to a situation in which Russian pressures against Berlin would increase until the Western nations might be confronted with the prospect of war over something trivial such as who stamped the passes on the Berlin autobahn. Moreover, Macmillan was a great believer in personal contacts and intimate, easy conversation. (The technique worked well enough for him with President Eisenhower, but it did not work with either Nikita Khrushchev or Charles de Gaulle.) Macmillan drew considerable popular political support in Britain by taking a position from the first that he wanted more flexible diplomacy to meet the crisis. The British felt, moreover, that there was not merely inflexibility at this point in Washington, but a kind of malaise in judging the implications of the new Russian offensive. Neither Macmillan nor anyone else knew then that John Foster Dulles had entered the next-to-last phase of cancer, with his energies already undermined.

In late December, without any prior consultation with any of his Allies, Macmillan instructed the British Ambassador to Moscow, Sir Patrick Reilley, to make careful inquiries to find out if the Russian Government would like to invite him to pay a visit to Moscow, returning the visit which Khrushchev and Bulganin had made to Britain in 1956. Macmillan at the same time advised Washington, Paris and Bonn of his move, and explained why he was taking the initiative and what he had in mind. President de Gaulle was indifferent. His policy was to ignore the Russian threat to Berlin completely. Chancellor Adenauer reacted with dismay. As far as he was concerned, any negotiation with the Russians could only work to Germany's disadvantage and he mistrusted the British anyway. John Foster Dulles boarded an airplane for his last trip to Europe.

Dulles was scarcely able to eat, needed periods of rest after each meeting (in contrast to his inexhaustible energy in previous years), and conducted his talks while in almost constant pain on that last visit in February, 1959, to London, Paris and Bonn. He was to resign from office two months later. Meanwhile, the Russian invitation to Macmillan had been delivered and accepted for the last week of February. All that Dulles could do was reassure himself on Macmillan's intentions and the fact that the British would give nothing away in Moscow, and then fly on to reassure Chancellor Adenauer as best he could that the British would not sell out Berlin. His final theme to Macmillan was: "I see nothing to negotiate over Berlin."

Macmillan arrived in Moscow wearing a jaunty white fur caracul hat, and though at one point in the few days which followed he almost left for England, in the end the British got the one result which they hoped for—Russian agreement to hold a Big Four Foreign Ministers' Conference on Berlin at Geneva in the summer of 1959. After that long exercise in diplomatic futility, President Eisenhower kept the dialogue going by inviting Khrushchev to visit the United States, and then General de Gaulle invited him to Paris. At last the Summit Conference was set for Paris in May, 1960.

On the way up the slope Macmillan, with his usual sense of political timing, called a General Election in October of 1959. Suez was forgotten. Prosperity glittered in every British shopwindow. Anglo-American happiness prevailed. And Britain was giving the lead in East-West diplomacy. Macmillan and the Conservatives won a sweeping victory, increasing their House of Commons majority from 60 to 102 seats.

The Summit Conference turned out to be one of the most bizarre tragicomedies of diplomatic history. Two weeks before it was due to open, Russian air defense rockets brought down an American U-2 photo reconnaissance plane from the skies 70,000 feet above the Siberian city of Sverdlovsk. The pilot, Francis Gary Powers, parachuted to safety, a show trial for espionage, and eighteen months in a Russian jail until he was eventually exchanged for the Russian spy Abel. Arriving in Paris, Khrushchev bombastically declared that he would not attend any summit meeting until President Eisenhower personally apologized and announced punishment for all those responsible. Eisenhower responded to the extent of stating that U-2 flights over Russia would not be resumed, but this was not enough for Khrushchev, and the Summit Conference never met at all.

Considering how little Khrushchev's actions affected the Berlin situation, or the course of history, it is surprising to recall and difficult to recapture the emotions and the tensions which swirled in Paris that wild Summit week. Nobody maintained as much poise or dignity as President Charles de Gaulle. Khrushchev held one of the most outrageous and obscene press conferences in the annals of the art, his little eyes blazing with anger, his face red with rage, his fists waving as he shouted threats at the Western powers in language so foul that the interpreters winced as they cleaned it up. President Eisenhower badly wanted to go out and play golf in the lovely May weather and was restrained only by the insistence of his press secretary, James Hagerty, who felt that golf might not make a good impression at such a time. In the end, when all had collapsed and Khrushchev had stormed off to Berlin and Moscow, the U. S. Strategic Air Force had been put on a war alert for seven hours. But President Eisenhower organized a cookout on the lawn of the American Embassy Residence in Paris and jauntily grilled steaks for his gray and exhausted Secretary of State, Christian Herter, and other more lighthearted members of his official circle.

The debacle was worst of all for Macmillan. The Prime Minister walked around the British Embassy gardens with tears literally streaming down his face, agonizing to Ambassador Sir Gladwyn Jebb about "little people in the thatched cottages and parish churches of England praying for peace and my success in this venture." The three old comrades of Algiers gathered in the Élysée Palace, while Khrushchev roared off for a drive in the Paris countryside to visit a farm and demonstrate his strength at chopping wood. Macmillan pleaded with De Gaulle and Eisenhower to authorize him to go to Khrushchev on their behalf and make one more try to get him to come and hold a meeting. Eisenhower began to nod sympathetically, but Charles E. Bohlen, the chief Soviet adviser on the American delegation, quickly slipped a note to Secretary Herter urging "Please do not let the President agree." Bohlen reasoned that the Russians were out to break up the conference anyway, and an appeal to keep it going would be futile and undignified and would only look like supine weakness.

But he need not have worried. President de Gaulle raised his hand and remarked loftily to Macmillan: "I think that would be somewhat Byzantine, and we all know what happened to the Byzantine civilization." The role of the honest broker was over.

Eighteen months of dipomatic effort (and considerable public money) had been expended to reach the abortive heights of the Summit Conference. The result had been a cruel and painful exposure of how little the Soviet Union cared for British common sense, good manners and diplomatic leadership—unless they also happened to serve Russian interests. The collapse of the Summit Conference left Harold Macmillan in search of a policy for Britain.

He had brought the Anglo-American "special relationship" to a new closeness for the British, but this scarcely constituted a role of

Britain's own in world affairs. The periodic flight to Washington to confer with the President in the White House of course had its usefulness on both sides of the Atlantic. It could not solve Britain's economic problems, however, and it was no substitute for a strong Britain able to speak with its own influence, prestige and authority in the world.

Macmillan had also devised a forward-looking British policy for the Commonwealth and the colonies, but essentially this was a reflection of the decline of British power rather than the creation of any new role for Britain in the world. The Commonwealth, in fact, was decreasing in importance to the British in direct ratio to the increase in the number of its new members and the diversity of their interests. The prewar Commonwealth of five members had been an essential instrument of British foreign policy, with a cohesiveness and homogeneity of men and nations around the world whose interests were tied directly to those of Great Britain. This could scarcely be said today of Nkrumah of Ghana, or Makarios of Cyprus, or Madame Bandaranika of Ceylon.

Nor was the changing Commonwealth any longer of the same economic importance and usefulness to the British. Commonwealth trade still loomed large in the statistics—38 percent of British imports and 41 percent of its exports in 1960. But the value and the pattern of the trade had altered considerably since the Commonwealth Preferential Tariff system was inaugurated in 1933.

For example, in the prewar days Britain exported quantities of cheap cotton, tariff free under Commonwealth preferences, to India. But by the mid-1950's, India was selling vast quantities of cheap cotton goods, tariff free, to Britain, and the British textile industry was slowly being forced to the wall by this competition from the old Empire. The result was a major and costly reorganization and rationalization of the Lancashire textile mills, carried out with a large government subsidy in 1959, to close down cheap production and concentrate on high quality. The changing Commonwealth was a considerable monument to British political skill, but it was no longer "British," it commanded none of the old loyalties or mutual dependence, and it no longer constituted any extension of British power or symbol of British economic strength in the world.

Britain's problem lay in Europe. The blunt truth was that there had been no genuine or realistic British policy toward Europe since the days of the Marshall Plan. Britain had led Europe actively and successfully in 1947, 1948 and 1949. The British had provided the diplomatic blueprint and taken the lead in establishing the Organization for European Economic Cooperation to coordinate the receiving end of the American aid program in 1947. Britain had proposed the Brussels Treaty of 1948—a fifty-year military alliance with France, the Benelux nations and Italy that was the forerunner of the NATO Pact. Somewhat reluctantly, in 1949, the Labour Government had joined in establishing the Council of Europe at Strasbourg. In 1951, Britain made the key decisions to provide technical and monetary support for a European Payments Union, to operate short-term trade credits for all of Europe on a multilateral basis.

British policy in those days was one of active cooperation and collaboration in European affairs. But this was precisely the problem. Britain was prepared to *cooperate*—but not to *join*.

In the immediate postwar years, European cooperation developed along British lines. But the issue presented itself clearly between Britain and Europe when Robert Schuman and Jean Monnet launched the European Coal and Steel Community plan in May, 1950. This was not to be another cooperative venture, but a breakthrough at last in the direction of a truly united Europe, with the surrender of national sovereignty and the creation of "supranational" control over a vital segment of European heavy industry. For three weeks, French and British diplomats struggled to find a formula under which the British Labour Government would agree to participate in the Schuman Plan negotiations. But no matter how the words were juggled, there was no bridging the gap between "cooperating" and "joining." In retrospect, it would have been far better for Britain if the Labour Government had joined and negotiated the terms and conditions and functions and structure of the Coal and Steel Community inside with The Six. But the idea of surrendering any part of sovereign control over the British economy to a High Authority sitting on the Continent of Europe was anathema to the Labour Government, and Britain's self-exclusion from the mainstream of European affairs began.

Moreover, the British handled the issue in a lofty and superior tone which did much to increase resentment and antipathy on the other side of the Channel. First the British took the attitude that the Europeans did not know what they were doing or what was good for Europe. Then, when "united Europe" began to work, the British returned, resentful that British interests were being ignored. The British could never bring themselves to believe or understand what was happening in Europe.

France's attitude toward Britain when the Schuman Plan was launched was typified by a pungent diary entry made at the time by a senior French diplomat, Jacques Dumaine:

> Recent British policy has been conspiring against all attempts to unite Europe, by skillfully demolishing any plans to that end, either in the Marshall Plan organization or before the Council of Europe. It has been deliberately negative and depressing, which is the reason why the other members are now determined to overcome British objections. Implicit, therefore, in the Schuman Plan is this resolve to force the hand of the British Government, which constitutes its weak link.

In June of 1955, less than a year after the death of E.D.C., Paul-Henri Spaak, the Belgian foreign minister, took the initiative to get European unity moving again. He proposed a meeting of the foreign ministers of the six Coal and Steel Community countries to be held at Messina in Sicily to discuss a new treaty for European economic integration—the formation of a European Common Market. Great Britain was invited to attend. Eden, then prime minister, loftily responded that the British would be pleased to have a junior minister from the Foreign Office or the Board of Trade present as an observer. Spaak answered vigorously that the meeting was to be a serious policy discussion at top level. If Britain was not prepared to send her foreign minister to participate in preliminary discussions, then it would have to be assumed that she would not be prepared to join in serious treaty negotiations which were expected to follow. As far as the Europeans were concerned, it had to be top-level representation or nothing. It was nothing. The British stayed away.

Eden, fresh from the E.D.C. affair, simply did not believe that yet another supranational treaty would ever get through the governments and parliaments of Europe. Moreover, looked at from the London viewpoint, there was already ample machinery for sound economic cooperation in Europe without all of the fuss of a complicated treaty. There was the Marshall Plan organization which Britain had taken the lead in founding, and there were stacks and stacks of recommendations for reduction of trade quotas and tariffs and elimination of national restrictions. There was the GATT organization—the General Agreement on Trade and Tariffs—which was working away to free international trade channels. The British found it impossible to believe that France, with the most protectionist economy in Europe, would ever throw open its doors to competition in a common market with Germany. Equally they found it impossible even to contemplate opening the British market to continental agriculture and farm products. The Commonwealth and the British farmer of course had to come first.

But although the E.D.C. treaty had failed, the economic integration of Europe had moved successfully forward and the mood and attitude toward more integration was much more receptive and positive in Europe than Eden and the British realized. The Coal and Steel Community had been in operation for two years, under Jean Monnet's rigorous direction, and the results had wholly supported all that its founding fathers had preached and promised. Everybody had benefited and no scars or wounds had been inflicted. Patriotism and national sovereignty had not disappeared. Industry had prospered. Trade had expanded. No vast new cartel was strangling the growth or expansion of European heavy industry. Moreover, the Coal and Steel Community had at its disposal in Europe a vast fund of money to help resolve such local problems as the closing down of uneconomic and redunant coal mines in Belgium—a problem which never could have been solved unless it had been placed in an international framework.

A great change was taking place in the attitude of industry all over Europe to the idea of integrating and accepting competition in a common market—particularly in France. The French steel industry had come through the first blast of competition with Germany extremely well, managing, even, to undersell the Germans in the south of their own country in Bavaria. Eden was quite right in assessing that France wanted no more supranationalism in the military or political sphere after the death of E.D.C., but in pragmatic matters of economic unity, supranationalism raised few national emotions. The Messina conference came to quick agreement on the principles of "a gradual fusion of national economies through the creation of a common market," and set a committee of experts to work in Brussels to draft a treaty under Spaak's direction.

At the invitation of the Six, the British did send a Foreign Office official as an observer to Brussels. But as Spaak later remarked to a British minister, "Nothing could have demonstrated more clearly the attitude of total British indifference to Europe than the series of negative interventions made by this unfortunate representative." * Britain was still talking about cooperation. Europe was talking about economic integration. In the remarkably short span of eight months, the Spaak Committee produced a full technical report on the outlines of a Common Market treaty. The foreign ministers of the Six met in Paris in May, 1956, to consider the report and direct that it be completed in treaty form.

At this point, in the summer of 1956 as Britain and France headed into the Suez crisis together, the Eden Government hastily trotted out a counterplan for the formation of a European Free Trade Area for all seventeen members of the Organization for European Economic Cooperation. But agricultural products were to be specifically excluded from the free trade plan, and everybody in Europe recognized that basic British policy had not changed. Britain was still moving on lines of cooperation rather than integration. The best that could be said of the Free Trade Area plan was that it constituted a growing recognition in Britain of the fact that a fundamental change was taking place in Europe, and an uneasy awareness that Britain was increasingly isolated and excluded from an effective voice in European affairs.

Here matters stood when Harold Macmillan succeeded Eden in January of 1957. The Free Trade Area plan had been initiated by Macmillan when he was Chancellor of the Exchequer. When he became prime minister, he sought almost immediately to put some impetus behind it by proposing a European conference to start negotiating a Free Trade Area agreement. But the French Foreign Ministry saw this as nothing but another British blocking effort against European integration, and Foreign Minister Christian Pineau, who had collaborated so closely with the British over Suez, sent word back that France would have nothing to do with the Free Trade Area plan until the European Common Market treaty had been ratified by the Parliaments of the Six. Macmillan was forced to lay the plan to one side for the time being, but by the summer of 1957 the Common Market Treaty was an accomplished fact and he returned to the attack. He named Reginald Maudling to a special ministerial post in the cabinet, with responsibility for negotiating the Free Trade Area Plan.

Maudling began a round of European capitals which, unhappily,

* Quoted by Anthony Nutting, Minister of State at the Foreign Office 1951–56, in *Europe Will Not Wait.*

left the impression that Britain's main objective still was to undermine or sabotage the Common Market before it could be effectively established. In particular, the British aroused the special resentment and suspicions of the French by tactics of seeking to play Common Market members off against each other in support of the Free Trade plan, with the apparent aim of isolating France. These were tactics which the British were to repeat when they began negotiating for full entrance into the Common Market four years later, and on neither occasion did they help their case or their diplomatic position.

In May, 1958, all the political equations in Europe changed with the return to power of General de Gaulle. Although De Gaulle was no enthusiast for integration, he was not blind to the enormous economic and political advantages for France in the Common Market. He had strong ideas about France's place of leadership in Europe, and after a brief period of uncertainty while he surveyed the scene, De Gaulle threw his weight behind France's commitments under the Common Market treaty with far greater strength and certainty than any government of the Fourth Republic had ever been able to muster. De Gaulle moreover had his suspicions and antipathies toward the Anglo-Saxons. These were amply confirmed in his mind when he dispatched a proposal in September, 1958, to President Eisenhower and Prime Minister Macmillan for the formation of a special triumverate to direct global Western strategy. Whatever the merits or drawbacks of the De Gaulle proposal, he received little more than uncomfortable and embarrassed replies from Washington and London. But in European affairs, France had a voice and De Gaulle was determined to make the most of it. In November, 1958, at a meeting of the OEEC countries in Paris, France rejected the Free Trade Area plan out of hand.

Britain was now isolated from Europe. Maudling undertook to pick up some of the pieces by negotiating a European Free Trade Association of seven members outside the Common Market: Sweden, Norway, Denmark, Austria, Switzerland, Portugal and Britain. EFTA is a straight multilateral trade treaty, more elaborate than most with an organization to run it, but on the traditional lines of cooperation with none of the features of economic integration which stamp the Common Market. At first, Britain wanted to put the EFTA headquarters in Paris, to keep in close touch with OEEC headquarters and work for the day when the Common Market and the Free Trade Association might negotiate some kind of a merger. But the French never entertained the slightest idea of any such agreement between the two blocs and denied even this crumb to the British. They politely told the EFTA group to take their headquarters elsewhere. It was then established in Geneva.

For fifteen years from the end of World War II, British policy had been aimed at preserving sovereign cooperation in Europe, while the Europeans labored to break it down and substitute integration and supranationalism in its place. What persuaded Harold Macmillan to reverse this policy—indeed, to reverse British history—and apply to join Europe as a full member of the Common Market in the summer of 1961?

The answer boils down to the fact that Britain's policy toward Europe had failed to achieve anything, was dead-ended and no longer accorded with the facts and the trends of the future, while European integration was succeeding beyond all results which Britain had believed possible. The failure of the Summit Conference, like Suez, had been another exposure of Britain's declining effectiveness and role in world affairs. At a time when the old Empire and the old power base had practically disappeared for the British, they also faced increasing economic and political isolation from their closest neighbors in Europe. It was time that Britain face up to the problems of a positive and forward-looking European policy.

Joining Europe never was and never will be a popular cause or a popular demand in Britain—any more than integration wins elections in the Deep South.* The sense of insular security and self-satisfaction is part of British life, and antipathies toward foreigners who do not speak English are strong. But from 1959 onward, intellectual opinion in Britain began moving steadily toward getting into Europe. Until that time, the Eden approach of three concentric circles or the three-legged stool (the Commonwealth, the Anglo-American relationship and Europe) had been the picture-image of British foreign policy. But after the French killed the European Free Trade Area plan, it was increasingly clear that the only way Britain was going to maintain any European policy would be to join Europe.

In the summer of 1959, shortly before calling the General Election, Macmillan instructed the cabinet secretariat to organize a study of long-term trends and problems of British foreign policy. A special committee was formed, with some of the best brains of the Foreign Office, the military services, the Colonial Office, the Treasury and

* There is an old British traveler's motto, "Blacks begin at Calais."

other departments. For three months the committee sifted through every British problem and position paper in every area of the world. Its report concluded that the world struggle with Communism during the 1960's would center on the problem of attracting and holding the emerging nations of Africa, Asia and elsewhere. But, the report asserted —and this was the central point—the problem of meeting the needs of the underdeveloped nations could only be solved by the resources of a strong and viable Europe. Britain did not even begin to have the resources to play a strong role among the emerging nations. Therefore, the report reasoned, Britain's first interest lay in establishing close relations with a strong Europe, and taking the lead through Europe, or with Europe, in the world at large.

The report did not make any specific recommendations that Britain join the Common Market. But it did serve to focus behind-the-scenes thinking in the British Government. During the 1950's, the British spent their time thinking about almost every part of the world but Europe. Never once was a cabinet committee formed or a cabinet discussion held or a government study initiated on the question, "Should we join Europe?" Plans like the Free Trade Area were thought up, but never did the British study the initiatives coming from Europe—what was developing in Europe, its effect on Britain, its implications for British foreign policy, and the pros and cons of joining.

The policy study of 1959, therefore, started the ball rolling. There were plenty of European-minded men in the British Foreign Office, the Treasury, the Board of Trade and elsewhere, but as long as the Eden approach dominated thinking and policy-making there was not much they could do. Now the need to shape a European policy was becoming obvious, and ideas and discussion became popular. The same thing was happening in public discussion. Books and pamphlets, editorials and articles, discussion meetings and political speeches were focusing increasingly on the question of Britain and Europe. Industrialists began to seek Common Market mergers and open branch factories on the Continent in order to get inside Europe even if Britain stayed out. The economic comparisons between Britain and Europe were painful. The British, with a stop-and-go policy of expansion and then a check on inflation, had plodded along at an average growth rate of 2.5 percent each year, while the Common Market countries galloped upward in the 1950's at rates of 7 or 8 percent.

Finally, candidates in Parliamentary by-elections began taking up the Common Market issue and speaking out for a policy of joining

Europe. By the summer of 1960, a conviction was growing among the senior political strategists of the Conservative Party that, difficult as it might be to get the Party to swallow it, a bold bid for Europe would give the Conservatives the kind of new look and forward policy which they would need to win yet another General Election. In 1959 they had won on a combination of "you never had it so good," restoration of Anglo-American special relations, the liberal policy toward the colonies and the new Commonwealth, and Macmillan's role of "honest broker." Now the party strategists sensed the chance to get out in front once again by seizing the political leadership on the question of Europe.

They calculated, moreover, that the Labour Party would ultimately remain insular toward Europe as it had done in the days of Ernest Bevin, and they turned out to be correct. Hugh Gaitskell, the Labour leader, did not commit himself on the question of joining Europe until October of 1962, and when he came out against membership in the Common Market on the terms which had thus far been negotiated in Brussels, his stand was a great disappointment to the moderate, intellectual wing of his party. Gaitskell had discussed and analyzed the problem endlessly before he finally made up his mind, and he acted out of deep intellectual conviction. But he gave the Tories a free run as "the party of the future."

This upsurge of discussion and public opinion took place in an absence of leadership from the Prime Minister. Macmillan was sitting back and following his usual political instinct of allowing public opinion to form itself. Behind this façade, however, Macmillan had begun very cautiously to shift. The first movement could be detected after the Prime Minister visited Bonn in August, 1960, and found that despite the mistrust which his "honest broker" efforts had created in Chancellor Adenauer, the Germans were ready to encourage and welcome British entry into the Common Market. Careful diplomatic soundings then began in other European capitals, but these were accomplished with the most soothing reassurances to the Conservative Party.

"We have a very modest target. It is to try and find a positive position from which we can move into negotiations. But we are a very long way from that," the Party was told at its annual conference in October, 1960, by Edward Heath, who was to become Britain's chief negotiator at Brussels.

In March, 1961, George Ball, the new Undersecretary of State in the Kennedy Administration, flew to Europe on a general reconnaissance for the new President, and when he arrived in London he was confronted by Heath and a roomful of senior Foreign Office officials and the question: "What will American reaction be if we apply to join Europe?" The United States had to decide whether on balance the advantage of Britain becoming an active member of the European Economic Community would outweigh the disadvantages which the United States might later face in trading and competing with an enormous European market with one set of trade restrictions and a single outer tariff wall. In fact, the Americans never did more than pose the problems which they thought would arise. The United States never raised any serious arguments against Britain joining Europe if it wanted to and never doubted that the British ought to wind up in Europe. The British, on the other hand, constantly used the "special relationship" as one of their excuses for not joining Europe. At that London meeting, however, Ball had no instructions so he simply listened to the British, posed some questions and flew home. In April, Macmillan visited Washington for his first meeting with President Kennedy, and after their talks he confided that "we are going to do it." Politician that he was, Macmillan later made much of how he had only taken his decision when it was clear that the United States would not object. Actually he could have had that assurance any time he really wanted it.

In June, the Prime Minister dispatched five of his cabinet ministers to various Commonwealth capitals around the globe to discuss the problems which would arise in Commonwealth trade if Britain decided to join. The signals for a change of course were now all set, but the Conservative Party was still not fully braced for what was to come.

In fact, the "Conservative News Letter," which goes out monthly to all the local party branches, said in its issue of July, 1961: "The Liberals call on the government to apply forthwith to join the Common Market. It is foolish advice which the Government is wise to reject." But on July 27, Macmillan at last made his formal move. Characteristically, he timed his announcement for the very end of the Parliamentary session just before the House of Commons recessed until late October. Thus, he gave himself a period which would be uninterrupted by any awkard Parliamentary debates or questions. And at the same time, he couched his announcement in familiar involuted terminology, designed to minimize the fact that anything very important was happening.

"During the past nine weeks we have had informal talks," he said. "We have now reached the stage where we cannot make further progress without entering into official negotiations. The majority of the House and country will feel that they cannot fairly judge whether it is possible for the United Kingdom to join the European Economic Community until they have a clearer picture before them of the conditions. . . ."

Formal application for negotiations with the Community for full British membership was sent to Brussels on August 9, 1961. After preliminary discussions on how to organize the negotiation, the first session took place on October 10. The end came almost exactly fifteen months later, with President de Gaulle's press conference of January 14, 1963.

President de Gaulle took the ultimate responsibility for breaking off the negotiations and forcing the British back to isolation, but the fact remains that the British did not handle their case at Brussels with insight or negotiating skill. The root of the difficulty was the fact that Harold Macmillan was really conducting three negotiations at once. First he was negotiating British entry into the Common Market. Next he was negotiating the withdrawal of British economic concessions and special privileges from the Commonwealth. And finally he was negotiating politically, every day, to get the Conservative Party to accept these vast changes in national policy and tradition without a real revolt. Moreover, in a typical political maneuver Macmillan had reshuffled his cabinet to immobilize the doubters about British entry by giving them direct responsibility for carrying out the new policy. Butler, who had opposed going into Europe all along, was put in charge of a cabinet coordinate committee which decided on the instructions for the Brussels negotiators. Maudling was made Chancellor of the Exchequer where he fixed Treasury policy on the necessary economic concessions to enter Europe. All of this was good domestic politics and would have given Macmillan a firm base of support for joining Europe if the negotiations had succeeded, but it was not good for the conduct of the negotiation in Brussels. Macmillan sought to back into Europe, inch-by-inch, instead of marching in boldly. Perhaps he could not take the political risk which the bold approach would have required, but the result was that his negotiators were limited in Brussels to niggling arguments and penny-package concessions, instead of the animation of European enthusiasm and a positive sense of venture for their task.*

Nevertheless, until the summer of 1962, a certain optimism prevailed in Brussels. Macmillan visited General de Gaulle in June of that year and found him friendly and cooperative, talking on the assumption that Britain would make it. The central problem of the negotiation for both the British and the Common Market countries was agriculture—the harmonization of Britain's highly subsidized farming industry and the low-cost producers of Europe, with special privileges for entry of Commonwealth farm products into Britain for a transitional period after the British joined the Common Market. Slowly the negotiators circled these issues. But by now both optimism and enthusiasm for joining Europe were running high enough for Iain Macleod, who was then leader of the House of Commons and chairman of the Conservative Party, to urge in cabinet discussions in July that Britain switch to bold tactics, make some crash concessions on the farm question, and seek quick agreement in Brussels by the end of August. Had his advice been taken, Britain might well be in the Common Market today. But the rest of the cabinet—with Butler in the lead—favored a cautious line to await the results of a Commonwealth Prime Ministers conference scheduled for September and the annual Tory Party conference in October. Accordingly, the Brussels talks bogged down and were recessed in late August.

Macmillan steered his way through a difficult Commonwealth meeting with great skill, and although there was plenty of beefing over the effect of British entry on Commonwealth trade, nobody sought to impose a veto or block the policy. Hugh Gaitskell then came out against joining the Common Market at the Labour Party conference in October, and the Conservatives met the following week in an exultant mood over their new European policy. "For them, a thousand years of history. For us, the future!" cried Butler.

But when the British returned to the negotiating table in Brussels in late October, the optimism of early summer quickly faded. Both sides had misjudged. The Common Market countries believed that the British were simply waiting until they got through the Commonwealth meeting and the Conservative political conference before offering the last big concessions on agriculture. But the British came back to Brussels in very much the opposite frame of mind. Macmillan had

* For detailed accounts of the Brussels negotiations, see *Atlantic Crisis* by Robert Kleiman (Norton, 1964) and *The General Said No* by Nora Beloff.

all but turned his back on the Commonwealth, and the September meeting had been a demonstration of the dangers which Britain faced on going much further. Instead of returning with new concessions, the British stiffened, in the hope or belief that the Common Market governments would be sympathetic over the difficulties which the Commonwealth conference had demonstrated. Sympathy the British might have had, but new concessions they could not get. They sought support from the Germans, the Dutch, the Italians, but these tactics, with the apparent aim of isolating the French, simply did not work. The French had an extremely strong and able negotiating team, and the Common Market members were not going to admit Britain at the expense of their own unity and strength or the watering-down of the Rome Treaty.

In this bleak atmosphere, the negotiations dragged on through November and December of 1962, when Prime Minister Macmillan made his last visit to France to confer once more with General de Gaulle.

A turning point of history—for Britain, for France, for the United States, for Europe—lay just ahead.

PART II

TEN DAYS THAT SHOOK THE WESTERN WORLD

1. The Hidden Crisis

By the end of 1962, the tide was at the flood, and Europe and the Atlantic Alliance—it seemed—were poised for a crowning moment of uniting fortune.

The British were doggedly bargaining in Brussels, determined to make their way into Europe, and although difficulties clouded the prospect there was no talk of any breakdown or crisis. The goal which almost every European statesman, politician and diplomat had sought for more than a decade would be achieved—a Europe united, Britain included.

Across the Atlantic, President Kennedy, in a far-reaching Fourth of July speech at Independence Hall in Philadelphia, had proclaimed a lasting goal of Atlantic interdependence as the basis of United States foreign policy. The new Trade Expansion Act had finally passed the Congress. It gave the President a practical instrument with which to begin negotiating an economic link across the Atlantic, a tie-in between the United States and an enlarged European Common Market.

Western strength and unity had been tested continuously for more than a year since the Berlin wall went up in August of 1961. Although there had been differences with the French over talking to the Russians, the Alliance was firm, the position strong. Then in late October, the Cuban crisis suddenly brought the whole of NATO to the brink of war. President Kennedy's actions were swiftly and solidly supported in Europe (particularly by President Charles de Gaulle) and as the episode reached its climax a sense of tense exhilaration swept through NATO from Oslo to Ankara, a feeling of cohesive power which had never quite been shared before. Not just the United States but the whole of the Atlantic Alliance was eyeball-to-eyeball with the Russians, and the Russians knew it.

The end of 1962 approached, therefore, in an atmosphere of surging optimism. Cuba looked to be a triumph not only for American power but for Atlantic unity. Surely, it seemed, this unity should now be reinforced and buttressed, should move swiftly forward in an hour of history when the monolithic Communist world was showing fissures of its own. Britain was ready to enter Europe. The United States was ready to forge new transatlantic economic links. And to cap the Kennedy administration's "Grand Design," the long-standing idea of creating some kind of a purely NATO nuclear force—a sharing of nuclear power in the Alliance—was about to be taken out of the bottom drawer, dusted off and made active American policy.

But beneath the floodtide an undertow was running.

Neither Washington nor London assessed it fully. It was too easy to explain away some of the underlying forces at work in Europe as mere expressions of the personality and "grandeur" of President de Gaulle. Certainly he was the epitome, the personification, of the trend away from the kind of unity of which Robert Schuman and Jean Monnet had dreamed. It was easy, too, to equate De Gaulle's ideas and policies with outmoded historical concepts that, seemingly, could never again be applied in Europe. Accustomed to a decade of support and reassurances from the Spaaks, Schumans, Adenauers, Erhards, Stikkers, De Gasperis, Fanfanis and Monnets of Europe, Washington and London could scarcely visualize how one man alone could thwart the combined historical will of Western statesmen.

But by the end of 1962, De Gaulle had become a force and a power in Europe in his own right. He had consolidated his hold on France. Moreover, he represented a new subsurface current—European nationalism. Essentially this current was hidden. De Gaulle, the vigorous and outspoken exponent of Europe standing between the two superpowers, found little visible or public support in Europe, and even the fashion in which Adenauer had shifted from European multilateralism to Gaullist bilateralism had been carefully managed so as not to burn any NATO bridges or undermine relations with the United States. Perhaps this was why, in the exhilaration of the post-Cuban atmosphere, the occasionally arrogant young men of the New Frontier began committing one tactical diplomatic and psychological error after another, playing straight into De Gaulle's hands. In the end, events moved with invisible but inexorable momentum toward the climactic De Gaulle press conference of January 14, 1963: the veto of British entry into the Common Market, the rejection of the

NATO nuclear force idea, and afterward Chancellor Adenauer's Paris visit to conclude the Franco-German Treaty of Cooperation—all coming in ten days that shook the western world.

These ten days constituted a turning point for postwar Europe, and it will be a long time before history can truly assess whether Charles de Gaulle was intuitively right or tragically wrong. By his actions, by his lone decisions, he halted the historic evolution of European unity in its tracks, turned it 180 degrees to one side, and left it to find a new course, new objectives and new momentum. As far as De Gaulle was concerned, France had had enough of unity and integration. National salvation and strength lay in national independence and national effort. And so he moved to impose France's example and France's policies on the rest of Europe.

The clouds began gathering almost as soon as the Cuban crisis was resolved. Washington drew one set of lessons from the Cuban affair. President de Gaulle drew another, almost diametrically opposed. In Washington, Cuba was proof that there could be only one finger on the nuclear trigger for all of NATO. To De Gaulle it was proof that Europe could not leave its nuclear defenses to the United States. Moreover, at Brussels the price of British entry into the Common Market rose higher and higher as the negotiators reached the central economic issues. And in Britain, the Labour Party had now united behind Hugh Gaitskell in unexpected open opposition against entry into Europe on the terms which had thus far been obtained. All of these fundamental differences and arguments in the Western camp rose into focus in Paris in late November and early December through the words of three important opinion-makers: Walter Lippmann, Raymond Aron, and Gaitskell.

Lippmann came to Paris in late November to deliver a special address to the Anglo-American Press Association at a luncheon marking the 75th anniversary of the founding of the European Edition of the New York *Herald Tribune*. Virtually the entire diplomatic press of Paris attended. While Lippmann himself would never lay claim to speaking for the Kennedy administration, it was nevertheless assumed by his audience that he had full knowledge of how the President and his advisers interpreted the Cuban affair.

"If anyone wishes to understand the American position in the Cuban crisis and the American attitude toward military power in the world today," Lippmann said, "he must remember that responsible Americans do not dare forget the reality of the nuclear age. I know these men. They live with these realities. For that reason they do not find themselves in close sympathy with those Europeans who talk as if nuclear weapons were merely a bigger and better kind of artillery, and that the new weapons are subject to the same rules of warfare and of diplomacy as were the old."

During the Cuban confrontation, Lippmann went on, it was evident that the crucial decisions were being taken in Washington without consultation with Europe. He said he would not for a moment minimize "how hard it is for great and proud nations to feel that they are being taken to the brink of catastrophe while the outcome is being determined in Washington and Moscow," but he added:

"Whether you think the American reason for not consulting Europe was a good reason, I think I am right in saying that our experience in the confrontation has confirmed us in the view that the command of nuclear power to balance the Soviet nuclear power cannot be divided or shared. The direction of the nuclear power of the Western world is like driving a car on a hair-raising mountain road. Only one man can sit at the wheel. Others in the car can help to decide before he starts whether to take the mountain road or to seek a safer though longer one. But once the road is chosen—once the objective, the policy, the strategic play have been agreed to by consultation—there can be only one driver at the wheel."

The other passengers might not like the driver, Lippmann went on, "but it is still safer for all concerned than if there were two or three drivers trying to grab the steering wheel at the same time."

He then turned to a comparison uppermost in the minds of Europeans—Cuba and Berlin. Lippmann declared it to be his opinion that "the United States will not risk a nuclear war in Europe over anything less than that for which it risked war in Cuba—that is to say a radical move against the balance of strategic power." He reasoned that the United States would defend "the physical freedom of West Berlin," but that "it will not risk a nuclear war over political and juridical issues."

Lippmann said that "for some years to come" it would be unavoidable that Europe should leave nuclear defense of the Western world to the United States.

"We become restless at being told again and again that we cannot be relied upon to fulfill our commitments involving Berlin and Germany and France, that we are soft and weak, that we care about Cuba and the Western Hemisphere but not about Europe, that we do not understand Communism and its challenge," he concluded. "We feel that we have earned the right to be trusted when we say that the vital interests of European security and prosperity are also the vital interests of the United States. Trust us not to desert you and to betray you."

As viewed from Washington, the Lippmann logic was undoubtedly fundamental and persuasive—and of course clear, as Lippmann always is. But his good friend Raymond Aron, who by no means can be called a Gaullist, counterattacked in an unusually sharp article in *Le Figaro* four days later, marshaling the European arguments against the Lippmann thesis.

Aron cuttingly wrote that his friend Lippmann was "a great mind entangled in his own arguments, letting himself be carried away trying to demonstrate something which cannot be demonstrated." The chief fallacy in Lippmann's case, Aron said, was his effort to liken the problem of Berlin to that of Cuba. The only similarity, he said, was that the United States was involved in both.

To Lippmann's statement that the United States would not risk nuclear war in Berlin over political or juridical issues—only to defend the physical freedom of the West Berliners—Aron retorted that "there is no lack of political and juridical issues which ultimately do compromise the physical freedom of Berliners." Berlin, he declared was exactly the kind of "political" rather than "strategic" question which involved the risk of nuclear war.

"In asking the Europeans to let President Kennedy act as the driver, Walter Lippmann is asking of them in fact a sort of abdication," Aron continued. "In measures where diplomacy must make use of the nuclear threat, the American monopoly, combined with the rule of nonconsultation of the Allies, finally reduces the European countries to the status of protectorates. General de Gaulle, whose nuclear projects worry our friend so much, could scarcely wish a more brilliant confirmation of his point of view [that Europe must have its own nuclear weapons]. Why should not our American friends offer Europe something else than blind confidence in the driver, and a renunciation to all autonomy? If the American policy is as Walter Lippmann put it, then the Europeans will undoubtedly do what he is trying to dissuade them from doing. They will accept the greatest sacrifices in order to acquire nuclear forces which may not even be effective."

Raymond Aron is one of the most Atlantic-minded of the European intellectuals, yet he sensed strongly that nuclear dependence on the United States, of the sort that Lippmann outlined, simply was not acceptable to Europe. General de Gaulle was to make much of this six weeks later. Meanwhile, on the same day that Aron wrote his reply to Lippmann, Hugh Gaitskell came to Paris, also to address the Anglo-American Press Association, with the British Labour Party's case against entry into the Common Market on the terms so far obtained at Brussels. It was Gaitskell's last major speech before his tragic death a few days after the De Gaulle press conference, and he deployed his case with a ringing, cutting clarity that had the shock of cold water for his Paris audience. In particular he aimed his remarks at the Americans, and American pressure for British entry.

"I cannot help feeling that there is an element of wishful thinking about the whole approach of many people in the United States toward political integration in Europe," Gaitskell said. "They appear to suppose that if only Britain enters the Common Market, all the problems of political disunity and disagreement within the Atlantic Alliance will somehow magically disappear. I'm bound to say there seem to me to be no grounds for assuming anything of the kind. These difficulties are due neither to the European Economic Community nor to our absence from it, and they will not be resolved by our entry."

Gaitskell reiterated that the Labour Party would support British entry into the Common Market "only if certain specific conditions are fulfilled, and if our conditions are not fulfilled, we believe that Britain should not enter." He asserted that if the economic concessions which Britain had already made in Brussels had been announced at the beginning of the negotiations, "they would have been rejected out of hand by the British people."

Turning to the political argument over British entry, Gaitskell continued:

> "It seems to me that those who argue for Britain's entry on political grounds must logically assume the existence of a new European federal state. We have the gravest doubts whether Britain should enter such a federation. They do not derive from any hostility to internationalism. The truth is that no one can really say what exactly the consequences of a new European state on international relations would be. To predict the foreign policy of the new state would be the wildest speculation. But the idea that it will necessarily be just what the British or the Americans want seems to me to have no basis in reality.

"I believe too that a new powerful European state may well seek to become that 'third force' after which, I think mistakenly, some Europeans have long hankered. It is highly probable that the new state would insist on having its own powerful armory of up-to-date nuclear weapons. It is possible that far from leading to a strengthening of the Western Alliance, it would prove a most unstable influence on world affairs. I do not pretend to be sure, but we cannot ignore these possibilities."

The next day I met Gaitskell for a long talk alone. Between his speech and our meeting, he had seen both Prime Minister Pompidou and Foreign Minister Maurice Couve de Murville. From Couve de Murville, he told me, he had received a strong hint that, were the Common Market negotiations to fail, France would be ready to talk about generous association arrangements between Britain and the Six. It was the first direct suggestion of such an arrangement by a responsible French official to the British, and it was of course developed by De Gaulle at his press conference.

"Why we do not see what there is in this and start talking about it, finding out about it, I cannot understand," Gaitskell said to me. We went on then to discuss the nuclear problem, and relations among Britain, France and the United States. It had been, he said, a fundamental error that Britain and the United States had failed to respond positively to President de Gaulle's famous letter of September, 1958, in which he had in effect proposed a three-power global strategic partnership. Gaitskell said that if he became Labour Prime Minister, he would try "a completely pragmatic approach to the nuclear problem—a meeting of the President of the United States, the President of France, and the British Prime Minister, and instructions to their military staffs to go to work on plans for nuclear cooperation and coordination of forces."

He told me that he planned to visit the United States in February of 1963 to deliver a lecture to the combined Georgetown Foreign Service Institute and the National War College in Washington. I remarked that he had better be prepared to find himself accused of being "the man who wrecked British entry into the Common Market," and his popularity low among his friends of the New Frontier. He smiled a little bleakly and said he planned to concentrate in his Washington lecture on the future if—as he already firmly felt would be the case—Britain did not make it into the Market. He did not rule out eventual British entry, but he felt strongly that now was not a moment of historical necessity for Britain to take the plunge. One day, Gaitskell said, the United States might be very glad that Britain had stayed out of Europe and independent of what he felt to be an essentially conservative and protectionist strain in European thinking. He thought that combined Anglo-American liberalism was a strong and useful force in the world and ought to remain so, and that this would suffer if Britain entered Europe.

Four days after Gaitskell's Paris speech, the hidden crisis began to move into the open. On December 7, 1962, the news broke from Bonn that Chancellor Adenauer at long last had been forced to give a firm pledge that he would retire from office when the parliamentary year ended in the summer of 1963. For almost a month, Germany had been floundering in a cabinet crisis, and now the old chancellor had paid the extreme price of a commitment to quit in order to hold his government together for a few more months. German and French experts were still at work on the text of an agreement for close co-operation between the two nations, and Adenauer was determined to stay in power until this crowning work had been achieved. But the fact that he had been forced to give a pledge of retirement made him very much an "old man in a hurry" for his next visit to Paris to meet De Gaulle—already scheduled for the third week of January, 1963.

Meanwhile from Washington that same day—the twenty-first anniversary of the Pearl Harbor attack which had allied Britain and the United States in war—another story broke which was to alter the whole political outlook in the Atlantic Alliance. On that day, although nobody in Washington or anywhere else could have guessed it, the Kennedy Grand Design began to fall apart. The headline from Washington read: SKYBOLT PROGRAM IN DOUBT—U. K. COUNTING ON U. S. WEAPON. In an instant, Britain was in a political uproar.

Defense policy had long been the most vulnerable spot in Prime Minister Macmillan's rusting political armor, and his relations with the United States supposedly had been his strongest political asset. Now, it seemed, the rug was being pulled unceremoniously from under the whole Anglo-American "special relationship" which he had so assiduously cultivated and fostered.

The Skybolt story went back to 1960, when the British defense minister of the day, Harold Watkinson, took a major decision to scrap the development of an independent British medium-range ballistic missile, known as Blue Streak, and rely instead on a joint production program with the United States of Skybolt as a means of extending the useful life of the existing Royal Air Force Bomber Command—the Vulcans and the Valiants—into the 1970's. At that time the British were well aware that the United States Air Force was strongly backing Skybolt as an airborne answer to Polaris. But although Watkinson's decision was logical, it meant that the British had put all their slender stack of defense chips on an American program.

The technical problems of Skybolt were indeed formidable. Launched from an aircraft traveling near the speed of sound or faster, the missile was supposed to take off and arch in on a target 1,000 miles or more away. A fantastic "flying computer" system was required to set it on course, and if the launching was only a few inches incorrect, the missile would miss its target by more than a mile.

By November of 1962, half a billion dollars had been spent on Skybolt, and the Pentagon estimated that the program to make the missile operational would eat up another $2 billion. And at that point, the Pentagon reasoned, Skybolt would still only accomplish what Polaris or the Minute Man intercontinental missiles could already do with greater certainty. The 1963 defense budget was under discussion, and a decision had to be taken as to whether to include a "line" for Skybolt, continuing the program, or whether to cut losses and get out. Thus, the timing and the manner of the decision became one of superbureaucracy—and at the flick of a slide rule, with no top-level political or diplomatic discussions of the consequences and no consultations with the British, Britain was suddenly denuded of her last small pretense to nuclear independence.

The Pentagon subsequently asserted that the Skybolt decision should have come as no surprise to the British—that as far back as September of 1962 Defense Minister Peter Thornycroft, on a visit to the United States, had been thoroughly briefed on the mounting technical and military doubts about the program, as well as the soaring costs. But nonetheless, when the blow fell, it was handled in the worst possible way, making temporary nonsense of the "Anglo-American special relationship" and putting the Macmillan government in a humiliating public position.

At this point, former Secretary of State Dean Acheson added insult to the British injury with a brutally penetrating speech at West Point in which he analyzed the post-Cuban power relationship in the world.

"Great Britain has lost an Empire and not yet found a role," Acheson told the cadets at the United States Military Academy.

"The attempt to play a separate role—that is, a role apart from Europe, a role based on a 'special relationship' with the United States, a role based on being the head of a 'Commonwealth' which has no political structure or unity or strength and enjoys a fragile and precarious economic relationship by means of the sterling area and preferences in the British market—this role is about played out. Great Britain, attempting to work alone and to be a broker between the United States and Russia, has seemed to conduct policy as weak as its military power. Her Majesty's Government is now attempting—wisely in my opinion—to reenter Europe from which it was banished at the time of the Plantagenets, and the battle seems to be about as hard-fought as were those of an earlier day."

Coming from a man of Acheson's stature and political experience, the speech threw the Conservative press and British public opinion into an uproar. Prime Minister Macmillan hit back in a roundabout way—a letter to one of his old political associates, Viscount Chandos, President of the Institute of Directors in Britain. Acheson, said Macmillan, "has fallen into an error which has been made by quite a lot of people in the course of the last four hundred years, including Philip of Spain, Louis the Fourteenth, Napoleon, the Kaiser and Hitler." He said that the former Secretary of State "seems wholly to misunderstand the role of the Commonwealth in world affairs," adding:

"Insofar as he referred to Britain's 'attempt to play a separate role . . . is about played out,' this would be acceptable if he had extended this concept to the United States and to every other nation of the free world. This is the doctrine of interdependence which must be applied in the world today if peace and prosperity are to be assured. I am sure it is fully recognized by the United States administration and by the American people."

But to Charles de Gaulle, the position in which Britain found itself at the hands of the United States—stripped to its military underwear and shivering piteously about the treatment it was receiving—was eloquent justification of his own determination to achieve nuclear independence for France, and a clear indictment of the pitfalls and fallacies of interdependence. For more than a decade, De Gaulle had argued that no self-respecting nation could afford to leave basic nuclear decisions in the hands of an ally, no matter how close and no matter how determined its protestations of unshakable fidelity and support. Interdependence of the Macmillan pattern had no place in the De Gaulle concept of national strength and national will. And ironically, it was the actions of the Kennedy administration itself which were providing De Gaulle with the proof of his arguments.

The foreign ministers and defense ministers of the NATO Alliance gathered in Paris on December 10 for a routine semiannual meeting which was overshadowed by the Skybolt affair. As the ministers scattered to their respective capitals on the afternoon of Friday, December 14, Prime Minister Macmillan flew across the Channel from London to Paris with Lady Dorothy Macmillan and drove to the British Embassy, that spendid old mansion on the rue Faubourg St.-Honoré, for a quiet social evening with Ambassador Sir Pierson and Lady Dixon. The Macmillans rose early on Saturday morning, breakfasted, and departed by Rolls-Royce for the Château de Rambouillet, thirty miles southwest of Paris, to spend the weekend with President and Madame de Gaulle.

The Rambouillet meeting, which had been arranged more than a month earlier, could scarcely have taken place at a worse time for Macmillan. Apart from the Skybolt affair, which had dealt such a political body blow to the Prime Minister and lodged so heavily in De Gaulle's sense of power realities, the Common Market negotiations in Brussels had grown steadily more acrimonious. Only the previous Monday the Ministers of the Six had met the British and deadlocked quickly over the old agricultural problem. Couve de Murville delivered a blunt attack on the British, accusing them of demanding so many privileges for their farmers that the net effect would be to exclude British agriculture from the Market completely for the first six years after British entry. Two days of wrangling ended with no further progress, except for an agreement to meet again later in December.

As Macmillan disappeared behind the walls of Rambouillet that Saturday, Couve de Murville saw a few of the American correspondents in Paris for one of his periodic background talks. It seemed to me, listening to him discourse on the state of the Brussels negotiations, that the French position had definitely hardened against British entry. Again and again, in the quiet of his high-ceilinged office, lighting and relighting his pipe as he lounged behind a vast Louis Napoleon table, Couve de Murville kept coming back to the fact that there would be no watering-down of the Rome Treaty to accommodate the British, and that even if the French found themselves alone on this stand, it was still up to somebody to defend the treaty and preserve what had already been accomplished. He added, somewhat bitingly, that if Mr. Macmillan raised the agricultural problem at Rambouillet, he would undoubtedly find that President de Gaulle knew much more than he about the issues and the arguments. We trooped out into a cheerless, cold, windy, rainy December evening, little knowing that prospects for British entry were going to be much worse after Rambouillet.

Charles de Gaulle is a gracious and thoughtful old-fashioned host who likes to do things in the Grand Manner. He chose Rambouillet for the talks as a particular gesture to Macmillan, who enjoys shooting. The seventeenth-century château, which has been the pride of French kings and presidents for decades, is surrounded by a vast hunting preserve abounding in pheasants, quail, hare and other game. De Gaulle, with his poor eyesight, does not attempt to shoot, but he arranged things for Macmillan in good "English weekend" style. Even the weather should have made Macmillan feel at home—chill, dripping rain. In no time the Prime Minister was out in the fields of Rambouillet in those baggy Edwardian plus-fours and gum boots and a floppy hat. He shot 77 pheasants before lunchtime.

Macmillan, despite the relaxation of the shooting, was drawn and strained. He had originally intended that the Rambouillet weekend be a simple and convivial affair, designed largely to reassure De Gaulle that he was being kept in the picture before a meeting the Prime Minister had scheduled for the following week at Nassau with President Kennedy. But now, after Skybolt, Macmillan found himself in an awkward and indeed somewhat inferior political position vis-à-vis his host. Moreover, in the brief time since the American decision to cancel Skybolt, the British had not yet had time to prepare any firm studies or position papers for the Prime Minister. Macmillan arrived at Rambouillet, therefore, with a general idea of what he would have to try to do at Nassau, but without any real preparation.

The second big topic for Rambouillet would have to be the state of the Common Market negotiations. Macmillan would have preferred to avoid the subject entirely and leave it to Edward Heath and the British negotiating team at Brussels. But Ambassador Sir Pierson Dixon and the Foreign Office advisers had urged Macmillan that he could not ignore the subject with General de Gaulle, that it had to be raised and discussed. Still it was Macmillan's intention to stick to generalities rather than specific issues of the Brussels talks.

When the morning's shooting was finished, the Macmillans returned to the Château for luncheon with General and Madame de Gaulle, and then the two men settled down in front of a blazing fireplace in one of the smaller salons, with an interpreter and aides present on either side, for the start of serious discussions.

The Saturday afternoon conversation went relatively harmoniously, largely because the Prime Minister did most of the talking and De Gaulle said little to show his hand. They began with such matters as the atmosphere of East-West relations since the Cuban crisis, the Russo-Chinese dispute. Then Macmillan took up the Skybolt problem and the outlook for his meeting with President Kennedy. He reviewed for De Gaulle the general background of Britain's decision to scrap its own medium-range ballistic missile program and purchase Skybolt from the Americans instead, and the effect of the American decision on British defense plans.

Finally, Macmillan told the French president that it was his intention to seek in Nassau the American Polaris missile as a substitute for Skybolt and switch the British nuclear deterrent force from airborne to seaborne. De Gaulle listened to this review without any comment. He responded by talking about France's nuclear program and the necessity for France also to have her own deterrent. Neither the Prime Minister nor the French president suggested any kind of joint Anglo-French nuclear program or nuclear cooperation. The first round ended amicably, with each man having stated his position and no arguments or objections.

On Sunday morning, after the De Gaulles had attended a private mass in the chapel of Rambouillet, the two heads of government were joined by ambassadors and ministers, and the talks resumed. They began with a discussion of the possibilities of closer Anglo-French cooperation in various fields. De Gaulle took the lead. France and Britain were cooperating on the Concorde supersonic jet airliner, he said, and in an almost offhanded way he added: Could they not cooperate in the joint development of a guided missile suitable for European defense?

After General de Gaulle's January press conference, much was made of this offer at Rambouillet and whether or not it constituted a serious proposal to the British. In fact, De Gaulle spoke so offhandedly that the remark did not appear in the French record of the talks. It was noted in the British record, which was kept by Macmillan's French-speaking private secretary. But Macmillan did not even respond to the idea.

Nevertheless, at a reception at the Élysée Palace after he had vetoed British entry into the Common Market, De Gaulle remarked to one of his guests: "Macmillan said to me at Rambouillet, 'You are right to make a nuclear strike force. We are trying to make our own. We should try to associate them within the European framework, independent of America.' "

To another guest, De Gaulle said: "Macmillan came to Rambouillet to discuss European unity with me, and then went on to the Bahamas and made the Polaris deal with the President of the United States. Naturally that brought my press conference forward a little and changed its tone."

On the basis of these remarks the Gaullists later sought to link the Nassau decisions with De Gaulle's veto of British entry into the Common Market. They contended that at Rambouillet, De Gaulle offered the British a chance to cooperate with France and Europe, which Macmillan ignored, and that De Gaulle then decided that Britain would only be a Trojan horse for the United States inside the Common Market. The record shows, however, that no serious offer of nuclear or missile cooperation was made or discussed, and that De Gaulle raised no objection to Macmillan's disclosure that he intended to seek the Polaris from the United States.

From the theme of Franco-British cooperation, the two men then turned to the question of Britain and Europe.

De Gaulle began with a long, philosophical discourse on whether or not Britain was really ready to enter the Common Market. The tired and harassed Macmillan listened, increasingly grim and irritated. De Gaulle talked on about the kind of Europe he envisaged, a loose confederation of truly independent states. The trouble, he said, was that the European states were not truly independent. France herself had only started to recover her independence; Germany was dependent on the United States; and the Benelux countries were dependent on Britain or America. Italy he dismissed as "not counting for anything," according to the British record, and he had some implied criticism for Macmillan's "special relationship" with the United States.

De Gaulle then revealed himself in a pointed and fundamental statement. France, he said, was in a position now to veto the Germans in the Common Market, and even when the veto right ended and

Market decisions were taken by majority vote, France could still be certain of a dominant position. But, he declared, this would not be the case if the British entered the Market. Macmillan retorted with some heat, "Are you now raising a matter of principle with me after sixteen months of negotiations?" De Gaulle reflected in somewhat haughty silence, and then declared flatly to Macmillan that he did not think Britain was ready to enter Europe.

In this bleak and uncompromising atmosphere, the statesmen and diplomats adjourned for Sunday dinner *à la grande cuisine française.*

Subsequently, some French officials said that President de Gaulle was really trying to prod Macmillan to respond to his discourse and arguments and to put the British countercase of intentions and faith in membership in Europe. If this was the case, it reflected a profound gap in De Gaulle's psychological understanding of Macmillan and the British, who above all were not going to come into Europe as supplicants. Some weeks later, De Gaulle said in conversation with one of his cabinet ministers:

"On the doorstep of Rambouillet as Macmillan was leaving, I asked him the question, 'Are you really capable and really ready, Monsieur le Prime Minister, to make the transformations and changes you have to make to enter Europe?' I was probing for some promise that his Commonwealth ties would take second place to his European ties. His answer was evasive, and at that moment as I walked back into the Château after bidding him good-bye, I decided that Britain would not enter the Common Market."

So ended the fateful Rambouillet weekend. At 4 o'clock the Rolls-Royce swept out of the Château gates and straight to Villacoublay airfield near Versailles to the west of Paris, where a Royal Air Force Comet was waiting to fly Macmillan back to London. He drove to Admiralty House, his residence while No. 10 Downing Street was being rebuilt, arriving in the heavy gloom of a London December evening. On Monday, he spent the day in consultation with Thorneycroft and Lord Home, the Foreign Secretary, who had been preparing papers for the Nassau meeting. On Tuesday, December 17, the three men took off for Nassau where the talks with President Kennedy opened on Wednesday.

The American delegation arrived at Nassau still expecting the British to seek continuation of Skybolt, and they had worked out three different offers: to turn the whole program over to the British; to place it on a 50-5 basis until a further evaluation could be made;

or to give the British the Hound Dog, a relatively unsophisticated short-range air-to-ground rocket, in its place. But as Macmillan had already informed De Gaulle, the British defense experts had urged that he seek Polaris. The submarine missile suited the seafaring instincts of the British, and above all it was a thoroughly developed weapon which would remain effective well into the future. Nearly three days of argument were required to work out an agreement.

In the end, the deal turned on British agreement to support the American plan for creating a multilateral nuclear force under NATO. This idea, which had originated with General Lauris Norstad and NATO Secretary-General Paul-Henri Spaak in the days of the Eisenhower administration, had been restudied by the Kennedy administration and proposed to the NATO powers with one important change. Instead of a force of land-based nuclear missiles in Europe, owned, financed and controlled by the NATO countries, the multilateral force was now to be a fleet of missile-bearing surface ships.

In the wake of President Kennedy's interdependence speech on the Fourth of July and the passage of the new Reciprocal Trade Act, the NATO nuclear force project had become part of the Kennedy Grand Design for Atlantic unity. Britain, however, had shown only polite interest and no enthusiasm for the nuclear force project up to the Nassau conference. But as the discussion went round and round over the Polaris missiles, President Kennedy and his advisers made it increasingly clear to Macmillan that he could only have the missiles if he agreed to some kind of nuclear integration under NATO.

Macmillan subsequently claimed the initiative in offering to assign British nuclear forces to NATO. But in fact he had exhausted the arguments for getting Polaris from the United States on an independent basis and realized that unless he changed his position on integration, he was likely to return to London empty-handed. On the American side, the New Frontiersmen saw a chance to drive a bargain. A long argument ensued, and a senior British official later said that it resulted "in an agreement which bore all the signs of having been drafted by harassed and tired men who were not in any position to give careful consideration to all of the complications it was bound to raise." In any event the deal was made. In return for Polaris, Britain would assign her Bomber Command to NATO, with the right to withdraw the force in a national emergency outside the NATO area, and then would cooperate in the American proposal to establish a mixed-manned multilateral force of missile-carrying surface ships with crews from all NATO countries wishing to join. The British did not commit themselves to joining the force, but they did agree to join the studies to see if it would work.

Such were the results of Nassau. But there remained the French, and General de Gaulle's well-known policy of nuclear independence. President Kennedy and Prime Minister Macmillan dispatched parallel letters to Paris, explaining their decisions and enclosing a copy of the Nassau communiqué. President Kennedy then made the same offer to President de Gaulle which he had arranged with the British: Polaris missiles for French submarines, provided they were placed under a NATO nuclear command. The letters were delivered to the Élysée Palace by the American and British chargés d'affaires. Charles E. Bohlen, the American ambassador, in Washington for Christmas leave, flew to Nassau, joined the Kennedy party, and returned to Palm Beach for an evening with the President to discuss the outlook for French cooperation. Neither put the chances very high.

Meanwhile, as the Nassau meeting was ending, another unsuccessful and dismal round of meetings was taking place in Brussels between Britain and the Six. The main result again was an agreement to meet in January. Optimists were still taking odds of 60–40 that the British would make it. Some of the key British negotiators felt differently, but they all kept smiling.

Christmas of 1962 was now at hand, and after the tumult of diplomatic activity in November and December, everybody needed a quiet break and a period of reflection. Macmillan reached London on December 23, hailing the Nassau agreement as "a good one for Britain and for NATO." De Gaulle retired to his country home at Colombey-les-deux-Églises to prepare for his regular New Year's message to the country, in which he declared that France was "ready to receive in the future a Britain which could and would join Europe without reservations and definitively." But nobody realized then that he had a much more distant future in mind than January, 1963.

On New Year's Day in Palm Beach, meanwhile, President Kennedy invited a group of White House correspondents for a background talk, to reflect and ruminate on the dramatic events of 1962 and the outlook for 1963.

"I think we are more aware, probably, that we are going to incur at intervals people's displeasure," the President said. "This is a sort of revolving cycle. At least I think that the United States ought to be more aware of it, and I think too often in the past we have defined our leadership as an attempt to be rather well regarded in all countries. . . . So I think that what we have to do is to be ready to accept a good deal more expressions of newspaper and governmental opposition to the United States in order to get something done than we have perhaps been willing to do in the past. I don't expect that the United States will be more beloved, but I would hope that we could get more done."

Meanwhile, Ambassador Bohlen returned to Paris from his Washington leave and sought an appointment with President de Gaulle on January 4 to explain and discuss President Kennedy's views and the Polaris offer. The administration was smarting from suggestions that the offer to France had been "backhanded" or an "afterthought," and above all Bohlen wanted the door kept open. As a preliminary to the Bohlen-De Gaulle meeting, however, came a rather tart press statement from Information Minister Alain Peyrefitte, who seldom says anything that does not reflect De Gaulle's views:

"France at present has neither the submarines required for Polaris missiles, nor the warheads, so that one cannot see how the offer has any immediacy. France is busy with her own efforts and there is no reason why she should give them up. There is obviously no question of closing the door to anything, but France adheres to the principle of independence of her own defense."

Still, the door was not closed, and Bohlen came away from his meeting with De Gaulle with a hopeful feeling. He stressed to De Gaulle that there was no need for any quick answer to the Polaris offer, and he also hinted obliquely that a positive French response in due course could open up broader cooperation—by implication, the whole nuclear field.

On Monday, January 7, Undersecretary of State George Ball flew to Paris with NATO Ambassador Thomas K. Finletter to launch the multilateral nuclear force proposal formally before the NATO Permanent Council. On Wednesday, the French cabinet held its regular weekly meeting, and President de Gaulle informed his ministers that at his Monday press conference he would discuss Britain and the Common Market and the French response to President Kennedy's Polaris offer. He did not tell them what he would say.

On Thursday evening, De Gaulle held a reception at the Élysée Palace for the Corps Diplomatique, the first of the big formal events of the presidential season. A number of Paris diplomatic correspondents were invited, and during the evening, De Gaulle beckoned to one of them, Harold King of Reuters. King had known the General since the early days of World War II in England and later in Algiers. Now, with Couve de Murville at his side listening, the French president remarked to King that he "did not think Britain was ready to enter Europe." King took this to mean simply that another tough round of bargaining at Brussels would start on Monday and indicated as much in his response. But De Gaulle added: "No, I intend to discuss this on Monday, and I hope you will not take what I will say as a catastrophe. It is only a step along the way for your country." They shook hands, and King moved back into the crowd.

The next morning, Friday, Britain's tireless Common Market negotiator, Edward Heath, flew to Paris for a working lunch at the British Embassy with Couve de Murville and the head of the economic section of the Quai d'Orsay, Olivier Wormser. Ambassador Sir Pierson Dixon and Sir Eric Roll of the British Brussels negotiating team were present on the British side. Heath speaks very little French, and the diplomats worked entirely in English, which both Couve de Murville and Wormser speak fluently. The men stayed at the Embassy dining room table after lunch, talking until 4 o'clock. At the end, Heath put a point-blank question to Couve de Murville. Would anything happen on Monday at the De Gaulle press conference, he asked, to alter the picture? Was there any basic reason of principle why the negotiation could not go forward and succeed? Couve de Murville replied, in one of the strange footnotes to the whole story, that he knew of nothing that would happen to affect the negotiations, and on the basis of the luncheon discussion he saw no reason why the remaining difficulties could not be overcome.

In view of what had happened at Rambouillet, and in view of what was about to happen at the Monday press conference, Couve de Murville's declaration to Heath can be explained only as a statement of complete innocence of understanding or of subtle diplomacy. It seems impossible that the French foreign minister had not at least sensed that a French veto over British entry was in the making in De Gaulle's mind. In fact, his economic deputy, Wormser, had flatly told two experienced British correspondents two days before that the French were contemplating the veto. Couve de Murville is a diplomat of great precision, technical skill and subtlety all rolled into one. If he sensed what was coming, he at least appeared to have nothing to do with it.

At the same time, the British are no fools at diplomacy. They had by now begun to feel that a French veto of their entry into the Market was in the making somewhere, in some form. But they were determined not to be booby-trapped or maneuvered into a mistake on which the French could pounce. British tactics were to hang on without being rattled no matter what happened in Brussels in the crucial days ahead. They believed in the possibility of a solution, given a little flexibility and goodwill from the French. Moreover, an agricultural compromise formula had been secretly worked out by their technicians. They therefore were expecting to move forward, but at the same time they were prepared for a rearguard action which would make it absolutely clear if and when the break came that the onus would rest unequivocally on France.

Edward Heath crossed back to London to prepare for the Brussels meeting on Monday, and the De Gaulle press conference.

2. The Ten Days

Charles de Gaulle uses press conferences as no other man in history. He holds them about twice a year, and they form a specific part of the pattern by which he expounds and explains and develops his policies. This, of course, is what press conferences are for, but in the case of De Gaulle the process is much more precise and managed, and the very atmosphere and form tend to elevate and dramatize the occasion. When he tours France, De Gaulle is the noble *seigneur*, visiting his domains and bestowing the blessing of his presence on populations and town councils. In his speeches and television appearances there is another De Gaulle, reporting directly to the people of France on his stewardship, appealing for their support, and reassuring and explaining what France is doing.

Press conferences fall into a different category. It was not for nothing that the term "Fourth Estate" was invented in France, and just as De Gaulle travels to the towns and cities to meet the mayors and the bourgeoisie, and then speaks over television to keep up his contacts with the Second and Third Estates of France, periodically he calls in the Fourth Estate. Moreover, a press conference has the advantage for De Gaulle in that he seemingly subjects himself to discussing what others want to talk about. In fact, however, a De Gaulle conference is so managed that it is much more a royal audience than a public cross-examination.

On Monday, January 14, 1963, De Gaulle was holding his first press conference since May, 1962. Much had happened: the final referendums ending the Algerian war; the murderous Secret Army Organization terror attacks in Algeria and France itself; the August assassination attempt upon De Gaulle; the October constitutional referendum which decided that future French presidents would be elected by direct popular vote; and then the sweeping Gaullist victory in the November parliamentary elections. On top of all this had come the Cuban crisis, and now the Common Market negotiations with Britain were clearly moving to a decisive stage. President Kennedy's offer of Polaris missiles for France obviously had to be discussed.

Early that Monday morning, Undersecretary Ball and Ambassador Finletter took off from Paris for Bonn to confer with Chancellor Adenauer and West German Defense Minister Kai-Ewe von Hassel on the NATO nuclear force plan. They felt that the first round at NATO had gone well, although there was a little American resentment at the fact that the British were putting much more emphasis on the multinational idea rather than the fully integrated multilateral plan. Also that Monday morning, Edward Heath and the British negotiating team flew from London to Brussels, and other top ministers converged from the capitals of the Six. Maurice Couve de Murville, however, stayed behind in Paris to attend the press conference. France was to be represented in the opening stages of the Brussels round by Agriculture Minister Edgar Pisani (who brought with him no fewer than fourteen new amendments to previous agreements with the British).

Shortly after 2:30, newspaper correspondents began crossing the great courtyard of the Élysée Palace to get the best of the spindly little gilt chairs arranged in the splendid Salon de Fête—four pairs of magnificent crystal chandeliers down the center of the room, columns of gold fluting and green alabaster, one wall hung with vast Gobelins and Aubusson tapestries, ceiling frescos trimmed in gilt, and an opposite wall draped entirely in red plush. Television cameras and lights jammed one end of the room, and in the center of the red drapes a dais had been placed, two steps high, on which a table and a high armchair awaited the President of France.

To the right of the dais were ranged chairs for his ministers. They entered looking a little sheepish and uncomfortable and out of place, like schoolboys waiting for the headmaster to call the class to order. Promptly at 3 o'clock the curtains behind the dais parted, and De Gaulle lumbered up the two steps into the room with that giraffe-like gait, holding his glasses in his hand and acknowledging with short nods in all directions his audience, which of course rose as a matter of respect.

In Brussels, the Common Market ministers had met and decided to recess immediately and watch the press conference on television.

De Gaulle sat down and at once proposed a familiar procedure—that correspondents all ask their questions first so that he could group the questions under headings and discuss them in order. It is part of his "audience" technique, which automatically gives him full control over the flow of the conference and effectively eliminates any cross-examination or give and take. When all the questions were in on that historic Monday, he settled back and remarked pleasantly, "Well, now I am informed. I shall now endeavor to see that you are informed in turn."

General De Gaulle first spent fifteen minutes discussing French domestic and social matters, as part of the warm-up, and then turned to a questioner who asked: "Can you explicitly define France's position concerning the entry of Britain into the Common Market and the political evolution of Europe?" Commenting that "this is a clear question which I am going to try to answer clearly," De Gaulle launched into a dissertation which, in twenty minutes, had ended with crushing finality a decade of hope for the Monnet cause of European unity, and sixteen months of active negotiation for British entry into the Common Market.

"Sentiments, as favorable as they might be and as they are, cannot be put forward in opposition to the real factors of the problem," he began. "What are these factors?

"The Treaty of Rome was concluded between six continental States, States which are economically of the same nature. Whether in terms of their industrial or agricultural production, of their foreign trade, of their commercial customs and clients, or of their living and working conditions, there are many more similarities than differences among them. Moreover, they are adjacent, they interpenetrate, they are extensions of each other through their communications. Thus it has been psychologically and materially possible to organize an economic community of the Six. . . .

"The application of Great Britain undoubtedly raises for each of the six States and for England problems of a very great dimension. England is, in effect, insular, maritime, linked through its trade, markets and food supply to very diverse and often very distant countries. Its activities are essentially industrial and commercial, and only slightly agricultural. It has, throughout its work, very marked and original customs and traditions. In short, the nature, structure and economic context of England differ profoundly from those of the other States of the Continent.

"What is to be done so that Britain, such as it lives, such as it produces and such as it trades, be incorporated into the Common Market such as it has been conceived and such as it functions? For example, the means by which the people of Great Britain nourish themselves is in fact by importing foodstuffs purchased at low prices in the two Americas or in the former dominions, while still granting large subsidies to British farmers. This means is obviously incompatible with the system the Six have quite naturally set up for themselves. . . .

"Once again, what is to be done to make Britain, such as it is, enter that system? One was sometimes led to believe that our British friends, in applying for membership in the Common Market, agreed to change their own ways even to the point of applying all the conditions accepted and practiced by the Six, but, the question is to know if Great Britain can at present place itself, with the Continent and like it, within a tariff that is truly common, give up all preference with regard to the Commonwealth, cease to claim that its agriculture be privileged and, even more, consider as null and void the commitments it has made with the countries that are part of its Free Trade Area. That question is the one at issue. One cannot say that it has now been resolved. Will it be so one day? Obviously Britain alone can answer that.

"It must be agreed that the entry first of Great Britain and then that of those other States will completely change the series of adjustments, agreements, compensations and regulations already established among the Six, because all these States, like Britain, have very important traits of their own. We would then have to envisage the construction of another Common Market. But the 11-member, then the 13-member and then perhaps 18-member Common Market that would be built would, without any doubt, hardly resemble the one the Six have built.

"Moreover, this Community, growing in that way, would be confronted with all the problems of its economic relations with a crowd of other States, and first of all with the United States. It is foreseeable that the cohesion of all its members, who would be very numerous and very diverse, would not hold for long and that in the end there would appear a colossal Atlantic Community under American dependence and leadership which would soon completely swallow up the European Community. This is an assumption that can be perfectly justified in the eyes of some, but it is not at all what France wanted to do and what France is doing, which is strictly a European construction. . . .

"It is possible that Britain would one day come round to transforming itself enough to belong to the European Community without restriction and without reservation, and in that case the Six would open the door to it and France would place no obstacle in its path. It is also possible that England is not yet prepared to do this, and that indeed appears to be the outcome of the long, long Brussels talks.

"Whatever decision Britain finally makes in this regard . . . the consideration and respect due that great State and that great people will not be altered in the least. . . . If the Brussels negotiations were not to succeed at this time, nothing would prevent the conclusion of an agreement of association between the Common Market and Great Britain in such a way as to safeguard trade; neither would anything prevent the maintenance of close relations between Britain and France. . . .

"Lastly, it is highly possible that Great Britain's own evolution and the evolution of the world would lead the British to the Continent, whatever may be the delays before complete realization. For my part, this is what I am inclined to believe, and that is why, in my opinion, it will be in any case a great honor for the British prime minister, for my friend Harold Macmillan and for his Government, to have perceived this so early, to have had enough political courage to proclaim it and to have had their country take the first steps along the path that, one day perhaps, will bring it to make fast to the Continent."

So much for Britain and the Common Market. British correspondents almost winced at the words *"mon ami,* Harold Macmillan."

De Gaulle did not actually veto British entry that day. This was a formal matter of diplomatic negotiation and procedure which was carried out by Couve de Murville in Brussels two weeks later. But the General had laid down conditions and terms for British entry into Europe which were clearly intended to bring the long, long Brussels negotiations to an end. His audience shifted in tense expectation as he pointed to another questioner who rose and repeated a question: "What is France's position concerning the Kennedy multilateral formula—that is to say, on the Nassau agreements?"

The French president rolled relentlessly on: "To have allies goes without saying for us in the historic period we are in. But also for a great people to have the free disposition of itself and the means to struggle to preserve it is an absolute imperative, for alliances have no absolute virtues, whatever may be the sentiments on which they are based. We are in an atomic age and we are a country that can be destroyed at any moment unless the aggressor is deterred from the undertaking by the certainty that he too will suffer frightful destruction. This justifies both alliance and independence. . . .

"We have just witnessed the Cuban affairs. The Americans, finding themselves exposed to a direct atomic attack from the Caribbean, acted in such a way as to rid themselves of that menace and, if it had been necessary, to crush it without it having occurred either to them or to anyone else that the game would necessarily be played in Europe and without recourse to the direct assistance of the Europeans. Moreover, the means which they immediately decided to employ in order to counter a direct attack, whether it came from Cuba only or was combined with another originating elsewhere, these means were automatically set aside for something other than the defense of Europe even if Europe had been attacked in its turn. . . .

"In these conditions, no one in the world—particularly no one in America—can say if, where, when, how and to what extent the American nuclear weapons would be employed to defend Europe. This does not in the least prevent the American nuclear weapons, which are the most powerful of all, from remaining the essential guarantee of world peace. But it remains that the American nuclear power does not necessarily and immediately meet all the eventualities concerning France and Europe. . . .

"Thus principles and realities combine to lead France to equip herself with an atomic force of her own. This does not exclude, of course, the combination of the action of this force with the action of similar forces of its allies. But for us in this specific case, integration is something that is unimaginable.

"It is completely understandable that this French undertaking does not appear to be highly satisfactory to certain American circles. In politics and in strategy, as in the economy, monopoly quite naturally appears to the person who holds it to be the best possible system.

"It is quite true that the number of nuclear weapons with which we can equip ourselves will not equal—far from it—the mass of those of the two giants of today. But since when has it been proved that a people should remain deprived of the most effective weapon for the reason that its chief possible adversary and its chief friend have means far superior to its own? France, when formerly it was its turn to be world colossus, often experienced the worth of either the resistance of a less powerful but well-equipped adversary, or the support of an ally lining up inferior but well-tempered and well-employed weapons. I only want to say that the French atomic force, from the very beginning, will have the somber and terrible capability of destroying in a few seconds millions and millions of men. This fact cannot fail to have at least some bearing on the intents of any possible aggressor."

Having restated France's nuclear policy in the light of Cuba, De Gaulle turned to the specific matter of the Nassau agreement, the offer of Polaris missiles for French submarines which President Kenney had made, conditioned on French participation in the multilateral nuclear force project.

"France has taken note of the Anglo-American Nassau agreement. Undoubtedly no one will be surprised that we cannot subscribe to it. It would truly not be useful for us to buy Polaris missiles when we have neither the submarines to launch them nor the thermonuclear warheads to arm them. Doubtless the day will come when we will have these submarines and these warheads. But that day will be long in coming. When we will have these submarines and these warheads, what will the Polaris missiles then be worth? At that time we will have missiles of our own. . . .

"But also it does not meet with the principle about which I just spoke and which consists of disposing in our own right of our deterrent force. To turn over our weapons to a multilateral force under a foreign command would be to act contrary to the principle of our defense and our policy. It is true that we too can theoretically retain the ability to take back in our hands, in the supreme hypothesis, our atomic weapons incorporated in the multilateral force. But how could we do it in practice during the unheard moments of the atomic apocalypse? And then, this multilateral force necessarily entails a web of liaisons, transmissions and interferences within itself, and on the outside a ring of obligations such that, if an integral part were suddenly snatched from it, there would be a strong risk of paralyzing it just at the moment, perhaps, when it should act.

"In sum, we will adhere to the decision we have made: to construct and, if necessary, to employ our atomic force ourselves. And that without refusing, of course, cooperation, be it technological or strategic, if this cooperation is, on the other hand, desired by our Allies."

The door which Ambassador Bohlen and President Kennedy hoped to keep open was now closed, along with the door on British entry into Europe. There were one or two anticlimactic questions, and then De Gaulle rose and said with old-fashioned courtesy: "Well, ladies and gentlemen, I believe I have satisfied your curiosity as far as I was able to do. I thank you for the kind attention you accorded me and bid you good-bye." The audience rose and the General disappeared behind the red drapes in that lumbering but dignified gait. His ministers shuffled out to their cars in the courtyard, looking grim and far from elated or stimulated. The conference had lasted one hour and twenty minutes.

In Washington, White House aides were hovering over the morning news ticker, stripping off take after take of the story as it came in from Paris. President Kennedy was preparing to depart for Capitol Hill to deliver the annual State of the Union message to Congress, and as the news from Paris became grimmer and grimmer for the Grand Design, the President added one word in one sentence to his prepared text when he spoke two hours later: The word "fortunately" in the sentence, "The unity of freedom has never relied on uniformity of opinion—fortunately."

As we shuffled out of the Élysée Palace into the cold January air, a British correspondent remarked bitterly, "Well, about the only thing he didn't demand was that we all learn French before he'll let us join Europe." But whether one agreed with De Gaulle or not, he had put on a superlatively impressive performance of classic textbook clarity. He never had looked as well physically in his five years in power, had never been more confident, serene and lucid—and never more devastating in the brutal force of his words.

Usually press conferences are offshoots of history, the reflections or reactions of men in office to events which have happened, to decisions which have been made. At best they are the tactical maneuvers and developments by which governments operate. But on January 14, 1963, we walked into the Élysée Palace, into the presence of the President of France, all of us thinking, living, speculating, and covering one kind of a western world, one kind of an Atlantic Community, one concept of a United Europe, one dream of the 20th Century. More than a decade of effort and struggle had gone into that dream—a generation of postwar education, a vast interweaving of policies of fifteen nations, years and years of tireless diplomacy, the travels and discussions of countless legislators and businessmen and journalists, the appropriation of millions and millions of dollars, the studies and the wealth or great universities and public foundations, the service of soldiers, the prayers of churches, the eloquence and emotion of politicians and statesmen, schoolchildren and public heroes, editorialists and propagandists. When we walked out, it lay as shattered as the pebbles which crunched under our feet in the cold forecourt of the Élysée Palace.

In Brussels, stunned ministers of the European Economic Community filed back into their conference room, after the television set had been snapped off, to face Mr. Heath and the British delegation in embarrassed shame and anger. Olivier Wormser of the French delegation departed in haste for his Brussels headquarters to telephone Paris for instructions. The dark-bearded French agriculture minister, Edgar Pisani, meanwhile tabled his amendments to the existing drafts of agricultural agreements with the British, and in effect everybody threw up his hands.

"If De Gaulle means what he says, we might as well pack in," one of the ministers remarked angrily as he left the room. In the pall which was cast over Brussels, there was little to do but await the arrival from Paris of Couve de Murville and a declaration of a formal French position with regard to the negotiations.

Meanwhile, in Bonn, Ball and Finletter were closeted with Chancellor Adenauer on the NATO multilateral force question. They emerged from "a very successful talk" with Adenauer's pledge of West German cooperation. Informed of what De Gaulle had said in Paris, Ball remarked to American reporters that "we developed our ideas of Nassau on the assumption that the French might not participate and we will go ahead." He then boarded a plane and headed back to Washington.

In Brussels, Tuesday, January 15, was given over almost entirely to one speech after another from the Common Market ministers denouncing the French stand. It was perfectly clear that France was isolated; what was also clear was that President de Gaulle didn't give a damn, and nothing was going to influence or alter his decision. Belgium's Paul-Henri Spaak called it a "policy of intransigence," and West Germany's Gerhard Schroeder rebutted the French accusation that Britain had so far given only insignificant or inadequate concessions. Luns of the Netherlands echoed Spaak. The Italian, Emilio Colombo, one of the best-informed men in Europe on the agricultural problem, heatedly declared that "a press conference on television does not constitute an act of this conference—the position of the Community has to be established by the Six and not by one member."

Heartwarming as all this was for the British it did not, in fact, take matters very far. In Paris on Wednesday, with all of the western world in an uproar, De Gaulle was haughtier than ever. The cabinet met to hear the General's instructions to his foreign minister for the Brussels meeting, plus a little lecture which he told Information Minister Alain Peyrefitte to pass on to the waiting press. De Gaulle remarked to his ministers that there "is a sort of convention in the world" by which nations "try to hide from realities." Thus, he said, when the President of France speaks of England as being an island, or the North Atlantic Treaty Organization as being under American command, "there is a cry of scandal and shock."

That same afternoon, Jean Monnet, the "Father of Europe," issued a statement declaring that De Gaulle was completely wrong about the state of the negotiations with the British, and that it was "inconceivable" that they should now fail on matters of minor importance in comparison with the great objective of unification of the West. Nearly all of the big questions were settled, Monnet said, and the remaining issues "can be quickly concluded." He went on:

"We must understand clearly that for the peace of the world it is imperative that Britain join the European Economic Community and that an equal relationship of partners be built between a united Europe, including Great Britain, and the United States."

With that, Monnet took an evening train to Brussels in a forlorn but determined behind-the-scenes effort to work out some kind of a common front, to block the French and keep the negotiations going.

But on Thursday morning, Couve de Murville arrived and his instructions from De Gaulle were ruthless and uncompromising: Break off the negotiations, bring them to a halt. His position was thoroughly unenviable and to any other man would have been untenable. Here, only six days before, he had given his professional assurances to Heath and the British that he knew of no reason why the negotiations would not go on, and no reason why they could not succeed. Now, while his colleagues boiled and seethed with emotion—and the British delegation cooled its heels at the Metropole Hotel waiting for the Six to decide the fate of the talks—Couve de Murville went to work with the methodical professional skill of a pathologist conducting a post-mortem on a poisoned corpse. As a career diplomat in the service of the President of France, he was the perfect subordinate.

Suavely he offered one solution: Transfer the discussions from Brussels to Luxembourg, and there let the Six continue the debate as to whether Britain was ready to join Europe and whether to go on negotiating. But the transparency of the move, which would bury the whole problem, was perfectly clear to the other ministers, who insisted as a rearguard action that the Common Market Commission should draw up a balance sheet on the state of the negotiations, and that this should be used as a basis for deciding whether or not to carry on. Couve de Murville held out unyieldingly for burial or break, and the ministers argued on in an angry and unsettled mood until nearly midnight, when they broke without a decision, to meet again on Friday.

That Thursday evening, De Gaulle was holding another reception at the Élysée Palace, this time for parliamentarians of the National Assembly. When he was asked by one if it was not the case that agreement had been very close with the British, he replied haughtily: "You believe that, but in reality, they multiply the exceptions of every proposal. That has been going on long enough. There is the Rome Treaty, and it must be accepted. Either the English will sign, or they will leave Brussels, and after that they will think. They will enter the Common Market one day—but I will certainly not be here!"

On Friday, the argument resumed in Brussels. The five held firm, refusing to break the negotiations or transfer them to Luxembourg. They insisted that the Common Market Commission draw up a report on outstanding issues, and they insisted that the ministers go through with their agreed timetable with the British and meet again in ten days' time on January 28. The French foreign minister finally announced disdainfully that the Commission could go ahead with its study, but he was returning to Brussels in ten days' time only for an adjournment of the talks with the British. At the same time, the French announced that they would boycott a meeting scheduled in Luxembourg on Monday to discuss British entry into the European Coal and Steel Community, and a Tuesday meeting of the Common Market negotiating team to discuss relations between the Community and the British Crown Colony of Hong Kong. In this angry mood, the Brussels round, which was supposed to have produced "one good heave" on British entry, ended.

The drama now shifted back to Paris. On Sunday, January 20, Chancellor Konrad Adenauer flew to the French capital in a special Lufthansa flight for a long-arranged visit, returning President de Gaulle's fabulously successful state visit in September. The Social Democratic Party in Bonn had demanded three days before that Adenauer postpone his trip in view of De Gaulle's treatment of the British, but the old chancellor, of course, had paid not the slightest attention. He had watched the events unfolding in Paris and Brussels in a silence which left no doubt that, while he had nothing against British entry into the Common Market, De Gaulle's attitude was quite acceptable to him. Adenauer did not regard the French veto of the British as any kind of a disaster for history, and in the long sixteen months of negotiation in Brussels he had been much less helpful to the British than his two senior cabinet ministers, Foreign Minister Gerhard Schroeder and Economics Minister Ludwig Erhard.

Moreover, Adenauer was now on the eve of what he believed to be the crowning achievement of his long years in office. West Germany and France had been working for many weeks on a government cooperation agreement, growing out of the De Gaulle visit to Bonn, and the main purpose of the Chancellor's trip to Paris was to sign the document. But it was not known on that rainy Sunday evening when Adenauer flew into Orly Airport that a secret decision had been taken to upgrade the agreement into a full-scale treaty between the two countries. Since the German cabinet crisis in November, and his pledge of December 7, 1962, to retire from office at the end of the parliamentary year, Adenauer had determined to press as far and as fast as he could in his remaining months to consolidate Franco-German rapprochement. Experts had been shuttling between Paris and Bonn putting together the bilateral agreement for cooperation in a variety of fields: political, cultural, military, economic. The document was in more or less final form by early January (incidentally, it was never shown to any of France's and Germany's Allies), but four days before the De Gaulle press conference the legal department of the West German Foreign Ministry deposited an opinion on the desk of Foreign Minister Schroeder, to the effect that the agreement should be made a treaty if it were to conform with the Bonn constitution. The advisers said that unless the document were given formal ratification and treated as a treaty, then it might be challenged in the Constitutional Court at Karlsruhe and invalidated as unconstitutional. The problem of what constitutes an "agreement" and what is a "treaty" is a familiar one to American Presidents and the United States Senate. It was up to Adenauer to decide.

Anxious to press forward with France, he now had a ready-made legal reason to upgrade the negotiations and seek a treaty. The French Ambassador to Bonn, the experienced and astute Roland de Margerie, was called in, told of the Foreign Ministry legal opinion, and asked if the French Government would agree to converting the draft document into a treaty.

Couve de Murville had some genuine doubts when the German request reached Paris as to how De Gaulle would respond. The French president above all does not like to be rushed, and at stake was a decision of historic importance. It was with some uncertainty, therefore, that the question was placed before De Gaulle for a decision at the Wednesday cabinet meeting following his press conference. But De Gaulle saw in it a chance for a new move in his own Grand Design and quickly sent Adenauer his approval. Experts now went to work frantically to make the necessary language changes, the final legal studies, and prepare the new treaty in bound volumes ready for signature.

All of these developments, of course, had taken place in complete secrecy. But when Adenauer disembarked from his aircraft on Sunday evening, an unusual semantic slip occurred. He remarked that he was in Paris to sign a "Vertrag"—the German word for treaty, which also translates as "agreement." First bulletins from the airport, sent out in English by a German-speaking reporter, spoke of a "treaty" to be signed. But the official spokesman of the Quai d'Orsay a short time later used the French word "accord" rather than "traité" in describing the document. The English news bulletins were then amended back to the word "agreement," and that Sunday evening the fact that a treaty was now afoot still remained a closely held Franco-German secret.

On Monday the two leaders began their talks at the Élysée Palace, and that afternoon the news was out. The reaction in the embassies of Paris was another round of shock and dismay. Did Adenauer, the faithful European and NATO partner of the past, not realize the implications of what he was about to do? Was De Gaulle now on his way to creating some kind of an axis or bloc within NATO?

The new treaty appeared to go far in that direction. It required, among other things, that the French president and the West German chancellor meet twice every year to coordinate policy, that their foreign ministers meet every two to three months, their military staff chiefs every two months, and that detailed consultations be instituted in all sorts of cultural and economic fields. French and German were to be raised to the status of second language in each country, and university degrees were to be standardized and made interchangeable. Without any "federation" or "integration," the treaty was a model of the Gaullist concept of how Europe ought to be organized along confederation lines.

On Tuesday, January 22, at 5 o'clock in the afternoon, De Gaulle and Adenauer sat down at a huge Louis Napoleon table in the gilded Murat Salon of the Élysée Palace, and under blazing television and camera lights, with their senior ministers and officials flanking them and standing behind them, they scratched their signatures in two bound volumes—one red, one blue. They exchanged volumes and signed again, their foreign secretaries signing after them.

De Gaulle rose and said, "There is not a man in the world who does not realize the fundamental importance of this act, not only because it turns the page on a long and bloody series of conflicts, but also because it opens the door wide to a new future for France and Germany, for Europe and consequently for the whole world."

Adenauer, who had devoted thirteen years to this supreme moment, rose with the briefest of responses, taking nothing away from his French host. All he said was: "President de Gaulle has expressed the feelings of all on both the French and German sides in such a perfect manner that I have nothing to add to his words."

Then as the aged but straight and vigorous old chancellor half turned to resume his seat, he suddenly found De Gaulle's arms outstretched in an embrace. The tall and austere President of France bent forward, and in the French manner he kissed the surprised and deeply moved Chancellor of Germany on each cheek. It was a moment of history—and of very mixed emotions for French viewers on their television screens that evening.

The next morning, as the other capitals of the Atlantic Alliance reacted in dismay and confusion at what seemed to be happening to Atlantic unity and the great enterprises of postwar European political construction, the Chancellor called at the Éysée Palace for a brief farewell meeting with the French president. They met alone for half an hour, and then, as they came through the great glass door to the Élysée courtyard to say good-bye, at the top of the short flight of steps leading down to Adenauer's car there occurred a poignant scene, in itself meaningless, yet oddly symbolic and suggestive of the relationship between the two great men.

The Garde Republicaine, in their plumed helmets, blue coats with red facings, white breeches and high black boots, were lining the steps at attention, drawn swords at their chests in salute to the German chancellor. Adenauer's black Mercedes limousine waited with the chauffeur holding the door. The two men paused, shaking hands and chatting for the benefit of the photographers. Then Adenauer started down the red-carpeted steps to his car. De Gaulle waved a brief parting farewell, turned the other way and headed back into the Élysée Palace. At the foot of the steps, Adenauer turned around with his hand half outstretched—obviously expecting to find the French president there for a last handshake. No one would pretend that it was a deliberate act. Adenauer probably had not been briefed on the formula of a De Gaulle farewell. But all that the old chancellor saw was De Gaulle's back, disappearing through the glass doors.

He dropped his hand, turned quickly away and settled himself in his car. The tires crunched on the gravel, and the Mercedes sped out through the gates with an escort of police.

The ten days were over.

That afternoon, President Kennedy hit back. Barely controlling his anger, he told a press conference in Washington:

"President de Gaulle may not believe that the United States' commitments to Europe are good, but Chairman Khrushchev does and Chairman Khrushchev is right. There may be reasons for a country to wish a nuclear force of its own, and France has put forward its reasons, but in my judgment it is inaccurate and not really in the interests of the Alliance to justify itself on the grounds that the United

States would fail to defend Europe by whatever means are necessary."

The President then announced that American nuclear power in Europe was about to be reinforced with the arrival of Polaris submarines on station in the Mediterranean. And he also announced that Ambassador Livingstone Merchant was coming out of retirement to fly to Paris on the following Monday to work in the U. S. NATO delegation on negotiations to establish the multilateral NATO nuclear force, as envisaged in the Nassau agreement with Britain and rejected by General de Gaulle.

The French, for their part, remained unmoved, unimpressed, uninfluenced and in fact, it seemed, a little self-satisfied and smug over the rumpus they had caused. At the regular weekly cabinet meeting, De Gaulle reaffirmed his instructions to break off negotiations with Britain and chided Couve de Murville for not having lowered the guillotine the week before.

On Sunday, January 27, Edward Heath and the British negotiating team were back in Brussels for the last time. The British in the intervening two weeks since the press conference had avoided any recriminatory or accusative or inflammatory response to De Gaulle, hoping, not without results, for a swing of support to their side. From Bonn, The Hague, Rome and Brussels this support had emerged. But it was not enough to influence events.

The British turned to the Germans for primary support, and on Sunday evening Heath had dinner with Ludwig Erhard. They agreed on a counterattack against the French, and Erhard raised British hopes somewhat with assurances that Adenauer believed he had an agreement with De Gaulle to allow the negotiations to continue. Monday, when the conference was due to resume, was a dank and foggy day in Brussels, and the aircraft bringing Foreign Minister Schroeder from Bonn had to be diverted. When Schroeder reached Brussels several hours late, he drove straight to the French mission to confer with Couve de Murville.

At times like these the French foreign minister—and he has been through a number of such times in the service of General de Gaulle—exudes an impression of icy enjoyment at playing the isolated role. He has great intelligence and years of negotiating experience, and a formidable capacity for sustained argument. He is an ideal Gaullist foreign minister. "Couve," a fellow diplomat once remarked, "is an exponent of the art of how to influence people without winning friends."

He would have none of the British-German formula for resuming negotiations after receiving a report from the Common Market Commission on what had to be done. He told Schroeder bluntly that France simply would not negotiate any further. They then drove to the Common Market headquarters together for a long wrangle over procedure which lasted until midnight. The next morning, Tuesday, Schroeder and Erhard asked Couve de Murville to meet at the German Embassy for one last try. While they were talking, Erhard was called out and handed a personal message from Secretary of State Dean Rusk.

The effort was sadly reminiscent of October, 1954, when Dulles dispatched Ambassador Bruce to Brussels with a special message to try to save the European Defense Community treaty. Rusk did not go quite so far as Dulles, but he did tell the Germans that he did not want to leave any doubt of the seriousness with which the United States regarded the prospects of a breakdown and the blow that rejection of British entry into the Common Market would be to the unity of the Atlantic Alliance. Nothing, however, could change General de Gaulle.

The talks among the Six resumed after lunch on Tuesday. Ministers are only human and can sustain anger, argument and indignation for only so long. Couve de Murville knows this perfectly well, and all he had to do was wait the argument out.

By now, the atmosphere was one of discouragement and disillusionment rather than the anger and bitterness which had marked the previous day or two weeks. Couve de Murville summarized the French position: "Replying to criticism which is being directed at us on all sides, which alleges that we French have a bias toward a little Europe, I would like to say once again that what we are concerned with is not to promote either a big or a little Europe, but to make sure that the Europe we are about to create is European. This, in our view, is the proper criterion for dealing with the problem of Britain's entry."

He then declared flatly and with finality that France would not participate in any further negotiating meetings with Britain. This was the veto and this was the end.

It was late afternoon. Since the other five Common Market countries could not negotiate British entry without the French, there was nothing more to be done. Word was sent to Edward Heath and the British delegation, who had been waiting at their own headquarters while the Six argued the death verdict. The British delegation took its place at the conference table for the last time. One by one, various ministers spoke in sorrow and sympathy, leaving the French coldly isolated. Heath spoke last. He is a quiet man, not given to oratory or bombast, and his soft reserved tone of speech added much emotion to what he had to say:

"There have been times in the history of Europe when it has been only too plain how European we are; and there have been many millions of people who have been grateful for it. . . . We told you at the very beginning of these negotiations that we wanted to go forward with you in the building of a new Europe. Our words were very carefully weighed. They remain true today.

"We have been encouraged by the upsurge of support for the fullest British participation in a united Europe which has been demonstrated in so many quarters in these recent weeks. And so I would say to my colleagues: They should have no fear. We in Britain are not going to turn our backs on the mainland of Europe or on the countries of the Community. We are a part of Europe; by geography, tradition, history, culture and civilization. We shall continue to work with all our friends in Europe for the true unity and strength of this continent."

Ministers crowded around Heath to grip his hand. Couve de Murville rose, snapped his briefcase shut, and circled out of the room in the opposite direction.

3. The Summing-up

From the launching of the Marshall Plan in 1947 until the De Gaulle press conference in 1963, a broad fundamental harmony of purpose and political strategy prevailed among the governments of the Atlantic Community.

They were agreed on the necessity of NATO unity to meet the challenge of Communism. They agreed that this unity should continue to strengthen and grow and not be allowed to wither away. They agreed on the need for collective security and an integrated defense system, and they poured billions into its infrastructure for everything from oil pipelines to a radar network that extends from the North Cape to the Black Sea. They agreed that the economies of Europe should be progressively integrated and that membership in a united Europe should expand. They agreed that NATO unity and the economic dynamism of the Western democracies had helped to produce the polycentrism—the growing fissures of nationalism and independence—which had begun to appear in the Communist bloc. They agreed that a strong American military presence on the Continent of Europe was a necessity for the peace of the world. As a corollary, the political leadership of the United States was accepted in the Alliance. The governments agreed that the NATO system was working well, and that closer ties and greater unity should be forged in the Alliance between North America and a united Europe—whether this be called "interdependence" or the "dumbbell concept" or "The Grand Design."

Of course there had been many arguments and difficulties in the Atlantic Alliance. Resentment had frequently run high in European capitals against United States leadership and tactics and the demands which America often placed on its Allies. These differences burst out in the 1950's over Suez, Indochina, diplomatic tactics in dealing with the Russians, colonialism and decolonization, the Baghdad Pact, the Algerian war, the European Defense Community treaty, negotiations for a nuclear test ban, disarmament policies, terms for a possible Berlin settlement, East-West trade restrictions, the role of neutralism in the world, recognition of Red China, and many other inter-Allied arguments that never made headlines. General de Gaulle added to the problems when he returned to power in 1958: his refusal to accept United States nuclear warheads on French territory, withdrawal of the French Mediterranean Fleet from NATO command, his attitude toward the United Nations and its peace-keeping operations, French withdrawal from the Geneva disarmament talks.

But with all the problems, there remained a strong fundamental sense of unity of purpose in the Atlantic Alliance, considerably reinforced during the Cuban crisis of 1962. United States leadership had frequently been questioned by the Allies, but there had been no real or lasting breach in Atlantic unity, and no NATO government had declared its basic policies to be different from those of the other members of the Alliance. The arguments of the 1950's on the whole were tactical rather than strategic—over matters of architecture and blueprints rather than whether or not to build the building.

This great postwar harmony of outlook and political strategy in the western world ended with the De Gaulle press conference. Nothing was the same in NATO or in Europe after January 14, 1963.

General de Gaulle's actions on that January day went far beyond the mere blocking of British entry into the Common Market and rejection of an integrated NATO nuclear force. These were simply the percussion caps which De Gaulle used for exploding the whole concept of integration, Atlantic unity and American paramountcy in the non-Communist world on which NATO had been built. The De Gaulle press conference brought a postwar era to an end and marked the beginning of Gaullist foreign policy and strategy in the West—separate and distinct from the established NATO policies under the leadership of the United States.

Far from supporting closer ties of transatlantic unity, General de Gaulle was determined on a policy of European political independence in world affairs. The key words in the De Gaulle press conference were these: "It is foreseeable that [if the Common Market were to be enlarged] the cohesion of all its members, who would be very numerous and diverse, would not hold for long, and that in the end there would appear a colossal Atlantic Community under American dependence and leadership which would soon completely swallow up the European Community. This is an assumption that can be perfectly justified in the eyes of some. But it is not at all what France wanted to do and what France is doing, which is strictly a European construction."

At some point in the long Brussels negotiations, De Gaulle made up his mind that British entry into the Common Market would be incompatible with his own grand plan for an independent Europe, free of United States influence or, as De Gaulle thinks of it, "domination." As De Gaulle pondered his moves, possibly he reflected on a fierce argument which he had held with Winston Churchill on the eve of the invasion of France, on June 4, 1944. De Gaulle had flown from Algiers to England and arrived at the invasion headquarters in the forest outside Portsmouth to join Churchill and the Allied commanders, who were anxiously watching the weather reports while the vast invasion armada loaded and prepared to sail. After hearing the invasion plans for the first time, De Gaulle immediately raised the question of recognition for his Committee of National Liberation as the governing authority for France. The British were prepared to grant recognition, but President Roosevelt had grimly set himself against De Gaulle. The argument reached its climax, according to De Gaulle's memoirs, when Churchill cried: "How do you expect that the British should take a separate position from that of the United States? There is something you ought to know: each time we have to choose between Europe and the open sea, we shall always choose the open sea."

De Gaulle and the Anglo-Saxons shared many bitter mutual recollections of the war days, and these strongly color De Gaulle's present-day determination to assert French strength and independence in the world. Eventually, De Gaulle concluded, once the British were inside the Common Market, they would be pushing constantly to support American interests instead of putting the interests of Europe first.

Was De Gaulle right or wrong in his assessment? France had almost no support for its action in vetoing the British. The other five governments were all prepared to accept the fact that Britain did have its outside special relationships which she would not abandon lightly, and that if Britain did enter the Common Market this might well cause new difficulties in shaping Common Market policies. But the other five also shared Jean Monnet's belief that once the British were inside the Market, many things would change and problems would look entirely different in London.

New trading partners for Britain, new outlets for British goods, new competition, membership in a new organization with rules of partnership and a new common interest to be shared, the opportunity to wield renewed political and economic influence on the Continent—all these, in Monnet's view, could not help but alter the traditional policies, thinking and national attitudes in Britain. In short, the other five Common Market countries did not question Britain's "European" credentials as did General de Gaulle, and they did not share the General's fear of "an Atlantic colossus under American dependence and leadership which would soon completely swallow up the European Community."

If the Brussels negotiations had gone on, would they have succeeded, could the British have made it into Europe? Here again, everybody but the French agreed that the economic concessions could have been worked out. On the eve of the De Gaulle veto, the Common Market Commission had drafted a secret agricultural compromise which was yet to be discussed by the ministers, but which experts on both sides believed could be made to work. The five did not share De Gaulle's view that it was pointless for the negotiations to go on. But they did believe that success could only come through much more hard bargaining and some further basic concessions by the British, and they did not agree with Prime Minister Macmillan when he told the British nation the night after the talks had ended that "the long and complicated negotiations broke down not because they were going to fail—but curiously because they were going to succeed."

The Italian minister of foreign trade, Emilio Colombo, who had been one of the most helpful of all the negotiators in working out compromises to get Britain in, disagreed strongly with Macmillan's contention that success was just around the corner.

"Had this been the reason there would have been no need for such a violent and immediate break by the French," Colombo summed up after it was all over. "A large number of problems were still unresolved, and France could easily have taken one of these as a pretext for stiffening her attitude and eventually closing the door to further negotiations. On the contrary, the requirement that economic negotiations also stimulate political integration, and a common defense, led during the last months of the negotiation to a crisis of mistrust that was at the basis of the failure." *

The five were willing to go on, in the belief that the economic difficulties could be overcome and the "crisis of mistrust" resolved. They were dedicated to the concepts of Atlantic unity which had prevailed in Europe since the Marshall Plan. They believed with Jean Monnet that "for the peace of the world it is imperative that Britain join the European Economic Community and that an equal relationship of partners be built between a united Europe, including Great Britain, and the United States."

But General de Gaulle did not. His veto of British entry was a political act. He never gave the negotiators in Brussels a chance to find out whether the secret agricultural compromise might have worked, whether the crisis of mistrust might not have been overcome, what the limits were to which Britain would go in making national sacrifices to join Europe. In the end, De Gaulle simply decided that Britain inside Europe did not fit his concept.

For the British, there was both bitterness and relief: bitterness

* Quoted by Robert Kleiman in *Atlantic Crisis.*

over the treatment handed down by General de Gaulle, but a certain relief that the nation was not going to be jogged out of its traditional ties and habits. Thinking Britons knew that the country badly needed the kind of jogging which entry into Europe would have given, but when the veto fell in Brussels there was little that the London intellectuals could do but retire to their universities, libraries and editorial offices in sadness and shock.

Macmillan went on television to warn Britons against "vindictiveness," but in the heat of the moment he added: "We have seen these attempts before of one nation—or sometimes one man—to dominate the whole of Europe, to create a kind of sham United Europe. They seem to think one nation can dominate Europe and, equally wrongly, that Europe can live alone without friends and without allies. I'm sorry to say it, but I fear that it is true that France—or at least the present Government of France—is looking backward, not forward."

These were strong words for the "old comrades of Algiers" and the "friends of Rambouillet."

Across the Atlantic, President Kennedy, who had wound up 1962 speculating that "I don't expect that the United States will be more believed but I would hope we could get more done" during 1963, fell back on the multilateral nuclear force project as the only available instrument to shore up transatlantic unity in NATO. Ambassadors Finletter and Merchant began the rounds of London, Bonn, Brussels, The Hague, Rome, Athens and Anakara. But in the wake of the De Gaulle press conference, governments all over Europe turned inward to domestic problems and issues of internal politics which had been buried or bypassed in the dramatic months of the Berlin crisis, the Summit Conference, the Cuban confrontation, and Britain's efforts to join Europe.

Kennedy flew to Europe in June, 1963, hopeful, at first, that he might at least find an agreement-in-principle on MLF. But in stops in Britain, Germany and Italy, he found instead that the momentum and impulse for new ventures in NATO integration and unity were lacking. Hints went from Washington to President de Gaulle that President Kennedy would be ready to stop off in Paris if there was anything to talk about, but there was no response from the Élysée Palace.

A few weeks before President Kennedy was assassinated, he had a long talk in his White House office with one of France's most distinguished journalists, Jean Daniel, then the foreign editor of the weekly *L'Express.* Couve de Murville had been in Washington to confer with Kennedy a week or two before, and the President talked at length to Daniel about France and the problems of Franco-American relations. At the time, the interview was off-the-record, but after the President was assassinated, Daniel felt that it should be part of the record of the times.

"Both Couve de Murville and myself had to admit that we were not in agreement on anything," the President said. "And we both accepted the fact that this total disagreement should not damage the friendship between two great Western countries. I came to the conclusion that the strategy of General de Gaulle, which I do not quite understand, needs a certain tension between France and the United States. Apparently he thinks that only this tension can give Europeans the will to think for themselves instead of relying lazily on American dollars and political leadership. But we are going to give less and less occasion for France to create this tension."

Two leaderships, two policies, two strategies, two different concepts of the Atlantic world, were now at work where only one had existed before.

PART III

FROM THE ATLANTIC TO THE URALS

1. De Gaulle's France and Europe

The central feature of the European diplomatic landscape is De Gaulle's France. It is likely to remain so for some years to come. Great Britain is passing through a nadir of decline and reassessment from which it is yet to begin emerging. Germany is divided, restive and uncertain of itself or its future. France, on the other hand, has not known such economic health, political stability and diplomatic ascendancy in Europe in this century. General de Gaulle is ruthless in asserting France's renewed strength against the uncertainties and difficulties which prevail in London and Bonn. The very depth from which France has risen in a quarter of a century gives a bitter, vengeful quality to De Gaulle's diplomacy and the exercise of his extraordinary power. He cannot be said to be leading Europe. But he is dominating it.

Gaullism does not attract much popular enthusiasm or political acclaim in Europe any more than Bonapartism did a century and a half ago. But popularity has never preoccupied De Gaulle. Power and the exercise of power has been the fascination of his life. The exclusion of Britain from the Common Market stands as one of those acts of naked Gaullist power which shape the Europe of our times. Others will follow from De Gaulle before this decade is out, and they will be taken in the same lonely eminence and handed down in the same imperious manner without reference to public opinion and with the same obdurate assertion of "the interests of France."

Twice De Gaulle has gained power in France as the result of disaster—not through any normal or peaceful process of politics. His contempt for the politicians of the Fourth Republic is complete.*

* Lord Attlee, former Labour prime minister of Britain, once reviewed a volume of De Gaulle's memoirs and commented that the General was a great general but no politician. Subsequently he received a letter from De Gaulle thanking him for the review, and commenting in a dry inversion of Clemenceau's famous epigram: "I have come to the conclusion that politics is too serious a business to be left to the politicians."

Unfettered by politics and at the pinnacle of power at last for himself and for France, De Gaulle asserts a nationalism that is deep-seated, traditional and fundamental. Gaullism, indeed, might be said to have its roots in the Political Testament which Cardinal Richelieu left behind when he died in 1642. The Cardinal, who was the first to practice diplomacy on a systematic and continuing basis and who dominated the European scene for France much as De Gaulle is dominating it today, laid down that the only basis for the effective exercise of power is the nation-state. The interest of the State is primary and eternal, he asserted, and the State therefore must be kept strong within and preserved from any outside interference or entanglement which might limit or constrain the exercise of national power and decision. Richelieu was against political integration. He taught that the interests of the State are above sentimental, ideological or doctrinal prejudices and affections, and that if national interest demands an alliance with an obnoxious state, then no feelings of like or dislike should be permitted to blur necessity. Allies are chosen not for integrity or charm but for physical or even geographical value. Richelieu preached these principles in an age of undisputed autocracy. Two centuries later, Lord Palmerston put it more succinctly for Britain in Victoria's time: "England has no permanent enemies and no permanent friends—only permanent interests."

A century after Palmerston's day, General de Gaulle applies this same principle to the protection and furthering of "the interests of France"—which he and he alone decides. De Gaulle is no more inhibited by public opinion or politics than Richelieu was, and probably less than Palmerston. Accordingly he is able to direct French policy and French diplomacy with an autocratic ruthlessness all but forgotten in modern times. It is easy enough to ridicule De Gaulle as an outmoded Bonapartist seeking to recreate some nineteenth- or eighteenth-century Europe. One of the most popular features of the French press is a weekly satire of life in De Gaulle's France which appears in *Le Canard Enchainé,* written in the style of Saint-Simon's famous diaries of the court of Louis XIV and illustrated with bitterly funny caricatures of De Gaulle and his ministers in the court dress and surroundings of Versailles. All of this is enhanced, of course, by De Gaulle's determined restoration of the trappings, decorations and ceremonials of the State. But the fact that Gaullism has its roots in past traditions and teachings of French history does not detract from the realities of De Gaulle's power.

Gaullism is, in fact, more of a study in exercise of power than it is a political philosophy. Having achieved power without the normal processes of politics, De Gaulle shows little or no interest in perpetuating the Gaullist political party in French national life. He pays almost no attention to his political followers except to make sure of their disciplined votes in the National Assembly. The leaders of his Union for the New Republic make a constant effort to establish their party with the kind of organization and political permanence which is enjoyed in other democracies by Republicans and Democrats, Conservatives and Labourites, Christian Democrats and Social Democrats. But the UNR is basically only a reflection of the power of De Gaulle, and De Gaulle concerns himself not with trying to build a political organization to carry on after he goes, but in acts of national policy which will shape France and Europe no matter who follows him.

The Fifth Republic is already half as old as the Fourth. Yet after seven years of Gaullism there is still a remarkable absence of political life in France. The Fourth Republic was of course a madhouse of politics in which nobody could exercise power. Now France is a power without politics. For the first time in French history, the National Assembly is controlled by one party instead of a coalition—the Gaullist UNR—and there need be no elections for a new Assembly before 1967. In the face of the overwhelming political strength behind General de Gaulle, it would seem to make common sense for the fragmented parties left over from the Fourth Republic to get together and unite behind a candidate and a program as an alternative to Gaullism. By such a process of political polarization, France might conceivably find its way to an effective two-party system. But this has not happened. Only one man declared himself well in advance to be a presidential candidate—Gaston Defferre, the Socialist mayor of Marseilles. And not only has he failed to attract any broad support of the anti-Gaullist parties, he cannot even count on the unanimous backing of his own Socialist Party. De Gaulle has not polarized French politics; he has pulverized French politics.

Accordingly, the political leaders of France are completely numbed. They see little hope for active political life until De Gaulle leaves the scene. Instead of moving toward a two-party system, the politicians appear to count on a breakup of the Gaullist UNR when De Gaulle goes, and with that, perhaps, a return to something akin to life in the Fourth Rebulic with a variety of parties once again actively vying and consorting for votes and power. But the politicians will have a long time to wait. Everything De Gaulle has said and done indicates that short of a physical collapse or an act of God, he will run for another seven-year term of office before the end of 1965 and be re-elected with a sweeping majority.

De Gaulle at the age of seventy-five is in excellent health despite a prostate operation in April, 1964. Apart from the period in which he was in the hospital, there has not in seven years been a single announced cancellation of a cabinet meeting or a public function because of any interruption in his health. He has eye cataracts which have been operated on and which impair his vision, but this does not hinder his work or his close watching of French television. After his prostate operation he tested his health with a rigorous month-long gallop around South America, visiting every one of its lands (something no President of the United States has yet done). As he moves on in years, his activities remain unchanged and undiminished. Six of his immediate forebears lived to an average age of eighty.

Gaullism in the form of General de Gaulle will be with Europe for some years to come, and Gaullism in the form of De Gaulle's effect on French policies and European history will last well beyond the General. There are reasonable doubts whether he would, in fact, serve out another full seven-year term of office. It is quite likely that he would decide to retire at some particular moment during a second term of office when he believes that he has accomplished most things within his grasp. Though contemptuous of politicians, he has an acute sense of history and political timing and no wish to preside over a bickering or squabbling nation. He walked out abruptly on France in 1946 when he decided that he could no longer make the postwar political situation work to his satisfaction. He would most probably want to go while his ascendancy over the country was still complete, and the power of his name still sufficient for him to insure that a successor of his choice is elected to the presidency. But at that point, political life will become active again in France, and no successor to General de Gaulle will be able to wield power and decide policies with the autocratic force and single-minded indifference to outside opinion that dominates France today.

The vacuum of political opposition in which De Gaulle wields his power extends to a large degree to French public opinion as well. There is frequent grumbling and dissatisfaction in France over internal problems such as wages, prices, rents, social security and the rest. But as a people the French pay very little attention to De Gaulle's foreign policies and the issues of Gaullism which concern the outside world. De Gaulle, moreover, arranges the affairs of France to leave the conduct of disagreeable problems to his prime minister, who has to say "no" to the trade unions and the farmers, introduce and defend unpopular legislation in the National Assembly. When De Gaulle does deal with the economic state of France, it is usually to report to the French people over television that "they never had it so good"—which, indeed, they have not.

Since De Gaulle returned to power in 1958, French social security allowances for families have increased from $1.8 billion to $3 billion annually. There has been a 25 percent increase in the French gross national product. Five out of every seven French homes now have refrigerators or washing machines, usually both. The government is spending twice as much today on expansion of the telephone and telecommunications system as it was spending in 1958. Direct-dial phoning is now complete throughout all of France, and is beginning to extend from France to Britain, Switzerland, Germany and Belgium.

In the last two years, another 1,500 miles of the French railway system has been electrified. In 1962, some 700,000 Algerian French flocked back to France in the wake of the ending of the Algerian war and they were absorbed into the burgeoning French economy with scarcely a ripple. By December of 1963, only 5,000 Algerian repatriates were listed as unemployed. French gold reserves which were practically exhausted when De Gaulle took over have increased to $5 billion today.

The government's power of direction over the French economy is enormous. A Frenchman uses gas, electricity, water, coal, railroads and buses which are owned and operated by the state. A portion of the gasoline in his car comes from government-owned supplies. The car itself may well have been manufactured by the state-owned Renault factory, which provides one-third of the French automobile output. A Frenchman smokes cigarettes (including American brands) which are manufactured or marketed solely through a nationalized French tobacco monopoly. He is insured by a state-owned insurance company, keeps his money in a bank which is probably owned or controlled by the government, and if he is a manufacturer and wants to borrow money for plant expansion, then the government is his main source of credit. But with all this concentration of economic power in the hands of the government, the economic cake is cut pretty well in France. Public dissatisfaction with this or that price increase and this or that wage decision does not by any means yet represent a ground swell of political opposition to De Gaulle. If it did, the politicians would be much more active trying to get out in front and lead the anti-Gaullist chorus. Significantly, the only two Gaullist programs which have been subject to much public criticism are French aid to its former African colonies and other undeveloped nations (which is the highest per capita aid program of any country in the world), and the expensive atomic program to build an independent nuclear strike-force. But neither of these has been opposed by the public for political reasons—only because they take money away from housing, hospitals, schools, social security, roads and other national needs of France.

General de Gaulle in fact permits no debate in advance on his big decisions of foreign policy. These he takes alone after long periods of watching, waiting and meditating. He listens, but he does not consult, and he seldom reveals himself in advance even to his close entourage.

Such was the case with his veto of British entry into the Common Market, and from there on, the list of his one-man acts of foreign policy is enormous: rejection of the multilateral nuclear force project; the decision to withdraw the French delegation from the Geneva disarmament negotiations; refusal to take part or pay for the United Nations "peace-keeping" operation in the Congo; withdrawal of the French fleet and French naval officers from NATO; recognition of Red China; support of neutralism in Southeast Asia; refusal to participate in discussions with the Russians over Berlin; rejection of any East-West nonaggression pact; refusal to permit the stockpiling of American nuclear weapons in France unless they were placed under French control; the fixing of various deadlines against his Common Market partners for the conclusion of various economic agreements. These all spring from secret decisions taken by De Gaulle and De Gaulle alone, and then announced to the cabinet or handed to various ministers and departments as the instructions of the Head of State. De Gaulle's instructions are carried out with a truly ruthless efficiency. His government is a very strong instrument of power, uninhibited by problems of public opinion, parliamentary debate, appropriations difficulties, by-elections, six-vote margins of security or any of the other weaknesses of democratic flesh.

The French radio and television are directly controlled by the government, and not only are acts of government policy presented without any critical questioning, but foreign reaction of a harshly critical nature is also politely filtered over the French TV screens to leave the viewers with the impression that De Gaulle is operating in an atmosphere of approbation, if not applause, all over the world. The hostility and mistrust which De Gaulle's acts arouse in other capitals somehow is lost in the offices of Radio Diffusion Television Francaise.

Nor is the French press much more active in criticizing Gaullism. The press is neither censored nor controlled, but either through lack of interest on the part of its readers or indifference on the part of its editors, there is no paper in France which can be pointed to as leading any coherent or consistent critical opposition. There is comment and criticism of specific acts and the handling of specific problems. But the simple fact is that there is not much opposition to Gaullism in France. De Gaulle has broad popular support for whatever he does, and he is going to continue to enjoy that support for the foreseeable future.

He can count, moreover, on strong nationalist feelings among the French people to back his intensely nationalistic policies. For example, his veto of British entry into the Common Market came as a shock to the intellectual opinion-formers of France and was generally judged to be unreasonable, high-handed and unjustified treatment of an ally. No politicians applauded De Gaulle's action, and his own supporters were uncomfortable and reserved. But when the public opinion polls arrived two weeks after his famous press conference, they showed that 64 percent of the French people were satisfied with De Gaulle's direction of French affairs, and on the specific question of approving his action against Britain, 40 percent backed him and 39 percent were in the "don't know" category. Only 21 percent disapproved of what he had done.

The majority of the French simply do not concern themselves about the larger problems such as the effect of De Gaulle's actions on the state of the Atlantic Alliance, on French security or the balance-of-power in the world, about whether or not France is isolated, about France's good or bad relations with its neighbors and Allies. The majority applaud De Gaulle's challenges to the Anglo-Saxons and the Russians, and the reassertion of French power, prestige and independence.

France has been subjected to military defeat, and then to so much diplomatic pushing-around, to so much loss of prestige and self-respect, to so many years of political chaos, that the French now take quiet pleasure in the fashion in which De Gaulle asserts "French interests"—even though they poke fun at his grandeur and *gloire* at the same time.

De Gaulle's France, a French pun puts it, is a "*mon*-archy." De Gaulle has succeeded as no other head of a democratic state in the world today in reducing politics to the vanishing point. The forms and liberties of democracy are fully preserved in France. But none of the checks and balances of the American Constitution impede De Gaulle's exercise of power, nor is there any union of parliament and government such as exists in Britain. In France, De Gaulle's government decides almost everything from wages to television programs. There is a legislature which legislates in rubber-stamp fashion. There are elections in which anyone can stand for office. There is ex post facto debate and discussion about the great decisions of state which are made by De Gaulle alone. There is freedom of the press, freedom of criticism, freedom of strike, freedom of political activity, free movement of citizens and independence of the judiciary and the law. But the nation which turned to De Gaulle in 1958 and entrusted its future entirely to his hands still trusts his absolute exercise of power and shows no signs yet of using its political freedom and its right of democratic expression to bring about a change.

In the nuclear age, De Gaulle has shaped an autocratic eighteenth-century instrument of power in France which he uses sometimes as a rapier, sometimes as a bludgeon. He bludgeoned Great Britain, but in the Cuban crisis he showed his rapier qualities in the manner in which he instantly supported President Kennedy. Yet in declaring his backing of the United States, De Gaulle never for an instant relaxed this intensely personal style of his exercise of power.

President Kennedy sent former Secretary of State Dean Acheson flying to Paris with a briefcaseful of photos of the Cuban missile sites to brief General de Gaulle on the grave decision to move to a nuclear showdown with the Russians. There were five people in the room at the Élysée Palace for the crucial conference—Acheson and two other Americans, President de Gaulle and a French aide-interpreter. Acheson outlined the situation and President Kennedy's plans. De Gaulle peered with fascination at the blown-up photos. In the end he nodded to Acheson and said:

"You may tell the President that he has the full support of France. I would do exactly the same if I were in his position."

De Gaulle then paused and added a final word: "I must note that I have been advised, but not consulted."

Power increases through its use. De Gaulle's memoirs, as well as the writings of those who have worked with him or had to deal with him, are replete with one example after another of the style and manner in which this remarkable general created power time and again out of the most trivial issues, often with nothing but what the British would call "sheer bloody-mindedness." De Gaulle's watchword, on the other hand, was "We are too weak to compromise." One of his earliest wartime showdowns with his Allies came in July, 1941, after the British, accompanied by Free French troops, invaded what was then the French Mandate territories of Syria and Lebanon and overthrew the regimes controlled by Vichy France and Marshal Petain.

But once the Vichy French had been overthrown, the British proceeded to act as if they had taken over conquered enemy territory. De Gaulle named the respected General Georges Catroux as high commissioner for the territories, but the British simply refused to permit any French administration to function. They took over the office buildings and the telephone exchanges, and even hauled down the Tricolor and hoisted the Union Jack. De Gaulle, who was in Brazzaville, flew to Cairo and confronted the British Minister of State in the Middle East with a serious ultimatum. He announced that in three days' time he intended to order the Free French forces in Syria and Lebanon to withdraw from British command and assert *their* authority over the territory, no matter who opposed them. In effect, this was a threat of war between the French and British forces in the midst of the war against Germans. De Gaulle announced his ultimatum in frigid anger, and although he had only a handful of troops, clearly he was not bluffing. The Minister of State hastily cabled London urging some kind of a compromise. In a flurry of cables, an agreement was worked out to permit General Catroux to exercise French authority once again. But at the height of the crisis, the Free French Committee of National Liberation, sitting in London and subject to quite understandable pressures from the British Foreign Office and Winston Churchill, nervously cabled De Gaulle pointing out that the Free French could not exist without British supplies, and urging him to modify his intransigence. De Gaulle sent back a memorable reply: "We shall have need of this intransigence up to the Rhine inclusive."

Intransigence was one of De Gaulle's few instruments of power in 1940 and the rest of the war years. He has many more weapons in his armory today, but intransigence is still one of his favorites.

The catalog of troubles between De Gaulle and the Anglo-Saxons throughout World War II constitutes one of the strangest records of obtuseness, pettiness and personal vindictiveness among great men in all history. Whether it is read from De Gaulle's memoirs, Churchill's *War History,* Harry Hopkins' White House papers, or in any of the many other chronicles of those times, the same judgment applies to all the main characters involved. But there is also grim fascination in going back over the record of the years 1940–45 and finding in those bitter exchanges between De Gaulle and the Anglo-Saxons the same fundamental historic attitudes and arguments which constitute De Gaulle's policies today. He has, for example, consistently berated the United States for its failure to come to the aid of France and Europe in good time in both world wars. But he has also consistently held that the United States has no fundamental role in the political affairs of Europe and, having saved Europe, should properly leave Europe to its own affairs.

De Gaulle tells of a conversation with Churchill at Downing Street in November, 1942, shortly after the Anglo-American landings in North Africa and the American deal with Admiral Darlan and General Giraud. He says that Churchill counseled him, "Don't confront the Americans head on. Be patient! They will come to you, for there is no alternative." De Gaulle continues:

" 'Perhaps,' I said. 'But how much crockery will be broken in the meantime? And I fail to understand your own position. You have been fighting this war since the first day. In a manner of speaking, you ARE this war. Your Army is advancing in Libya. There would be no Americans in Africa if, on your side, you were not in the process of defeating Rommel. Up to this very moment not a single one of Roosevelt's soldiers has met a single one of Hitler's soldiers, while for three years your men have been fighting in every latitude of the globe. Besides, in this African campaign it is Europe that is at stake and England belongs to Europe. Yet you let the Americans take charge of the conflict, though it is up to you to control it, at least ethically. Do so! All of European public opinion will follow you!' "

De Gaulle asserts that "this sally struck Churchill" and that they parted agreed that "Franco-British solidarity was more than ever in accord with the natural order of things when the United States intervened in the affairs of the Old World." No doubt the sally did strike Churchill, but probably not in the manner De Gaulle suspected. Churchill was seeking to draw an isolationist America as deeply as possible into Europe's affairs, while De Gaulle—before any Anglo-Saxons had yet landed in Europe—was looking to a Gaullist reconstruction of Europe.

But at least De Gaulle's wartime arguments with Churchill had something of the grand manner of eloquent and intelligent statesmen, rooted in history and the experience of war and European politics. De Gaulle's arguments with the United States, on the other hand, have a quality of bitter contempt. He records, in his memoirs, a particularly indignant and sardonic exchange which he had with Harry Hopkins in Paris one week before the opening of the Yalta Conference, from which, of course, France was excluded. Hopkins had been sent to Paris by President Roosevelt on one of the many futile missions to explain United States policy and induce his support. De Gaulle writes:

> I said this to the special envoy of the President. You have explained to me why, from your point of view, our relations have deteriorated. I am going to tell you what, on our side, contributes to the same result. Let us leave aside the occasional and secondary frictions which are due to the abnormal conditions in which our Alliance is functioning. For us, here is the essential: in the mortal dangers which we French have been passing through since the beginning of the century, the United States has not given us the impression that it considers its fate linked to that of France, that it wants a great and strong France, that it is doing what it could to help France remain so or to become so again. Perhaps indeed we are not worth the trouble. In that case, you are right. But perhaps we will rise again. Then you will have been wrong. In any case, your behavior tends to estrange us from you.

De Gaulle then went on to give Hopkins a De Gaulle's-eye view of the history of American interventions in the two world wars: in the First World War "only because of the interference with trade by German submarines, and after having been tempted to impose a compromise peace under which France would not even have recovered Alsace and Lorraine"; in the Second World War "when the Japanese, allies of the Germans, sent your ships to the bottom at Pearl Harbor." In between, De Gaulle informed Hopkins, "we had seen the Americans refuse France the security guarantees which they had formally promised her, exercise stubborn pressure on France to surrender the cards she held, and finally furnish Germany with all the help necessary for the restoration of her power." Hopkins listened to this blast, and then asked how the two nations might in the future act in agreement and confidence. De Gaulle rolled relentlessly on:

> "If such is the intention of the United States," I replied, "I cannot understand how they can undertake to settle the fate of Europe in the absence of France. I understand this all the less since after having appeared to ignore France in the forthcoming discussions [at Yalta] of the "Three" they will have to turn to Paris to ask its agreement on what will have been decided. You have come on behalf of the President of the United States in order to clarify the crux of the matter with respect to our relations. I think that we have done this. The French have the impression that you no longer consider the greatness of France as necessary for the world and for yourselves. Hence the cold wind which you feel on our approach and even in this office. If you want the relations of America and France to be established on a different basis, it is up to you to do what is necessary. Pending your choice, I send President Roosevelt greetings of friendship on the eve of the conference for which he is coming to Europe."

The date of that conversation was January 27, 1945.

De Gaulle waited nearly twenty years before he was able to make good his warning to Harry Hopkins: "Perhaps we will rise again. Then you will have been wrong." It was a long way from the Hopkins mission before Yalta to the Acheson mission before Cuba.

Although De Gaulle's acts of power are stamped with a quality of vengeful self-interest, they nevertheless are part of a coherent strategic pattern, with well-defined objectives for France—a particular Gaullist vision of the construction of Europe which De Gaulle has held for a very long time. In 1942 he was exhorting Churchill that "Britain is part of Europe" and he should not allow the Americans to take over running the war, and twenty years later one of his excuses for vetoing British entry into Europe was his contention that Britain remained too close to America. In 1945 he was berating Harry Hopkins and the United States for attempting to decide the future of Europe at Yalta without France, and in 1965 he was again telling a press conference audience that the German question "can only be solved by joint action of the peoples who have been there for all time; that is, the European peoples." For more than a quarter of a century, through defeat and victory, self-imposed political exile and then a return to power, De Gaulle has moved with extraordinarily sustained effort to push and prod history into the pattern of his own vision of Europe's future. He outlined this "Grand Design"—or more specifically, his "Grand Strategy" for Europe—very concisely in the final volume of his war memoirs, which appeared in 1959 but had been written before his return to power:

> To guarantee French security in Western Europe by preventing the rise of a new Reich which might again threaten it;
> To cooperate with East and West and, as need occurs, to make necessary alliances with one side or the other without ever accepting any kind of dependence;
> To transform the French Union into a free association in order to avoid the still unspecified dangers of its disintegration;
> To induce the states along the Rhine, the Alps and the Pyrenees to form a political, economic and strategic bloc;
> To make this organization one of the three world powers, and, if need be, the arbiter between the two Soviet and Anglo-Saxon camps.

Such is De Gaulle's strategic design. Significantly, he does not even mention the Atlantic Alliance, which plays no part in the aims of his policy. On the contrary, in De Gaulle's long-term strategy, the Atlantic Alliance is to wither away in order that Europe may take its independent place in the scheme of world affairs.

Everything General de Gaulle does in the field of diplomacy and international politics, every move he makes, has a tactical place in achieving these strategic objectives. Veto of British entry into Europe, his opposition to the American multilateral nuclear force project in NATO, his journey around South America, withdrawal of French naval forces from NATO, his independent nuclear policy for France, recognition of Red China—all these actions are part of the broad Gaullist strategy. At the end of his first term of office, De Gaulle has succeeded in two of his basic aims. He has transformed the French Union into a free association of fourteen African nations, and with the ending of the Algerian war he has restored peace to France for the first time since 1939. He has made a treaty ally out of France's old enemy, Germany. The Franco-German Treaty of Cooperation may not always seem to produce much cooperation, and relations between Bonn and Paris often look like a fever chart. But whatever the semi-annual ups-and-downs, nevertheless there is now a treaty where there had been four hundred years of war, and this treaty forms an integral part of the Gaullist construction of Europe which neither France nor Germany has the slightest intention of abandoning.

These, however, were relatively limited objectives of Gaullism. The means of their accomplishment lay primarily within France itself. General de Gaulle's broader aims "to induce the states along the Rhine, the Alps and the Pyrenees to form a political, economic and strategic bloc," and "to make this organization one of the three world powers" are of a very different order. Here Gaullism clashes with the Monnet concept of the construction of a federated Europe, and more importantly, it clashes with the strategic aims and concepts of the Atlantic Alliance under which the United States has guaranteed Europe its security since 1949.

This clash of two strategies, which was joined when De Gaulle vetoed British entry into the Common Market, will dominate the affairs of the Alliance as long as De Gaulle remains in power, and beyond. The clash will intensify as the end of the first twenty-year period of the North Atlantic Treaty approaches in 1969, and De Gaulle moves—as he certainly intends to move—to force changes in Supreme Allied Headquarters in Europe, the military organization of NATO, and its political structure as well.

There is no dearth of criticism and condemnation of General de Gaulle's aims. In both Europe and the United States there is plenty of analysis and political writing to prove that he is wrong in his concepts of history, wrong in his ideas of the future, wrong in his appreciation of the East-West struggle and the nature of the Communist challenge, wrong in his belief that any nation can play an independent role between the two blocs. But De Gaulle holds to his long-term ideas with remarkable persistency. If he declined to make concessions to his Allies in the war because he was too weak, he is even less inclined to modify his aims now that he is strong. He is, however, a realist and he adjusts his policies to power realism. With General de Gaulle, it is more important to see where he is trying to go, and what the power realities are, rather than debate whether he is right or wrong.

The next immediate phase of Gaullism will be played out in the organization of Europe. In the two years following De Gaulle's veto of British entry into the Common Market, little of significance happened on the European political front. De Gaulle's partners resented his ruthless treatment of Britain. They remained basically loyal to the Monnet federalist principles and opposed to De Gaulle's approach of confederation. Above all, they had no wish to enlarge the division in the Atlantic Alliance between Europe and North America. They stood out against De Gaulle's ideas of European political unity, therefore, in the belief that Europe should include Britain and that Europe's ties with the United States should be strengthened and not weakened. But in early 1965, a slow shift in European opinion began to emerge, and a certain political momentum took hold again among the Six.

There were a number of reasons for this restoration of political momentum. First and foremost, although Europe was at a political dead end after the De Gaulle press conference, the Common Market made very rapid and substantial progress toward full integration on the economic front. The Market is two and a half years ahead of schedule toward its ultimate goal of a single external tariff structure for all the six nations and the abolition of all internal tariffs and trade restrictions. The Rome Treaty of 1956 fixed 1970 as the target date, but at the present pace it will be accomplished by the middle of 1967. Moreover, under massive pressure from De Gaulle, the Common Market also reached agreement on a single grain price for all of its farmers by 1967, so that both agriculture and industry will be fully integrated among the Six. The finance ministers are already beginning to talk about establishing a single currency unit and one central reserve bank for Europe by 1970. These successes on the economic front inevitably produced a change in the political atmosphere among the Six, and a feeling that whatever the arguments about the form or substance of political unity, it was time to try to make progress.

The next factor which changed the situation in De Gaulle's favor was the election of the Labour Government in Great Britain. Labour's determined antipathy toward joining Europe, or even having much of a "European policy," has made it all but impossible for the pro-British members of the Common Market to hold out against De Gaulle's pressures for purely European political unity. As the Dutch foreign minister, Joseph Luns, remarked rather bitterly after a visit to London in 1964: "We cannot be expected to be more British than the British."

Finally, the Monnet Federalists—Luns, Paul-Henri Spaak of Belgium and Giusèppe Sarragat of Italy, who moved from foreign minister to president at the beginning of 1965—slowly came to the conclusion that it would be better politically for the future of Europe to take what they can get in the way of a Treaty of Political Unity from

De Gaulle rather than stand out forever on issues of Federalism-versus-Gaullism. For example, the governments of the Six have long been agreed in principle that the three European communities—Common Market, Coal and Steel, and Euratom—should be merged into one organization with one executive commission and one president. But the Federalists have insisted up to now that when the Communities merge, the Parliamentary Assembly of the Six, which meets twice a year at Strasbourg, should also be given enlarged powers and responsibilities and even that a portion of its members should in future be elected by direct European voting. They have proposed that the parliament be given the right to approve the nomination of the president of the combined Executive Commission and its members, and that parliament have the right to debate and approve the budget of the Community, which soon will include vast sums in an agricultural equalization fund to even out grain prices for farmers all over Europe. But these enlargements of parliamentary authority in the direction of federalism have been stiffly rejected by De Gaulle. The General defined his ideas about the political structure of Europe at a press conference in May, 1962:

"Let us begin at the beginning. Let us organize our cooperation, let our Heads of State or of Government meet periodically to examine our problems together and to make decisions with regard to those problems which will be the decisions of Europe. Let us set up a political commission, a defense commission and a cultural commission just as we have formed an economic commission in Brussels.

"I am more attached to France than ever, and I do not believe that Europe can have any living reality if it does not include France and her Frenchmen, Germany and its Germans, Italy and its Italians and so forth. Dante, Goethe, Chateaubriand, belong to all Europe to the very extent that they were respectively and eminently Italian, German and French. They would not have served Europe very well if they had been stateless or if they had thought and written in some kind of integrated Esperanto or Volapuk.

"On what elements can Europe be built? The States, of course! For in this respect it is only the States that are valid, legitimate and capable of achievement. At the present time there cannot be any other Europe than a Europe of states, apart, of course, from myths, stories and parades. What is happening with regard to the Economic Community proves this every day, for it is the States and only the States that created this Community, that furnished it with funds, that provided it with staff members; and it is the States that give it efficiency, all the more so as it is impossible to take any far-reaching economic measure without committing a political action. Would the French people, the German people, the Italian people, the Dutch people, the Belgian people, or the Luxembourg people dream of submitting to laws voted by foreign deputies if these laws were to run contrary to their own deep-seated will? Let us place reality at the basis of the edifice of a united Europe, and when we shall have completed our work, this will be time for us to lull ourselves to sleep with tales of *The Thousand and One Nights* and the marvelous lamp of Aladdin."

This vigorous slap in the face for the European Federalists produced for De Gaulle in May, 1962, the first and only cabinet crisis of his seven years in power. Within hours after the press conference, Pierre Pflimlin abruptly resigned from De Gaulle's government, which he had been serving as minister of state. Pflimlin was the last premier of the Fourth Republic before De Gaulle returned to power and the only remaining non-Gaullist political figure in the government. But he quickly put his loyalties to his own political party—the Popular Republican Movement (MRP), the party of Robert Schuman and other leading Europeans of France—above his loyalty to De Gaulle's government. Somewhat taken aback, ("The first time I ever heard him use the telephone," an Élysée Palace official later recounted), De Gaulle regrouped his cabinet, and since that time he has been served only by loyal Gaullists, nearly all of them technicians rather than politicians, drawn from the ranks of business, finance, the diplomatic corps and the civil service.

But De Gaulle was not in the slightest influenced by Pflimlin's resignation. He pressed steadily forward from this press conference to enlist Konrad Adenauer's support for his ideas about the construction of Europe, culminating in the signing of the Franco-German Treaty of Cooperation as a kind of pilot model for the future of Europe in January, 1963. By 1965, Europe had begun to move again in his wake. As has been the case so often in the past, De Gaulle's intransigence and refusal to compromise his position has slowly worn down his opponents. He has not led Europe, but he has dominated it.

The next years will therefore probably see the emergence of some kind of an organization of "the states along the Rhine, the Alps and the Pyrenees to form a political, economic and strategic bloc." There remains the question of where De Gaulle intends to try to lead, or force, this Europe, and the extent to which Europe is prepared to substitute Gaullism for Atlanticism.

There is no discernable support or enthusiasm anywhere for De Gaulle's strategy of "making this organization one of the three world powers, and, if need be, the arbiter between the two Soviet and Anglo-Saxon camps." Taken literally, this would mean nothing less than complete European withdrawal from the Atlantic Alliance, for Europe could not be a third power or a third force otherwise. How would such a third world power defend itself? Not with De Gaulle's independent nuclear deterrent. France's bomb is solely a political weapon acquired for the purpose of prestige, not a military defense weapon. De Gaulle knows as well as every other responsible European statesman that Europe is overwhelmingly dependent on the protective nuclear power of the United States. No European government, least of all Germany, De Gaulle's closest European ally, is prepared to run the risk of denuding Europe of American nuclear power and America's defense guarantee in the ephemeral hope of being able to act as arbiter between Russia and the United States.

On the other hand, among European governments there is genuine fundamental support for the idea of greater European political independence from American policies, greater freedom of action, and an end to the constant American expectation of NATO support for American leadership. The difference between a "third force" in Europe and an "independent Europe" may be subtle, but it is real. Moreover, De Gaulle has recognized the reality, and he has made a careful adjustment to define his aims accordingly. This Gaullist retuning reflected particularly in a speech which he delivered in the city of Strasbourg on the twentieth anniversary of its liberation, in November, 1964. French policy, he declared, was a "very old and also very modern" ambition:

"The construction of a Europe which is European, in other words a Europe independent, powerful and influential within the world of liberty. France considers it essential that the Six should as soon as possible achieve and put into practice among themselves in the political domain—which is first that of defense—an organization, *certainly allied to the New World,* but which would be truly theirs, with its objectives, its resources and its obligations."

An independent Europe allied to the New World is very different from a third world power acting as an arbiter between the two camps. True, General de Gaulle's skill with words and his passion for historic consistency is such that he and his interpreters might profess to see no difference at all. They could contend that an independent Europe and a third world power are the same thing, and that being allied to the New World need not at all prevent an independent Europe from acting as arbiter. But this argument or interpretation can be left to General de Gaulle's semantical specialists, who are legion in Paris.

The reality is that while Europeans are now beginning to move ahead on a political organization along Gaullist, rather than Monnet, lines, there is no support whatsoever for cutting this organization off from the United States and making it a third force. Without much doubt there will be a great deal of argument among the Six on the central problem of organizing defense. De Gaulle will try to force the creation of a purely European defense organization to supersede Supreme Allied Headquarters and the command structure which is run by the United States under NATO. The Europeans will resist making any new defense arrangements among themselves, at De Gaulle's behest, which might weaken or lessen the security which only America can give and guarantee.

Utimately, the real problem of creating European independence lies not in opposing Washington, but in Moscow. Europe will gain no independence by opting out of NATO, cutting defense ties with the United States, and accepting De Gaulle's arbitration between East and West. Far from independence, Western Europe would wind up a strategic hostage to the military power of the Soviet Union. The Europeans know this and so does General de Gaulle. This rather grandly anachronistic twentieth-century autocrat may expend his political bitterness and energy in the practice of throwing rocks across the Atlantic and demonstrating his independence of the United States. But he does so because he knows that it is perfectly safe.

De Gaulle is a realist who well knows what the realities of power are in the world today. He knows that the hope of Gaullism and an independent Europe lies not in any process of arbitration, but only if he can bring about a separation of the two superpowers which will release the Continent from the grip of the military and political confrontation of Russia and the United States in the center of Germany. Hence the increasing emphasis on one of those recurring Gaullist catchphrase picture images: "Europe from the Atlantic to the Urals." De Gaulle described this vision of the future of Europe with his usual sweeping vigor at a press conference in February, 1965, held, incidentally, on the twentieth anniversary of the Yalta Conference. He was asked what he considered to be the path to the reunification of Germany, and how he saw relations developing with Eastern Europe. He replied:

"Russia must evolve in such a way that it sees its future not through the totalitarian constraint imposed on its own land and on others, but through the progress accomplished in common by free men and peoples. The nations which it has satellized must be able to play their role in a renewed Europe.

"It must be recognized first of all by Germany that any settlement of which it would be the subject would necessarily imply a settlement of its frontiers and of its armament in agreement with all its neighbors, those on the East and those on the West.

"The six nations which, let us hope, are in the process of establishing the economic community of Western Europe must succeed in organizing themselves in the political domain as well as in that of defense, in order to make a new equilibrium possible on our continent. Europe, the mother of modern civilization, must establish herself from the Atlantic to the Urals in harmony and cooperation with a view to the development of her vast resources and so as to play, in conjunction with America, her daughter, the role which falls to her in the progress of two billion men who desperately need it.

"These conditions appear very complex and these delays seem quite long. But after all, the solution to a problem as vast as that of Germany can only have large dimensions and consequences. France, for her part, believes that this problem cannot be resolved except by Europe herself, because it is on the scale of the whole of Europe. This, ultimately, is the basic objective on this continent of the policy of France."

Such is the Gaullist vision of Europe. Such will be the direction of De Gaulle's diplomacy for as long as he continues in power. Already it can be seen in the intensification of French diplomatic activity in the satellite states, in trade, culture, commerce, official visits and diplomatic consultations. It will intensify, too, in his continued demonstrations of independence, in his policy of "being in NATO less and less" as he once described it to Harold Macmillan, in his pressures to bring other European governments to follow his lead.

What reality is there behind this Gaullist vision? Only the unfolding years of this decade will tell. General de Gaulle has seen history catch up with his vision before in the last quarter of a century. It is certain, at least, that Germany will not be reunified and the future of Europe arranged by any advance of the NATO frontier to the east, or by any advance of the Communist frontier to the west. General de Gaulle may not be talking about *THE* future, but he is talking about *A* future.

2. The New Germany and Europe

Fifteen years after Konrad Adenauer formed the first Bonn Government, I was back in the West German capital talking to a Western European ambassador who had dealt with German affairs for many years. His, like many other foreign governments, had long since accepted the permanence of Bonn as a German capital and had built a rather undistinguished modern embassy building that takes full advantage of the city's best asset—the view of the Rhine. Outside the big picture windows of the ambassador's office the barges crowded up and down the river. Trucks and cars streamed along the road in front of the embassy, and in the distance across the Rhine a freight train ran south, hauling car after car loaded with brightly colored new automobiles. I remarked to the ambassador that across the years since 1949 everything in West Germany had seemed to expand, grow and improve except the government itself, which did not yet appear to be attracting new talent for careers in the civil service and diplomatic corps.

"Ah," he smiled, "but this is an economy—not a state."

West Germany, with its population of 55 million, is by far the biggest, most productive economy in Europe and confidently expects to grow by another 7 percent during 1965. With 420,000 men under arms, West Germany also maintains the largest military establishment in Europe outside the Soviet Union. But there remains an elusive quality of political rootlessness and impermanence about the country. It is not yet a nation-state, and the Germans know it.

Since the end of the war, preoccupations with survival, security, materialism and the *wirtschafswunder* have been more than enough to absorb the well-known frenetic energy of the German people. The Cold War and successive Berlin crises forced them to keep their political heads down and pray that the shooting would not start all over again. Their country, their land, the German nation, had become little more than a piece of military geography in which vast foreign armies faced each other. The division of Germany is arbitrary and unreal. It bears no relation to politics, geography, history, nature, culture, race, tradition or language. Yet it exists.

In this situation the Germans as a people have so far found it neither practical nor desirable to devote thought or personal involvement to their political history, to the problems of democracy, to their own responsibility for the destruction and division of their nation, or to Germany's political future. In East Germany the Communists manipulated political thought by force. In the West the people on the whole were relieved to be able to leave the construction of a new democratic state, the definition of its ideals, its policies and its political objectives, almost exclusively in the hands of Konrad Adenauer, while they plunged on with the job of rebuilding the economy.

There were other deeper reasons for this intellectual vacuum. To begin with, the Nazis had not merely wiped out all but 33,000 German Jews in the ghastly twelve years of the Third Reich; they had also all but wiped out German intellectualism and the intelligentsia, the democratic political leadership of the country, the old liberal aristocracy, the strong-minded churchmen, the writers and poets, the thinkers and critics, the publishers and editors and even the comedians.

Those who spoke out for political idealism and human rights were silenced or disappeared. Those who tried to live with the system and soften its excesses while concealing their inner beliefs wound up too compromised to attempt intellectual or political leadership in postwar Germany. The Nazis left an indelible moral stain on the civil service, the judges and the diplomatic corps. They turned government into a monstrous evil instead of a regulator of society for the maximum human good, and they left Germany an intellectual desert, a political wasteland. When it came to building the new West German state, the German people, almost to a man, wanted nothing to do with politics and government. They would give their new democracy their votes, but the favorite political motto of the early 1950's was *"Ohne Mich"* —without me. In those days, when the Rhine River pleasure boats sailed past the new parliament building on the riverbank in Bonn, the citizens of the Federal Republic would laugh themselves silly singing an old drinking song across the waters: *"Wer hat das bezahlen, wer hat das bestellt"*—Who has paid for this, who has ordered this?

Nor could Germans with more intellectual dignity and introspective concern, or slightly longer memories turn with hope or satisfaction to pre-Nazi history. The Weimar Republic had its high-minded men who sought to plant democracy in the stony soil of inflation, unemployment, reparations, and rising Communism and Nazism. But these factors, and the multiplicity of democratic political parties and factions, made parliamentary government as unworkable as it eventually proved to be in the Fourth Republic of France. Time and again the Weimar democrats found themselves turning to the old authoritarian elements for stability and support—to the German General Staff and the Army, to the industrial barons and the Prussian aristocracy whose figurehead, with the Kaiser gone, was Hindenburg.

German political history before the Weimar days is even less fruitful in searching for the roots of a viable democratic life. The era of Bismarck and the Kaisers saw successive waves of industrialization and economic development in Germany, but virtually no change in the structure of German politics, government or society. The land barons became industrial barons and the wealthy grew more wealthy. The masses never had a political voice. Imperial rule was stable and despotic, and the political character of Germany remained essentially feudal. True, there were liberalizing movements in German politics. The Social Democratic Party, the oldest political party in Germany, was formed in 1863. But German liberalism remained in the realm of political theory, thinking and writing, and never was translated into political action. Germany never experienced the popular uprisings which have given France its democratic traditions, or the parliamentary evolution of British democracy. In the end, all that can be said for Hitler is that he completely smashed everything he inherited—the feudal structure of German society, the grip of the old authoritarianism on the machinery of government, the economic domination of the industrial barons, the frail beginnings of parliamentary democracy under the Weimar Republic, the power of the German General Staff, and in the end, of course, the political structure of the Third Reich. But in the ruins there was nowhere for Germans to turn and say: "This is our democratic tradition, this is what our nation stands for, this is where we begin again."

And so the Germans submerged themselves in building an economy—not a state. To lose national identity became almost a political narcotic to Germans after so many years of virulent Nazism. To sleep comfortably on, rocked in the cradle of a united Europe, seemed a soothing and peaceful solution to the problem of seeking political roots which could not be found.

Hans Magnus Enzensberger, one of the new Germany's younger Left poets and literary critics, who was born in 1929, wrote:

> We were late in acquiring our national identity and we have never felt very secure in it. In 1945 we were divested of this identity so thoroughly that the question arises whether there is any point left in speaking about a German nation. Nations can be destroyed from one year to the next; the very concept of nationality has become vulnerable.
>
> We are not thereby made into cosmopolitans. The idea of the nation-state may have ceased to correspond to any concrete reality, but it lives on obstinately in the form of an illusion, and illusions on this scale deserve to be taken seriously. They constitute realities in their own right, psychological realities with explosive potential: and I have often asked myself what binds us so fast to them. Presumably it is too troublesome for us to develop our own individual resentments and complexes, our own idiosyncrasies and neuroses. The phantom of the State provides every man with spiritual lodgings among whose furniture he can make himself at home; what's more, it's a ready-made assortment with no necessity for individual choice and with the enormous advantage of being shared with many others.
>
> To be a German does not seem to me to be a harder or an easier lot than any other. It is not a condition *à part;* it is one fate among many. I see no occasion to bemoan it or to disclaim it, and not at all to regard it as a distinction. I have no wish to quarrel with those who attach more importance to the fact that I am a German than I do. I will accept this fact whenever possible and ignore it whenever necessary.*

This political rootlessness, this *"ohne mich"* attitude in a divided country, has been reflected continuously in the way the Bonn Government has had to conduct German affairs—in fact, in the very selection of Bonn as the capital of the Federal Republic in 1949 and in the Bonn Basic Law itself. The West German constitution was drafted with the deliberate aim of constraining the powers of the central gov-

* In *Encounter* magazine, April, 1964.

ernment and enhancing the importance of the provincial governments of the ten *laender,* or states.* The Western Allies wished to reestablish some of the old separatist feelings from the days when Germany was a collection of principalities and small states. At the same time, the Germans themselves were anxious to avoid the consequences of a strong state, of too much power at the top. Today most of the functions of government which involve direct contact or interference with people's daily lives are in the hands of the individual states: education, radio, television, cultural activities, the administration of justice (with the exception of crimes against the Federal Constitution). With the exception of the Federal Border Police, the police are under the control of the individual states. The Federal Government can only requisition land for military purposes through the *laender* administrations. In the case of taxation, the constitution provided that, while the Federal Government would legislate the tax rates for all of Germany, the receipts would then be divided two-thirds to the states and one-third to the central government, and that the ratio could not be changed in less than two years. When German rearmament began in 1955, the Federal Government negotiated a 65–35 split with some difficulty, and today it is trying to bring the ratio down to a more realistic 60–40 basis.

Even in recruiting a civil service, the Federal Government is restricted by an agreement with the states not to offer higher pay for the same civil service grade than is paid in the state capitals. This means that, in order to attract trained personnel to Bonn, the Federal Government has to promote out of grade in order to pay more money. More often than not, such promotion is not deserved, yet even for more money, it is difficult to persuade trained *beamters* to give up homes and work in the state capitals at Munich, Hannover, Hamburg, Stuttgart or Düsseldorf to move to Bonn.

Still, the problem facing the Bonn Government is not wholly one of money or the location of the capital. The root of the problem lies in a fundamental disinterest among the German people in working for the state or serving the state, either as civil servants or politicians. The Foreign Ministry, which can offer postings to more than 100 embassies, legations or consulates all over the world, is barely able to fill its training course for the diplomatic corps. Young men coming out of universities find careers in the economy more attractive than

* Originally there were eleven *laender,* but in 1956 the states of Baden and Württemberg voted to merge.

the state. Industry offers travel, security, more money and faster promotion. The state, for once in German history, takes a back seat.

The choice of Bonn as the location of the West German capital was suitable to the role which the Germans and the Western Allies anticipated of the new regime in 1949—that of an administration rather than a government. The city is not without its charm, but it is scarcely a center of German cultural life or social activity. It has only recently acquired that status symbol of national capitals—its first traffic underpass. The total population of the Bonn area is only a little over 200,000, and big stores, theater, music, the arts, nightclubs, society—these are not to be found on the banks of the Rhine.

Bonn became the capital largely at the personal insistence of Konrad Adenauer. Frankfurt was the only other city to put in a strong bid, but whatever its practical advantages of size and location, the politicians found it unsuitable because it was the headquarters of the United States Military Government. An atmosphere of political tutelage already surrounded the new Federal Republic, and it therefore suited the political conditions of occupation Germany to tuck the new capital off in a small provincial university town, almost out of sight and out of mind. It also suited Adenauer's Rhineland separatist feelings about the political balance with Prussian Germany, just as it suited the politicians who wanted to emphasize the temporary character of the new state, pending German reunification and a return to Berlin. No secret police headquarters would spring up on the banks of the Rhine, and no nationalistic thunderbolts would be hurled against the peace and harmony of Europe. So the Federal Republic has settled down to a kind of permanent impermanence. It is, in fact, a government in search of a nation.

The non-nationhood of Germany has suited almost everyone for the last twenty years. It has enabled the German people, unconcerned with issues of statehood, diplomacy, nationalism, to concentrate successfully on their material well-being. It has suited those inside and outside Germany who never want to see another concentration of German governmental power. It has suited Gemany's enemies of the last hundred years who feel more secure with Germany divided than united. It has suited the movement of European unity. And it has suited Germans like Hans Magnus Enzensberger who find that the idea of the nation-state, epitomized by De Gaulle's France, no longer corresponds to reality and is only an obstinate illusion.

But today the question arises whether these attitudes and precepts will much longer remain valid for Germany. For a slow thaw has begun. Germans are beginning to think again about their history and its lessons and about the future. And just as they are beginng to think, so in time will they begin to act. This does not mean that a hysterical revival of German nationalism is about to be loosed up on a peaceful Europe, or that cries of *"lebensraum"* and *"drang nach osten"* will again be shattering the airwaves. (One of the problems and risks of trying to assess the political realities and probabilities in Germany, however, is that the cliché attitudes remain, as dangerous and constant reminders of the past.)

Nevertheless, just as Gaullism has altered a whole range of fundamental attitudes and policies in France twenty years after the war, so must Europe and the United States anticipate the emergence of new political thinking, new ideas, new leadership and new attitudes in Germany. A change is under way. There is as yet no politician who is seeking to place himself at the head of a new movement or party and give definition and identity to a policy for Germany's future. There is no General de Gaulle waiting in the wings to proclaim a destiny for a revived German nation-state. There is no ideology or political philosophy for the change which is beginning to take place. At this point it can be defined only in the very broadest terms: a growing political conscience in Germany, and a growing determination by *Germans* to do something about the future of Germany instead of leaving their national destiny forever in the hands of outsiders.

This new attitude is to be found first of all in the postwar generation of German young people who are beginning to take their place in national life—people who had nothing to do with the Nazi past and its crimes and excesses, nothing to do with the war, nothing to do with the Bonn Government or the inheritance of contemporary Germany. It is a startling statistical fact that 45 percent of West Germany's population is comprised of young people who have just entered their thirties or are below the age of thirty. The war gutted the German nation of six million people—most of them in their twenties and thirties when they died. That is why the political life of the Federal Republic has so far been almost entirely in the hands of men who were in their forties and fifties when the war ended and are now in their sixties. The middle group was either wiped out or was politically useless in postwar Germany. Today this gap is beginning to fill up with young men and women who were children or babies when the war ended and were only in their teens when the Bonn Government was formed and Berlin was blockaded.

To generalize about German youth, or youth anywhere for that matter, is difficult and perhaps risky, but a few cautious points seem valid. First of all, the political awareness of young people today in West Germany universities or just starting out their careers is very different from the *ohne mich* attitude of youth in the first decade after the war. Such idealism as the older group did muster centered on the cause of Europe, and entailed the submerging of their national identity as preached by Enzensberger, who is himself one of them.

Young Germans are not yet very active in politics. They do not run for seats in the Bundestag or local municipal councils. They are not flocking to join the diplomatic corps, work for the government or take up politics as a career. But neither are they turning their backs blindly on Germany's past or refusing to think about the problems of Germany's future. This emerging generation has a better chance, perhaps, than any in German history of thinking and acting objectively rather than out of blind tradition. Young Germans can look at the excesses and the bestiality of the Nazi era the way the French can look at the Terror of the Revolution and the guillotines in the Place de la Concorde, or the British can look back on Newgate Prison, the slave trade or the exiling of early trade union leaders to Botany Bay. This does not mean that the Nazis can be considered as parallel to British judges or French revolutionaries. But it does mean that the sordid and grisly Third Reich is part of German history and cannot and should not be ignored or treated as a bad dream.

In the immediate postwar period, the policies of Allied Military Government on the question of Nazi history were curiously ambivalent. On the one hand, Germans were loaded down with national guilt. On the other hand, Hitler's name was only whispered, lest the very sound might stir a revival of National Socialism. School textbooks were expunged of any examination of what had happened. Nowhere could the Germans read about or examine the rise of Nazism in historical terms.

It was not until 1953 that a German film company felt that it could challenge Allied misgivings and put together a first documentary feature-length film on the Nazi period. As a particular tidbit, the company obtained some of Eva Braun's home-movie shots, showing Eva at play with Hitler and his entourage in a Bavarian hideaway complete with an exotic waterfall. Some Allied officials feared that all this excitement would be too much for German instability. I went to the first public showing in Berlin. Eva Braun turned out to be a dumpy, frowzy, tasteless hausfrau who looked almost repulsive in a bathing suit. Certainly she was no Nordic goddess. And far from being aroused by the sight and sound of the old banners and torch-light parades, the audience shuffled out silent and shamefaced. Recordings of Hitler and Goebbels are easily obtainable in Germany now, but young people have a typical common-sense reaction: "What is he shouting about? Why did he scream like that?"

The silent treatment on the history of the Third Reich is over in Germany. A great deal of detailed, sober, analytical study and research is under way to bring the full story into the open in textbooks, histories and special quarterlies. The Institute of Contemporary History at Munich regularly produces lengthy studies on such subjects as the Nazi system of justice, the organization of the Gestapo under Himmler, the fate of the trade unions in the Third Reich, German administration of Poland, the origin of the race laws, the Jewish question. In Berlin another institute has produced a detailed examination of the decline of the Weimar Republic and the technique of National Socialism's seizure of power. At Hamburg, Göttingen, at universities all over Germany, there is a growing, almost Germanic determination to uncover the facts. The Federal Republic has established an eight-story Public Records Office in Coblentz where almost all of the documents which the Western Allies seized from the old Foreign Ministery, Hitler's Chancellery, and the German military commands have now been placed.

The emphasis of this research is not to whitewash or apologize but simply to establish the facts, which speak with enormity for themselves. This emphasis, this tone, is communicated in university seminars and studies, student discussion, lectures and themes. The result is that the young people of the new German generation are exposed to a great deal more factual, historic evidence of what happened in the Nazi times than their parents ever knew. Moreover, this scholarly, academic study is taking place against the public background of the Nazi crimes trials, in particular the Auschwitz trial at Frankfurt. Day after day, night after night, in the newspapers and on the television screen, Germans have seen the truth unfold in their own courts, from their own neighbors, in their own records. It is perfectly true that on any public opinion poll the majority of the Germans would like to have done with these trials twenty years after the war. But still the trials go on, and their fundamental effect is to burn the facts of what happened into German minds and, it is to be assumed, German consciences.

The evolution in attitude can be seen in the fashion in which the German people now approach the plotters of July 20, 1944. In the immediate postwar years, only those few who had been associated with the plot and had survived were prepared to speak out vigorously to honor the plotters as patriotic heroes. Germans who fought the war, supported Hitler, and applauded the work of the Gestapo and the People's Courts when the plot failed had to regard them as traitors who deserved to hang. Slowly the perspective has changed. More and more has been dug up and written about the plot. Germans have been reading and pondering the writings and the smuggled prison letters of Pastor Dietrich Bonhoeffer, Count Helmuth von Moltke, Colonel Claus von Stauffenberg who planted the bomb, Adam von Trott of the old German Foreign Ministry, Count Peter Yorck von Wartenburg and others. If the idealism of these men seems to a non-German murky, involving belated discovery of obvious truths, nevertheless their writings do make clear to Germans that there were other Germans in their midst who had the courage to put loyalty to the higher aspirations of human life above loyalty to the Führer and the Nazi system. Gradually, therefore, it has begun to be accepted in Germany that the plot was indeed not treason but high patriotism. The new generation can come to this conclusion more readily and objectively than the older generation. But everybody now knows what it was the July plotters were trying to overthrow. The cause of moral integrity stands out more clearly every day against the dark stains of the Auschwitz trial. In 1964, on the twentieth anniversary of the plot, July 20 became a national holiday in West Germany. Mayor Willy Brandt of West Berlin used the occasion to tell Germans that "there has been no German self-cleansing and the power has failed to confront the people in all factual severity and with human sincerity with its own past. . . . There is too much opportunism and too little courage to face unpleasant facts."

In the summer of 1964, the United States Embassy in Bonn asked all of its consulates in West Germany to prepare special reports on German youth. These were not public opinion poll surveys. They were based on the conversations and impressions which the consuls in the state capitals of Germany derived from grass-roots contacts in German universities, with youth groups, or through personal experiences. Every one of the dozen or so reports which arrived at the Embassy in Bonn stressed one basic theme. Reunification of Germany had replaced European unity and all other topics as the No. 1 political concern of German young people. This is a very considerable change from the immediate postwar period, when a united Europe was the great urge and outlet for a kind of *ersatz* German patriotism. Today, this European idealism has faded into a maze of economic obscurities over agricultural subsidies, frozen chickens and tariff percentages. The change in the attitude of young people is not yet reflected in any particular political activity in Germany, and it is too early to predict what direction it is going to take and what it is going to mean. But a search for German national identity, which was so rigorously thrust to one side by German youth fifteen years ago, is now beginning.

This new German generation is not likely to accept for long the status of national penitence as a permanent condition of German national life. It bears no responsibility for Nazi crimes, the origins of the Second World War, or the division of Germany. But it does bear a moral responsibility for the future, and it is not going to remain content, as the present generation of German political leaders, to be frozen in the attitudes of defeat and the political conditions of the Cold War.

For the last twenty years reunification has been regarded as one of those subjects about which German politicians had to talk but Germans did not really care. Historians could point to the past and the fact that Germany did not become a united country until Bismarck's time. Politicians could point to the fact that Adenauer was a Rhinelander and a Catholic Christian Democrat who had no particular wish to have the balance upset by the Prussian, Protestant, Social Democratic traditions of East Germany. Industrialists and economists could point to the difficulties of re-merging the free-enterprise, capitalist, booming West with the stagnant, Communist East. And Germany's neighbors could agree that a divided Germany was safer for Europe than a united Germany.

Today neither the German Government nor German politicians can treat reunification as a lip-service political problem. That is why the Bonn Government, in advance of the 1965 election campaign, began to press so actively with the British, the French and the Americans for a new round of talks with the Russians on German reunification. That is also why President de Gaulle decided that it was time that he define his "Atlantic to the Urals" concept more clearly and stated that "it must be recognized first of all by Germany that any settlement of which it would be the subject would necessarily imply a settlement of its frontiers and of its armament in agreement with all its neighbors, those on the East and those on the West." That is why the Bonn Government is so active in trade contacts in Eastern Europe.

The policy of the Bonn Government toward East Germany and the reunification question has been enshrined since 1955 in what is known as the Hallstein Doctrine—devised by Dr. Walter Hallstein who was then the powerful state secretary in the Foreign Ministry and is now President of the European Common Market Executive Commission. The doctrine, which aims at the diplomatic isolation of the East German Communist Government, resulted from the one and only visit which Chancellor Adenauer made to Moscow, in 1955. Almost as a ransom to obtain the release of German war prisoners still in Soviet hands, Adenauer agreed to the establishment of full diplomatic relations between Russia and West Germany. Thus, in effect, Russia recognized the sovereignty of the Federal Republic even though there was no German peace treaty. But the Russians immediatey opened a campaign for similar diplomatic recognition in the West of their East German satellite. In effect, this would also amount to legalizing the division of Germany and elevating the Ulbricht regime to equal status in the world. To head off any such development, Hallstein pronounced as a fixed rule of West German foreign policy that any country which recognized East Germany—except the Soviet Union—would automatically forfeit diplomatic recognition and the economic help and goodwill of West Germany. For ten years, the doctrine has been effectively applied. East Germany has of course gained formal diplomatic recognition in the Communist capitals, but it has remained almost completely cut off from the rest of the world. In some instances, the East Germans have managed to open consulates or trade missions outside the Communist bloc, but nowhere up to 1965 had they won diplomatic recognition.

The Hallstein Doctrine was a diplomatic application of John Foster Dulles's policy of "situation of strength" pressures against the Communist world. Dulles and Adenauer saw German reunification coming about as a result of the unyielding power of the NATO Alliance against the Iron Curtain, while in the Communist states, the inner weaknesses of the system would slowly produce an economic and political breakdown of Russian power and control over Eastern Europe. At this point, the NATO frontier would advance to the east, and West Germany would emerge as the inheritor of a reunited German state.

This Cold War policy was clear-cut, coherent and logical in the conditions of the times, when the United States led NATO and the policies of Europe. But the "Atlantic to the Urals" doctrine which is the objective of De Gaulle's foreign policy is based on a very different concept of Europe's evolution. Instead of an advance of NATO military power to the east, De Gaulle seeks a reduction or even a withdrawal of American strength, and at the same time a relaxation of Russia's grip on the satellite system of Eastern Europe.

Increasingly, the West Germans are finding the Hallstein Doctrine difficult to apply. The question often arises whether the interests of the Federal Republic would not be better served by a resumption of normal diplomatic relations with the Communist regimes of Eastern Europe, despite the fact that they recognize East Germany. For the moment the Bonn Government relies on its businessmen, with the firm of Alfred Krupp taking a strong lead, to establish back-door contacts and *de facto* recognition in Warsaw, Prague, Budapest, Bucharest and Sofia through trade agreements and trade missions which are accorded diplomatic status.

The application of the doctrine often becomes, therefore, a matter of strained legalisms rather than clear-cut policy. The first major challenge to it came when the Egyptian Government, at the urging of the Russians, agreed to receive Ulbricht in February, 1965, on what amounted to a formal state visit. East Germany has long maintained a trade mission in Cairo, while West Germany has an Embassy there with full diplomatic privileges. The West Germans dithered and debated whether their best interest lay in firm application of the Hallstein Doctrine (which would have meant breaking relations with Egypt) or in living a while longer with legalisms and diplomatic hair-splitting. In the end they decided to live with the situation, and from now on there will be a string of such moves and challenges inspired by the Communists in the noncommitted countries of Africa and Asia, with the aim of slowly building up a legal and diplomatic recognition of the division of Germany into two states.

But while the Bonn Government fights this diplomatic battle to keep East Germany in a state of isolation and nonrecognition, it faces the problem of increasing political sentiment among its own people for a more flexible and active policy toward East Germany. Nobody in West Germany remotely advocates conceding equality of legal or diplomatic status to the Communist regime, but two years after the Berlin Wall went up, Mayor Willy Brandt began outlining a policy which he called "change through closer relations." In a speech delivered by the West Berlin press chief, Egon Bahr, on July 15, 1963, in the West German city of Tutzing, this trend toward a more active policy was brought into the open and defined:

"If it is correct that the interests of the other side, too, have to be recognized and taken into consideration, then it is certainly impossible for the Soviet Union to have the zone of East Germany snatched away for the purpose of strengthening the western potential. The zone, with the consent of the Soviet Union, has to be transformed. If we could get that far, we would have advanced a great step toward reunification."

A direct outgrowth of this speech and other statements from Mayor Brandt himself was the first deal in 1963 for Christmas passes for West Berliners to go through the wall and visit East Berlin. A year later a new agreement was negotiated, and the wall is now opened up for one-way traffic, west to east, four times a year. Brandt came under heavy fire for the first pass deal, on the grounds that he had come very close to exceeding his authority in negotiating the agreement, that he risked establishing the principle that West Berlin could negotiate on its own in such matters instead of as part of the Federal Republic, and that his actions almost constituted legal recognition of the Communist regime. Brandt snapped back:

"One hears alarmed whispers here and there in the West, in my own city as well as elsewhere, that we in Berlin are playing a dangerous game with our own future safety and the viability of Western policy. I have little patience with this kind of complaint. It comes mainly, I think, from two kinds of people—those who are afraid to take a chance on extending freedom, the 'no-experiment' types, and those who, I am sorry to say, would rather see the Berlin Wall remain impenetrable until both it and the Communist regime behind it come tumbling down in one roaring crash. Neither side at this stage of events and at this level of action can expect to change the political order or solve any major problems. This will require negotiations on a higher level. But if we make it easier for others to reach higher ground in due time, we Berliners can only be grateful."

In the four years since the wall went up in Berlin, there has also been a definite rise in the productivity, the living standards and the general economic conditions of Communist East Germany. (In the long run, not even the Communist system, it seems, can stop Germans from building and producing.) By plugging the escape root, Ulbricht and the Communist regime have succeeded in stabilizing their economic situation. No one who has visited East Germany recently pretends that it is in any way comparable to the opulence and plenty of West Germany, but the contrast is less glaring. The political effect, is to disprove the theory that reunification will come about through collapse of the system or abrupt Soviet withdrawal. The "Atlantic to the Urals" approach, therefore, offers a framework for West Germany to pursue a much more active diplomatic and trade policy not only in Eastern Europe, which has always been a natural German Market, but also toward East Germany. Just as Mayor Brandt's 1963 deal for Christmas passes has grown into a regular system, so it will probably expand in another year or two to cover visits by East Germans to the West. Ulbricht is seventy-two years old and he is not immortal. He is the last Stalinist left in the Communist system, and his demise, along with the general easing of the Communist grip on daily life in Eastern Europe, will carry the atmosphere of "change through closer relations" yet another step.

Such is the trend among young people, among the German political intelligentsia, with Mayor Brandt and the Social Democratic Party, and in the Bonn Government itself. But the government, which has power and responsibility, must inevitably move more cautiously in feeling its way on reunification policy.

Bonn must try to keep a political and diplomatic balance between Gaullism and NATOism. It is NATO which has given security to the West German state. It is Gaullism which is encouraging a new nationalism and a new mobility of policy in West Germany, but these remain to be tried and tested in the arena of the future. The appeal of nationalism, its dominance of German politics in the past, needs no elaboration. In these postwar years the old nationalists have been noisy but unsuccessful, and that is the best harbinger of the future. The Bonn constitution provides that no party which draws less than 5 percent of the popular vote is entitled to seats in the parliament. The fragmentation of the German right wing has therefore been such that the parties which appealed to the refugees or the neo-Nazis or the separatists (such as the Bavarians) have died out one by one.

This was the great strengthening contribution of the Adenauer era to the democratic processes in Germany.

Today the ultra-Rightists are making an effort to group into a common front. They have a newspaper called the *Deutsche Nachrichten* and they have amalgamated into the "National Democratic Party." They see hope in the fact that the total ultranationalist vote in Germany has run well over 10 percent in the past, though too split to be effective. But these nationalists have nothing to offer, and broadly speaking the German people know it. The man who hopes to be the NDP figurehead is Friedrich Thielen, who is forty-eight years old, and who says that "the time is ripe for a strong hand over our nation, for clear and firm leadership." In the meantime, every one of the ultranationalist political parties or groups in Germany has gone down and down in membership and voting support since the elections of 1949. Not one has improved.

The old nationalism has very little appeal to the pragmatic and somewhat materialistic new generation in Germany. It will not be banners, speeches and torchlight parades which create the problem. Germany is moving from the period in which it has recovered its economy to a period in which it is going to try to find its nationhood again. It will be a period of confusing and uncertain political pressures—such as what to do about the Hallstein Doctrine if India, for example, decides to recognize East Germany, or how far the Federal Republic should go in a normalization of contacts with East Germany. And there will be pressures from the right-wing extremists who think that the Germany of 1937 is the only Germany that ever really existed.

The strength of the German economy in the center of Europe is very great, and the Germans are again beginning to sense the realities of power. They know that they are needed and are even sought after again as a strong partner. They know that they are being watched sharply and critically in Paris, Washington, London and Moscow. They know that they are the only great power, the only modern state, which is arbitrarily cut in two by the military occupation of the superpowers.

The question remains whether the Germans themselves will have the stability, the national repose, to move from their past history to a new plateau of pan-European peace and harmony. On the whole, they have gained the confidence of their neighbors to the West. They must now adopt the attitudes and make the sacrifices to achieve the same in the East. When Germany has settled on its own size and shape and destiny it will be a nation again. Until then, the only attitude which it can expect is a combination of confidence and suspicion.

3. Britain and Europe

Big Ben was stilled. From St. James's Park behind the silent tens of thousands who lined Whitehall, Trafalgar Square, The Strand, Fleet Street and Ludgate Hill, the first gun from the saluting battery broke the somber quiet—one gun a minute, ninety guns in all, one for each year of the great man's life. The young Grenadier Guardsmen bore the heavy casket from the catafalque in Westminster Hall to the waiting gun carriage in New Palace Yard, their faces tense with emotion and physical strain as they pressed against the Union Jack which draped the great burden of his frail remains. They lowered it carefully, reverently, to the caisson and the naval ratings shuffled to close ranks and grasp the white ropes to draw him on his last journey. A bass drum boomed and a band began the Funeral March from Beethoven's *Eroica* Symphony. "Let there be plenty of music," he had said, and twelve bands were in the long line of march.

In stiff slow stride, sixty-five paces to the minute, they drew the gun carriage into Parliament Square and turned up Whitehall past the Treasury and the Home Office where he had served as a minister, past Downing Street where he had presided over years of tumult and years of peace, past the Admiralty where he had mobilized the Fleet in 1914 and taken charge again in 1939. With poignancy and magnificence his last processional unfolded—the saluting guns echoing in the clear cold January air, the clatter of horses' hoofs, the bands, the determined and stately cadence of the slow march of thousands of men, the muffled drums, the cry of "IN . . . VER . . . TARMS" from rank to rank of the soldiers, the sailors, the airmen and marines lining the route through London's famous streets.

They bore him up the steps of St. Paul's Cathedral to lie for a brief half hour under Sir Christopher Wren's great fire-scarred dome in the presence of kings whose thrones he had saved, presidents and prime ministers whose governments he had restored and traditions preserved, admirals and generals he had sent into battle. They sang, at his request, "The Battle Hymn of the Republic"—". . . I have seen him in the watchfires of a hundred circling camps. . . . He hath sounded forth the trumpet that shall never call retreat. . . . Let us die to make men free. . . His soul goes marching on. . . ." And then they bore the casket back to the gun carriage and drew him to the Tower of London where the massed pipe bands of the British Army played him aboard a launch for a silent journey up the Thames as the dockside cranes dipped in salute. From Waterloo Station, he returned to the place of his birth and lies in a country churchyard by the walls of Blenheim Palace.

England's Age of Churchill is ended.

In the life of nations, as in the life of men, there comes a time when pause, reflection, rest and reassessment has to follow great historic exertion. Winston Churchill, first by his leadership and then by his very presence, extended England's past role in history years beyond its inherent life. But his age is over now, and for England a new age must begin.

Churchill wrote in *My Early Life:*

> I was a child of the Victorian era, when the structure of our country seemed firmly set, when its position in trade and on the seas was unrivalled, and when the realization of the greatness of our Empire and of our duty to preserve it was ever growing stronger. In those days the dominant forces in Great Britain were very sure of themselves and their doctrines. They thought they could teach the world the art of government and the science of economics. They were sure they were supreme at sea and consequently safe at home. They rested therefore sedately under the convictions of power and security. Very different is the aspect of these anxious and dubious times.

England's structure is no longer firmly set and its position in world trade has steadily declined. England no longer has an Empire to preserve and no longer commands the seas. It is no longer sure of itself or its doctrines. The world no longer learns either government or economics from the British. Britain enjoys neither the convictions of powers nor its own security. The times are indeed anxious and dubious. England starts again—without Churchill.

The most vivid asset which England displays at this unhappy time of national reappraisal is the intelligence of its people, and a fierce, almost masochistic determination that nobody is going to outdo the British themselves in harsh examination of Britain's problems. The result is an unending flood of self-analysis, self-criticism, self-satirization, self-deprecation. No thinking person in England is in the slightest illusion about the decline of British power and Britain's role in the world, the weakness of the pound sterling, the monotonous recurrence of economic crisis and squeeze, the worsening competitive position of British industry in world markets, and the frustrations of life with an island rather than a world horizon.

Unhappily, the British are finding it much easier to catalog their shortcomings, weaknesses, mistakes and failures at home and abroad than they are able to devise imaginative solutions. It is impossible to picture them having the kind of modern revolution of enforced, pressurized, necessary change in outlook which De Gaulle has worked in France in the last seven years. As a nation, Britain worships stability and declines to examine the positive results and realities which change can bring. It is not so much the case that Britain today is a prisoner of nostalgia or of past historic greatness and attitudes. But it is the case that the virtues on which the British built their past strength now work steadily against the process of change. The British had their revolution in 1642, and since then their great strength has been their ability to adjust and evolve socially and economically as a nation while preserving stability, continuity, steadiness, faith in tradition and a fundamental belief which has grown with the ages in the ultimate soundness of British judgment and the triumph of British values. But this long stability and continuity have created a stifling atmosphere of conformity in British life, from top to bottom. This is all the more sad for Britain because it has only been the great nonconformists and reformers who have really made the English system work. Churchill's greatness and strength, which he imparted to his country in such enormous historic measure, lay in his magnificent ability to combine England's traditions with sweeping nonconformity—whether he was introducing its earliest social security measures, deserting one political party for another, landing a British

Army at Gallipoli and trying to force the Dardenelles, or warning against Hitler and leading the opposition to appeasement. He gave life to the system.

There are no great radical nonconformist political leaders at work in England today, focusing the difficulties, tickling the senses, stirring imagination, raising the sights, fixing on new horizons. Even with all the immense output of critical self-analysis which floods England, there are not yet any great new social writers who have emerged with the creative penetration and literary quality of George Orwell, Bernard Shaw or Matthew Arnold. There is plenty of brilliance, plenty of wit and satire. But the vogue of the "Angry Young Men" of the late 1950's, for example, thrived not on any new ideas about England's future, but on sticking pins in English conformity. It was good fun to go and watch John Osborne's hero Jimmy Porter, in *Look Back in Anger,* wallow around the stage in self-indulgent weakness, blaming everybody from the Archbishop of Canterbury to *The New Statesman and Nation* for the kind of cigarettes he had to smoke in his seedy attic room. But as a writer, who would John Osborne be without the English way-of-life to rail about, and what ideas has he contributed to the future, a future, any kind of future for England? In the end, Osborne and the other "Angry Young Men" wind up as court-jesters to the system, as much a part of the Establishment which runs England as the British Broadcasting Corporation. This sense of their own imprisonment of course deepens their bitterness.*

At the other extreme, take C. P. Snow, the novelist, dramatist and scientist who stimulated so much thought with his essays warning of the autocratic power of science over decisions of government. He is now Lord Snow and a minister in the Labour Government in a newly created Ministery of Technology. In a House of Lords debate, he rose to argue the case for educational reform and Labour's plans to introduce a system of comprehensive schools which will enable children to pursue their studies on a broader curriculum, instead of being filtered out through a testing system between the ages of eleven and twelve. A Conservative peer interjected that Lord Snow sent his son to Eton.

"It seems to me," Lord Snow replied, "that if you are living in a

* "Damn you, England," Mr. Osborne once wrote from the Riviera in an open letter to "my fellow countrymen." "There is murder in my brain, and I carry a knife in my heart for every one of you. Macmillan, and you, Gaitskell, you particularly."

fairly prosperous home it is a mistake to educate your child differently from the mass of people whom you know socially."

There is nothing wrong with Eton as a place to get a good education and still less is there anything wrong with Lord Snow deciding to send his son there. But as a Labour Government minister who is supposed to be creating new technological horizons and visions for England, it was disappointing to find him reflecting one of the stuffiest of all principles of British social conformity in defending his choice for his son. Even Queen Elizabeth and Prince Philip have shown more imagination. They have sent Prince Charles, the future King of England, not to Eton but to a little-known non-Establishment school called Gordonstoun, in the north of Scotland, in order to get him away from "the mass of people whom you know socially."

In previous times, this fundamental English conformity was much less noticeable, less dominant and suffocating because the British were involved in great enterprises of world power, running an empire or fighting wars, which produced invigorating challenges from the outside. They offered adventure and demanded initiative. Seldom for more than a century—even today in Malaysia—has there been a time when British soldiers were not getting a whiff of grapeshot somewhere in the world. Englishmen went out from England with a sense of power and greatness, and with a self-confidence that was rooted in part in the conformity and stability from which they were sprung. Britain has left more monuments of law, government, civil service, police, language, armies and civilization around the world than any nation since ancient Rome. And at the same time, England also scattered the globe with some of the greatest offbeat oddball nonconformist characters of all history, from Lord Byron to Orde Wingate.

Conformity was also under constant political and intellectual attack at home in Britain, particularly during the depression years of the 1920's and 1930's, when the breakdown of Edwardian wealth and economic order followed the First World War. There were enormous problems to attract nonconformist intellects, and fortunately for England there were whole schools of penetrating minds to probe questions of distribution of national wealth, the social structure of the nation, the organization of its economy. This was the period when the British Labour Party did most of its thinking out of the future, with the Fabian Society taking the lead. But radical thinking was by no means confined to the trade unions and the working class. It was going on in the universities, among philosophers and economists, among upper-class rebels, poets and writers, social thinkers, people like Sidney and Beatrice Webb, G. D. H. Cole, Bernard Shaw, and most powerfully of all, John Maynard Keynes.

But these outlets and stimulations which have kept conformist England a place of challenges and ideas have been closed off today from two directions. With the loss of British power in the world, there has been a loss of national purpose. This was one reason why the mess at Suez left such bitterness in England. A nation of dashing adventurers had staged a fiasco and bungled the job. Britain's old role in the world truly did end not with a bang but a whimper. Afterwards, a kind of chauvinistic, petulant, frustrated nationalism took hold in England, and it continues to mark popular British reaction to events in which Britain does not participate and cannot control.*

At home, the Welfare State has added mightily to England's conformity. It has brought English living standards to the highest of any nation in the world outside the United States, but it has also made the British working class and middle class almost more resistant to change, more conformist, than the upper classes. The old intellectual ferment of social and economic problems has been stifled by the successes of full employment and social security which minds like the Webbs, Beveridge and Keynes helped to devise. Today there is plenty of self-analysis and self-criticism of English attitudes, but there is precious little self-denial or self-sacrifice or readiness to part with outmoded encumbrances, be they inefficient machine tools or old ideas. Every segment of British society now has its own conformities and resistance to change, except change by which somebody gains a little bit more of the economic cake.

The horizons closed in with Suez, and it fell to Harold Macmillan not merely to preside over the declining Age of Churchill, but to personify the comforts of conformity. "You never had it so good," the slogan which won Macmillan the general election of 1959, was one of the most misleading and unkind political soporifics ever administered to the voting public. But the shops were full of television sets and washing machines and refrigerators and the country was happily

* "In a troubled world, what a blessing it is that the Prime Minister can pick up the telephone and talk at once to the President of the United States," editorialized *The Daily Express* at the height of the Vietnam crisis. "It is called the hot line. In truth it is an assurance that coolness and common sense will prevail when dangers seem to be near. How happy we should be every time we read that Mr. Wilson and Mr. Johnson have been talking on the telephone. Upon their calls the peaceful evolution of the world may depend."

loaded down with installment buying. In the end, to his credit, Macmillan saw that the challenge of entering Europe, which Britain had repeatedly passed up, alone offered a restoration of national purpose and the kind of change which would stir England from the slow decline of conformity. Churchill had perceived this in 1946, when Britain could have had the leadership of a united Europe and dictated the terms of its organization for the asking. But when Macmillan undertook the job, he was too much a prisoner of conformity to declare boldly that he was out to change Britain's traditional political alignment, now that the Empire was gone, and completely overhaul the competitive, trading, agricultural and economic structure of England. This, in fact, is what membership in the Common Market eventually would have meant. But England was not to be so rudely shaken. Macmillan sought to back into Europe instead of marching in. It was a historic misfortune that he did not make it, and a bitter slap in the face for a great nation to which Europe owes so much that one man could have vetoed such a great enterprise. But the fault ultimately lay in the fact that Britain and Macmillan, through caution, indifference, suspicion or misjudgment vis-à-vis Europe, had worked themselves into a position where such a one-man veto was possible. Macmillan subsequently moved off the public stage in England to a chorus of raucous national laughter. The British turned around and convulsed themselves at one of the wildest and most bitterly funny bouts of self-satirization in the cultural life of any nation.

Macmillan almost invited imitation and caricature, with his floppy cardigan sweaters and droopy moustache and Edwardian manners. His political speeches and style of delivery were wide open for parody. The London stage and nightclubs and television screens were flooded with Macmillan satire:

"I flew to Washington, on your behalf—and at your expense—and told President Kennedy of our wish to be the honest broker. He remarked to me that we certainly were honest, and I ventured to chaff the President by replying, 'And never broker!' " . . .

"At Nassau, the President was kind enough to show me an actual photo of the Polaris missile." . . .

"I have received a letter from an old-age pensioner which will be engraved on my memory forever. I will read it to you." . . .

"This decision of the government means that in seven or eight years' time, Great Britain will have its own independent missile with a range of approximately 200 miles, or enough to hit Paris—and hit Paris we will!" . . .

"I have to announce to the nation that we have just been through the shortest war on record—one hour and twenty-three minutes including the signing of the peace treaty." . . .

If none of this took Britain very far out of its troubles, at least the sound of laughter was a certain relief and reassurance. The Conservative Party added to the general hilarity by thinking up a new slogan for the next general election: "Modernize with Macmillan." But illness struck the prime minister down and he never got a chance to try his electoral luck again. Sir Alec Douglas-Home who succeeded him will at least go down in the history books as the first British peer to give up his title in order to become prime minister. In his year in office, perhaps his most dynamic act was a law to end wholesale price-fixing and introduce a little competition in the stores. But this gesture against conformity seems to have cost the Conservatives votes in the nation of shopkeepers.

After thirteen years of Conservative rule, the British ought to have been able to turn to the Labour Party with confidence and relief. But Labour's last two big men were gone. Aneurin Bevan died of cancer in 1960, and Hugh Gaitskell died at the age of fifty-seven, a few days after the De Gaulle press conference in January, 1963, of a virus which was never identified.

Bevan was in the great radical nonconformist tradition. He was a Welshman whose soul burned with social reform. Up from the coal pits, he was educated on funds collected penny by penny from trade union members, and the class struggle was his life. But he was the kind of radical who made the English system work. He was a great debater and parliamentarian, and he loved the House of Commons and the struggles of democracy. Like Winston Churchill, with whom he clashed in some of the most memorable and lively of all Commons exchanges, he raised the level of the whole House and gave it life and vitality. Bevan was temperamentally the very opposite of the intellectually donnish, upper-middle-class Hugh Gaitskell. The son of an Indian civil servant, Gaitskell was a product of the English system, educated at Winchester and Oxford. He liked society and a gay life. But intellectually he was a nonconformist who had become a Socialist not because of class struggle, but out of a cold passion of logic, study and intellectual conviction that Socialism was the best democratic and economic hope of man. Bevan, with his burning social conscience, looked on Gaitskell with suspicion and disdain and the two men clashed frequently and angrily. But Gaitskell won the Labour Party leadership hands-down over Bevan when Clement Attlee retired in 1955. Bevan was too far to the Left for the party image or the leadership. Afterward, although they could scarcely be called friends, they settled down to work in harness, and by 1959 they had achieved a relationship of mutual respect and understanding and confidence which had given the party great strength at the top.

Each man needed the other, and the Labour Party badly needed them both. Bevan came to accept the balance-of-power and took charge of foreign policy for the party at the time of Suez. He would have made a very considerable and vigorous British foreign secretary. Gaitskell once told me that the turn in their personal relationship came when they traveled to Russia in 1959, and found in long conversations on the airplane and in dealing with the Russians face to face together that they thought and felt a great deal more alike than either had suspected in their years of feuding. They were big men. Labour lost the General Election in 1959, but Gaitskell and Bevan had gained in mutual confidence, and had they lived they would have swept the country for Labour the next time around.

Gaitskell, to his political courage, directed his nonconformity against the Labour Party itself—which frequently behaves as if it got its last new idea during the General Strike of 1926. After the 1959 election defeat, Gaitskell opened up an audacious attack on the most sacred of the party's political tenets: nationalization of industry. Gaitskell reasoned with plenty of political evidence to support him that a "nationalization scare," a fear in the electorate that if Labour were returned to power it would embark on a new round of wholesale state takeovers of all kinds of industries, cost the party more votes in 1959 than any other single issue. He had also concluded, with plenty of economic evidence to support him, that apart from the steel industry, nationalization had served its basic purpose in the British economy and was no longer germane to a solution of Britain's economic problems. He went before a full Party Conference to fight almost completely alone to have the nationalization policy clause removed from the party constitution. He lost the fight and in the process was called some of the nastiest names in the political lexicon by party Left Wingers. But the effect of his one-man stand was to furl the flag of nationalization once and for all. He had struck a blow against outmoded Labour conformity.

Harold Wilson succeeded to the leadership of the Labour Party and the prime ministership of England by death and death alone. "A little round hard ball bearing like Harold Wilson, that's what the Labour Party needs as leader," Richard H. S. Crossman, one of the Leftist Labourites, said to me at the height of Hugh Gaitskell's fight with the party over nationalization. Wilson not only has no friends or confidants, he prides himself on avoiding them. In all my years in England, I never heard anybody speak of him with any warmth or personal liking or enthusiasm or affection. The best that he ever aroused was admiration for his undoubted intelligence, and praise for his carefully prepared House of Commons wit. He rose to prominence in the Labour Party first in Bevan's shadow, as a man of the Left. As he neared the top, it was almost amusing to watch Harold Wilson modulate his extremism and roll like a hard ball bearing to the center. As a political personality, he resembles Richard Nixon. He does not inspire instinctive confidence and trust. With good reason, too. Once, by accident, I watched while he almost literally stabbed Hugh Gaitskell in the back.

The incident took place at the Labour Party conference at Scarborough on the northeast coast of England in October, 1960. Gaitskell, harried and pummeled by the party Left Wing on the nationalization issue, faced a new fight on a matter of basic principle over a left-wing resolution fixing unilateral disarmament for Britain as the aim of the Labour Party. Such a policy was ludicrous for a great nation, and Gaitskell had painfully worked out a compromise resolution which the Executive of the Labour Party, including Harold Wilson, was pledged to support. But Gaitskell knew that he did not have the votes on the floor from the membership and that the unilateralist Left Wingers would almost certainly carry the day. In the face of this situation, he delivered one of the most passionate and electrifying speeches of political courage and principle that the Labour Party ever heard, ending with the cold ringing words:

"We may lose this vote today . . . but some of us will fight and fight and fight again so that our party, with its great past, will retain its glory and greatness and reject a suicidal path of unilateral disarmament which leaves our country defenseless and alone."

I had taken a place in the balcony above and behind the platform to listen to the speech and watch what we all knew would be a boisterous reception from the floor. When Gaitskell concluded, applause broke out from his supporters who, if they did not have the votes, at least had the spirit of integrity and determination of their leader. Members of the Labour Executive were ranged on either side of Gaitskell behind a long platform table, Harold Wilson to the left of the rostrum. Wilson had puffed on his pipe with pained indifference throughout the forty-minute speech. The principle for which Gaitskell was fighting did not trouble him. As cheers and counter-cheers swelled from the floor, two or three of Gaitskell's loyal supporters on the Executive rose and, motioning those in the hall to follow, gave the party leader a standing ovation. Wilson at that point took his pipe from his mouth with his right hand, and then dropped his left hand behind his chair, behind Hugh Gaitskell's back, and unseen from the floor of the hall he feverishly wigwagged to the other members of the Executive to keep their seats.

Wilson came out in the open a few weeks later and ran against Gaitskell in the annual leadership election—"the only time I couldn't sleep; I didn't want to oppose Gaitskell but I felt I had to." He of course knew that he would be soundly defeated, but it was a political maneuver to put himself at the head of the Left Wing of the party with Bevan gone. To the Bevanites it was an act of courage; to Gaitskell's supporters it was cheap betrayal.

Gaitskell brushed off the leadership challenge and magnanimously kept Wilson at his side in the post of foreign policy spokesman in Commons. Meanwhile, Gaitskell fought and fought back hard against the unilateral disarmers and routed them completely at the next annual conference in 1961. By these lonely battles of political courage and integrity, Gaitskell had gained ascendancy over the Labour Party and enormous respect and confidence in the country when suddenly he died. Labour's Left and Right leaders were gone, and Harold Wilson rolled into the leadership. But he could never inherit the trust and confidence which Gaitskell enjoyed. The country voted accordingly in October, 1964—and gave him a tiny six-seat majority in the House of Commons. He would not even have had that had Hugh Gaitskell not been enough of a nonconformist to fight the Labour Party over nationalization of industry, and fight again over unilateral disarmament.

The economic situation which Harold Wilson and the Labour Party inherited in October, 1964, would tax the strength, confidence and ingenuity of a government with a House of Commons majority of 100. Starting out with a majority of only six, which was promptly cut to four as the result of a by-election loss, the Labour Government could fall as the result of an automobile accident, a couple of heart attacks or a flu epidemic. More important than physical precariousness, however, is the fact that such a narrow House of Commons majority inevitably inflicts political caution and uncertainty on any government, and works against innovation, strong radical measures, and the introduction of change. But England's need for radicalism—whether it comes from the Labour or Conservative Party—is great.

From 1953 to 1963, across the years of "you never had it so good," Great Britain's share of world export markets in manufactured goods fell from 21 percent to 15 percent. During that same period West Germany, with about the same population and industrial capacity and not even enjoying Commonwealth preferential tariffs, *increased* its share of world trade by almost exactly this same amount, from 13½ percent to 20 percent. It does not take any industrial or efficiency expert to deduce that this represents a serious and fundamental decline in the competitive state of British industry. It has been failing to expand, failing to modernize, failing to seek technical improvements, failing to cut costs, failing to sell and failing to develop new competitive lines in world markets. Of course Great Britain has many bright and spirited industrial exceptions, such as Unilever, Rolls-Royce with its jet engines, Imperial Chemical Industries. But the basic downward trend of Britain's competitive position in the world is not the kind of pattern on which a great trading nation can go on living, and it is only going to be reversed by considerable effort and original measures.

The effect of these progressively worsening trade figures on the strength of the pound sterling is bleak indeed. When the Labour Government took office and looked at the books, it found that as a result of the decline in exports and an import buying spree, the country faced a balance-of-payments deficit of at least £700 million in 1964. In a series of dramatic international phone calls to the International Monetary Fund and central banks all over the world—even including little Austria—the Bank of England hastily lined up the enormous credit of $4 billion, or twice the total sterling area reserves, in order to maintain the strength and value of the pound.

In 1956, after the Suez crisis, Britain had to arrange external credits totaling $1.3 billion to maintain sterling. In 1961, the balance-of-payments problem caught up with the country again and $2 billion had to be raised. Then came the 1964 operation of $4 billion which had to be extended and revised a few months later in 1965. Each time the problem has progressively deepened, and each time the British have just about had to double the ante in order to go on.

Britain's economic problem can be elaborated endlessly, and London abounds in statistical material and learned analysis which proves to the British over and over again that their national economic record has been frighteningly bad and that something has to be done to reverse the downward trend before devaluation, deflation and the disaster of economic shrinkage impose themselves. There is no dearth of diagnosis. The British problem lies in lack of leadership and cure.

Harold Wilson's initial set of measures to meet the problem had the stamp of stereotype. He slapped a 15 percent import surcharge on practically everything coming into Britain except foodstuffs, making British tariff rates about the highest in the world, temporarily at least —and incidentally infuriating Britain's partners in the European Free Trade Area, who pointed out that the action was in direct contravention of the EFTA treaty. He raised the bank rate to 7 percent to cut down on internal credit and industrial expansion. He offered a new rebate for exporters. He distributed a small increase to old-age pensioners to meet an election pledge and announced some emergency tax increases with the introduction of a new excess profits tax to follow. He established a separate Ministry of Economic Affairs and a new Ministry of Technology. He announced a Royal Commission to review Britain's labor laws and trade union practices and recommend government action. He appealed for "the Dunkirk spirit" in the country to meet the crisis.

All of these measures are necessary, obvious and unexceptional. But they do not exactly promise an expanding and prosperous British future. They fail in one great respect. In requiring sacrifice, they do not offer opportunity. Broadly speaking they are conformist measures which tend to narrow Britain's already diminished horizons. They may be Socialist-Left-Labour measures in their effect on distribution of national wealth and incomes and the management of the economy. But they are not radical measures in the sense that they break any new ground or represent any fresh thinking or change in tackling Britain's problems. The Labour Party ought to be the breeding ground for imagination in Britain, but the unhappy fact is that its thinkers—Wilson included—have devoted themselves almost exclusively to the business of tinkering around with ideas about new divisions of wealth in an economy which is already too static, instead of preparing to take radical decisions which would force change and introduce some new competitive dynamism in the industrial structure and in the national outlook.

Wilson himself is consumed with middle-class suspicion and resentment of wealth. He makes a fetish of releasing all kinds of figures about his personal living arrangements. He sends his two sons to school as day students and spends £174 a year in fees for each of them. In 1948 he bought a three-bedroom house in Hampstead Gardens in London for £5,100 and in 1953 he bought the four-bedroom house next door for £5,300 on a 90 percent mortgage which, in 1965, still had fourteen years to run. He kept the first house until 1957, renting it, and then sold it at a loss (for some unexplained reason) at £4,500. He has purchased a small three-room vacation bungalow in the Isles of Scilly off the extreme west coast of Cornwall for £2,000, which he is also financing on a mortgage. He buys his suits at Montague Burton, a London men's wear chain store. He is on his third Gannes macintosh overcoat, having paid £15 for the first one in 1958. He dislikes what the economists call "conspicuous consumption."

"Conspicuous consumption by a small but highly regarded class is not merely repugnant to the vast majority but makes it harder for us to do our job," Wilson said to one of his many interviewers. "There are many more important things to do. What is wrong with our society is that those who make the money are more regarded than those who earn the money." Nobody knows yet exactly how Harold Wilson might seek to translate these sentiments into government policy. But among Leftist Labour thinkers, there is a theory that the British people consume too much of the wrong things, and that the way to solve the economic problem is to cut down on this consumption and spend the money elsewhere. The Leftist Labourites conveniently combine this pseudo-economic philosophy with denunciation of American materialism and pious assertions that this must not be allowed to happen in Britain.

Typical of this thinking is the following, written by Richard Crossman in a Fabian Society pamphlet, "Labour in the Affluent Society":

> A mass demand for profitable but inessential consumer goods and luxuries has been stimulated by extravagantly expensive

> mass advertising and satisfied at the cost of the public services, but at a satisfactory rate of profit to private industry. The commercialized media of mass communications have been systematically used to dope the critical faculties which would normally have been stimulated by the improvement of popular education since 1945. By the continued application of these methods it may well be possible to keep the British people complacently apathetic, while the social and moral sinews of the national organism are rapidly weakened by fatty degeneration.

If the best that Harold Wilson and the Labour Government can offer England—in a period when almost every other modern state in the world, except for the Communist bloc, is expanding faster—is a large dose of economic contraction with a new apportionment of an even smaller cake, then Britain's future will be a bitter one indeed. Conformity will have won a complete victory over radicalism.

Harold Wilson's ability and intellectual bent lie in the mastery of specific issues and problems rather than innovation or originality on a wide scale. He will bring thorough study and technical expertise to a measure such as the introduction of the excess profits tax into Britain. But he has a distinct lack of interest in the idea that Britain needs new political relationships and associations to replace its defunct Empire. Great Britain is no longer able to operate a take-it-or-leave-it foreign policy in the world, whereas the Labour Party's thinking, except for a small articulate few, has almost always stopped with the English Channel. When Labour was in power from 1945 to 1951, and the first chance to join Europe came along in the form of the Schuman Plan, the first and most basic reaction of the Labourites was: "We can't have any outsiders interfering with British economic planning." Today the Labour Government has had to turn, cap in hand, to central banks all over Europe. But suggestions from these moneylenders that Britain is not being very realistic about its problems and might have something to learn from outside are greeted with cold resentment. The idea that continental economists or Zurich bankers can teach anything to British Socialists is not regarded as worth considering.

In foreign policy, therefore, Harold Wilson is trying to balance on two of the legs of Anthony Eden's old three-legged stool. Like every British prime minister, whatever his politics, he is grateful for that telephone line to Washington. And he hopes to "strengthen the Commonwealth" and Commonwealth trade. Europe is only a place to borrow money and not, evidently, a source of ideas, associations or opportunity for Britain.

For the moment, the British have the Malaysia operation in Southeast Asia to keep up some of the old imperial illusion—and a very useful and necessary operation it is, too. More than 50,000 British troops and airmen have now been deployed in the Far East, and that gutty, Kiplingesque phrase, "British power east of Suez," looms as large to Harold Wilson as it did to Anthony Eden. But one day the Malaysian situation will be stabilized, or so it is hoped, and one day the British troops will begin going home. Britain will not find its future role in the world east of Suez. As for the Commonwealth, one of Wilson's first suggestions—that a permanent Commonwealth secretariat be organized in London—was immediately greeted with loud cheers from Ghana and a demand that an African and preferably a Ghanian be given the post. Ghana is not exactly regarded by the rest of the Commonwealth as a model of emergent democracy. Not only that, the Ghanians said they thought it would be essential that the proposed Commonwealth secretariat be empowered to study Commonwealth political disputes and make recommendations for their settlement. Far from strengthening the Commonwealth, such a structure would be more likely to produce its breakup and demise.

In trade, as in foreign policy, England's real challenge today lies not in the far reaches of the old Empire but on the doorstep at home. Exports, and a change in the long, steady decline of Britain's share of world markets, will be the only genuine index of Britain's capacity to maintain its economic life. In 1963, the year of the De Gaulle veto, the British had a 15 percent rise in exports to the Common Market, but in 1964 the rise was only 2 percent. Common market tariff walls, and more especially the reduction of barriers and increased trade inside the Market, are closing in against the British.

In every direction, England is living on narrow margins—in trade, in its military establishment, in its balance-of-payments, in sterling area reserve figures and the value of the pound sterling, but most narrowly of all in its political thought and leadership and its four-vote government majority in the House of Commons. The narrow margin of this political confrontation makes for political excitement for the British, but it also makes radicalism and originality a risk instead of a political reward.

By the normal swing of politics, after thirteen years of Conservative rule in which trade figures and pound sterling had gone steadily from bad to worse, the Labour Party should have come into power with a solid majority, mandate for change, and the strength to carry out bold programs in the internal reorganization of the British economy. The Conservatives should have been put into the wilderness to scrape off their political barnacles and think about Britain's future. Sir Alec Douglas-Home, who once blandly asserted that he uses matchsticks to try to understand economics, is no man to cling to power, and as the former fourteenth Earl of Home he would have returned quite comfortably to the patriarchial life which he inherited even though he has shorn himself of his title. But with England locked in the tightest of political situations, where the slightest absenteeism in the House of Commons can determine the fall of the government and the timing of a quick General Election, Sir Alec is there on the firing line, with his matchsticks, and the Conservatives are ready for a quick turnover.

What, then, is the hope of radicalism, which England so badly needs?

The answer, I think, is to be found in the ferment with which the British are debating and discussing their situation and their future. They have gone through the "Angry Young Men" period of railing at the system. They have gone through the satire phase, laughing at the very pretentiousness of Britain's condition. Today the need, the demand, for something better than a "Little England" future and a "Little England" outlook is slowly focusing the realities of England without an empire, England without Churchill. The more the British ponder and debate these realities, and argue what to do about them, the more the realization grows that Britain's challenge and Britain's future role lie with Europe. Just as the British were irresistibly drawn, from Marlborough to Churchill, into a succession of continental wars across two and a half centuries, so must they be irresistibly drawn into the construction of Europe's future economic and political life, the construction of wide European peace and understanding.

But writers, poets, economists, playrights and comedians are not enough. England cries out for political leadership—for a humanizing, adventurous, larger-than-live revival of opportunity and national purpose from which all else can then begin to flow.

> Men at some time are masters of their fates:
> The fault, dear Brutus, is not in our stars,
> But in ourselves. . . .

4. The United States and Europe

In the 186 years since the adoption of the American Constitution, the foreign policy of the United States has fallen into three broad historic phases, and today a new fourth phase appears to have begun.

The first extended roughly from George Washington's Farewell Address to the time of the Spanish-American War, and was a period of almost complete isolation from world affairs in which America, secure behind British seapower, concentrated on building its own nationhood, expanding to the west, fighting a Civil War and laying the groundwork for the mightiest industrial society on the globe. The second phase, coinciding with the first half of the twentieth century, was a period of ad hoc American intervention in world affairs: the imperialist ventures of the Philippines, the Pacific islands, Cuba, China, the Panama Canal; the start of a two-ocean navy as British seapower gradually withdrew from the Far East to face the menace from Germany; American intervention at a late hour in the First World War followed by another bout of proud isolation; and finally the Second World War from which the United States emerged with a determination to shoulder world responsibilities in the face of the Communist challenge, as the strongest power in a world which was almost completely in ruins.

The third phase of American foreign policy—the Cold War with the Soviet Union—opened with the Truman Doctrine in 1947 and reached its climax in the Cuban confrontation of 1962. The Cold War involved the United States for the first time in its history in a whole series of permanent diplomatic and military commitments all over the world, coupled with enormous defense expenditures and $45 billion in aid to Europe alone. It produced eruptions and tests of strength all around the perimeter of the Communist bloc: Western Europe and Berlin, the Korean war, the offshore islands of China, the first Indochina war from 1947 to 1954; Tibet and India and the Middle East. But as far as the two superpowers were concerned, the decisive strategic theater of the Cold War remained in Europe. If Europe had not been secured against Communist pressures, then the strategic balance would have swung decisively against the United States. It was in Europe, therefore, that the main postwar effort of American aid and involvement was placed. And America looked in turn to a revived Europe to help hold the line against Communism around the globe.

In the Cuban confrontation, the United States and Russia faced each other across a Western Europe which had rebuilt its industrial and military capacities and was politically stable and secure. American power overwhelmingly decided the outcome of the crisis, but Europe represented a strategic barrier to Russia which the Russians did not dare risk crossing to go to Castro's aid. The NATO Alliance which had stood firm for more than a decade in the defense of Berlin also stood firm over Cuba. The aftermath has been a tacit acceptance by Russia and the United States and their respective allies of a stalemate in the power contest in Europe.

A new historic fourth phase of foreign policy appears, therefore, to be under way for the United States. As the Cold War with Russia in Europe has receded, the arena of primary strategic concern in foreign policy has shifted to the challenge of Chinese Communism in the Far East. Moreover, this is just as true for Russia as it is for the United States. Red China is challenging the interests of *both* America and the Soviet Union in the world, and this is likely to be the most important single factor in the shaping of foreign policy and the conduct of world diplomacy for ten years to come and longer.

The Chinese clash with the United States in Asia is of course classic Marxist anti-Imperialist doctrine, a continuation of the Communist dream of world revolution. It is being conducted with the language and ideological drive of Stalinism—a policy which the Russians have certainly muted in their relations with Europe and the West, if not abandoned. As Russian living standards have gradually improved, and in particular since the Russians went to the brink of war over Cuba, the Soviet leaders have talked less and less about world revolution and more and more about the eventual triumph of Communism through peaceful demonstration of the validity of the system. Such a "soft sell" is anathema to the Red Chinese, who roundly condemn the Russians for abandoning Communist militancy, and who seek everywhere to seize the ideological leadership of the world Communist movement, particularly in the emerging nations of Africa and Asia. The Sino-Soviet split is very deep, and there are no signs yet that the quarrel can be patched up. When Khrushchev fell from power in October, 1964, it was widely believed that his handling of the China question was a key factor, and that his successors would set about improving relations with Peking. But the split is now five years old, and even Soviet efforts to maintain a certain modulation in the argument with Peking has been to little avail. The Red Chinese respond with attacks on the Russian leaders couched in the same style and ideological language which Stalin once used to denounce Tito.

If the Sino-Soviet split merely involved interpretations of Communism and tactics against the non-Communist world, it probably would have been smoothed over by now. But with every month that it continues, it becomes more and more a fundamental clash of *national* rather than ideological interests. The Chinese are no longer subservient to Russian leadership, and they have entered the ranks of the nuclear powers without any recent help from their closest ally. All over the world they are stepping up their own particular brand of political and military pressures and asserting Chinese national interests against the Russians in the infighting in the Communist movement, and against the Americans at points where they find themselves encircled or contained by American power, as in South Vietnam.

Time and again events in Southeast Asia produce the diplomatic evidence of how little the Russians are now able to control the aggressive nationalism of Peking. In 1954 when Pierre Mendès-France went to Geneva to negotiate the armistice which ended France's Indochina war, he negotiated with the Russians. In the final dramatic hours at Geneva it was Molotov, Mendès-France and Eden who hammered out the terms of the agreement. The Red Chinese were in the shadowy background. Out in the Tongking Delta of Indochina, the Vietminh rebels with Chinese backing clearly held the upper hand militarily after the fall of Dienbienphu, and the French shuddered to think what the situation would be if they did not get an armistice and the fighting went on. But Moscow had decided in that year after Stalin's death that it was time to bring the war to a halt, and so the armistice terms were agreed and Vietnam was divided into North and South. The difference between the war of 1954 and the war of 1965 is the difference of the Communist ideological split and the explosion of

China's first nuclear device. China is now deciding its own policy—not Russia.

Nor can the Russian General Staff allow itself to forget the problems of the 6,000-mile frontier between China and Russia across Central Asia and Siberia. On Chinese maps, there are vast areas of this frontier territory which China has disputed since the days of the imperialist clashes between the Moguls, the Manchus and the Czars. Just as the Chinese descended on India's frontiers in 1961 waving maps which predated the borders drawn by imperialist Britain, so one day might Peking confront Moscow with maps of Central Asia which predate the Czars. At any rate, the Russians must take into account the possibility that their bitter ideological quarrel with China, with all its nationalistic overtones, could suddenly erupt into an aggressive military threat from the enormous mass of the Chinese Armies backed by nuclear weapons in the open and isolated Asian countryside.

It is far too early for the United States or the West to draw any conclusions or base any expectations or policies on the future development of the Sino-Soviet split. For the present, it undoubtedly suits the Russians quite well to have China and the United States locked in fighting in Southeast Asia. It serves to divert China's military resources to the south, away from Russia's frontiers, and it serves as a temporary rallying-point for Communist unity in the world despite the ideological split.

Nevertheless, in the long run it may be that both Russia and the United States will find themselves with a parallel interest in checking and containing the expanding nationalist pressures of a nuclear-equipped Communist China. Meanwhile, in the short run, this shift of strategic emphasis to Asia appears to have reinforced the acceptance of the power stalemate in Europe.

This was demonstrated during the period when President Johnson was gradually stepping up the retaliatory air strikes and military pressures against North Vietnam. The Russians made some moves in the direction of reconvening the 1954 Geneva Conference, and quickly discovered that the Chinese would have none of it. Russia then settled back to a position of diplomatic solidarity with the Chinese to the extent of echoing China's call for a halt to air strikes and an end to American intervention in South Vietnam. But the Russians acted in a rather tentative *pro forma* manner without much militancy, and above all they refrained from any action to create counterpressures against the United States in Europe—for example, a renewal of the harassment of West Berlin.

In the course of this new phase of American foreign policy, what will be the trends and the problems which will confront the United States in Europe?

Above all, Europe must be held, and the balance of power must be maintained. America's primary concern is not how the European states organize themselves, whether it is federation or confederation, whether it is six, seven or eleven. These are questions for the Europeans and the Europeans alone to decide. They are of importance to the United States only insofar as they might affect good relations and the harmony of Europe. Ultimately, the basic American interest in Europe, and the only reason for a strong American presence on the Continent for the last twenty years, is the maintenance of peace and security.

Security can be achieved in two ways. It can be bought at the high price of a military deterrent, or it can be arrived at through political understanding which removes the threat of aggression. Usually one follows the other, or the two go hand in hand and develop over a long period of time. It took Western Europe a century and a half to get over Clausewitz's dictum that "War is an extension of politics by other means." But today, at least from the Atlantic to the Elbe, the states of Europe have achieved peaceful understanding and no nation threatens its neighbors, either politically, ideologically or territorially. Obviously if this situation could be extended from the Altantic to the Urals, and the Russian threat to Western Europe thus replaced by a broad political accord, then there would be no reason to go on maintaining a massive American military establishment in Europe. The Europeans would not need it or want it, and America would not go on paying for it.

Europe has entered a period of cautious diplomatic probing and testing of political ground in both the East and the West. America, for its part, has long since given up trying to "roll back" Communism, and the Soviet Union has given up trying to "bury" Western civilization. After the Cuban confrontation, the Berlin crisis went off the air almost overnight and the city has been allowed to go on developing its life and commerce undisturbed inside the Communist wall. Official visits, cultural exchanges and trade missions have multiplied back and forth between East and West to a point where nobody bothers to keep track of them anymore. French has been restored as the second language in Romanian schools, replacing Russian, and dozens of French teachers have been sent to Romania from Paris. Every one of the Communist countries advertises avidly in newspapers and magazines in Western Europe for tourists to cross the rusting Iron Curtain and bring hard currency with them. Who, a few years ago, would have believed that entry visas would be offered at the borders and airports of Eastern Europe?

The vibrant productive wealth of Western Europe has become of enormous attraction and importance to the flagging Communist economies of the East. The barrier on long-term commercial credits for the Communist bloc was broken at the end of 1964 by Great Britain, after long arguments in the NATO council. France, Italy and West Germany quickly followed in offering seven- eight- or nine-year credit deals to Russia and Eastern Europe to finance such projects as fertilizer, synthetic fiber and rubber factories. For the Bonn Government, trade with Eastern Europe is a major instrument in its efforts to build a diplomatic position in the Communist world, and to outflank East Germany in a part of Europe where German interests have always predominated.

Poland has turned, of all places, to the Ruhr firm of Alfred Krupp for an experiment in a mixed free-enterprise–Communist deal in which Krupps will not only build an entire new Polish manufacturing complex but will provide German managers to run the plant along private enterprise lines, technicians to train the workers, marketing experts to design the products and sales experts to go after trade and exports. Even on the question of East Germany there is a note of cautious flexibility in West Germany. The determination to keep the Ulbricht government in the pariah state it has earned for itself is unchanged. But in matters which concern the people of East Germany rather than the government, a distinction is being made. It can be seen in the Berlin pass agreements, in trade and credits which West Germany extends to East Germany, in Mayor Willy Brandt's enunciation of a policy of "change through closer relations," in the more questioning attitude of West German public opinion on the problems of Germany's future.

In summary, a whole new texture of contacts of many kinds at many levels in many directions is being woven among the states of Europe. The post-Cuban cessation of Communist pressure tactics has now lasted three years with no very disturbing setbacks or interruptions, and this continued atmosphere of *détente* has opened up for the Europeans at least a possibility of working toward some normalization of relations among all the European states for the first time in more than a quarter of a century. The Europeans are groping to see if there is a basis for some wider political understanding, some context in which the German question might eventually be solved, some progress toward pan-European peace and security.

No very important, dramatic or immediate changes are likely to arise out of this process. The emphasis on both sides is on gradualism and caution, on what Secretary of State Dean Rusk once called *"status quo* in motion." But despite the military stalemate, in fact almost because of the military stalemate, there is a new diplomatic mobility in the European scene.

Its most striking feature is the rise of the new nationalism. In Eastern Europe this has been labeled "polycentrism" and in Western Europe it is of course well known as Gaullism. The common denominator is the challenge to the bipolar dominance of Europe's affairs from Washington and from Moscow. In seeking to break away from the established patterns of the last twenty years, the nations of Eastern and Western Europe are inevitably turning to each other for closer contacts, trade, tourism and understanding which will, hopefully, enable them to ease out from under the confrontation of the great powers.

The United States, to its discomfort, is going to have to get used to the idea that it will be increasingly excluded from this process. It cannot know and probably will not know what German businessmen, acting with the blessing of the Bonn Government, are saying in Prague, or what Romanian diplomats are proposing in Paris, or what the Poles will be discussing with the British. In the old days of the Cold War when satellite contacts of this kind were extremely limited and rigidly conducted, it was a simple and routine matter for governments to relay through the machinery of the NATO Council in Paris the results and analyses of what they were hearing and saying in Eastern Europe. Such cross-feeding of political intelligence was essential to the pattern of Alliance diplomacy. But the times are changing. The contacts have multiplied and diversified. More important, there is the growing tendency of governments to treat these as matters of *national* rather than NATO concern.

Paradoxically, while the United States has applauded and supported the rise of nationalism in Africa, Asia and the Arab world, it has reacted with surprise and even indignation that the same thing should now be taking place in Europe. This was not the outcome which Americans apparently envisaged from the Monnet process, from the revival of Europe and the movement toward European unity. Having become involved in two world wars which were brought about by excessive European nationalism, Americans have come to regard "nationalism" as a dirty word where Europe is concerned. But the new nationalism is a fact of political life in Europe and it is going to increase and not diminish, however much Americans may deplore it. It is a serious mistake to think that this is nothing more than a reflection of the nineteenth-century ambitions of General de Gaulle, foolishly loosed at the wrong time in history. De Gaulle epitomizes and drives this nationalism ruthlessly, often against the established interests of the United States. But if De Gaulle disappeared tomorrow there would still be a problem of nationalism in Europe. Moreover, if there are advantages to be found in nationalism for emerging nations, and if there are advantages in the polycentrism which is taking place in Eastern Europe, then it is difficult and indeed foolish for the United States to expect to stuff nationalism back into a bottle and put it on the shelf in Western Europe—the cradle of modern civilization and the birthplace of political democracy. De Gaulle once scoffed about protests against France's nationalistic policies: "Nationalism evidently was supposed to be reserved for the great powers and the underdeveloped countries."

This new mobility of diplomatic contacts in Europe between East and West, coupled with the new European nationalism, is slowly but steadily eroding much of the ground on which unity and the common policies of the North Atlantic Treaty Organization rested in the more cohesive days of the Cold War. This erosion reflects in many ways—for example, the failure of the NATO powers to agree to go on holding the line on long-term credits for the Communist bloc; the indifference, if not open opposition, of NATO members to American appeals for more support in South Vietnam. For the United States, however, the chief alarm centers on the nuclear question and on General de Gaulle's policy of building an independent nuclear force for France.

No subject has been analyzed by American experts with more fervor, intensity and automated equipment, and discussed with greater apprehension and anguish, than the problem of nuclear warfare. The

United States has displayed an almost obsessive fear of the proliferation of nuclear weapons and the loss of its nuclear monopoly in the West. (British nuclear cooperation with the United States has become so intimate and complete over the years that the Americans have come to regard the British, for all practical purposes, as simply providing another few squadrons under the control of the U. S. Strategic Air Command.) But whatever the sophistication of American arguments to prove the dangers of nuclear proliferation, the course of recent history has been like Canute and the tides. General de Gaulle is determined to break the American nuclear monopoly in the West and achieve nuclear independence for France. The more the facts and arguments of the nuclear problem are deployed, the more they serve to strengthen De Gaulle's determination that France must possess these weapons, and his assertion that Europe must have a nuclear capability which it can employ independent of any control from Washington.

In the highly complicated and theoretical world of nuclear decision-making, two basically important acts by the Kennedy Administration illustrate the dilemma of trying to arrive at a strategic doctrine which satisfies *both* the United States and Europe. These decisions pointed up, moreover, the extent to which Europe has been completely subservient to military policy-making in Washington. President Kennedy acted in matters which profoundly affected the military posture in Europe. He took his decisions unilaterally, without any consultation or exchange of views whatsoever with the British-French-American NATO Military Standing Group in Washington which is supposed to decide NATO strategy, or with the fourteen-member NATO Military Committee which also sits in Washington, or with the NATO Council in Paris.*

The first decision, made shortly after the President took office in 1961, was the implementation of the "pause theory" for the employment of nuclear weapons in a land battle in Europe.

President Kennedy inherited from President Eisenhower a series of NATO defense plans in which nuclear weapons under American control had been deployed in Germany as a built-in part of the military preparations to meet any attack across the Iron Curtain. Control over the weapons fell into three step-by-step stages. In the first stage, if there was sufficient warning or signs of a buildup for a possible attack

* Iceland, the fifteenth member of NATO, is not a member of the Military Committee.

on NATO, General Lauris Norstad, then Supreme Allied Commander, would seek from President Eisenhower the precautionary authority to "release nuclear warheads to units." This would put the NATO forces in a state of nuclear readiness. Then if an attack began, General Norstad would next ask for Presidential authority to fire nuclear weapons. Firing would then be ordered only by higher headquarters, under American control, as the battle developed. This did not mean that some trigger-happy lieutenant in the field would be able to start a nuclear exchange.

In the meantime, in the forward areas of Germany, commanders had made their battle plans with nuclear weapons as an integral part of the planning. For example, a battalion commander assigned to hold a particular piece of strategic terrain would map where he intended to place his troops and artillery and plan his defensive action. Then if he failed to hold an advance by conventional means, and if a breakthrough began to develop across a bridge, or through a road juncture, he could call for nuclear fire from Corporal or Honest John short-range missiles, from nuclear howitzers, or from an air strike. He could not himself order such a nuclear strike. That would be a matter for higher headquarters to determine in the light of developments all along the front. But in terms of planning the NATO defense of Europe, nuclear firepower was built in with conventional weapons, and was considered to be immediately available.

President Kennedy, alarmed at what he felt to be an excessive leeway for commanders in the field over employment of nuclear weapons, made a sweeping change. At his decision, the Pentagon laid it down at once that battle planning was to be based on conventional weapons and conventional weapons alone. Nuclear weapons were withdrawn from lower-echelon planning, and the "pause theory" became the new strategy. The point at which nuclear weapons would be released and employed in battle would in future be determined by the President, after an attack had developed. This, it was argued by theoreticians, would permit the "appreciation of the wider risks involved" before nuclear war was begun. The Americans kept explaining over and over to the Europeans that the "pause" might last only one hour, or it might last twenty-four, but a pause there had to be.

Whatever the logic of the pause theory from the point of view of the responsibilities of the President of the United States, the effect on the military staffs in Europe and in Germany in particular was disturbing and upsetting—particularly as nobody in Europe was even consulted. The plans which had been worked out under General Norstad and approved by President Eisenhower did not in the least envisage that nuclear weapons would go off when the first Russian soldier crossed the frontier. They provided that the initial attack would be met entirely by conventional methods, and that only in the event of a clearly identified decisive strategic breakthrough against conventional forces, which established that a major assault was underway, would nuclear firepower then be brought into play. Up and down the center of Germany there are dozens of towns and cities which could be seized in a matter of hours by a determined attack: Lubeck, Hamburg, Göttingen, Wolfsburg Goslar, Fulda, Coburg, Hof, to name a few. The pause theory, by removing nuclear weapons from battle planning, introduced a new element of delay and uncertainty in the defense of these towns. Would nuclear weapons be employed quickly enough to stop their seizure? Would the President of the United States regard their defense as worth the risk of a nuclear exchange with the Soviet Union?

The adoption of the pause theory was accompanied by great American pressure on the NATO Allies to build up their conventional forces to a strength at which even a conventional attack by the Russians in Europe would be unthinkable. And at the same time, America poured more and more nuclear warheads into Europe, and the Pentagon devoted itself to repeated reassurances of the colossal American superiority and the fullest American nuclear backup for Europe.

But instead of being reassuring to Europe, the effect was just the opposite. To most European military men, the pause theory *decreased* the validity of America's vast deterrent strength, and the new American emphasis on conventional warfare (including stockpiles for a ninety-day war) was an increase in the temptation to the Russians to attack. The Europeans are all for "flexible response" and "pause" by the United States in Laos or Vietnam or the Middle East or Africa. But Europeans cannot envisage an attack in Europe (as distinct from minor border incidents) as meaning anything but total and general war. They have sought, therefore, to make America's nuclear response as total, automatic and decisive as possible. Under the Eisenhower-Norstad planning there had been some assurance of such an automatic response. But with the pause theory, the issue of use of nuclear weapons in the defense of Europe came out into the open, and U. S. strategic policy in NATO came under explicit and fundamental questioning.

For General de Gaulle, the pause theory was added proof that Europe could not wait for the President of the United States to decide whether to respond with nuclear weapons to an attack on the other side of the Atlantic. The President of France had to have the same power and the same choice.

President Kennedy's second major decision affecting the military posture in Europe concerned land-based missiles. In the wake of the Cuban confrontation, he abruptly pulled American Thor and Jupiter missiles out of Turkey, Greece, Italy and the United Kingdom and assigned their targets to Polaris submarines at sea. The Italian Foreign Minister was told of the decision by the President very casually in the middle of a formal official dinner at the White House, as he was ending a three-day visit to Washington.

More important from the long-term military standpoint, the President took a secret decision at the same time that, as Khrushchev had withdrawn Russian missiles from Cuba, the United States would not place *any* missiles on land in Europe again which would directly threaten the Soviet Union.

As a result of this Kennedy decision, which has remained American policy under President Johnson, the longest range ballistic missile in Europe today is the American Pershing, which can hit targets to a depth of about 450 miles behind the Iron Curtain, in East Germany, Poland, Czechoslovakia, Hungary and Romania but not in Russia. On the other hand, the Russians have upwards of 800 medium-range missiles on their soil which are targeted on Paris, London, Rome, Oslo, Hamburg, the Ruhr, airfields all over Europe and any other points which they deem to be of strategic interest. Since 1960, first General Norstad and then the present Supreme Allied Commander, General Lyman L. Lemnitzer, and successive SHAPE planning staffs, have urged that NATO forces be equipped with similar land-based medium-range missiles to counter this Russian threat in Europe. For the present, and perhaps for another five years or so, it will be possible for low-flying tactical bombers to penetrate Soviet air defenses and knock out at least a percentage of these missile sites. But in the long run, the only effective defense against Soviet missiles in Europe will be NATO missiles of similar range and precision. The Polaris and the Minuteman missiles, fired from American submarines or from silos buried in the center of the continental United States, are massive anti-city weapons which do not have the precision to hit small, widely dispersed Russian missile sites. But they remain the only missiles which can reach the Soviet Union. The United States not only continues to oppose placing on the Continent missiles which can hit Russia. It has so far declined even to develop a missile of this type and range. Thus, the means of counterattacking against a Russian missile strike against Western Europe lies exclusively in American hands—in American submarines and the Minuteman silos deep in the United States.

The pause theory and American policy against land-based missiles on the Continent of Europe are both, no doubt, logical and sound from the point of view of American efforts to devise a coherent and flexible global military strategy. The very vastness of America's nuclear arsenal, with its hair-raising "overkill" capacity, makes the Pentagon even more impatient at the questioning of American strategic doctrine for the defense of NATO and Europe. Above all, the United States shows itself to be nervous, almost frantic, at the possibility that America might lose that total control over strategy, deployment and use of nuclear weapons in the West which it has enjoyed for twenty years.

Nevertheless, serious differences over nuclear doctrine and strategy have now arisen between the United States and Europe. American theories for the defense of NATO are challenged not only by General de Gaulle, who now has a few nuclear bombs and a button of his own to press, but also by military men, political leaders and diplomats who do not possess nuclear weapons and have no intention of trying to acquire them.

The American response to the complexity of questions which have arisen in NATO was to try to shore things up through a sharing of nuclear responsibility. Eventually this idea came to rest in the form of the proposal to create a multilateral nuclear force—to consist of twenty-five surface ships, each to be armed with ten or more Polaris missiles, to be manned by mixed crews of American, British, Dutch, Italian, Greek and Turkish sailors and anyone else who might join, to be built, financed and owned jointly by the countries participating. Everybody would have a veto over firing the missiles, with the American veto, of course, remaining supreme. The MLF proposal pretty much dominated American diplomatic activity in NATO and Europe for two years, from just after the famous De Gaulle press conference until President Johnson decided that the policy probably wasn't going to succeed, and called a halt in December, 1964.

There were a number of uncomfortable parallels between the MLF plan and the European Defense Community treaty for a European

Army which floundered ten years earlier, despite all-out American backing. EDC and MLF were even to an extent the product of the same official and unofficial State Department advisers. Both projects were prompted by the belief that a military problem could be used to achieve greater integration and unity in the NATO Alliance. In both cases the reach exceeded the grasp.

The MLF plan suffered from many built-in contradictions from the first. For the Germans, it was supposed to offer the status symbol of joining the ranks of the nuclear powers with a voice in the control of nuclear weapons. For others in Europe it was supposed to be a way of denying Germany the possession of nuclear weapons, and thwarting some hidden future German desire for nuclear equality. It was supposed to be a reassurance for Europe of American nuclear backing for Europe's defense. For America it was supposed to be a way of satisfying the Europeans without giving up American strategic control of NATO. For NATO it was a way to increase NATO nuclear power, while the Russians were told it was a way of controlling nuclear power to make disarmament easier. First it was supposed to lead to a "European deterrent" which the Europeans might one day take over. Then it was supposed to establish a permanent European partnership with America in the field of nuclear weapons in which the American veto would hold forever. It was supposed to increase the validity of the deterrent by giving the Europeans a voice in the firing of nuclear weapons. But at the same time it decreased the validity of the deterrent by opening up the possibility that one of the participants in the MLF force might say No. ("Can Germany trust the firing of nuclear weapons in her defense to Harold Wilson?" the Germans asked.) The more the experts and idealists tinkered with the plan, the more it came to resemble a new model automobile to which designers go on adding bits of chrome and gadgets and brightwork and special features to improve the sales appeal for everybody.

As negotiations and debate and discussion wore on through 1963 and 1964, the MLF took on more and more of the aspect of an American effort to thwart General de Gaulle. It became more dis-uniting in NATO than unifying, and among the other NATO powers, those who were not participating in the scheme as well as those who were, the feeling grew that it was better to hold on to such unity as NATO had achieved rather than risk some large blowup over MLF. The plan never did obtain anything but reluctant backing from Britain, and despite the enthusiasm of West Germany, it was a mistake for the United States to embark on a policy for the Atlantic Alliance which would not command the support of the European "Big Three." This is one of the limits of Alliance diplomacy. Finally, Paul-Henri Spaak of Belgium, who, as a former NATO secretary-general could scarcely be accused of being anti-NATO, said openly that it was time to put European unity ahead of MLF. After that, Italy's Manlio Brosio, newly appointed as NATO secretary-general, declared it to be his opinion that MLF could be introduced into NATO or incorporated into the NATO forces only with the unanimous consent of its members. France was thus armed with a veto. The Turkish Foreign Minister flew to Moscow for the first such visit since before Ataturk, and soon after Russia's policy on the Cyprus question modified and Turkey decided to pull out of the MLF scheme. General de Gaulle, who had kept relatively quiet over MLF, then turned on it with heavy blows. He informed Chancellor Ludwig Erhard bluntly that he would regard German participation in MLF to be damaging to Franco-German relations and the spirit of their treaty of cooperation, and more than that, decisively damaging to Germany's chances for reunification.

In the face of this welter of contradiction and controversy, President Johnson called a halt. Washed of its high-mindedness and ideology, and its all-things-to-all-nations theories, the multilateral nuclear force plan was essentially a device to try to make the American nuclear monopoly and the American strategic hegemony over NATO and Europe more palatable to the Europeans. It did not succeed.

Times have changed in Europe since the NATO Treaty was signed in April, 1949, and Supreme Allied Headquarters was organized by General Eisenhower in 1950. The first basic problem which the United States faces in its future relations with Europe lies in accepting the change, analyzing both its problems and its opportunities, and adjusting its policies and attitudes toward Europe at floodtide.

To begin with, a very delicate and subtle shift is under way in Europe in the balance between dependence on purely *military* security and a new degree of confidence and trust in *political* security. United States policies in NATO are necessarily directed almost totally to the problems of Europe's military security. Europeans, on the other hand, are directing their policies toward trying to find a basis of political security. They play the game to the East—General de Gaulle in particular—with an irritating abandon, knowing that they can take chances, make sweeping declarations of independent policies, criticize, oppose, obstruct and deprecate, but still remain secure under the umbrella of American power. They know that ultimately, whatever the differences and arguments over NATO strategy and the rest, the United States in its own self-interest will not risk any withdrawal from Europe which risks the security of Europe and the maintenance of peace.

The simple fact is that the Europeans have almost totally written off the threat or possibility of war in the diplomatic calculations which will govern their actions in the period ahead. The Europeans may turn out to be wrong, but for more than a century they have been used to the rather cynical routine of placing odds on the timing of future wars. The British Government used to operate on what was known as the "five-year rule." Every five years, the Imperial Defense Committee would weigh all the available intelligence and political evidence and advise the government of the day whether it might expect another five years of peace, or whether it ought to begin getting ready for war. Until the Cuban confrontation, all the NATO governments had to think and act with the possibility of war in the background. But today, Europe feels an almost total release from this ultimate threat and fear, and this in turn makes Alliance diplomacy so difficult for the United States.

America, holding the ultimate responsibility for European security, cannot afford to make such easy calculations about war and peace. Nevertheless, the American focus and concern about the interdependence of NATO nuclear strategy, which may be completely valid from a military point of view, is no longer the central problem of the Alliance. However important the United States might consider it to be to have the capability of fighting a centrally controlled nuclear war, the practical problem and the much more important problem in the period ahead lies in devising common political policies with the European Allies at a time when trends and impulses lead to other directions—nationalism, independence, neutralism, pan-Europeanism, third force-ism, polycentrism, etc. If the Atlantic Alliance cannot be held together *politically* in this confusing and difficult period, then it matters little whether or not there is one American-directed NATO strategy, whether or not there is nuclear proliferation, whether or not there is a pause theory, or where the missiles are located.

Part of the American problem in adjusting to the changing outlook of the Atlantic Alliance lies in a tendency to try to deal with foreign policy by structure and organization. In part this is probably a reflection of America's own success with federalism and with its constitutional system. Americans are by nature builders, designers, engineers, production specialists. In the operation of government they like to have projects and programs for which money can be appropriated, results demonstrated and enthusiasm generated. In foreign policy and military policy this tendency spills over in a proliferation of expertise, in superanalysis and the preparation of "solutions" to problems, in putting together "grand designs." Sometimes these plans work quite well. The Marshall Plan was such a structure for organizing economic assistance for Europe. NATO was a structure for organizing the military security of Europe. The MLF was then supposed to be a structure for solving the problem of nuclear policy for Europe.

But this tendency in turn leads to sterile, useless arguments about "integration." Simply to put together an integrated structure is a meaningless operation unless there is some fundamental understanding that makes it work. This is being demonstrated over and over again in NATO today, which has plenty of structure but less and less political cohesion and purpose. In the period which Europe has entered today, problems of foreign policy and diplomacy will lend themselves less and less to structural solutions. The trend is back to bilateralism instead of forward to integrated multilateralism. In any case, for the Europeans, treaties and alliances come and go, and politics and diplomacy and relations among governments tend to be conducted by more cynical rules, with limited commitments and an expectation of human fallibility, rather than too much faith in structures and organizations.

Even today, the European Common Market, which is by far the most successful integrated structure ever built in Europe, is the exception that proves the rule. How well things are going on the economic front among the Six has almost nothing to do with the mercurial state of relations between France and West Germany. The Franco-German political debate is conducted on an entirely different wavelength from the operations of the Common Market in Brussels.

The long years of the success of NATO, the great debt of peace and security which all of Europe owes to the Atlantic Alliance, makes this rise of polycentrism in the Western camp all the more confusing for the United States. From the very beginning in 1949, NATO came to be regarded by the Americans as a kind of constitution and magna carta of the new American involvement in world affairs. Never in its history had the United States made a treaty commitment to go to war on behalf of some other nation. Throughout the Cold War, NATO became a chosen instrument of American foreign policy, reinforced by successive political parties, Presidents and Congresses. This makes it difficult to face the fact that times have changed in Europe and the problems of maintaining the Atlantic Alliance have changed also.

Nevertheless, a cool and rational reappraisal of NATO and its military and political organization will be far better than some future blowup in which General de Gaulle might, for example, withdraw France completely from any further participation in the NATO command structure and request the removal of SHAPE Headquarters from French soil. To sit down and discuss with France, Germany, Britain and the other Allies a new basis for military coordination and cooperation in the Atlantic Alliance is not unreasonable—particularly as NATO is lurching toward a situation in which the present structure might simply become unworkable.

Is it wise or right that an American general should go on being Supreme Allied Commander in Europe? Will the danger of war be increased if there are only three American divisions in Germany instead of six? Might it not in fact suit the long-term problems of American military strategy if the United States was *less* committed and *less* integrated in Europe's defense? If General de Gaulle detests the idea of integrated NATO forces, is it beyond the ingenuity of American planners to find a new system of NATO defense?

The first point to be clear about is that whatever happens to the *structure* of NATO, the North Atlantic Treaty will go right on. The treaty runs for an original span of twenty years, until April, 1969, and after that it continues in force automatically unless some nation decides to denounce it or opt out on one year's notice. The treaty provided that proposals for its revision could be made at any time after the first fifteen years of its life. Nobody has come up with any proposals for revising the treaty yet. The French argument about NATO does not center on either the language of the treaty or its commitments but on its organization and integration. General de Gaulle keeps repeating at almost every press conference that "the Atlantic Alliance exists. So long as the Soviets threaten the world this alliance must be maintained. France is an integral part of it. If the free world were attacked, on the old or the new continent, France would take part in the common defense of the coasts of her allies with all the means that she has." That being France's policy, it will be far better for the United States and for the future of the Alliance to clear the air and find out what the limits of future cooperation are going to be.

Nor should the United States blind itself to the fact that advantages in the conduct of American foreign policy may lie in a little less expectation or reliance on NATO unity. Such unity was essential in the conduct of the Cold War. But as the United States is finding in Southeast Asia, NATO is of very little help and indeed almost a hindrance. Europe has no vital interest in Southeast Asia and declines any longer to accept the Communist challenge as a monolithic threat-to-all. For the United States to expect a degree of help or support from NATO nations in areas outside of NATO, just because they are members of NATO, is going to put an increasingly heavy strain on the Alliance. More important, it can also wind up handicapping and even handcuffing the conduct of American diplomacy, and American actions and decisions in dealing with Chinese Communist pressures and other eruptions around the globe.

In short, there are limits to the usefulness of Alliance diplomacy, which tends to reduce actions to the lowest common denominator, and there are advantages in a certain freedom of action and political flexibility. To recognize this fact, and to adjust the structure and the operations of the NATO Alliance accordingly, does not mean that the work of a decade and a half is about to be junked and that Europe is about to be laid wide open to Russian invasion. On the contrary, a recognition of greater freedom of political action by all members of the Alliance—the United States as well as France, Germany, Britain and the rest—could have the paradoxical effect of improving the sense of unity by reducing the temptations and desires for autonomous action, and the arguments about "damage to NATO" when somebody decides to go it alone.

To examine these questions candidly and openly with the NATO Allies is certainly the responsibility of the strongest power in the Alliance. It would be poor leadership and unwise diplomacy simply to sit back and keep repeating that it is up to those who criticize NATO to make suggestions or keep quiet. While General de Gaulle makes most of the noise about overhauling NATO, he is not alone in his view that it is time for a new look. In any case, the Alliance will not work effectively or well without France. And even without such pressures from Europe, it is time that the United States accept and indeed require a recognition of the new balance and the changing NATO outlook.

The future of NATO will center on three broad objectives: an acceptance of independent policies within the framework of a free alliance; an overhauling of NATO machinery and the military organization to take into account the changed relationship between the United States and Europe; the continuance of an American military commitment to Europe which will satisfy the basic American interest in the maintenance of European peace and security. Contradictory as these objectives may seem, they can be resolved by understanding and confidence. Shortly before the First World War, a French general, when asked how many British troops he wanted, remarked: "We need only one, and we will make sure he is killed on the first day." Somewhere between the figure of one American soldier and six divisions, a new balance of America's commitments to Europe and a new balance of Europe's obligations to itself can certainly be found.

In September of 1958, General de Gaulle, back in power only four months, addressed a famous memorandum to President Eisenhower and Prime Minister Macmillan proposing that they form a global strategic triumvirate to coordinate policies outside the NATO area. He was politely turned down by Eisenhower, partly because he was asking for a voice in the use of nuclear weapons, partly because the United States felt that it was unwise to create such a directorate to the exclusion of the other NATO Allies.

De Gaulle's proposal came two years before France exploded its first nuclear device and five years before France had produced its first operational atomic bomb. In the meantime, the General has repeatedly stated his readiness to join in "cooperation, be it technological or strategic, if this cooperation is, on the other hand, desired by our Allies." Cooperation on nuclear targeting between the tiny French *force de frappe* and the massive U. S. Strategic Air Command is beginning. Is it not possible for allies to explore what more can be done without becoming bogged down in theoretical debate over whether integration is better than coordination, or cooperation less satisfactory than collaboration, or comradeship not as good as unity?

The world has reached a somewhat paradoxical state in which the removal of the threat of war is making it all the more difficult to maintain intimacy and harmony. In the prenuclear days, every nation had to calculate its foreign policy and diplomacy with the threat of war in the background, and this had the effect of acting as a brake on impulsive actions and policies. The brake did not, indeed, prevent war, but it did temper the conduct of diplomacy and relations among nations. But in the nuclear age this restraint is removed —particularly among those who do not possess the nuclear bomb. As a result, consultative machinery breaks down or is not heeded, and nations like France tend to spin off and go their own way, knowing full well that they are safe from any ultimate sanctions. This changed atmosphere presents an enormous challenge to American patience, leadership and diplomacy. The United States will have to concern itself less with organizations, and more with understandings. This will require more poise, more open-mindedness, more flexibility, and less concern when things do not go precisely as America would like.

But the position in Europe is strong and the base for understanding is great. The ties of heritage and civilization, of hopes and aspirations, of sentiment and intellect between the United States and Europe are very deep and abiding. The record of United States foreign policy in Europe since the Second World War is one in which Americans can rightly take historic pride. It is time, now, to show a new confidence in the fruit of this labor and the strength that has been won.

Bougival, France.
March, 1965

Index